RESTRUCTURING NETWORKS IN POST-SOCIALISM

Legacies, Linkages, and Localities

Edited by

GERNOT GRABHER
and
DAVID STARK

OXFORD UNIVERSITY PRESS

1997

Oxford University Press, Great Clarendon Street, Oxford OX2 6DP

Oxford New York

Athens Auckland Bangkok Bogota Bombay
Buenos Aires Calcutta Cape Town Dar es Salaam
Delhi Florence Hong Kong Istanbul Karachi
Kuala Lumpur Madras Madrid Melbourne
Mexico City Nairobi Paris Singapore
Taipei Tokyo Toronto

and associated companies in
Berlin Ibadan

Oxford is a trade mark of Oxford University Press

Published in the United States by
Oxford University Press Inc., New York

© the various contributors 1997

British Library Cataloguing in Publication Data
Data available

Library of Congress Cataloging in Publication Data
Restructuring networks in post socialism: legacies, linkages, and
localities/edited by Gernot Grabher and David Stark.
Includes bibliographical references.
1. Industrial organization—Europe, Eastern. 2. Industrial
organization—Former Soviet republics. 3. Privatization—Europe,
Eastern. 4. Privatization—Former Soviet republics. 5. Post-
communism—Europe, Eastern. 6. Post-communism—Former Soviet
republics. I. Grabher, Gernot. II. Stark, David, 1950–
HD70.E7R47 1996 96-24872
338.947—dc20

ISBN 0-19-829020-9

1 3 5 7 9 10 8 6 4 2

Typeset by Best-set Typesetter Ltd., Hong Kong
Printed in Great Britain by
Bookcraft, Bath Ltd., Midsomer Norton, Somerset

PREFACE

'Pets and Meat.' This is the message, at once naïve and unscrupulous, on a signboard advertising rabbits. These rabbits are bred by a young woman who fleetingly appears as one of the many tragic heroes of Michael Moore's documentary *Roger and Me*, which portrays the struggle for survival in the declining Detroit area.

'Pets and Meat' might serve as a kind of signboard for this volume as it illustrates an innovative character, born of necessity, that we find in the redefinition of economic assets in the transformations in contemporary Eastern Europe. Whereas the dominant view blames the ambiguity and multiplicity of orientations in post-socialism for the 'chaos' that hinders economic activity, this volume argues that ambiguity can also be a resource that facilitates economic action. As a pre-condition for the redefinition of assets, ambiguity is a constitutive element of the entrepreneurial moment—as, for example, when it permits the definition (and, with the appropriate skills, the selling) of rabbits as pets *and* meat.

'Pets and Meat' also signals our reluctance to pursue the scientific ambition of decomposing the ambiguities of change and transformation through concepts that are themselves devoid of ambiguity. Like the heroine of *Roger and Me*, we attempt to exploit the ambiguities of the organizing themes of this volume: legacies will be interpreted not simply as residues of the past but also as resources for the future; linkages will be examined through analytic lenses that highlight the absence or looseness of particular connections; and finally, localities will be explored not for homogeneity and coherence within certain sites, but for the multiplicity and ambiguity of meanings which are simultaneously present in them.

Despite such open tolerance of ambiguity, this volume is aware of the danger that an excess of ambiguity can erode coherence and cohesion. This appears to be true not only for economies and societies for also for edited volumes. For their efforts to keep ambiguities in bounds, the editors thank Wendy Carlin, Hartmut Haussermann, Claus Offe, and Endre Sík, who contributed as discussants at the conference at the Wissenschaftszentrum Berlin (WZB) where these papers were presented. Warm thanks for disciplining us in the editing of the manuscript are due to David Antal, Rebecca Matthews, and Angelika Zierer-Kuhnle. For fellowship support and funds for translation we thank the Institute for Advanced Study, Collegium Budapest, the Center for Advanced Study in the Behavioral Sciences, Palo Alto, and the Mario Einaudi Center for International Studies at Cornell University. Our special thanks to the WZB for hosting the conference and for its generous support in bringing this volume to publication.

G. G.
D. S.

Berlin and Palo Alto

CONTENTS

CONTRIBUTORS

VLADIMÍR BENÁCEK is Professor of International Economics at the Charles University, Prague.

ISTVÁN R. GÁBOR is Professor of Labour Economics and Chair of the Department of Human Resources at the Budapest University of Economics.

GERNOT GRABHER is Lecturer in Economic Geography at King's College, London (formerly Senior Research Fellow at the Social Science Centre, Berlin).

JERZY HAUSNER is Professor in Economics at the Cracow Academy of Economics.

THOMAS KOCH is Senior Research Fellow at the Berlin Institute of Social Science Studies (BISS).

TIBOR KUCZI is Lecturer in Sociology at the Budapest University of Economics.

TADEUSZ KUDŁACZ is Professor in Economic Geography at the Cracow Academy of Sciences.

GERALD A. McDERMOTT is Ph.D. candidate at the Department of Political Science at the Massachusetts Institute of Technology.

CSABA MAKÓ is Senior Researcher at the Centre of Social Conflict Research, Hungarian Academy of Sciences, and Professor of Organization and Management at the Budapest University of Economics.

CHRIS PICKVANCE is Professor of Urban Studies at the University of Kent at Canterbury.

PETER RUTLAND is Assistant Director of Research at the Open Media Research Institute in Prague.

JUDITH B. SEDAITIS is Research Associate at the Center for International Security and Arms Control, Stanford University.

WOLFGANG SEIBEL is Professor of Political and Administrative Science at the University of Constance.

DAVID STARK is Professor of Sociology at Cornell University.

JACEK SZLACHTA is Professor of Economics at the Warsaw School of Economics.

MICHAEL THOMAS is Senior Lecturer in Sociology at the Technical University of Dresden.

HELLMUT WOLLMANN is Professor in Public Administration at the Humboldt University, Berlin.

1

Organizing Diversity: *Evolutionary Theory, Network Analysis, and Post-socialism*

GERNOT GRABHER *and* DAVID STARK

INTRODUCTION: LESSONS FROM LABRADOR

Each evening during their hunting season, the Naskapi Indians of the Labrador Peninsula determined where they would look for game on the next day's hunt by holding a caribou shoulder-bone over the fire.[1] Examining the smoke deposits on the caribou bone, a shaman read for the hunting party the points of orientation of tomorrow's search. In this way, the Naskapi introduced a randomizing element to confound a short-term rationality in which the one best way to find game would have been to look again tomorrow where they had found game today. By following the daily divergent map of smoke on the caribou bone, they avoided locking in to early successes that, while taking them to game in the short run, would have depleted the caribou stock in that quadrant and reduced the likelihood of successful hunting in the long run. By breaking the link between future courses and past successes, the tradition of shoulder-bone reading was an antidote to path dependence in the hunt.

Mainstream notions of the post-socialist 'transition' as the replacement of one set of economic institutions by another set of institutions of proven efficiency are plagued by similar problems of short-term rationality that the Naskapi traditional practices mitigate. As the economist's variant of 'hunt tomorrow where we found game today', neo-liberals recommend the adoption of a highly stylized version of the institutions of prices and property that have 'worked well in the West'. Economic efficiency will be maximized only by the rapid and all-encompassing implementation of privatization and marketization. We argue, by contrast, from an evolutionary perspective, that although such institutional homogenization might foster *adaptation* in the short run, the consequent loss of institutional diversity will impede *adaptability* in the long run (Grabher 1994). Limiting the search for effective institutions and organizational forms to the familiar Western quadrant of tried and proven arrangements locks in the post-socialist economies to *exploiting* known territory at the cost of forgetting (or never learning) the skills of *exploring* for new solutions.

With our Naskapi example we do not mean to suggest that policy-makers in contemporary Eastern Europe should select institutions with a roll of the dice. For us, the lesson from Labrador is that institutional legacies that retard the quick pursuit of immediate successes can be important for keeping open alternative courses of action. Institutional friction preserves diversity; it sustains organizational routines that might later be recombined in new organizational forms. Resistance to change, in this sense, can foster change. Institutional legacies embody not only the persistence of the past but also resources for the future. Institutional friction that blocks transition to an already designated future keeps open a multiplicity of alternative paths to further exploration.

Our neo-liberal colleagues would be quick to argue that such exploration is costly, inefficient, and unnecessary. In their view, the alternative, evolutionary course of search seems an indulgent squandering of resources, avoidable by exploiting institutions with proven returns. Given limited resources, the economies of Eastern Europe would do better to be quick to the chase, to learn from the leaders instead of the lessons of Labrador.

Recent studies in evolutionary economics and organizational analysis suggest, by contrast, that organizations that learn too quickly sacrifice efficiency. Allen and McGlade (1987), for example, use the behaviour of Nova Scotia fishermen to illustrate the possible trade-offs of exploiting old certainties and exploring new possibilities. Their model of these fishing fleets divides the fishermen into two classes: the rationalist 'Cartesians' who drop their nets only where the fish are known to be biting and the risk-taking 'Stochasts' who discover the new schools of fish. In simulations where all the skippers are Stochasts the fleet is relatively unproductive—for knowledge of where the fish are biting is unutilized; but a purely Cartesian fleet locks in to the 'most likely' spot and quickly fishes it out. More efficient are the models that most closely mimic the actual behaviour of the Nova Scotia fishing fleets with their mix of Cartesian exploiters and Stochastic explorers.

James March's simulation in 'Exploitation and Exploration in Organizational Learning' (1991) yields similar results when he finds that interacting collections of smart learners frequently underperform interactions of smart and dumb.[2] Organizations that learn too quickly exploit at the expense of exploration thereby locking in to suboptimal routines and strategies. The purely Cartesian fleet in Allen and McGlade's study, like the organizations of homogeneously smart learners in March's simulations, illustrate the potential dangers of positive feedback and the pitfalls of tight coupling. Like infantry officers who instructed drummers to disrupt cadence deliberately while crossing bridges lest the resonance of uniformly marching soldiers bring calamity, we draw the lesson that dissonance contributes to organizational learning and economic evolution.

This book counters the neo-classical prescriptions for the post-socialist economies with an alternative conception of development drawn from new insights in evolutionary theory and network analysis. These schools of analysis are not typically paired, and this introductory essay makes the case that their combination provides fruitful tools for understanding the post-socialist transformations.

As we introduce the major themes of the book and anticipate the substantive research findings of its chapters, we shall see that each of the papers contributes in its own way to elaborating the volume's title: *Restructuring Networks*. The starting premiss of this book is that the proper analytic unit, because it is the actual economic unit, is not the isolated firm but networks that link firms and connect persons across them.[3] Similarly, the unit of entrepreneurship is not the isolated individual but networks of actors. As such, our attention shifts from the attributes and motivations of individual personalities to the properties of the localities and networks in which entrepreneurial activity is reproduced (Stark 1990). It follows that the economic unit to be restructured is not the isolated firm but networks of firms linking interdependent assets across formal organizational boundaries.

The chapters in this volume also exploit the intentionally double meaning of the book's title: networks are not only the units to be restructured but also the agents to do restructuring. That is, in place of the dichotomously forced choice of restructuring directed by state agencies versus restructuring via market processes this book explores the possibilities of alternative co-ordinating mechanisms governed neither by hierarchy nor by markets (Powell 1987, 1990; Stark and Bruszt 1995).

The volume's subtitle, *Legacies, Linkages, and Localities*, serves as the organizing principle of this introductory chapter. As we make the case for incongruence and explore the possibilities that ambiguity can be a resource for economic action, the reader should be prepared for some dissonance between the conventional meanings of these terms and their usage here. In developing these themes, we shall discover processes and logics quite different from notions that come first to mind. As we have already mentioned, we shall see that legacies are not simple residues of the past but can serve as resources for the future. Similarly, the more systematically we pursue the logic of linkages, the more our analysis turns to the structural features produced by the absences of particular connections. And whereas 'localities' might evoke sites in which proximity shapes shared meanings, we examine localities as sites where the simultaneous presence of multiple logics (what we might think of as different 'species' of social action) yields complex ecologies of meaning.

Fitness Tests

In the neo-liberal prescription for the post-socialist transition, the persistence of organizational forms and social relationships of the old state-socialist system signals an incomplete change, a manifest symptom of a half-hearted implementation of the envisaged new social order. Accordingly, legacies indicate institutional pathologies contaminated with the deficiences of the old regime obstructing the process of transformation: the future cannot be realized because the past cannot be overcome. The legacies of state-socialism block the promising road to free markets.

Free markets, the prominent advocates of neo-classical economics incessantly repeat, are a synonym for efficiency. Notoriously suppressed during state socialism, competition in free markets guarantees that more efficient organizational forms will survive and that inefficient ones will perish. In the relentless struggle for survival only the fittest endure.

Ironically, while economists can still embrace the crude Darwinism of Spencer's 'survival of the fittest', contemporary biologists (see e.g. Smith 1984; Gould and Lewontin 1984; and the essays in Dupre 1987) have challenged the received evolutionary model arguing that evolution cannot simply be regarded as a one-dimensional process of optimization, a beneficent and unilinear journey from the lower to the higher form of organization, from the inferior to the superior. Natural selection does not yield the superlative fittest, only the comparatively and tolerably fit.

Evolution, in this sense, does not proceed along a single grand path towards perfection but along multiple paths which do not all lead to optimal change. That some developmental paths produce ineffective solutions and suboptimal outcomes is not an indication of evolutionary failure but a precondition for evolutionary selection: no variety, no evolution. Hence, the evolutionary process necessarily entails development through failure: 'imperfections are the primary proofs that evolution has occured, since optimal designs erase all signposts of history' (Gould 1987: 14).

This critique of the 'survival of the fittest' paradigm, offers an alternative evolutionary model for challenging the neo-classical assumptions of 'historical efficiency' (March and Olsen 1989: 5–6) in which survival implies efficiency and mere existence proves optimality (cf. Hodgson 1993). The lesson to be drawn from evolutionary theory is that competition in free markets does not necessarily favour the fitter and more efficient form of organization: market competition is not an optimizer (Barnett 1995).

Fitness is not an absolute and invariant quantity. Rather, fitness depends on the environment, and the environment may change during the course of the selection process (Carroll and Harrison 1994). Thus, even if the selected characteristics of an organizational form were the 'fittest', they would be so only in regard to a particular economic, political, and cultural context; they would not be the fittest for a changing or a different context. In fact, the very fitness of an organizational form might, through various mechanisms, induce environmental changes that undermine their efficiency.[4] It follows that organizational forms that are most fit for the 'transition' are quite likely to be suboptimal in the subsequently changed environment. In place of the search for the 'best' institutions to manage the transition, we might do better to reorient our analysis to identifying the types of organizational configurations that are better at search.

Evolutionary theory, moreover, turns our attention to how the future development of an economic system is affected by the path it has traced in the past. Once we reject the notion that 'from whatever starting point, the system will eventually gravitate to the same equilibrium' (Hodgson 1993: 204), we are alerted to the possibilities that free markets might lock in economic development to a particular path that does not gravitate to the optimum. Positive feedback can have negative effects. Increasing returns from learning effects and network externalities (Katz and Shapiro 1985; David 1992) yield real immediate benefits that can preclude selection in the long run of the most efficient organizational form (Arthur 1994; David 1986; Carroll and Harrison 1994). Once an economy is locked into a particular trajectory, the costs of shifting strategies outweigh the benefits of alternatives. This approach to economic history stresses the possibility that the very mechanisms that foster allocative efficiency might eventually lock in economic development to a path which is inefficient viewed dynamically. The mechanisms that are conducive for the synchronic adaptation of the economy to a specific environment may, at the same time, undermine an economy's diachronic adaptability.

The trade-off between allocative and dynamic efficiency[5] constitutes a fundamental tension in the current transformation in Eastern Europe. Murrell (1991) argues from empirical data that state socialism was no less efficient in allocating resources than capitalist societies. Where it lagged was in dynamic efficiency, in its capacity to promote innovation. This imbalance has survived state socialism: current reform efforts seem preoccupied with removing institutional legacies for the sake of improving allocative efficiency. But a purging of organizational legacies to gain allocative efficiency can come at the cost of undermining dynamic efficiency just as a narrow adaptation to a specific economic environment can jeopardize the economy's adaptability (Grabher 1994; Granovetter 1979: 498; Hannan 1986).

In the perspective developed here, we focus not on the problem of how to improve the immediate 'fit' into a new economic environment but on how to reorganize the institutional and organization structure of these economies to enhance their ability to respond to unpredictable changes in the environment. Although the institutional legacies of the East European

economies might hinder their adaptation in the short run, they could contribute to the economy's adaptability in the long run. We do not seek, of
course, to reverse the evaluation of historical legacies from universally
vicious to unequivocally virtuous. Instead we aim to highlight the dual
potential of legacies to block *and* to support transformation.

It follows that instead of examining organizational forms in Eastern
Europe according to the degree to which they conform to or depart from
the ideal types of organizing production in Western-style capitalism, this
book is concerned with variations and mutations emerging from the recombination of the inherited forms with emerging new ones. Instead of simply
conceiving these recombinations as accidental aberrations, this book
explores their evolutionary potentials.

Compartmentalization: The Organization of Diversity

We thus shift from the preoccupation with the efficiency of an individual
organizational form to a concern for variety and diversity of forms[6] central
to the perspective of 'population thinking' (Mayr 1984, 1985; Sober 1984:
155–69).

As we shall see, the recombination of old organizational forms in the
reorganization of the large state enterprises increases variety and diversity
within the 'genetic pool' for the evolution of new organizational forms. For
evolution to work there must always be a variety of forms from which to
select: 'Selection is like a fire that consumes its own fuel . . . unless variation
is renewed periodically, evolution would come to a stop almost at its incep-
tion' (Lewontin 1982: 151). Diversity and variety allow evolution to follow
at the same time different paths which are associated with different sets of
organizational forms. When selection starts off not simply from a single
trajectory but from a broad and diverse range of evolutionary alternatives,
the risk decreases that local maximization results in an evolutionary dead
end. Two or more evolutionary trajectories are thus able to cope with a
broader array of unpredictable environmental changes than is the case with
a single one.

In this perspective, different levels of efficiency associated with the different evolutionary paths are not symptoms of an inefficient selection mechanism. Rather, they are a pre-condition for improving overall efficiency since
'the rate of increase in fitness of any organism at any time is equal to its
genetic variance in fitness at that time' (Fisher 1930: 35). The merciless
competition evoked by the crude Darwinism of the 'survival of the fittest'
is, according to neo-Darwinism, mitigated by the biological principle of
compartmentalization.[7] Compartmentalization buffers the various sub-
populations from each other and, hence, allows less efficient ones to coexist
with the currently most efficient ones without being exposed to selection
immediately. Compartmentalization allows for an increasing diversification

of the evolutionary selection (Mayr 1980). In a compartmentalized genetic pool, rare genes have a greater chance to influence subsequent evolution than is the case with a non-compartmentalized genetic pool.[8] Although compartmentalization detracts from the fitness of the entire system, the sum of the subsystems keeps ready a broader spectrum of answers to environmental challenges and, thus, ultimately arrives at an even higher level of fitness (Weizsaecker and Weizsaecker 1984: 188). Similarly, but from a game-theoretic perspective, Boyer and Orlean (1992) argue that a new convention is more likely to take hold in a population of organizations not when it attempts to invade the entire population immediately but when it begins in a relatively buffered subfield of organizations. In different terms: containment can be an important element of contamination.

The principle of compartmentalization suggests that it is not simply the diversity of organizations but the *organization of diversity* that is relevant for the recombination of organizational forms in Eastern Europe. The reproduction of diversity depends on the ability of different levels of efficiency to coexist. On the one hand, evolution comes to a stop in cases where less efficient forms are eliminated through selection immediately: too little diversity, no evolution. On the other hand, however, the absence of any evolutionary selective comparison might turn diversity into 'noise' in which none of the organizational forms would be able to influence the direction of any evolutionary trajectory: too much diversity, likewise, no evolution.

This tension between too little diversity (emerging from a too low degree of compartmentalization) and too much diversity (resulting from a too high degree of compartmentalization) is exemplified by the analysis of the restructuring of the large state-owned corporations in East Germany (Grabher, Chapter 4 of this volume) and in Hungary (Stark, Chapter 2). The resolute East German approach led to a rapid dissolution of the old hegemonic form of the *Kombinat* and (through the establishment of Western branch plants) to an increasing diversity of organizational forms. But, as Grabher argues, this diversity might yet shrink again in the medium term. The superior efficiency of the Western branch plants could lead—due to a lack of compartmentalization—to a further crowding out of other organizational forms located mainly within the indigenous small-firm sector. The great disparity between the invading front-runner and the indigenous laggards could produce a winner-takes-all situation that once again suppresses organizational diversity.

Seen from this perspective, the current Eastern German economy echoes the relative paucity of organizational forms of the old GDR economy whereas the transformation of the large enterprises in contemporary Hungary builds on the previous decade of organizational experimentation that allowed not only for competition among *firms* but also for competition of *forms* (Stark 1989). This competition of forms created a broad spectrum of variants in organizing production that increasingly overlapped in terms of personnel, supplier relations, and property rights. With this blurring of boundaries came greater organizational diversity. In contrast to the more recent experience in Eastern Germany, moreover, this diversity of forms has not been challenged by the emergence of a vastly more efficient form. That is, there is greater diversity of organizational forms in Hungary, but there is also much less obvious disparity of 'fitness' among them. Whereas in Eastern Germany a preponderant disparity runs the danger of suppressing diversity, in Hungary a 'noisy' diversity runs the danger of suppressing selection with the result that less efficient forms might deprive more efficient forms of resources to an extent that blocks the evolution of the entire economy.

Legacies for Entrepreneurial Careers

The notion of compartmentalization also figures implicitly in proposals for a 'two-track strategy' whereby resources are channelled into the indigenous small-firm sector (the former second economy) while adopting more stringent administrative measures to harden the budget constraints of large firms remaining in the state sector. That strategy builds on the pioneering work of István Gábor, who was among the first to perceive and analyse the significance of the second economy. In a series of brilliant studies, Gábor (1979, 1985, 1986) demonstrated that the developmental potential of the second economy rested not in some spirit of individual entrepreneurship but in a *dynamic tension* between the twinned economies of late state socialism. Subsequent advocates of the two-track strategy such as Kornai (1990, 1992), Murrell (1992*a,b*, 1993), and later Poznanski (1993) argued that this dynamic tension would evaporate if privatization and marketization would be attempted throughout the entire economy. That is, the transformative potential of the emerging marketized sector would dissipate if it was not buffered from the sphere of the large public enterprises (Stark 1990). Attempts to 'privatize' everything at once would lead to privatizing little at all. A strategy of non-compartmentalized privatization would yield firms that were private in name only. Similarly, expectations are not likely to change when those with new behaviours are scattered throughout the population. Actors are more likely to change their expectations when the probability of encountering a new behaviour trait is higher (Boyer and Orlean 1992). Buffering the sub-population of market-oriented actors increases this likelihood; and compartmentalization (buffering that is not absolute but porous) increases the chances that the new patterns of behaviour can take hold in the broader population.

But the two-track strategy was nowhere adopted as official policy.[9] Nor can we assume, in any case, that a compartmentalized strategy would have selected behavioural traits of market orientation. What we can do is to examine actual behaviour in the emergent small-firm sector. Doing so, we see (1) that the second economy has not necessarily promoted a dynamic capital-accumulating stratum and (2) that the second economy has not been the primary source of the new economic élite as successful entrepreneurs are likely to come from the ranks of the socialist cadre. Each illustrates the ambiguous legacy of state socialism.

First, as we shall see in Gábor's analysis below in Chapter 6, the small-firm sector in post-socialist Hungary is marked by fragmentation and 'over-tertialization'. Instead of finding small-scale proprietors growing into medium-size employers, Gábor identifies an increasing tendency for small entrepreneurs to shun productive lines of business that involve higher investment intensity.[10] He traces these features, at least partially, to economic preferences inherited from the second economy of the past regime including the income-maximizing consumption orientation of households; aversion to long-term business investment and risk-taking; the low appreciation of free time compared to income; and the poor tax morale. Much of the entrepreneurship in this overly tertiary small-firm sector means 'moving things', not making them (Maruyama 1993: 166; see also Gábor 1994).

Second, technocratic expertise acquired during state socialism provides an important source of entrepreneurship in the post-socialist period. As in advanced market economies, the élite in state socialism was an educated élite—in the early years, partly because party membership in their youth enabled some to receive higher education, in the later years, because the ambitious joined the party to promote their careers after completing their formal education.[11] That is, under socialism, education and party recruitment went hand in hand. It now appears, and not surprisingly so, that under post-socialism, education and entrepreneurship are closely linked. The legacy of socialism is that the former élite are well endowed to convert the cultural capital of the education and training acquired in the old order to advance to prominent positions in the new (Bourdieu 1986; Szelényi *et al.* 1995; Li and White 1990; and for a discussion of recent debates see Hanley 1995).

Empirical studies conducted in Hungary, the Czech Republic, and East Germany are now providing evidence to support an argument that it is the common technocratic character of both party *and* entrepreneurial recruitment that is a main source of this continuity. Róna-Tas (1994: 62), for example, concludes from a study on Hungary that 'cadres are more enterprising both as non-corporate and corporate entrepreneurs'. Starting a corporate business upholds the technocratic continuity argument, as the effect of cadreship takes place through education. The new élite of entrepreneurs will substantially overlap with the old one, 'because in the transition from socialism the first shall not be last, but rather the first shall last' (Róna-Tas 1994: 65). In a similar vein, Vladimír Benácek's study of new entrepreneurs in the Czech Republic (Chapter 9 below) and Thomas Koch and Michael Thomas's analysis of their counterparts in Eastern Germany

(Chapter 10) present findings of a strong connection between managerial or technocratic positions in the state-socialist past and success in entering private entrepreneurship in post-socialism.

Taken together, the studies in this volume point to several legacies of state socialism in the field of entrepreneurial careers: whereas the old socialist hierarchies seem a launching-pad for careers in the larger, legal firms of the emerging entrepreneurial sector, the heritage of the second economy pushes towards further fragmentation within the semi-legal sector of micro-firms.

LINKAGES

Loose Coupling

In the predominant view, the implosion of state socialism has left behind an institutional vacuum and a social *tabula rasa* of atomized economic and political actors. Instead of atomization and paralysis, this book examines the embeddedness of actors in social ties, whether official or informal. Instead of a social *tabula rasa*, the volume focuses on how actors attempt to recombine resources, especially by reorganizing the networks that link individuals and firms within and across localities and economic spheres. By examining the constraining *and the enabling* dimensions of patterned relationships, we emphasize that actors are vividly involved in restructuring networks.

The relational approach adopted here starts not with the personal attributes of actors but with the networks of interaction that link actors (Emirbayer and Goodwin 1994). From this perspective, very strong and dense social networks facilitate the development of uniform subcultures and strong collective identities. But network analysis does not begin and end with social cohesion. A particularly dense and tightly coupled network (in the extreme, where every actor in the network has a direct tie to every other) might promote cohesiveness while hindering the ability to gain information and mobilize resources from the environment.[12] Recent trends in network analysis posit an inverse relationship, in general, between the density and intensity of the coupling of network ties on the one hand and their openness to the outside environment on the other. Similarly, in contrast to conventional cliquing models (e.g. 'who knows whom'), new research in the field is more likely to focus on absent ties in a network social space where actors lack direct connections. Research within this more robust relational analysis is now demonstrating that 'weak ties' (Granovetter 1973) indirectly connecting actors or bridging the 'structural holes' (Burt 1992) that become 'obligatory passage points' (Callon and Latour 1981; Latour 1988) between relatively isolated groups of actors are crucial for the *adaptability of networks*.

The evolutionary advantages of loosely coupled networks were early appreciated and systematically differentiated by Weick (1976). First, a loosely coupled network is a good system for *localized* adaptation. If the elements in a system are loosely coupled, then any one element can adjust to and modify a local contingency without affecting the whole system. Loose coupling thus lowers the probability that the network will have to (or even be able to) respond to every minor change in the environment. A second advantage is that loosely coupled networks preserve many independent sensing elements and therefore 'know' their environment better. Third, in loosely coupled networks where the identity and separateness of elements is preserved, the network can potentially retain a greater number of mutations and novel solutions than would be the case with a tightly coupled system. As such, loosely coupled networks 'may be elegant solutions to the problem that adaptation can preclude adaptability' (Weick 1976: 7). When a specific network fits into an ecological niche, adaptation can be costly because resources that are useless in the current environment might deteriorate even though they could be crucial in a modified environment. Finally, it is conceivable that loose coupling preserves more diversity in responding than do tightly coupled networks and therefore can adapt to a considerably wider range of changes in the environment.

Network concepts of strong and weak ties, of tight and loose coupling, can thus be translated back into the problem of compartmentalization in population thinking even as the latter can be expressed in network terms: just as new traits enter a population by enough buffering for them to take hold within a sub-population and diffuse throughout a species by enough contact across substructures, so change in the organizational field is fostered by enough strong ties for social cohesion and enough loose coupling for adaptability.[13]

Again, however, we are not claiming an unequivocably positive relationship between the loose coupling and the adaptability of a network. Although diversity and loose coupling might, on a structural level, support adaptability by allowing different levels of efficiency to coexist, they can also, on a cognitive level, result in a cacophony of orientations, perceptions, goals, and world-views that confounds even minimal cohesiveness. Such is the danger noted by some observers of the East European transformation (e.g. Henderson *et al.* 1995) who identify the 'chaos' resulting from the multiplicity and ambiguity of orientations and perceptions as a major obstacle to future-oriented economic action. None the less, the chapters in this volume invite a tolerance of ambiguity. That tolerance is not an unqualified embrace[14] but an explicit ambivalence: it acknowledges that ambiguity can be an asset even while it recognizes that these gains can come at the expense of accountability. Aware that an excess of ambiguity can dissipate social cohesion, it is none the less alert to the possibilities that ambiguity can be a resource for credible commitments. Just as tolerance for ambiguity is regarded, on an individual level, as an attribute of a mature and robust personality (Loevinger 1976: 23), so here it is seen, on the system level, as a central cognitive pre-condition for adaptability. Similar to the ways that tolerance for different levels of efficiency enhances the evolutionary potentials of a network, so tolerance for ambiguous or even contradictory perceptions and goals facilitates the search for new answers to new questions (Grabher 1994: 37–41). Organizational research 'leaves little doubt that an increase in subgoal diversity and attendant conflict can enhance the quality of search' (Cohen 1984: 436). The communication of contradictions and conflicts, sparked by the ambiguity of goals, could act as a sort of an 'immune system' for a network (Luhmann 1986: 185). In a sense, tolerance for ambiguity constitutes the 'intelligence' of a network reducing the chance that contradictory signals are suppressed in favour of a singular but distorted knowledge and an internally consistent but mistaken interpretation.[15]

Loose Coupling in Entrepreneurial Networks

As we shall see in the chapters in this volume, rather than being extinguished for the sake of the logical principle of *tertium non datur* (there is no third case), ambiguity can be deliberately reproduced in particular situations by the *tertius gaudens* (the third who benefits). Taken from the work of Simmel (1923/1950: 154, 232) the *tertius* role is instructive in the East European transformation because it points to an ambiguity from which 'the third who benefits' leverages off a stable entrepreneurial position. In certain situations, emerging as the *tertius* depends on creating competition: 'Make simultaneous, contradictory demands explicit to the people posing them, and ask them to resolve their—now explicit—conflict' (Burt 1992: 76). Entrepreneurship, in this perspective, emerges from *tertius* brokering contradiction and ambiguity between others: no ambiguity, no *tertius*.

As Judith Sedaitis's analysis of the emergence of new market organizations in Russia suggests (Chapter 5 below), such a *tertius* strategy and the strategic utilization of ambiguity seems more easily practised in loosely coupled networks than in tightly integrated ones. According to her study of the new commodity exchanges in Russia, exchanges organized around loosely coupled networks differ from tightly coupled networks in crucial aspects. Loosely coupled networks (with less density of direct ties among their founders) enjoy greater immediate returns on investment due to their greater manœuvrability and more varied access to resources. They are able to serve market demand more directly and to exploit the lucrative opportunities in the disruption of established distribution patterns. With minimal constraints both internally and externally, they are relatively free to pursue *tertius* strategies in a manner which has been labelled 'shark behavior'

(Kozminski 1993). At the same time, however, their extraordinary diversity in turn provides little basis for social cohesion.

Commodity exchanges organized around the tightly knit networks grounded in past institutional arrangements, by contrast, inherit institutional legitimacy yet they suffer a limited profitability. Sedaitis argues that the lower profitability of these tightly knit networks is due less to the constricted range of talent of their personnel than to the structural incapacity of their networks to pursue the aggressive *tertius* strategy favoured by the loosely coupled networks. Moreover, for the tightly knit networks, limited outside interaction inhibits processes of learning and unlearning: 'Shared past histories constrain the range of future possibilities . . . old ties limit organizational flexibility and maintain a 'segmented' system of circumscribed action and responsibility that limits the potential of management to respond creatively to the new environment and the problems it poses' (Sedaitis, Chapter 5).

Sedaitis's analysis of the Russian commodity exchanges thus marks an important departure from conventional approaches to entrepreneurship in two respects. It can be contrasted, first, to the research tradition that attributed entrepreneurship to the behavioural features of certain personality types, featured prominently, for example, in the early writings of Schumpeter (1912/1961: 137), who provided a rich source of iconographic portraits of entrepreneurs as 'whole-hearted fellows' (*ganze Kerle*) combining the genius of creative discovery with the courage of 'creative destruction'. For Sedaitis, entrepreneurship is not a function of an individual personality but of a social network. Second, Sedaitis's use of network concepts departs dramatically from a recent tendency to view network connections as the property of individuals. In that view, 'social capital' (Coleman 1988) is a new individual-level variable that interacts with other assets ('human capital') in the process of status attainment or career mobility (for a critical assessment, see Baron and Hannan 1994). Accordingly, researchers can now develop measures of the 'volume of network capital' (Sík 1994) in the possession of individual research subjects. However innovative in the field of mobility studies or the analysis of entrepreneurship, the addition of this new variable brings the notion of 'network' into the picture in a manner that neglects the relational dimension that is the fundamental insight of network analysis. In Sedaitis's study, by contrast, our attention shifts from *networks as property* to the *properties of networks* as she demonstrates that the shape, structure, and characteristics of *different kinds of networks* make possible different economic activities.

Asset Ambiguity

If the legacy of old networks and the structure of new ties are important for determining the types of entrepreneurial activity in post-socialism, might they also figure prominently in the restructuring of large corporations? This is the question posed in the studies by Gerald McDermott (Chapter 3 below) and David Stark (Chapter 2) on the Czech Republic and Hungary respectively.

In Czechoslovakia during the 1970s and 1980s, under the umbrella of meso-level 'industrial associations', constituent suppliers and customers, managers and workers, state bank branches, firms, and local Communist Party members formed alliances to gain privileges from the centre and created informal compacts of economic co-ordination to limit and adjust to the uncertainties of an economy of shortage.[16] McDermott argues that, over time, these informal networks became institutionalized, though not necessarily legally recognized, and became the frameworks to define and renegotiate claims to individual units of the large state-owned corporations. To the extent that these tightly coupled networks are also sources of mutual hold-up power among the actors, the discretion and the necessary knowledge to reorganize production are bound up in these relationships. Hence, the policy of the state to end-run the potential hold-up powers of firm actors—through rapid privatization—would be 'one-legged' (McDermott, Chapter 3).

McDermott demonstrates that, despite its neo-liberal rhetoric, Vaclav Klaus's voucher privatization programme did not eliminate the ties that bind so much as rearrange them.[17] The outcome is a web of connections through which a multiplicity of actors are renegotiating not simply contractual ties but their mutual claims on interdependent assets.[18] Through that web, firms, banks, investment companies, local governments, and parts of the state bureaucracy identify firms that should be saved, devise strategies for restructuring assets, bargain about the allocation of resources, and renegotiate the very rules and governance institutions for resolving disputes among them.

The Janus face of networks also influences the Hungarian process of property transformation and corporatization, driven by key actors in the old formal and informal networks who constituted the best organized social group in Hungary during the last decades. As Stark documents in Chapter 2, managers of the large state-owned enterprises are breaking up their organizations—along divisional, plant, or even workshop lines—into numerous satellite corporations. Although these newly incorporated entities with legal identities were nominally independent, they combined private, semi-private, and state property in a complex manner. Property shares in these satellite organizations are not limited to the founding enterprise but are also held by top and mid-level managers, professionals, and other staff. In the typical pattern of this particular form of 'recombinant property', these private persons were joined in share ownership by other corporations and corporate satellites which were spinning around some other enterprises. At the same time, large enterprises are acquiring shares in each other, creating extensive inter-enterprise ownership networks. Like the ropes binding moutain climbers on a treacherous face, these ties reduce risk, they buffer the networks from the uncertainty of the transformation shock, and they can facilitate innovation for some, even while retarding the selection process for many (Miner *et al.* 1990; Ickes and Ryterman 1994).

In contrast to the essentialist categories of private versus state property, these recombinant practices create networks of horizontal ties of cross-ownership intertwined with vertical ties of nested holdings in which the boundaries between state and private property are increasingly blurred.[19] Recombinant property is not, however, a simple mixture of public and private: it is a hedging strategy that also blurs the boundaries of organizations themselves and blurs, as well, the boundedness of justificatory principles. As Sabel (1990) and Kogut *et al.* (1992) demonstrate in their studies in Germany and the United States,[20] under conditions of extreme market volatility or of extraordinarily rapid technological change, economic actors engage in hedging strategies such as cross-ownership. In cases of extremely complex asset interdependence, it is not clear-cut property claims but an ambiguity of property claims that provides flexible adaptation. Stark argues that Hungarian recombinant property displays similar features of organizational boundary blurring. Such *asset ambiguity* should not be interpreted, however, as the simple polar opposite of Williamson's 'asset specificity' for it occurs in a volatile environment where the state's paternalistic efforts at the centralized management of liabilities creates incentives for managers to employ a multiplicity of justificatory principles to acquire resources. To survive in such an environment, managers become equally skilled in the language of profitability for credit financing as in the syntax of eligibility for debt forgiveness. When they attempt to hold resources that can be justified by more than one legitimizing principle, they make assets of ambiguity.

It is this ambiguity, together with the network properties that underlie it, that forms the basis for a kind of strategic play that Padgett and Ansell (1993) label 'robust action'. At the core of robust action is the fact 'that single actions can be interpreted coherently from multiple perspectives simultaneously, the fact that single actions can be moves in many games at once, and the fact that public and private motivations cannot be parsed' (Padgett and Ansell 1993: 1263). The outcome is flexible opportunism, that is, maintaining discretionary options across unforeseeable futures in the face of hostile attempts by others to narrow those options. Crucial for maintaining discretion is not to pursue any specific goals: 'For in nasty strategic games . . . positional play is the maneuvering of opponents into the forced clarification of their (but not your) tactical lines of action' (Padgett and Ansell 1993: 1265). Victory, hence, means locking in others, but not yourself, to goal-oriented sequences of strategic play that become predictable thereby.

The same opportunistic blurring of boundaries that leads to a recombination of assets and a decomposition of the large corporations also bears a social cost: it erodes (or, in the post-socialist case, retards) accountability. As Stark demonstrates (Chapter 2), the problem with the peculiarly diversified portfolios in the 'polyphonic discourse of worth that is post-socialism' is that actors can all too often easily and almost imperceptibly switch among the various positions they hold simultaneously in the coexisting moral economies. To be accountable according to many different principles becomes a means to be accountable to none. Unless we are willing to posit 'flexibility' as an overriding value and a meta-legitimizing principle, we cannot escape the challenge that post-socialism poses, not uniquely[21] but acutely, for our epoch: if networks are viable economic agents of permanently ongoing restructuring, how can we make networks (as a new kind of moral actor) accountable?

LOCALITIES

Locality as Ecology

In the dominant view, localities are irrelevant in constructing transition strategies. When not centred squarely at the level of the individual firm, analysis of the post-socialist transformations typically focuses on policies and institutions at the level of the national economy such as monetary policy, legal frameworks for corporate governance, or regulatory institutions for banking and finance. Place, the problem of localities, is out of place in these perspectives.

The chapters in this volume, by contrast, bring localities into focus as sites of economic action. In so doing, they draw on the new economic sociology which demonstrates that globalization does not displace the properties of localities but makes them all the more salient. As greater market volatility shifts strategic action from economies of scale to economies of scope and then to economies of time (Storper 1989; Teece 1993; Sabel 1994; Gereffi 1994), local knowledge, local culture, and local networks give shape to the new organizational forms of flexible specialization.

It was with the analysis of the industrial districts of northern Italy that the potential of localities to contribute to economic development most dramatically entered the research literature in the 1980s. The stories of regional production systems concentrated in the province of Emilia Romagna have typically been written as success stories of a coherent system of economic institutions whose compatibility makes for the decisive transaction cost efficiency of the regional co-operative networks. These networks are deeply embedded within an institutional infrastructure that effectively provides for support services.

But the story of the Italian industrial districts might also be read in a different light (Grabher 1994: 70–8). The Italian textiles and clothing districts in particular are composed of an extremely broad and heterogeneous spectrum of diverse institutions and organizational forms ranging from internationally renowned design ateliers and technologically highly advanced medium-size firms at one pole to small artisanal firms and illegal homeworkers at the other. Instead of regarding this spectrum as a coherent set whose efficiency is based on the transaction cost savings gained through the compatibility of the various organizational forms, the evolutionary strengths of the industrial district might be based on the very incompatibility of these forms. In this view, not systemic coherence but organizational discrepancy is the effective evolutionary anti-body against hegemonic 'best-practice solutions'. By preserving the richness of diverse organizational routines for the evolution of new organizational mutations, discrepancy increases the adaptability of the region.

The resistance against the economistic temptation to streamline, at least in the Italian industrial districts, seems not to be an entirely intentional product of institutional design. In these districts, the spatial proximity of closely knit co-operative networks in small neighbourhoods is seen as a major source of their transaction cost efficiency. From an evolutionary perspective, however, the transaction cost effects are less important than the fact that spatial proximity allows for a continuous exchange of resources, information, and personnel across these diverse, even incompatible, forms of production. Whether or not proximity economizes on transaction costs, its long-term benefit is to facilitate a cross-fertilization across disparate forms less likely if spatially dispersed. Like the Naskapi caribou ritual of our introduction, spatial proximity in the northern Italian districts acts as a sort of random generator disrupting the tendency towards transaction cost-efficient relations with compatible firms. In preventing hyperefficient behaviour, spatial proximity does not dissolve incompatibility but enhances it.

Expressed in different terms, this view of industrial districts analyses localities as ecologies of diverse organizations. Localities are sites of interdependence of even greater complexity than the proprietary ambiguities of complementary and co-specialized assets across the boundaries of enterprises. The interdependencies within localities are more complex because they entail ambiguities across *different social logics*, routines, and practices involving not only business firms but political, religious, residential, and family life. Because these logics cannot be reduced to each other or expressed in the equivalents of a common currency, localities are not simply compartmentalizing buffers separating sub-populations of the *same* species of organization but are complex ecologies of *diverse* 'species' of social ordering principles.

Post-socialist Localities

In the post-World War II era, two major policies had inordinate weight in shaping the economic geography of state socialism: the vigorous rationalization of industries and the clustering of new, interrelated plants in the countryside. To facilitate central administration of industries, the authorities consistently decreased the number of firms while increasing their size. Once labour shortages developed in traditional regions of industrial manufacturing, the government could tap into excess rural labour by grouping plants around small, isolated communities. This was particularly possible with the so-called footloose industries such as textiles, engineering, or electronics. Subsequently, communities became increasingly isolated from one another at the same time that they became increasingly dependent on these local firms or plants for employment, economic resources, and social services such as housing, medical services, kindergartens, sport facilities, and the like (McDermott, Chapter 3 of this volume).

The 'company town' syndrome emerging from state-socialist policies in the recent past explains the importance of the local level in the restructuring of the large state-owned corporations in the present. Whereas enterprise directors were formerly confronted by compulsory co-ordination with state ministries, provincial party committees, and the central management of the large combines, the collapse of the socialist hierarchies has the consequence that managers of individual plants now frequently face only the representatives of local government (Burawoy and Krotov 1992; Berezin and Kaganova 1993; and for an interesting comparison to China, see Walder 1995). Under conditions of high concentration and industrial mono-structures, privatization and restructuring do not result in a competitive market structure but rather in a new pattern of interaction between state and economy which is often confined to the local level (Wiesenthal 1993: 10). According to Shleifer and Boycko (1993: 48), for example, in Russia, local governments have legitimacy as elected bodies and have been given control over electricity, water, and other utilities which they can translate into influence over firms: as a result, they 'have found tremendous room to govern their localities'. As the papers on local governments in Eastern Germany by Hellmut Wollmann (Chapter 14 below) and in Hungary and Russia by Chris Pickvance (Chapter 13) indicate, with the central-state bureaucracy having lost many of its functions but with market transactions between enterprises only poorly developed, the emerging governance structures of post-socialism are shaped by a growing number of decentralized and local actors who try to find a position in the uncertain and volatile conditions *beyond* plan and market.

Entrepreneurs in Localities, Entrepreneurial Localities

The emerging localized governance structure based on horizontal rather than on hierarchical or market co-ordination can contribute to the mobilization of resources in the formation of new entrepreneurial units. In their study of a small community near Budapest, Tibor Kuczi and Csaba Makó

(Chapter 7 below) indicate how local network ties reduce uncertainties and risks facing start-up ventures. That is, network linkages act as buffers retarding selection and reducing the 'liability of newness'—a problem facing new firms in any economy but particularly acute in the volatile uncertainties of post-socialist economic transformation. Kuczi and Makó point to trust-based relations where patterns of economic exchange are interwoven with ties of kinship and friendship. In the local community they studied, new contractual arrangements often follow informal relations among actors with shared experiences in the recent past whether at the locally dominant state enterprise or through joint participation in the second economy. In such conditions, trust reduces the risks involved in the selection of suppliers, business partners, and employees. Kuczi and Makó conclude that among these local networks, economic transactions are regulated by 'relational contracting' in which the stronger partner does not exploit situations where the weaker partner is vulnerable and where maintenance of the tie itself is a value that regulates exchanges and moderates disputes.

The networks of small-scale proprietors in Kuczi and Makó's study bear some resemblance, at first glance, with the north Italian industrial districts—for example, their preference for localized business contacts in the absence of a strong state, and the importance of traditional relations in contract enforcement. But the traditional elements are only a part of the success story of the north Italian districts. And although Kuczi and Makó indicate that an entrepreneurs' club and a local foundation were in the planning stages at the time of their study, the community they examined showed few signs of the highly organized craft associations, trade unions, and administratively competent local authorities so important in the north Italian district.

Moreover, there are reasons to question the causal connection between traditional ties, relations of trust, and local development. For Gábor (Chapter 6), the liabilities of traditionalism are likely to outweigh the benefits. First, to the extent that second-economy producers continue their old habits of making market transactions only where social relations have preceded, they might be disadvantaged in establishing business ties where arm's-length transactions are entirely appropriate (even to the point of forgoing advertising, for example). Second, in the absence of strong civic associations (blocked under communism, but thriving in Italy),[22] Gábor is unwilling to assume that the legacy of the proximate ties of the second economy are relations of trust. It might just as well be that the most salient 'shared experiences' from the past are relations of *mistrust* and that new exchanges based on them will bear that stamp (Kemény 1996). In slightly different terms, instead of the north Italian route to prosperity, for some post-socialist economies the road to Europe might run through Sicily.

Finally, what if the direction of causality does not run from local identities to co-operative development strategies but the reverse? This is the question posed by Charles Sabel in rethinking the dynamics of the Italian districts and other regional developmental associations. Co-operative relations, Sabel argues, are not based on primordial loyalties but on 'studied trust' (Sabel 1992). One of the clues to these processes is that Sabel and his colleagues (Sabel 1992; Hirst and Zeitlin 1991; Sabel and Zeitlin 1996) find co-operative regional development projects in districts whose recent histories were marked by intense conflicts. Yet contemporary accounts by actors in these same localities repeatedly refer to harmonious pasts as history is reconstructed in line with the present. Thus, instead of shared identities giving rise to social relations of trust, this work suggests that co-operative configurations reshape identities that can then be shared. Although historically inaccurate, these identities are no less real in their effects as templates for current co-operative action.

In this alternative view, localities contribute to innovative and co-operative development strategies not because they are a locus of shared meanings but because they are sites of interdependence among different social groups and different social logics. Because localities cannot be indifferent to this interdependence, we can say that localities are means for organizing diversity. Several of the chapters in this volume develop these insights—from Stark's notion that actors are manœuvring not only through an ecology of organizations but through an ecology of ordering principles (Chapter 2) to McDermott's analysis of how localities are the sites for complex negotiations among actors whose claims are not only competing but also very heterogeneous (Chapter 3).

A similar conception of localities as ecologies of social logics informs the study of regional development in Poland by Jerzy Hausner, Tadeusz Kudłacz, and Jacek Szlachta (Chapter 8 below). Hausner and his colleagues examined economic development in nine provinces in south-eastern Poland in a study that takes the locality not only as the unit of observation but also as the unit of analysis. In seeking to explain why economic development takes off in some regions and not others, they turn from the properties of individuals to the properties (characteristics, qualities) of the localities themselves (for an earlier ecological study of rural entrepreneurship in China, see Nee and Young 1991). In contrast to Kuczi and Makó, who provide such a rich community study of *enterpreneurs in localities*, Hausner, Kudłacz, and Szlachta might be seen to study *entrepreneurial localities*. Hausner *et al.* conclude that the best regional development strategies are not led by yet another administrative or quasi-governmental unit in the form of intermediate-level 'Regional Development Authorities'. Instead, a major factor explaining the differences in regional restructuring was the presence of networks linking diverse types of organizations.

CONCLUSION: FRICTION

In the opening pages of *The Economic Institutions of Capitalism*, Oliver Williamson (1985: 18–19) observes that

Transaction costs are the economic equivalent of friction in physical systems. . . . But whereas physicists were quickly reminded by their laboratory instruments and the world around them that friction was pervasive and often needed to be taken expressly into account, economists did not have a corresponding appreciation for the costs of running the economic system. Thus, although positive economics admitted that frictions were important in principle, it had no language to describe frictions in fact.

Williamson's contribution to economics has been to develop an analytic strategy to understand 'friction' in economic transactions—with the aim of guiding policies and promoting institutions that minimize these transaction costs. The chapters in this volume can be seen as bringing the analysis of friction into the study of the transforming post-socialist economies. They differ from Williamson's project, however, in two fundamental ways. First, the friction they examine is not that of economic exchanges *per se* but the friction of economic restructuring: that is, whereas Williamson turns our attention to *transaction* costs, we are concerned here with *transformation* costs. In fact, to the extent that institutionalization is a kind of 'investment in forms' (Thévenot 1984) that reduces the costs of future transactions, such transformation costs might be conceptualized as sunk transaction costs. Second, unlike the Williamsonian tendency to assess as superior those forms that minimize friction, these chapters see a positive role for economic friction. To be sure, we are not advocating higher transformation costs or seeking to promote institutions with steep transaction costs; but it does seems to us useful to question the notion of a 'smooth' or frictionless 'transition'.

That position begins from the insight that some friction may be essential for the functioning of markets by undermining positive feedback loops that can lead to lock-in. Such was the lesson drawn by the federal Securities and Exchange Commission in the aftermath of the 508-point crash of the New York Stock Exchange on 19 October 1987. As trading in some fields was approaching an almost frictionless character with advances in 'programme trading'—computerized, high-speed trading of baskets of stock by major investors with simultaneous and nearly identical information—the Securities and Exchange commissioners saw a danger that some markets could pass from volatility to chaos. To maintain orderly markets, the commissioners designed a set of 'collars' that trigger temporary halts in computerized index arbitrage when the Dow skips more than a certain number of points in either direction. Like the Naskapi caribou shoulder-bone that disrupts the negative effects of positive feedback, these so-called circuit-breakers bring time, and hence friction, back into the Exchange.[23]

Our aim in this introductory chapter has been to begin the analysis of the circuit-breakers that bring friction to the post-socialist transformations. Institutional legacies produce the friction that grinds against a smooth transition but preserves diversity for future recombinant strategies. Inter-enterprise linkages buffer firms and retard selection, but the redundant relations of loosely coupled networks produce the friction of ambiguity that facilitates entrepreneurial strategies. And the multiple ordering principles of localities produce the friction that inhibits too simple harmonizations but yields more complex ecologies that are the basis for regional development strategies. With the concepts of compartmentalization, asset ambiguity, and local ecologies of meaning we can proceed to analyse how actors reconfigure legacies, linkages, and localities to forge pathways from state socialism.

NOTES

We wish to thank Bill Barnett, Pascal Boyer, Geoff Fougere, István Gábor, Szabolcs Kemény, Gerald McDermott, and Monique Djokic Stark for their criticisms of an earlier draft. This introductory essay was completed while David Stark was a Fellow at the Center for Advanced Study in the Behavioral Sciences. He is grateful for financial support provided by the National Science Foundation #SES-9022192 and the USA Department of State Title VIII Funds Grant #1006-304101.

1. This account is drawn from Weick (1977: 45).
2. As John Padgett summarizes March's findings: '(A) Fast learners overspecialize into competency traps. Slow learners preserve collective wisdom. (B) Smart learners respond quickly to noise as well as to true data. They reinforce self-confidence in collective delusions. (C) Homogeneity in "smart" worldview limits the genetic variability necessary for future exploration. (D) Personnel turnover of dumb for smart is good up to a point, as long as others in the organization learn about whom to attend to when' (Padgett 1992: 746; see also Levinthal and March 1993).
3. See Grabher (1993). Here we join with economic sociologists and legal scholars studying East Asian economies from a network-centred approach in which social networks are the basic units of action. Redding and Whitley (1990: 79), for example, argue that 'Anglo-Saxon conceptions of the legally bounded firm as the basic unit of economic action are inadequate to explain the economic actions and structure of *chaebol* and Chinese family businesses, both of which have complex extra-firm linkages influencing decision making.' Gilson and Roe (1993) 'take as the Japanese structure not a single Japanese corporation in isolation, but the *keiretsu* structure—the interlocking webs of firms, which loom so large in the Japanese economy'. Hamilton and Feenstra (1995) offer a simi-

lar, but more general, argument: 'Inter-firm networks that rest on strongly normative bonds are better understood as economic organizations in their own right instead of a residual or intermediate category. Embedded networks become units of economic action rather than the firms that constitute them.... The network linkages are stronger than the firms that make up the networks. Firms come and go, but the networks persist over time.'

4. One of the better known of these mechanisms has been introduced in organizational ecology as the concept of 'density dependence' (Hannan and Freeman 1989). When the number of a specific organizational form is small (and its density in the population low), the rate of increase of this form will be slow. As the number increases, however, the rate of growth of this form will also increase because of complementarities and, as Alfred Marshall would have called it, positive external economies. As the density of the specific form increases further, however, the rate of increase will decline since competition for resources becomes tougher amongst a growing number of rivals. In summary, the viability of a particular form (as expressed in terms of rates of foundings and rates of failures) first increases and then decreases as a function of the frequency of that form in the population.

5. In the economic literature this tension has been described as 'a conflict between short-term "static efficiency" and long-term efficiency and . . . this property relates directly to the distributional characteristics of the firm population. Diversity at the micro level is a prerequisite for stable macro growth' (Eliasson 1984: 263; see also Eliasson 1991; Nelson 1991; Dosi 1991; Dosi and Marengo 1994).

6. As Michael Hannan argues, 'Having a range of alternative ways to produce certain goods and services is valuable whenever the future is uncertain. A society that retains only a few organizational forms may thrive for a time. But once the environment changes, such a society faces serious problems until existing organizations can be reshaped or new ones created. Since reorganization is costly and may not work at all for the reasons state above (and because new organizations are fragile), it may take a long time to adapt to the new conditions. A system with greater organizational diversity has a higher probability of having in hand some solution that is satisfactory under changed environmental conditions' (Hannan 1986: 85).

7. See e.g. Eigen *et al.* (1981). In contrast to the basic selection model, the subdivided population model relaxes the assumption of spatial homogeneity in the genetic composition of populations. Evolutionary biologists more frequently use the term 'structure' (see e.g. Wilson 1984 and essays in Brandon and Burian 1984) to refer to processes that we designate here as compartmentalization.

8. For related arguments in organizational ecology, see Barnett (1995).

9. A plausible argument might be made that, despite official rhetoric, Poland's *de facto* policies came closest to the two-track strategy.

10. Gábor's ecological analysis of the 'too many, too small' syndrome is an interesting application of the concept of density dependence. 'In the first place, parallel with the proliferation and shrinkage of undertakings, economic inefficiency became a less and less effective handicap to entry. In the second place, as the undertakings were growing in number and shrinking in size, it became easier for them to conceal incomes, which provided them a source of protection, inde-

pendent of economic efficiency, from larger organizations as competitors. . . . In the third place, the more fragmented they became, the less they could afford, by reason of their diminished incomes . . . to seek business expansion, while crowdedness may also have discouraged financially stronger firms as potential rivals from entering the market.'

11. For comparative studies of stratification see e.g. Haller *et al.* (1990); Blau and Ruan (1990); Treimann and Ganzeboom (1990).

12. On the weakness of strong (multiply connected) ties see Breiger and Roberts (1995). On the strength of weak (or indirect) ties, Granovetter (1973: 1366, 1376) writes: 'Weak ties are more likely to link members of different social groups than are strong ones which tend to be concentrated within particular groups.' Hence, 'whatever is to be diffused can reach a larger number of people, and traverse greater social distance (i.e. path length), when passed through weak ties rather than strong.'

13. It follows that the exploitation-versus-exploration problem of the Nova Scotia fishing fleet raised in the introduction could be re-examined through the concept of compartmentalization expressed in network terms. As such, the purely 'Cartesian' simulations in Allen and McGlade's models would be seen as too tightly coupled and the purely 'Stochastic' as too loosely so—with the actual fleet seen as a compartmentalized population with some subregions of the network space showing the density and intensity of strong ties within an overall network structure of loose coupling.

14. '[A]mbiguity is not satisfying in itself, nor is it, considered as a device on its own, a thing to be attempted; it must in each case arise from, and be justified by, the peculiar requirements of the situation' (Empson 1973: 235). Ambiguous and contradictory perceptions and world-views can isolate themselves from each other in a way that ends up in a sort of structural 'schizophrenia'. Systems might fall victim to a vicious circle of stagnation and fragmentation in which the subunits 'may fight the growing entanglement of stagnation by striving for independence. Fiefdoms evolve. Independence is gained, but synergy from interdependence is lost. . . . Buffers dissolve, and conflict may be triggered incidentally' (Masuch 1985: 29).

15. Chan (1979: 177) specifies the fatal consequences of suppressing ambiguity in pointing to the counter-productive effects of the preference of intelligence agencies for conformists who share the regime's values and belief system: ' "Deviants" in terms of class background, professional training, ideological committment (e.g. pacifists), or racial or ethnic origin are systematically underrepresented. Consequently, there is no reason to expect that tendencies of ethnocentrism will be ameliorated or that various cognitive biases will cancel each other out, if we simply increase the number of intelligence bureaus. In fact, the reverse may be true. Errors will be duplicated . . . leading to an illusory confidence in the intelligence product.'

16. As McDermott notes, 'one of the increasingly evident legacies of socialist economies is that while industrial concentration rigidified the economic and technical links among, say, customers and suppliers, the increasing self-coordination and autarky among interlinked firms within industrial associations allowed for the development of complex informal vertical and horizontal alliances among economic actors' (Chapter 3).

17. For an analysis of the new structure of concentrated ownership that resulted from voucher privatization see esp. Brom and Orenstein (1994); on the new 'investment funds' and problems of corporate governance in the newly 'privatized' Czech firms, see Coffee (1996); and for a comparative analysis of how the patterns of inter-enterprise ownership in the Czech Republic differ from those in Hungary, see Stark and Bruszt (1995).
18. See Sabel (1993) for a discussion of asset interdependence; Sabel and Prokop (1996) analyse similar organizational dynamics in the Russian setting.
19. For a related discussion of the blurring of the boundaries of public and private see Gieryn's (forthcoming) fascinating analysis of the architectural design of a biotechnology lab at a major US research university.
20. Gereffi (1994) presents similar findings in this analysis of East Asian supplier chains in the garment industry. His 'global commodities chain' approach 'looks at the configuration of economic and social networks, rather than the structure and strategy of isolated firms, as a key to understanding new patterns of global competition. . . . In summary, the transnational governance structures that define buyer-driven and producer-driven Global Commodity Chains (GCCs) make conventional boundaries between firms, industries, and countries obsolete' (Fonda *et al.* 1994).
21. See esp. Teubner (1993) for an insightful discussion of how new network forms of organization pose challenges for legal theory.
22. Trigilia (1986*a,b*); Stark (1990); Gábor (1994); Putnam (1993).
23. See Robb (1990) for an account of the Commission's decision. Heberlein (1995) and Petruno (1994) assess the impact on the New York Stock Exchange. Since it was put in place in 1990, the NYSE 'collar' has been triggered fewer and fewer times each year, as market swings have died down.

REFERENCES

ALLEN, PETER M., and MCGLADE, J. M. (1987), 'Modelling Complex Human Systems: A Fisheries Example', *European Journal of Operational Research*, 24: 147–67.

ARTHUR, W. BRIAN (1994), *Increasing Returns and Path Dependence in the Economy* (Ann Arbor: University of Michigan Press).

BARNETT, WILLIAM P. (1995), *The Dynamics of Competitive Intensity*, Research paper no. 1227 (Stanford, Calif.: Stanford Business School).

BARON, JAMES N., and HANNAN, MICHAEL T. (1994), 'The Impact of Economics on Contemporary Sociology', *Journal of Economic Literature*, 32: 1111–46.

BEREZIN, M., and KAGANOVA, O. (1993), 'Real Property Market as Capitalization Factor of Russian Cities', Paper presented to the Conference of the European Network for Housing Research, Budapest, 10 Sept. 1993.

BLAU, PETER M., and RUAN, D. (1990), 'Inequality of Opportunity in Urban China and America', *Research in Social Stratification and Mobility*, 9: 3–32.

BOURDIEU, PIERRE (1986), 'Forms of Capital', in J. G. Richardson (ed.), *Handbook of Theory and Research for the Sociology of Education* (Westport, Conn.: Greenwood Press), 141–58.

BOYER, ROBERT, and ORLEAN, ANDRÉ (1992), 'How do Conventions Evolve?' *Journal of Evolutionary Economics*, 2: 165–77.

BRANDON, ROBERT N., and BURIAN, RICHARD M. (eds.) (1984), *Genes, Organisms, Populations: Controversy over the Units of Selection* (Cambridge, Mass.: MIT Press).

BREIGER, RONALD L., and ROBERTS, JOHN M., Jr. (1995), 'Solidarity and Social Networks', *Journal of Mathematical Sociology*, 20: 215–56.

BROM, KARLA, and ORENSTEIN, MITCHELL (1994), 'The "Privatized" Sector in the Czech Republic: Government and Bank Control in a Transitional Economy', *Europe–Asia Studies*, 46/6: 893–928.

BURAWOY, MICHAEL, and KROTOV, PAVEL (1992), 'The Soviet Transition from Socialism to Capitalism: Worker Control and Economic Bargaining in the Wood Industry', *American Sociological Review*, 57: 16–38.

BURT, RONALD (1992), *Structural Holes: The Social Structure of Competition* (Cambridge, Mass.: Harvard University Press).

CALLON, MICHEL, and LATOUR, BRUNO (1981), 'Unscrewing the Big Leviathan: How Actors Macrostructure Reality and how Sociology Helps Them', in Karin Knorr and Aron Cicourel (eds.), *Advances in Social Theory and Methodology* (London: Routledge), 277–303.

CARROLL, GLENN R., and HARRISON, J. R. (1994), 'On the Historical Efficiency of Competition between Organizational Populations', *American Journal of Sociology*, 100/3: 720–49.

CHAN, S. (1979), 'The Intelligence of Stupidity: Understanding Failures in Strategic Warning', *American Political Science Review*, 78: 171–80.

CHIKÁN, ATTILA (1994), 'Supply Chain Development and the Theory of the Firm', MS, University of Economics, Budapest.

COFFEE, JOHN C., Jr. (1996), 'Institutional Investors in Transitional Economies: Lessons from the Czech Experience', in Roman Frydman, Cheryl Gray, and Andrzej Rapaczynski (eds.), *Corporate Governance in Central Europe and Russia*, Vol. I (Budapest: Central European University Press), 111–86.

COHEN, M. D. (1984), 'Conflict and Complexity: Goal Diversity and Organizational Search Effectiveness', *American Political Science Review*, 78: 435–51.

COLEMAN, JAMES (1988), 'Social Capital in the Creation of Human Capital', *American Journal of Sociology*, 94 (suppl.): S95–S120.

DAVID, PAUL A. (1986), 'Understanding the Economics of QWERTY', in W. N. Parker (ed.), *Economic History and the Modern Economist* (Oxford: Blackwell), 30–49.

——(1992), 'Path Dependence and the Predictability in Dynamic Systems with Local Network Externalities: A Paradigm for Historical Economics', in C. Freeman and D. Foray (eds.), *Technology and the Wealth of Nations* (London: Pinter).

DOSI, GIOVANNI (1991), 'Some Thoughts on the Promises, Challenges and Dangers of an "Evolutionary Perspective" in Economics', *Journal of Evolutionary Economics*, 1/1: 1–3.

——and MARENGO, LUIGI (1994), 'Some Elements of an Evolutionary Theory of Organizational Competences', in Richard W. England (ed.), *Evolutionary Concepts in Contemporary Economics* (Ann Arbor: University of Michigan Press), 157–78.

DUPRÉ, JOHN A. (ed.) (1987), *The Latest on the Best: Essays on Evolution and Optimality* (Cambridge, Mass.: MIT Press).

EIGEN, MANFRED, GARDINER, WILLIAM, SCHUSTER, PETER, and WINKLER-OSWATITSCH, RUTHILD (1981), 'The Origin of Genetic Information', *Scientific American*, 244/4: 88–118.

ELIASSON, G. (1984), 'Microheterogeneity of Firms and the Stability of Industrial Growth', *Journal of Economic Behavior and Organization*, 5/3–4: 115–51.

—— (1991), 'Deregulation, Innovative Entry and Structural Diversity as a Source of Stable and Rapid Economic Growth', *Journal of Evolutionary Economics*, 1/1: 49–63.

EMIRBAYER, MUSTAFA, and GOODWIN, JEFF (1994), 'Network Analysis, Culture, and the Problem of Agency', *American Journal of Sociology*, 99/6: 1411–54.

EMPSON, W. (1973), *Seven Types of Ambiguity* (London: Chatto & Windus).

FISHER, R. A. (1930), *The Genetic Theory of Natural Selection* (Oxford: Clarendon Press).

FONDA, STEPHANIE, GEREFFI, GARY, and NONNEMAKER, LYNN (1994), 'Tapping the Global Economy: An Analysis of Globalization Strategies among US Apparel and Retail Companies', Paper presented to the Conference on the New Institutionalism in Economic Sociology, Cornell University, Oct. 1994.

GÁBOR, ISTVÁN (1979), 'The Second (Secondary) Economy', *Acta Oeconomica*, 22/4: 91–311.

—— (1985), 'The Major Domains of the Second Economy', in Péter Galasi and György Sziráczki (eds.), *Labour Market and Second Economy in Hungary* (Frankfurt: Campus), 133–78.

—— (1986), 'Reformok második gazdaság, államszocializmus. A 80- as évek tapasztalatainak feljödéstani és összehasonlító gazdaságtani tanulságairól' (Reforms, Second Economy, State Socialism: Speculation on the Evolutionary and Comparative Economic Lessons of the Hungarian Eighties), *Valóság*, 6: 32–48.

—— (1994), 'Modernity or a New Type of Duality?: The Second Economy Today', in János Mátyás Kovács (ed.), *Transition to Capitalism? The Legacy of Communism in Eastern Europe* (New Brunswick, NJ: Transaction Books), 3–21.

GEREFFI, GARY (1994), 'The Organization of Buyer-Driven Global Commodity Chains: How US Retailers Shape Overseas Production Networks', in Gary Gereffi and Manuel Kornzeniewicz (eds.), *Commodity Chains and Global Capitalism* (Westport, Conn.: Praeger), 95–112.

GIERYN, THOMAS F. (forthcoming), 'Biotechnology's Private Parts (and Some Public Ones)', in Arnold Thackray (ed.), *Private Science: The Biotechnology Industry and the Rise of Molecular Biology* (Philadelphia: University of Pennsylvania Press).

GILSON, RONALD J., and ROE, MARK J. (1993), 'Understanding the Japanese *Keiretsu*: Overlaps between Corporate Governance and Industrial Organization', *Yale Law Journal*, 102: 871–906.

GOULD, STEPHEN J. (1987), 'The Panda's Thumb of Technology', *Natural History*, 1: 14–23.

—— and LEWONTIN, RICHARD C. (1984), 'The Spandrels of San Marco and the Panglossian Paradigm: A Critique of the Adaptationist Programme', in Elliott Sober (ed.), *Conceptual Issues in Evolutionary Biology* (Cambridge, Mass.: MIT Press), 252–70.

GRABHER, GERNOT (1993), 'Rediscovering the Social in the Economics of Interfirm Relations', in Gernot Grabher (ed.), *The Embedded Firm: On the Socioeconomics of Industrial Networks* (London: Routledge), 1–31.

——(1994), *Lob der Verschwendung. Redundanz in der Regionalentwicklung* (Berlin: edition sigma).

GRANOVETTER, MARK (1973), 'The Strength of Weak Ties', *American Journal of Sociology*, 78/6: 1360–80.

——(1979), 'The Idea of "Advancement" in Theories of Social Evolution and Development', *American Journal of Sociology*, 85/3: 489–515.

HALLER, M., KOLOSI, T., and ROBERT, P. (1990), 'Social Mobility in Austria, Czechoslovakia, and Hungary', in M. Haller (ed.), *Class Structure in Europe: New Findings from East–West Comparisons of Social Structure and Mobility* (Armonk: Sharpe), 153–97.

HAMILTON, GARY G., and FEENSTRA, ROBERT C. (1995), 'Varieties of Hierarchies and Markets: An Introduction', *Industrial and Corporate Change*, 4/1: 51–91.

HANLEY, ERIC (1995), 'Market-Maintained Inequalities in Eastern Europe: The Emergence of Small-Scale Entrepreneurship in Poland, Hungary, and the Czech Republic', MS, Department of Sociology, University of California, Los Angeles.

HANNAN, MICHAEL T. (1986), 'Uncertainty, Diversity, and Organizational Change', in *Behavioral and Social Sciences: Fifty Years of Discovery* (Washington: National Academy Press), 73–94.

——and FREEMAN, JOHN H. (1989), *Organizational Ecology* (Cambridge, Mass.: Harvard University Press).

HEBERLEIN, GREG (1995), 'Circuit Breakers don't Electrocute Investors . . . Yet', *Seattle Times*, 19 Mar. 1995.

HENDERSON, JEFFREY, WHITLEY, RICHARD, LENGYEL, GYÖRGY, and CSABAN, LÁSZLÓ (1995), 'Contention and Confusion in Industrial Transformation: Dilemmas of State Economic Management', in E. Dittrich, G. Schmitt, and R. Whitley (eds.), *Industrial Transformation in Europe: Process and Contexts* (London: Sage).

HIRST, PAUL, and ZEITLIN, JONATHAN (1991), 'Flexible Specialization versus Post-Fordism: Theory, Evidence, and Policy Implications', *Economy and Society*, 20/1: 1–56.

HODGSON, GEOFFREY M. (1993), *Economics and Evolution: Bringing Life back into Economics* (Cambridge: Polity Press).

ICKES, BARRY W., and RYTERMAN, RANDI (1994), 'From Enterprise to Firm: Notes for a Theory of the Enterprise in Transition', in Robert W. Campbell (ed.), *The Postcommunist Economic Transformation* (Boulder, Colo.: Westview Press), 83–104.

KATZ, M. L., and SHAPIRO, C. (1985), 'Network Externalities, Competition, and Compatibility', *American Economic Review*, 75/3: 424–40.

KEMÉNY, SZABOLCS (1996), 'Competition, Cooperation, and Corruption: Economic Practice in a Transforming Market in Hungary', Paper presented to the 10th International Conference of Europeanists, Chicago, Mar. 1996.

KOGUT, BRUCE, SHAN, WEIJAN, and WALKER, GORDON (1992), 'The Make-or-Cooperate Decision in the Context of an Industry Network', in Nitin Nohria and Robert G. Eccles (eds.), *Networks and Organizations* (Cambridge, Mass.: Harvard Business School Press), 348–65.

KORNAI, JÁNOS (1990), *The Road to a Free Economy* (New York: Norton).

——(1992), 'The Postsocialist Transition and the State: Reflections in the Light of Hungarian Fiscal Problems', *American Economic Review*, 82/2: 1–21.

KOZMINSKI, A. K. (1993), *Catching Up? Organizational and Management Change in the Ex-socialist Block* (Albany: State University of New York Press).

LATOUR, BRUNO (1988), *The Pasteurization of France*, trans. Alan Sheridan and John Law (Cambridge, Mass.: Harvard University Press).

LEVINTHAL, DANIEL A., and MARCH, JAMES G. (1993), 'The Myopia of Learning', *Strategic Management Journal*, 14: 95–112.

LEWONTIN, RICHARD C. (1982), *Human Diversity* (New York: Scientific American Books).

LI, C., and WHITE, L. (1990), 'Élite Transformation and Modern Change in Mainland China and Taiwan: Empirical Data and the Theory of Technocracy', *China Quarterly*, 121: 1–35.

LOEVINGER, J. (1976), *Ego Development* (San Francisco: Jossey-Bass).

LUHMANN, NIKLAS (1986), 'The Autopoiesis of Social Systems', in F. Geyer and J. van den Zouwen (eds.), *Sociocybernetic Paradoxes: Observation, Control and Evolution of Self-Steering Systems* (London: Sage), 172–92.

MARCH, JAMES G. (1991), 'Exploration and Exploitation in Organizational Learning', *Organization Science*, 2/1: 71–87.

——and OLSEN, J. P. (1989), *Rediscovering Institutions: The Organizational Basis of Politics* (New York: Free Press).

MARUYAMA, M. (1993), 'Survival, Adaptive and Maladaptive Strategies, and Pitfalls in Management Transfer: Lessons from Other Parts of the World and their Use in Management Reform in Central and Eastern Europe', in M. Maruyama (ed.), *Management Reform in Eastern and Central Europe* (Aldershot: Dartmouth), 163–75.

MASUCH, M. (1985), 'Vicious Circles in Organizations', *Administrative Science Quarterly*, 30: 14–33.

MAYR, ERNST (1980), 'Prologue: Some Thoughts on the History of the Evolutionary Synthesis', in Ernst Mayr and William B. Provine (eds.), *The Evolutionary Synthesis: Perspectives on the Unification of Biology* (Cambridge, Mass.: Harvard University Press), 1–48.

——(1984), 'Typological versus Population Thinking', in Elliott Sober (ed.), *Conceptual Issues in Evolutionary Biology* (Cambridge, Mass.: MIT Press), 14–18.

——(1985), 'How Biology Differs from the Physical Sciences', in David J. Depew and Bruce H. Weber (eds.), *Evolution at the Crossroads: The New Biology and the New Philosophy of Science* (Cambridge, Mass.: MIT Press), 43–63.

MINER, ANNE S., AMBURGEY, TERRY L., and STEARNS, TIMOTHY M. (1990), 'Interorganizational Linkages and Population Dynamics: Buffering and Transformational Shields', *Administrative Science Quarterly*, 35: 689–713.

MURRELL, PETER (1991), 'Can Neoclassical Economics Underpin the Reform of Centrally Planned Economies', *Journal of Economic Perspectives*, 5/4: 59–78.

——(1992a), 'Evolution in Economics and in the Economic Reform of the Centrally Planned Economies', in Christopher Clague and Gordon C. Rausser (eds.), *The Emergence of Market Economies in Eastern Europe* (Oxford: Blackwell), 35–54.

MURRELL, PETER (1992*b*), 'Evolutionary and Radical Approaches to Economic Reform', *Economics of Planning*, 25 (1992), 79–95.

——(1993), 'What is Shock Therapy? What did it Do in Poland and Russia?', *Post-Soviet Affairs*, 9/2: 11–140.

NEE, VICTOR, and YOUNG, FRANK W. (1991), 'Peasant Entrepreneurs in China's Second Economy: An Institutional Analysis', *Economic Development and Cultural Change*, 39: 293–310.

NELSON, RICHARD R. (1991), 'Why do Firms Differ, and how does it Matter?', *Strategic Management Journal*, 12: 61–74.

PADGETT, JOHN F. (1992), 'Learning from (and about) March', *Contemporary Sociology*, 21/6: 744–9.

——and ANSELL, CHRISTOPHER K. (1993), 'Robust Action and the Rise of the Medici, 1400–1434', *American Journal of Sociology*, 98/6: 1259–1319.

PETRUNO, TOM (1994), 'Is NYSE being Kept too Cool under its Collar?', *Los Angeles Times*, 26 Jan. 1994.

POWELL, WALTER W. (1987), 'Hybrid Organizational Arrangements: New Form or Transitional Development', *California Management Review*, 30/1: 67–87.

——(1990), 'Neither Market nor Hierarchy: Network Forms of Organization', in B. Staw and L. L. Cummings (eds.), *Research in Organizational Behavior*, xii (Greenwich, Conn.: JAI), 295–336.

POZNANSKI, KAZIMIEREZ Z. (1993), 'Restructuring of Property Rights in Poland: A Study in Evolutionary Politics', *East European Politics and Societies*, 7/3: 395–421.

PUTNAM, ROBERT (1993), *Making Democracy Work: Civic Traditions in Modern Italy* (Princeton, NJ: Princeton University Press).

REDDING, S. GORDON, and WHITLEY, RICHARD D. (1990), 'Beyond Bureaucracy: Towards a Comparative Analysis of Forms of Economic Resource Co-ordination and Control', in S. R. Clegg and S. G. Redding (eds.), *Capitalism in Contrasting Cultures* (Berlin: de Gruyter), 79–104.

ROBB, GREGORY A. (1990), 'Curb on Some Program Trades to be Tried', *New York Times*, 26 July 1990.

RÓNA-TAS, AKOS (1994), 'The First shall be Last? Entrepreneurship and Communist Cadres in the Transition from Socialism', *American Journal of Sociology*, 100/1: 40–69.

SABEL, CHARLES F. (1990), 'Moebius-Strip Organizations and Open Labor Markets: Some Consequences of the Reintegration of Conception and Execution in a Volatile Economy', in Pierre Bourdieu and James Coleman (eds.), *Social Theory for a Changing Society* (Boulder, Colo.: Westview Press and Russell Sage Foundation), 3–54.

——(1992), 'Studied Trust: Building New Forms of Co-operation in a Volatile Economy', in Frank Pyke and Werner Sengenberger (eds.), *Industrial District and Local Economic Regeneration* (Geneva: International Labour Organization), 215–50.

——(1993), 'Constitutional Ordering in Historical Perspective', in Fritz Scharpf (ed.), *Games in Hierarchies and Networks* (Boulder, Colo.: Westview Press), 65–123.

——(1994), 'Learning by Monitoring: The Institutions of Economic Development', in Neil J. Smelser and Richard Swedberg (eds.), *The Handbook of Economic Sociology* (Princeton, NJ: Princeton University Press), 137–65.

——and PROKOP, JANE E. (1996), 'Stabilization through Reorganization? Some Preliminary Implications of Russia's Entry into World Markets in the Age of Discursive Quality Standards', in Roman Frydman, Cheryl Gray, and Andrzej Rapaczynski (eds.), *Corporate Governance in Russia and Eastern Europe* (Budapest: Central European University Press), 151–91.

——and ZEITLIN, JONATHAN (eds.) (1996), *Worlds of Possibility: Flexibility and Mass Production in Western Industrialization* (Cambridge: Cambridge University Press).

SCHUMPETER, JOSEPH A. (1912/1961), *The Theory of Economic Development*, trans. R. Opie (Cambridge, Mass.: Harvard University Press).

SHLEIFER, A., and BOYCKO, M. (1993), 'The Politics of Russian Privatization', in Olivier Blanchard (ed.), *Post-communist Reform* (Cambridge, Mass.: MIT Press).

SÍK, ENDRE (1994), 'Network Capital in Capitalist, Communist, and Post-communist Societies', *International Contributions to Labour Studies*, 4: 73–93.

SIMMEL, GEORG (1923/1950), *The Sociology of Georg Simmel*, trans. Kurt H. Wolff (New York: Free Press).

SMITH, JOHN MAYNARD (1984), 'Optimization Theory in Evolution', in Elliott Sober (ed.), *Conceptual Issues in Evolutionary Biology* (Cambridge, Mass.: MIT Press), 289–315.

SOBER, ELLIOTT (1984), *The Nature of Selection: Evolutionary Theory in Philosophical Focus* (Cambridge, Mass.: MIT Press).

STARK, DAVID (1989), 'Coexisting Organizational Forms in Hungary's Emerging Mixed Economy', in Victor Nee and David Stark (eds.), *Remaking the Economic Institutions of Socialism: China and Eastern Europe* (Stanford, Calif.: Stanford University Press), 137–68.

——(1990), 'Privatization in Hungary: From Plan to Market or from Plan to Clan?' *East European Politics and Societies*, 4/3: 351–92.

——and BRUSZT, LÁSZLÓ (1995), *Network Properties of Assets and Liabilities: Interenterprise Ownership Networks in Hungary and the Czech Republic*, Working Papers on Transitions from State Socialism (Ithaca, NY: Cornell University, Einaudi Center for International Studies).

STORPER, MICHAEL (1989), 'The Transition to Flexible Specialization in the Film Industry: The Division of Labour, External Economies, and the Crossing of Industrial Divides', *Cambridge Journal of Economics*, 13/3: 273–305.

SZELÉNYI, SZONJA, SZELÉNYI, IVÁN, and KOVÁCH, IMRE (1995), 'The Making of the Hungarian Postcommunist Élite: Circulation in Politics, Reproduction in the Economy', *Theory and Society*, 24: 697–722.

TEECE, DAVID (1993), 'The Dynamics of Industrial Capitalism: Perspectives on Alfred Chandler's *Scale and Scope*', *Journal of Economic Literature*, 31: 199–225.

TEUBNER, GUNTHER (1993), 'Nouvelles formes d'organisation et droit', *Revue Française de Gestion* (Nov.–Dec.), 50–68.

THÉVENOT, LAURENT (1985), 'Rules and Implements: Investment in Forms', *Social Science Information*, 23/1: 1–45.

TREIMANN, DONALD J., and GANZEBOOM, H. B. G. (1990), 'Cross-national Comparative Status Attainment Research', *Research in Social Stratification and Mobility*, 9: 105–27.

TRIGILIA, CARLO (1986a), *Grand partiti e piccole impresse* (Big Parties, Small Firms) (Bologna).

Trigilia, Carlo (1986*b*), 'Small Firm Development and Political Subcultures in Italy', *European Sociological Review*, 2/3: 161–75.

Walder, Andrew G. (1995), 'Local Governments as Industrial Firms: An Organizational Analysis of China's Transitional Economy', *American Journal of Sociology*, 101/2: 263–301.

Weick, Karl E. (1976), 'Educational Organizations as Loosely Coupled Systems', *Administrative Science Quarterly*, 21/1: 1–19.

——(1977), 'Organization Design: Organizations as Self-Designing Systems', *Organizational Dynamics*, 6/2: 31–45.

Weizsäcker, C., and Weizsäcker, E. U. (1984), 'Fehlerfreundlichkeit', in K. Kornwachs (ed.), *Offenheit—Zeitlichkeit—Komplexitaet. Zur Theorie der Offenen Systeme* (Frankfurt-on-Main: Campus), 167–201.

Wiesenthal, H. (1993), *Die 'Politische Oekonomie' des fortgeschrittenen Transformationsprozesses und die (potentiellen) Funktionen intermediaerer Akteure*, Working paper, Max-Planck-Gesellschaft Arbeitsgruppe Transformationsprozesse in den neuen Bundeslaendern an der Humboldt-Universitaet zu Berlin.

Williamson, Oliver E. (1985), *The Economic Institutions of Capitalism* (New York: Free Press).

Wilson, David Sloan (1984), 'Individual Selection and the Concept of Structured Demes', in Brandon and Burian (1984: 272–91).

I

RECOMBINANT NETWORKS:

Property Transformation and Restructuring of Large Firms

2

Recombinant Property in East European Capitalism

DAVID STARK

INTRODUCTION: THE SCIENCE OF THE NOT YET

Sociology began as a science of transition, founded at our century's turn on studies of the epochal shifts from tradition to modernity, rural to urban society, *Gemeinschaft* to *Gesellschaft*, feudalism to capitalism, and mechanical to organic solidarity. For the founders of sociology, the crisis besetting European societies at the end of the nineteenth century was diagnosed as a normative and institutional vacuum. The old order regulated by tradition had passed, but a new moral order had not yet been established.[1]

During our own *fin de siècle*, not the crumbling of traditional structures but the collapse of communism gives new life to the transition problematic (Nee 1989; Lipset 1990; and see Alexander 1994 for an extended critical discussion). As the science of the not yet, transitology studies the present as an approximation of a designated future (Blanchard *et al*. 1994), risking an underlying teleology in which concepts are driven by hypostasized end-states.[2] In that framework, the transitional present is a period of dislocation as society undergoes the passage through a liminal state suspended between one social order and another (Bunce and Csanadi 1992), each conceived as a stable equilibrium organized around a coherent and more or less unitary logic.[3]

But is ours still the century of transition? And is that model of social change, so formative in the launching of sociology, still adequate for understanding the momentous changes in contemporary Eastern Europe?

Difficult to assimilate within the transition problematic are the numerous studies from Eastern Europe documenting parallel and contradictory logics in which ordinary citizens were already experiencing, for a decade prior to 1989, a social world in which various domains were not integrated coherently (Gábor 1979, 1986; Szelényi 1988; Stark 1986, 1989; Róna-Tas 1994).[4] Through survey research and ethnographic studies, researchers have identified a multiplicity of social relations that did not conform to officially prescribed hierarchical patterns. These relations of reciprocity and market-like transactions were widespread inside the socialist sector as well as in the 'second economy' and stemmed from the contradictions of attempting to 'scientifically manage' an entire national economy. At the shop-floor level, shortages and supply bottle-necks led to bargaining between supervisors and informal groups; at the managerial level, the task of meeting plan targets required a dense network of informal ties that cut across enterprises and local organizations; and the allocative distortions of central planning produced the conditions for the predominantly part-time enterpreneurship of the second economies that differed in scope, density of network connections, and conditions of legality across the region (Gábor 1979; Kornai 1980; Sabel and Stark 1982; Szelényi 1988).

The existence of parallel structures (however contradictory and fragmentary) in these informal and interfirm networks that 'got the job done' means that the collapse of the formal structures of the socialist regime does not result in an institutional vacuum. Instead, we find the persistence of routines and practices, organizational forms and social ties, that can become assets, resources, and the basis for credible commitments and co-ordinated actions in the post-socialist period (Bourdieu 1990; Nelson and Winter 1982). In short, in place of disorientation, we find the metamorphosis of *sub rosa* organizational forms and the activation of pre-existing networks of affiliation.

If by the 1980s the societies of Eastern Europe were decidedly not systems organized around a single logic, they are not likely in the post-socialist epoch to become, any more or less than our own, societies with a single system identity. Change, even fundamental change, of the social world is not the passage from one order to another but rearrangements in the patterns of how multiple orders are interwoven. Organizational innovation in this view is not replacement but recombination (Schumpeter 1934).

Thus, we examine how actors in the post-socialist context are rebuilding organizations and institutions not *on the ruins* but *with the ruins* of communism as they redeploy available resources in response to their immediate practical dilemmas. With such a conception of path dependence, we explain not the persistence of the past but how multiple futures are being contested in the present. Instead of paralysis and disorientation or of condemnation to repetition or retrogression,[5] we see ongoing processes of organizational innovation—for it is through adjusting to new uncertainties by improvising on practised routines that new organizational forms emerge (Nelson and Winter 1982; White 1993; Kogut and Zander 1992; Sabel and Zeitlin 1996). The analysis that follows emphasizes the organizational reflexivity that is possible when actors manœuvre across a multiplicity of legitimizing principles and strategically exploit ambiguities in the polyphony of accounts of work, value, and justice that compose modern society (Boltanski and Thévenot 1991; White 1992; Stark 1990; Padgett and Ansell 1993; Breiger 1995).

A New Type of Mixed Economy?

This chapter examines the recombinatory logic of organizational innovation in the restructuring of property relations in Hungary. It asks: are recombinant processes resulting in a new type of mixed economy as a distinctively East European capitalism?

For more than thirty years policy analysts in Eastern Europe debated the 'correct mix of plan and market' (Stark and Nee 1989). By the mid-1980s in Hungary, the debate had shifted to the correct mix of 'public and private property' as the earlier sacrosanct status of collective property eroded with the growth of the second economy. It was thus, in the waning years of state socialism, that Gábor (1986) and Szelényi (1988) coined the term 'socialist mixed economy' to designate the new economic configuration.[6] Meanwhile, Stark (1989: 168), amplifying Gábor's call to acknowledge a mixed economy 'as a viable hybrid form and not as inherently unstable and necessarily transitional', wondered, none the less, whether the concept of mixed economy was adequate to grasp the emergent phenomena of late socialism. On the basis of field research on 'intrapreneurial' subcontracting units in Hungarian firms, I argued that aspects of emergent private property were not respecting the boundaries of the second economy but were being fused with public ownership *inside* the socialist firm resulting in a 'diversification of property forms'. Identifying 'hybrid mixtures of public ownership and private initiative', Stark (1989: 167–8), I argued that, instead of a mixed economy with well-bounded public and private sectors, analysis should begin to address the growing plurality of 'mixed property forms' that transgressed and blurred traditional property boundaries.[7]

Scholars of economic reforms in China subsequently developed related concepts to analyse the fiscal reforms reshaping incentives among local governments giving rise to 'township and village enterprises'. Oi's (1992) concept of 'local corporatism', Nee's (1992) 'hybrid property', and Cui's (forthcoming) notion of 'Möebius-strip ownership' each illuminated a particular facet of Chinese property reforms that supported the general conclusion that China's is not a simple mixed economy but a kaleidoscope of mixed public and private property forms.

Of special relevance to my concerns is Walder's (1994) insight that property reform should not be equated with privatization. Walder argues that 'clarification of property rights' in the Chinese fiscal reforms can yield performance-enhancing incentives even while maintaining 'public ownership' without privatization. Our analysis of the Hungarian case also demonstrates that property transformation can occur without conventional privatization.[8] The difference, however, is that property transformation in Hungary does not necessarily clarify property rights. As we shall see, the emerging new property forms in Hungary blur (1) the boundaries of public and private, (2) the organizational boundaries of enterprises, and (3) the boundedness of justificatory principles. To denote these processes of triple boundary-blurring I adopt the term *recombinant property*.

Recombinant property is a form of organizational hedging, or portfolio management, in which actors respond to uncertainty in the organizational environment by diversifying their assets, redefining and recombining resources. It is an attempt to hold resources that can be justified or assessed by more than one standard of measure.

The distinctive variant of organizational hedging that is recombinant property in Hungary is produced in two simultaneous processes: parallel to the *decentralized reorganization of assets* is the *centralized management of liabilities*. On the one hand, decentralized reorganization produces the criss-crossing lines of inter-enterprise ownership networks; on the other, debt consolidation transforms private debt into public liability. Although these two dimensions are discussed separately, their simultaneity gives distinctive shape to Hungarian property. The clash of competing ordering principles produces organizational diversity that can form a basis for greater adaptability but, at the same time, creates acute problems of accountability.

My arguments are based on data collected during an eleven-month stay in Budapest in 1993–4. That research includes (1) field research in six Hungarian enterprises,[9] (2) compilation of a data set on the ownership structure of Hungary's 200 largest corporations and top twenty-five banks,[10] and (3) interviews with leading actors in banks, property agencies, political parties, and government ministries.[11]

PROPERTY TRANSFORMATION IN HUNGARY: THE POLICY DEBATE

My point of departure is a question central to contemporary debates in Eastern Europe and the former Soviet Union: by what means can private property become the typical form of property relations in economies overwhelmingly dominated by state ownership of productive assets?

Much of that debate can be organized around two fundamental policy strategies. First, the institutionalization of private property can best be established by transferring assets from public to private hands. Despite differences in the specific methods designated for such privatization (e.g. sale vs. free distribution, etc.), the various proposals within this radical perspective share the assumption that the creation of a private sector begins with the existing state-owned enterprises, that is, the basic organizational units of the emergent market economy will be the pre-existing but newly privatized enterprises.

The second policy strategy argues from the perspective of institutional (and, specifically, evolutionary) economics that, although slower, the more reliable road to institutionalizing private property rests in the development of a class of private proprietors. Instead of transferring the assets of a given organizational unit from one ownership form to another, public policy should lower barriers to entry for small- and medium-scale, genuinely private ventures. This perspective typically looks to the existing second-economy entrepreneurs as the basic organizational building-block of an emergent market economy.

Recent evidence suggests that Hungary is adopting neither a big-bang approach nor the policy prescriptions of evolutionary economics (Murrell 1990). Contrary to the optimistic scenarios of domestic politicians and Western economists who foresaw a rapid transfer of assets from state-owned enterprises to private ownership, the overwhelming bulk of the Hungarian economy remains state property. Two years after Prime Minister Jozsef Antall confidently announced that his new government would privatize more than 50 per cent of state property by 1995, the director of the Privatization Research Institute functioning alongside the State Property Agency (SPA) estimated that only about 3 per cent of the state-owned productive capital has been privatized (Mellár 1992). According to a recent study commissioned by the World Bank (Pistor and Turkewitz 1994), by mid-1994 the SPA had only sold about 11 per cent of the value of its original portfolio.

Contrary as well to the hopes of evolutionary economics, a considerable body of evidence now suggests that the second economy has not become a dynamic, legitimate private sector: although the number of registered private ventures has sky-rocketed, many are 'dummy firms', tax evasion is pervasive, and many entrepreneurs (a majority in some categories) still engage in private ventures only as a second job (Laky 1992; Gábor 1994; Gábor, Ch. 6 in this volume). And although employment is slowly increasing in the sector, most researchers agree that the proportion of unregistered work (for which the state receives no social security payments and the employee receives no benefits) is increasing faster (Kornai 1992: 13).

These tendencies together with new forms of corruption, extortion, and exploitation have prompted one researcher to label the transition as one 'from second economy to informal economy', arguing that it is now, under these new conditions, that Latin American comparisons are more applicable to the Hungarian setting (Sík 1992). When private entrepreneurs look to government policy they see only burdensome taxation, lack of credits, virtually no programmes to encourage regional or local development, and inordinate delays in payments for orders delivered to public sector firms (Webster 1992; Kornai 1992). Through violations of tax codes, off-the-books payments to workers, and reluctance to engage in capital investment, much of the private sector is responding in kind (Gábor, Ch. 6 in this volume). Such government policies and private sector responses are clearly not a recipe for the development of a legitimate private sector as a dynamic engine of economic growth.

THE DECENTRALIZED REORGANIZATION OF ASSETS

Although they fail to correspond to the policy prescriptions of either big-bang or evolutionary economics, significant property transformations are taking place in Hungary. Since 1989 there has been an explosion of new economic units. In Table 2.1 we see that:

- the number of state enterprises declined by about 60 per cent from the end of 1988 to the middle of 1994;
- the number of incorporated shareholding companies (*részvéntársaság*, or Rt) increased by more than twentyfold (from 116 to 2,679); and
- the number of limited liability companies (*korlátolt felelösségü társaság*, or KFT) increased most dramatically from only 450 units in 1988 to over 79,000 by the middle of 1994.

Table 2.1 clearly indicates the sudden proliferation of new units in the Hungarian economy. But does the table provide a reliable map of property relations in contemporary Hungary? No, at least not if the data are forced into the dichotomous public–private categories that structure the discussion about property transformation in the post-socialist countries. As we shall see, actors within the large formerly state firms are transforming property relations at the enterprise level. The results, however, are not well-defined rights of private property, yet neither are they a continuation or reproduction of old forms of state ownership.

New Forms of State Ownership

Take first the shareholding companies (Rts) on the second row of the table. Some of these corporations are private ventures newly established after the

TABLE 2.1. *Main enterprise forms in Hungary, 1988–1994*[a]

Organizational form	1988	1989	1990	1991	1992	1993	1994
State enterprises	2,378	2,400	2,363	2,233	1,733	1,130	892
Shareholding companies (Rts)	116	307	646	1,072	1,712	2,375	2,679
Limited liability companies (KFTs)	450	4,464	18,317	41,206	57,262	72,897	79,395

[a] Figures are for Dec., except 1994, when figures are for May.

Source: National Bank of Hungary (1994); Hungarian Central Statistical Office (1994).

'system change'. But many are the legal successors of the state-owned enterprises that would have been enumerated in the previous year on the first row of the table. Through a mandatory process of 'corporatization', the former state-owned enterprise transforms its legal organizational form into a shareholding company. The question, of course, is who is holding the shares? In most of these corporatized firms the majority of shares are held by the SPA or the newly created State Holding Corporation (AV-Rt). That is, as 'public' and 'private' actors co-participate in the new recombinant property forms, the nature and instruments of the 'public' dimension change: whereas 'state ownership' in socialism meant unmediated and indivisible ownership by a state ministry (e.g. the Ministry of Industry), corporatization in post-communism entails share ownership by one or another government agency responsible for state property.

Such corporatization mandated by a privatization agency in the current context has some distinctive features of renationalization. In the 1980s managers in Hungary (and workers in Poland) exercised *de facto* property rights. Although they enjoyed no rights over disposal of property, they did exercise rights of residual control as well as rights over residual income streams. In the 1990s corporatization paradoxically involves efforts by the state to reclaim the actual exercise of the property rights that had devolved to enterprise-level actors. Ironically, the agencies responsible for privatization are acting as agents of étatization (Voszka 1992).

The 'trap of centralization' (Bruszt 1988) already well known in the region, stands as a warning, however, that the effective exercise of such centralized control varies inversely with the scope and the degree of direct intervention. One encounters, therefore, proposals for privatizing the asset management function. In such programmes, the state retains the right to dispose of property but delegates its rights as shareholder to private consulting firms and portfolio management teams who oversee daily operations and strategic decisions on a subcontracting or commission basis.

Inter-enterprise Ownership

The state is seldom, however, the sole shareholder of the corporatized firms. Who are the other shareholders of the Rts enumerated on the second row of Table 2.1? To answer this question, I compiled a data set on the ownership structure of the largest 200 Hungarian corporations (ranked by sales).[12] These firms compose the 'Top 200' of the 1993 listing of *Figyelö*, a leading Hungarian business weekly. Like their *Fortune* 500 counterparts in the United States, the *Figyelö* 200 firms are major players in the Hungarian economy employing an estimated 21 per cent of the labour force and accounting for 37 per cent of total net sales and 42 per cent of export revenues (*Figyelö* 1993). The data also include the top twenty-five Hungarian banks (ranked by assets). Ownership data were obtained directly from the Hungarian Courts of Registry where corporate files contain not only information on the company's officers and board of directors but also a complete list of the company's owners as of the 1993 annual shareholders' meeting. The data analysed here are limited to the top twenty shareholders of each corporation.[13] In the Budapest Court of Registry and the nineteen county registries we were able to locate ownership files for 195 of the 200 corporations and for all of the twenty-five banks, referred to below as the 'Top 220' firms.

Who holds the shares of these 220 largest enterprises and banks? I found some form of state ownership—with shares held by the AV-Rt, the SPA, or the institutions of local government (who had typically exchanged their real-estate holdings for enterprise shares)—present in the overwhelming majority (71 per cent) of these enterprises and banks. More surprisingly, given the relatively short time since the 'system change' in 1989–90, we found thirty-six companies (i.e. more than 16 per cent of this population) in majority foreign ownership. Hungarian private individuals (summed down the top twenty owners) hold at least 25 per cent of the shares of only twelve of these largest enterprises and banks.

Most interesting from the perspective of this chapter is the finding of eighty-seven cases in which another Hungarian company is among the twenty largest shareholders. In forty-two of these cases the other Hungarian companies together hold a clear majority (50 per cent plus one share). Thus, by the most restrictive definition, almost 20 per cent of our Top 220 companies are unambiguous cases of inter-enterprise ownership; and we find some degree of inter-enterprise ownership in almost 40 per cent of these large companies.

Figure 2.1 presents two discrete networks formed through such inter-enterprise ownership. Arrows indicate directionality in which a given firm holds shares in another large enterprise. Weak ties (shareholdings with other firms that do not have at least one other tie, whether as owner or owned, to any other firm in the network) are not displayed.[14] The relations depicted in the figure, we emphasize, are the direct horizontal ties among the very largest enterprises—the superhighways, so to speak, of Hungarian corporate networks. The diagrams presented in Figure 2.1 indicate a different way of mapping the social space of property transformation than that suggested in Table 2.1. Whereas Table 2.1 grouped entities according to their legal corporate status, here we trace not the distribution of attributes but the patterns of social ties.

In analysing the relational dynamics of recombinant property, we now shift our focus from the corporate thoroughfares linking the large enterprises to examine the local byways linking spin-off properties within the gravitational field of large enterprises.

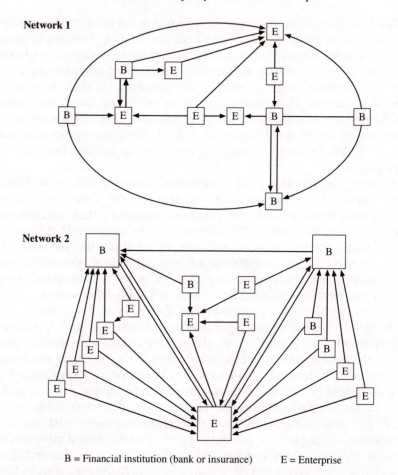

B = Financial institution (bank or insurance)   E = Enterprise

FIG. 2.1. Two inter-enterprise ownership networks among large Hungarian firms. Source: Corporate files of the largest 200 enterprises and top twenty-five banks in the Hungarian Courts of Registry

Corporate Satellites

We turn thus to the form with the most dramatic growth during the post-socialist period, the newly established limited liability companies (KFTs), enumerated on the third row of Table 2.1. Some of these KFTs are genuinely private entrepreneurial ventures. But many of these limited liability companies are not entirely distinct from the transformed shareholding companies examined above. In fact, the formerly socialist enterprises have been active founders and continue as current owners of the newly incorporated units.

The basic process of this property transformation is one of decentralized reorganization: under the pressure of enormous debt, declining sales, and threats of bankruptcy (or, in cases of more prosperous enterprises, to fore-stall take-overs as well as to increase autonomy from state ministries) directors of many large enterprises are breaking up their firms (along divisional, factory, departmental, or even workshop lines) into numer-ous joint stock and limited liability companies. It is not uncommon to find virtually all of the activities of a large public enterprise distributed among fifteen to twenty such satellites orbiting around the corporate headquarters.

As newly incorporated entities with legal identities, these new units are nominally independent—registered separately, with their own directors and separate balance sheets. But on closer inspection, their status in prac-tice is semi-autonomous. An examination of the computerized records of the Budapest Court of Registry indicates, for example, that the controlling shares of these corporate satellites are typically held by the public enter-prises themselves. This pattern is exemplified by the case of one of Hunga-ry's largest metallurgy firms represented in Figure 2.2. As we see in that figure, 'Heavy Metal', an enormous shareholding company in the portfolio of the AV-Rt, is the majority shareholder of twenty-six of its forty corpo-rate satellites. Like Saturn's rings, Heavy Metal's satellites revolve around the giant corporate planet in concentric orbits. Near the centre are the core metallurgy units, hot-rolling mills, energy, maintenance, and strategic plan-ning units held in a kind of geo-synchronous orbit by 100 per cent owner-ship. In the next ring, where the corporate headquarters holds roughly 50–99 per cent of the shares, are the cold-rolling mills, wire and cable production, oxygen facility, galvanizing and other finishing treatments, spe-cialized castings, quality control, and marketing units. As this listing sug-gests, these satellites are linked to each other and to the core units by ties of technological dependence. Relations between the middle-ring satellites and the company centre are marked by the centre's recurrent efforts to intro-duce stricter accounting procedures and tighter financial controls. These attempts are countered by the units' efforts to increase their autonomy—co-ordinated through personal ties and formalized in the bi-weekly meet-ings of the 'Club of KFT Managing Directors'.

The satellites of the outer ring are even more heterogeneous in their production profiles (construction, industrial services, computing, ceramics, machining) and are usually of lower levels of capitalization. Units of this outer ring are less fixed in Heavy Metal's gravitational field: some have recently entered and some seem about to leave. Among the new entrants are some of Heavy Metal's domestic customers. Unable to collect receiva-bles, Heavy Metal exchanged inter-enterprise debt for equity in its clients, preferring that these meteors be swept into an orbit rather than be lost in liquidation. Among those satellites launched from the old state enterprise

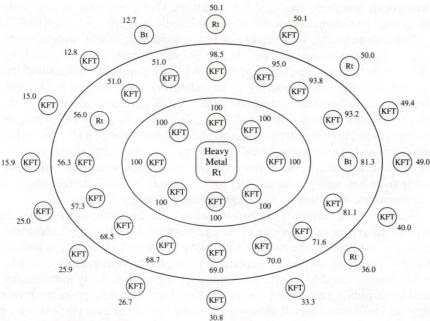

Rt = shareholding company
KFT = limited liability comapny
Bt = partnerships

FIG. 2.2. Corporate satellites at Heavy Metal. Numerals indicate Heavy Metal's ownership stage in a given satellite. Source: Internal company documents at Heavy Metal

are some for which Heavy Metal augments its less than majority ownership with leasing arrangements to keep centrifugal forces in check.

The corporate satellites among the limited liability companies enumerated on the third row of Table 2.1 are, thus, far from unambiguously 'private' ventures; yet neither are they unmistakably 'statist' residues of the socialist past. Property shares in most corporate satellites are not limited to the founding enterprise. Top- and mid-level managers, professionals, and other staff can be found on the lists of founding partners and current owners. Such private persons rarely acquire complete ownership of the corporate satellite, preferring to use their insider knowledge to exploit the ambiguities of institutional co-ownership. The corporate satellites are thus partially a result of the hedging and risk-sharing strategies of individual managers. We might ask why a given manager would not want to acquire 100 per cent ownership in order to obtain 100 of the profit, but from the perspective of a given manager the calculus instead is 'Why acquire 100 per cent of the risk if some can be shared with the corporate centre?' With ambiguous interests and divided loyalties, these risk-sharing (or risk-shedding) owner-managers are organizationally hedging (Sabel 1990).[15]

Not uncommonly, these individuals are joined in mixed ownership by other joint stock companies and limited liability companies—sometimes by independent companies, often by other KFTs in a similar orbit around the *same* enterprise, and frequently by shareholding companies or KFTs spinning around some *other* enterprise with lines of purchase or supply to the corporate unit (Voszka 1991). Banks also participate in this form of recombinant property. In many cases, the establishment of KFTs and other new corporate forms is triggered by enterprise debt. In the reorganization of the insolvent firms, the commercial banks (whose shares as joint stock companies are still predominantly state-owned) become shareholders of the corporate satellites by exchanging debt for equity.

We have used the term 'corporate satellite' to designate this instance of recombinant property. An exact (but cumbersome) terminology reflects the complex, intertwined character of property relations in Hungary: a limited liability company owned by private persons, by private ventures, and by other limited liability companies owned by joint stock companies, banks, and large public enterprises owned by the state. The new property forms thus find horizontal ties of cross-ownership intertwined with vertical ties of nested holdings.

Recombinets

The recombinant character of Hungarian property is a function not only of the direct (horizontal) ownership ties among the largest firms and of their direct (vertical) ties to their corporate satellites but also of the network properties of the full ensemble of direct and indirect ties linking entities, irrespective of their attributes (large, small, or of various legal forms) in a given configuration. The available data do not allow us to present a comprehensive map of these complex relations. Records in the Courts of Registry include documents on the owners of a particular firm, but enterprises are not required to report the companies in which they hold a stake. However, on the basis of enterprise-level field research, examination of public records at the SPA, and interviews with bankers and executives of consulting firms, we have been able to reconstruct at least partial networks represented in Figure 2.3.

For orientation in this graphic space, we position Figure 2.3 in relation to Figures 2.1 and 2.2. Figure 2.1 presented inter-enterprise ownership networks formed through horizontal ties directly linking large enterprises. Figure 2.2 zoomed in on the corporate satellites of a single large enterprise. With Figure 2.3 we pull back to examine a fragment of a broader inter-enterprise ownership network bringing into focus the ties that link corpo-

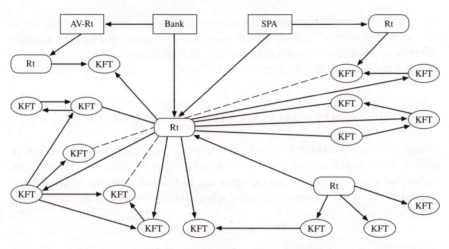

Fig. 2.3. A Hungarian recombinet. Source: Internal company documents; State Property Agency files; corporate files, Budapest Court of Registry

rate satellites to each other and that form the indirect ties among heterogeneous units in a more loosely coupled network.[16]

I label this emergent form of recombinant property a *recombinet*. Here we see that the limited liability companies that began as corporate spin-offs are oriented through ownership ties either to more than one shareholding company and/or to other limited liability companies. In the recombinet, actors recognize the network properties of their interdependent assets and regroup them across formal organizational boundaries. These creative regroupings fail to respect the organizational boundaries between enterprises as well as the boundaries between public and private.

With few exceptions (Sabel and Prokop 1996), the literature on postsocialist property transformation (most of it confined to 'privatization') assumes that the *economic unit to be restructured is the individual enterprise*. But the identification of inter-firm networks suggests that policies and practices aimed at restructuring should target not the isolated firm but *networks of firms*. Such an alternative strategy of restructuring recognizes that assets and liabilities have distinctive network properties.

The industrial structure of the socialist economy commonly grouped, within a single enterprise, assets that were incompatible (except within the logic of central planning). Merely separating or simply regrouping such assets within existing enterprises alone (on a firm-by-firm basis) cannot equal the more fruitful recombinations of complementary assets across a set of firms. Restructuring via the recombinet thus opens the possibilities of increasing the value of existing assets through their recombination. This regrouping does not necessarily imply bringing interdependent assets under the common-ownership umbrella of a hierarchically organized enterprise. As such, Hungarian recombinant property provides examples of inter-corporate networks as alternatives to a dichotomously forced choice between markets and hierarchies.

THE CENTRALIZED MANAGEMENT OF LIABILITIES

In the previous section, we examined the decentralized reorganization of assets. Property transformation, however, involves not only assets and rights but also liabiltities and obligations. In this section, we analyse what happens in a post-socialist economy when actors are called to account for enterprise debt.

Taking the Last Small Steps

The liabilities management story begins in 1991 when the Hungarian government fundamentally modified three important laws regulating the accounting of assets and liabilities in an attempt to maintain its lead in regional competition for foreign investments and international credits. Hungary's comparative advantage, it appeared, was its gradualism, which, across the decades of the 1970s and 1980s, had yielded a full range of market-like institutions. Admittedly, these were not the institutions of a market economy, but they were close; and so, the government reasoned, why not take the last small steps? As the pioneer attempt to bring post-socialist practice in full conformity with Western accounting and banking standards, the new measures could be cast as a bold move when appealing to international lending agencies. But because they were not big steps, the new measures could gain external legitimization without creating a domestic shock.

Thus, the new Accounting Law of 1991 (which took effect on 1 January 1992) required enterprises to switch to Western-style accounting principles. A simultaneously enacted tough new Western-style Bankruptcy Act similarly contained stiff personal penalties for directors of enterprises that failed to file for bankruptcy after the accountants (using the new accounting principles) sounded the alarm. At the same time, the new Act on Financial Institutions introduced in December 1991 was designed to put Hungary's commercial banks on a Western footing. In particular, the reserve requirements for measuring capital–adequacy ratios were modified and the securities and other financial instruments for provisioning against qualified loans were respecified.

The last small steps proved to be a leap into the abyss. Already reeling from the collapse of the Council for Mutual Economic Assistance (CMEA) markets, enterprise directors now learned from their accountants that the new accounting practices were colouring the companies' books even redder than expected. By the end of 1992 over 10,000 bankruptcies and liquidation proceedings had been initiated—a figure ten times higher than during the previous year when enterprises had experienced the worst shock of the collapsed Eastern markets (Bokros 1994). With one-third to one-half of enterprises in the red, the loss-making firms began to stop payment on their bank credits. By the end of 1992 the overdue loan stock of the banking system was 127 billion forints (Ft.) ($US1.5 billion), up 90 per cent from the previous year (National Bank of Hungary 1992: 109).

With thousands of firms filing for bankruptcy, the banks were forced by the new banking law to reclassify loans. The subsequent dramatic increase in the new legally required provisionings against poorly performing loans cut deeply into bank profits, slashed dividends and tax revenues from the banking sector to the state treasury, and turned the banks' capital–adequacy ratios from positive to negative. The banking system was in crisis—first announced, no less, in the *Financial Times* (Denton 1993).

From Small Steps to Big Bail-outs

The same government that had launched an unintended financial shock now initiated a bold plan to save the banks. In its 1992 loan consolidation programme the government bought 104.9 billion Ft. (about $1 billion) of qualified debt (almost all in the 'bad' debt classification) involving fourteen banks and 1,885 companies. In a related move in early 1993, the government also purchased the bank debt of eleven giant enterprises (the so-called dirty dozen) for roughly $300 million. But the loan consolidation and enterprise recapitalization programmes did not restore stability in the banking sector. By September 1993, only nine months later, financial experts were estimating that loans in arrears had once again soared to 20 per cent of total loan portfolios. And the ten largest banks were again hovering at or below the 0 per cent capital–adequacy ratio (a condition of technical insolvency).

For the government, the new banking rules did not exclude bailing out banks and enterprises again and again. But the big bail-out of 1993 had a new twist. Instead of buying the debt from the banks, this time the government adopted a two-stage strategy of first recapitalizing the banks and then using the banks to work out the enterprise debt. By injecting enormous sums of fresh capital into the banks, the Ministry of Finance became the dominant shareholder of the large commercial banks. The first stage of the strategy, then, could be summarized in a phrase: Don't acquire the debt; acquire the banks.

The second stage of the strategy was designed to harness the expertise of the banks to the service of the state. Because it was the banks, and not the state, that would be left holding the qualified debt, the banks would have an incentive to collect that debt, or at least the part they had not already

written off their books. And they would do so, this time, not with the state
as their sometime partner but with the state as their majority owner. But
efforts to exercise control through direct ownership do not equal more
effective state capacity. The conservative-nationalist government seemed
determined to learn the lesson of the 'trap of centralization' from its own
experience. Banks have shown almost no willingness to use the consolidation funds for actively restructuring firms; and despite the assumption that
the Ministry of Finance's ownership would yield control of the banks, the
government has been almost entirely ineffective in monitoring how the
banks use the recapitalization funds.

The massive bail-out programmes were not, of course, without effects: At
300 billion Ft. ($3 billion)—amounting to 10 per cent of Hungarian GDP
and 18.3 per cent of the 1994 national budget[17]—the bail-outs created a long
queue of banks and firms with their hands out, reaching for the state's
pocket-book.

Thus, at the same time that the corporate networks were engaged in the
decentralized reorganization of assets, the Hungarian state attempted
the centralized management of liabilities. That centralization has not left
the decentralized processes untouched. From the perspective of the enterprises, 'debt consolidation' triggers the organizational separation of debts
from assets. The Hungarian government's attempt at the centralized management of liabilities stimulates the networks to complement their strategies of risk-spreading with new strategies of risk-shedding. Two types of
strategy can be identified, each based on the organizational separation of
assets and liabilities. In one type, assets are distributed to the satellites and
debts are centralized, increasing the enterprises' chances of inclusion in the
government-funded debt consolidation. In the other, assets are closely held
by the enterprise centre and liabilities are distributed to the satellites where
network ties and political connections manipulate proceedings in a Hungarian version of 'bankruptcy for profit' (Akerlof and Romer 1993 coin the
term in their study of state-managed liabilities in the US savings and loan
bail-out).

We thus see a new paternalism in Hungary: whereas in the state-socialist
economy paternalism was based on the state's attempts to manage assets
centrally (Kornai 1993*a*), in the first years of the post-socialist economy
paternalism is based on the state's attempts to manage liabilities centrally.
Centralized management of liabilities will not continue indefinitely, but the
organizational dynamics of enterprises formed under the new paternalistic
conditions are likely to have strong path-dependent effects.

THE MULTIPLE ACCOUNTS OF RECOMBINANT PROPERTY

In the highly uncertain organizational environment that is the post-socialist
economy, relatively few actors (apart from institutional designers) set out

with the aim to create a market economy. Many, indeed would welcome such an outcome. But their immediate goals are more pragmatic: at best to thrive, at least to survive. And so they strive to use whatever resources are available. That task is not so simple because one must first identify the relevant system of accounting in which something can exist as a resource. At the extreme, it is sometimes even difficult to distinguish a liability from an asset. If the liabilities of your organization (enterprise or bank) are big enough, perhaps they can be translated into qualifications for more resources. And what could be more worthless than a bankrupted limited liability company—except, of course, if you have shed the risk to the banks (and then to the state) and put the assets in another form? Assets and liabilities have value not in themselves but in relation to legitimating principles.

To examine how economic actors in the post-socialist setting manœuvre not only through an ecology of organizations but also through a complex ecology of ordering principles we need to understand the doubly associative character of assets. There are no free-floating resources. To exist as an asset a potential resource must be mobilizable through ties of association among persons (Granovetter 1985). And to be of *value* a potential resource must also have relative worth according to a standard of measure. To be able to circulate through the ties that bind (and thus contribute to that binding) an asset must be justified within a relatively stabilized *network of categories* that make up a legitimizing principle (Thévenot 1985; Boltanski and Thévenot 1991; Latour 1988; White 1992).[18] Regrouping assets thus involves making new associations—not only by rearranging social ties among persons and things but also by drawing on diverse repertoires of justificatory principles.

To emphasize the patterned and the performative aspects of this process, I exploit a notion of *accounts*. Etymologically rich, the term simultaneously connotes bookkeeping and narration. Both dimensions entail evaluative judgements, and each implies the other: accountants prepare story-lines according to established formulae, and in the accountings of a good story-teller we know what counts. In everyday life, we are all bookkeepers and story-tellers. We keep accounts and we give accounts, and most importantly, we can all be called to account for our actions. When we make such an accounting, we draw on and reproduce social orders. We can competently produce justifications only in terms of established and recognized ordering principles, standards, and measures of evaluation. Because we do not simply give reasons but also have reasons for doing things, accounts are not simply retrospective; the imperative of justification (Boltanski and Thévenot 1991) structures what we do and not simply how we explain. We can never simply 'calculate' because we must do so with units and instruments of measurement that are deeply structured by accounts of what can be of value. We reproduce these units of measurement and we recalibrate the measuring instruments when we assert our worthiness, when we defer to the 'more worthy', or when we denounce their status according to some other standard of evaluation. When we give an account, we affirm or challenge the ordering criteria according to which our actions (and/or those of others) have been or will be evaluated. And it is always within accounts that we 'size up the situation', for not every form of worth can be made to apply and not every asset is in a form mobilizable for the situation. We *evaluate* the situation by manœuvring to use scales that measure some types of worth and not others, thereby acting to validate some accounts and discredit others.

The multiple accounts of recombinant property respond to and exploit the fundamental, though diffused, uncertainty about the organizational environment. In transformative economies, firms have to worry not simply about whether there is demand for their products, or about the rate of return on their investment, or about the level of profitability, but also about the very principle of selection itself. Thus, the question is not only 'Will I survive the *market test*?'—but also, 'Under what conditions is proof of worth on market principles neither sufficient nor necessary to survive?' Because there are multiply operative, mutually coexistent principles of justification according to which you can be called on to give accounts of your actions, you cannot be sure what counts. By what proof and according to which principles of justification are you worthy to steward such and such resources? Because of this uncertainty, actors will seek to diversify their assets, to hold resources in multiple accounts.

This ability to glide among principles and to produce multiple accountings is an organizational hedging. It differs, however, from the kind of hedging to minimize risk exposure that we would find within a purely market logic—as, for example, when the shopkeeper who sells swimwear and sun lotion also devotes some floor space to umbrellas. Instead of acting within a single regime of evaluation, this is organizational hedging that crosses and combines disparate evaluative principles. Recombinant property is a particular kind of portfolio management. It is an attempt to have a resource that can be justified or assessed by more than one standard of measure (as, for example, the rabbit-breeder whose roadside stand advertises 'Pets and Meat' in the documentary film *Roger and Me*). In managing one's portfolio of justifications, one starts from the dictum: Diversify your accounts.

The adroit recombinant agent in the transformative economies of East Central Europe diversifies holdings in response to fundamental uncertainties about what can constitute a resource. Under conditions not simply of market uncertainty but of organizational uncertainty, there can be multiple (and intertwined) strategies for survival—based in some cases on *profitability* but in others on *eligibility*. Where your success is judged, and the resources placed at your disposal determined, sometimes by your market share and sometimes by the number of workers you employ in a region;

sometimes by your price–earnings ratio and sometimes by your 'strategic importance'; and, when even the absolute size of your losses can be transformed into an asset yielding an income stream, you might be wise to diversify your portfolio, to be able to shift your accounts, to be equally skilled in applying for loans as in applying for job creation subsidies, to have a multilingual command of the grammar of creditworthiness and the syntax of debt forgiveness. To hold recombinant property is to have such a diversified portfolio.

To gain room for manœuvre, actors court and even create ambiguity. They measure in multiple units; they speak in many tongues. They will be less controlled by others if they can be accountable (able to make credible accounts) to many.[19] In so doing, they produce the polyphonic discourse of worth that is post-socialism.

We can hear that polyphonic chorus in the diverse ways that firms justify their claims for participation in the debt relief programme. The following litany of justifications are stylized versions of claims encountered in discussions with bankers, property agency officials, and enterprise directors. Our firm should be included in the debt relief programme:

because we will forgive our debtors (i.e. our firm occupies a strategic place in a network of inter-enterprise debt)

because we are truly creditworthy (i.e. if our liabilities are separated from our assets, we will again be eligible for more bank financing. Similar translations could be provided for each of the following justifications)

because we employ thousands

because our suppliers depend on us for a market

because we are in your election district

because our customers depend on our product inputs

because we can then be privatized

because we can never be privatized

because we took big risks

because we were prudent and did not take risks

because we were planned in the past

because we have a plan for the future

because we export to the West

because we export to the East

because our product has been awarded an International Standards Quality Control Certificate

because our product is part of the Hungarian national heritage

because we are an employee buy-out

because we are a management buy-in

because we are partly state-owned

because we are partly privately held

because our creditors drove us into bankruptcy when they loaned to us at higher than market rates to artificially raise bank profits in order to pay dividends into a state treasury whose coffers had dwindled when corporations like ourselves effectively stopped paying taxes.

And so we must ask, into whose account and by which account will debt forgiveness flow? Or, in such a situation, is anyone accountable?

AN EAST EUROPEAN CAPITALISM?

How are we to understand these unorthodox forms, these organizational 'monsters' regrouping the seemingly incongruous?

In this concluding section, we reconsider the three aspects of recombinant property (blurring of public and private, blurring of enterprise boundaries, and blurring the boundedness of legitimizing principles) in terms of three underlying concepts—mixture, diversity, and complexity.

Mixture

Imagine two economies, each of equal parts public and private. In one, half the firms are fully private, half are fully public. In the other, every firm is half-public, half-private. Each is a 'mixed economy'. Yet is it likely that their dynamics will be the same?[20] No two economies closely approximate the thought experiment's ideal types; but it none the less puts in sharp relief the question *What is the mix of the post-socialist mixed economy?*

My findings of corporate spin-offs and recombinant reorganization at the enterprise level, and of widespread public ownership combined with inter-enterprise ownership networks among the very largest enterprises, challenges the assumption, widely held on all sides of the privatization debate, that post-socialist economies can be adequately represented in a two-sector model. That analytic shortcoming cannot be remedied by more precise specification of the boundary between public and private: the old property divide has been so eroded that what might once have been a distinct boundary line is now a recombinant zone. Hungary is a post-socialist mixed economy not because of a simple dualism of well-bounded state-owned firms in one sector and privately owned firms in another but because many firms themselves exploit aspects of public and private property relations. What we find are new forms of property in which the properties of private and public are dissolved, interwoven, and recombined. Property in East European capitalism is recombinant property, and its analysis suggests the emergence of a distinctively East European capitalism that will differ as much from West European capitalisms as do contemporary East Asian variants.

The concept of a post-socialist mixed economy is a useful first approximation of an East European capitalism. But its essentialist categories of
'public' and 'private' (and the related dualisms of 'market' and 'redistribution')—even when opened up to the possibility of being mixed together in
the same organizational setting—may be more limiting than illuminating.

For decades, capitalism was defined *vis-à-vis* socialism, and vice versa.
Their systematic comparison enriched our understanding of both, but the
'methods of mirrored opposition' and similar constructs (Stark 1986;
Szelényi 1978, 1988) that worked with these dualisms are no longer fruitful.
The demise of socialism challenges that analytically forced choice, and it
offers an opportunity for enriching comparative institutional analysis.
When we stop defining capitalism in terms of socialism, we see that, in our
epoch, capitalism as a construct is only analytically interesting in the plural:
capitalisms must be defined and compared *vis-à-vis* each other.

Diversity

Our first analytic shift, therefore, must be from the conceptual tools around
the concept of *mixture* to those around that of *diversity*. Capitalisms are
diverse, and that diversity is manifested in forms that cannot be adequately
conceptualized as mixtures of capitalism and socialism.[21] By analysing
recombinant property not only as the dissolution and interweaving of elements of public and private but also as a blurring of organizational boundaries in networks of interlocking ownership, we can escape, for example, the
terms of the debate about whether the 'lessons of East Asia for Eastern
Europe' are the virtues of neo-liberalism or of neo-statism (World Bank
1993; Amsden 1994). Instead we join economic sociologists who are studying the East Asian economies from a network-centred approach in which
not markets, nor states, nor isolated firms, but social networks are the basic
units of analysis (Gereffi 1994; Hamilton *et al.* 1990; Hamilton and Feenstra
1995). In this perspective, the ability of the East Asian economies to adapt
flexibly to changes in world markets rests in the interlocking ties characteristic of corporate groups (Orru *et al.* 1991; Granovetter 1995), whether these
be the patterns of mutual shareholding within the Japanese *keiretsu*
(Gerlach and Lincoln 1992; Hoshi 1994); the ties of family ownership within
the more vertically integrated South Korean *chaebol* (Kim 1991; Hamilton
and Feenstra 1995); the social ties of the more horizontally integrated
Taiwanese *guanxiquiye* 'related enterprises' (Numazaki 1991); or the dense
ties that transgress organizational boundaries in the 'buyer-driven' and
'producer-driven' networks in Hong Kong, Singapore, and elsewhere in
South-east Asia (Gereffi 1994).

These recent studies of the social embeddedness and local organizational
innovation characteristic of East Asian corporate networks suggest that the

strategic choice is not plans or markets, or even clans or markets but clans for markets. Market *orientation* must be distinguished from market *co-ordination*: a broad variety of institutions of non-market co-ordination are compatible with high-performance market orientation (Schmitter 1988; Boyer 1991; Bresser Pereira 1993). Many of the most successful forms of network co-ordination in East Asia, moreover, appeared to early observers as highly improbable forms whose atavistic features could not possibly survive beyond the period of post-war reconstruction from which they arose.[22] Our point of departure, it should be clear, however, is not to look to Eastern Europe to find Hungarian *keiretsu* or Czech *chaebol*. Instead of searching for direct counterparts, East Asian–East European comparisons will yield new concepts when we grasp the specificity of the regional variants by explaining the differences among the various countries within a region.[23]

Future research must examine whether the East European corporate networks are becoming successfully oriented to the world market. But it is not too early to pose analytic dimensions along which we could assess the potential for recombinant property to contribute to economic development.

One starting-point, ready at hand from the burgeoning literature on the 'transitional' economies, would be to ask, 'Do they contribute to creative destruction?' That litmus test is based on a widely held assumption that economic development will be best promoted by 'allowing the selection mechanism to work' through bankruptcies of underperforming enterprises. Recombinant property would not receive an unambiguously positive score measured by this standard. Indeed, the kinds of inter-enterprise ownership described above are classic risk-spreading and risk-sharing devices that mitigate differences across firms. By dampening the performance of the stronger and facilitating the survival of the weaker firms in the inter-enterprise recombinet, they might even impede creative destruction in the conventional sense.

But there is some question that a tidal wave of mass bankruptcies is a long-term cure for the post-socialist economies. With the catastrophic loss of markets to the East and with the stagnation of the economies of potentially new trading partners to the West, the depth and length of the transformational crisis in East Central Europe now exceeds that of the Great Depression of the inter-war period (Kornai 1993*b*). In such circumstances, an absolute hardening of firms' budget constraints not only drives poorly performing firms into bankruptcy but also destroys enterprises that would otherwise be quite capable of making a high performance adjustment (see especially Cui 1994). Wanton destruction is not creative destruction, goes this reasoning; and recombinant property might save some of these struggling but capable firms through risk-sharing networks. Along this line of reasoning, we would want to assess whether the sacrifice in allocative efficiency by retarding bankruptcy is being offset by the preservation of assets with real potential for high performance in a situation of economic recovery.

A related, but analytically separate, point is that risk-spreading can be a basis for risk-taking. Extraordinarily high uncertainties of the kind we see now in the post-socialist economies can lead to low levels of investment with negative strategic complementarities (as when firms forgo investments because they expect a sluggish economy based on the lack of investments by others). By mitigating disinclinations to invest, risk-spreading might be one means to break out of otherwise low-level equilibrium traps.[24] Firms in the post-socialist transformational crisis are like mountain climbers assaulting a treacherous face, and the networks of inter-enterprise ownership are the safety ropes lashing them together. Neo-liberals who bemoan a retarded bankruptcy rate fail to acknowledge that there might be circumstances when this mutual binding is a pre-condition for attempting a difficult ascent. Along this line of reasoning, we would want to assess whether the opportunities for risk-shedding in the Hungarian setting can be offset when networks (rather than 'developmental states', Evans 1992) perform disequilibrating functions that facilitate and stimulate entrepreneurial risk-taking.

Economic development in East Central Europe does require more exit (some, indeed many, firms must perish) and more entry as well. But for destruction to be creative, these deaths must be accompanied by births not simply of new organizations but of new organizational forms. Organizational forms are specific bundles of routines, and the reduction of their diversity means the loss of organized information that might be of value when the environment changes (Hannan 1986; Boyer 1991; Stark 1989, 1992). From this perspective, an economy that maximized *allocative* efficiency (by putting all resources in the most efficient form) would sacrifice *adaptive* efficiency. Socialism, in this view, failed not only because it lacked a selection mechanism to eliminate organizations that performed poorly but also because it put all its economic resources in a single organizational form—the state enterprise. Socialism drastically reduced organizational diversity and in so doing prohibited a broad repertoire of organized solutions to problems of collective action. Along this line of reasoning, an assessment of forms of recombinant property in an East European capitalism should start not by testing whether they reproduce state socialism or harbour real private property but whether they contribute to adaptive efficiency.

For the property rights school, it is not destruction (bankruptcy) nor diversity but the *clarity* of property rights that will yield the right set of incentives to make restructuring in the post-socialist transformation performance-enhancing. Instead of reassigning property rights to an owner (an ironic legacy of an essentially Marxist notion of property), this school argues that property can be productively 'disintegrated' (Grey 1980) such that different actors can legitimately claim rights to different aspects and capacities of the same thing (Hart 1988; Comisso 1991). But however disaggregated, property rights must be clarified if accountability is to be ensured. Walder (1994), the leading proponent of this perspective in the post-socialist debate, for example, shows that it is not the privatization of assets but the clarification of property rights that has contributed to the dynamism of township and village enterprises in Chinese light industry.

Along this line of reasoning, we should assess whether recombinant property is leading to well-defined property rights. The initial evidence presented in this chapter suggests that recombinant property would fail such a test. But from another perspective in the debate over property rights, the blurring of enterprise boundaries might be a viable strategy to promote organizational flexibility. On the basis of research in advanced manufacturing fields in Germany and the United States, Sabel (1990) and Kogut *et al.* (1992) demonstrate that under conditions of extreme market volatility or of extraordinarily rapid technological change, economic actors engage in hedging strategies *vis-à-vis* other organizations (partners or competitors) in their organizational field. When the future is highly uncertain, it is far from clear at t_1 whether your assets will be interdependent with mine at t_2. In such situations, in addition to the dualism *make or buy* (hierarchy or market) there is an alternative—*co-operate*. Kogut observes that one manifestation of such a hedging strategy is cross-ownership (not simply among purchasers and suppliers but also among competitors), and he finds dense patterns of cross-ownership among competitors in the field of microprocessing, where firms cannot be certain whose standards will be the industry standards in the next round. Sabel goes even further, arguing that, in cases of extremely complex asset interdependence, it is not clear-cut property claims (however dense the cross-ownership) but an *ambiguity* of property claims that provides flexible adaptation to the market. Sabel's argument departs radically from the property rights school: he is claiming that actors are not assigned different rights over different aspects of an asset but are making overlapping claims on the same aspect. This is ambiguous property, not disaggregated property.

The hedging strategies and boundary-blurring in post-socialist reconstruction, it seems, find counterparts in some of the technologically most highly sophisticated sectors of North American and West European capitalism. Along the dimension of this line of reasoning, we should assess whether recombinant property is, in fact, contributing to flexibility and whether any gains that might so accrue are enough to offset the possible sacrifice of accountability. We re-encounter this trade-off of adaptability and accountability as we turn from the issues of organizational diversity and property rights to the problem of heterogeneous legitimizing principles.

Complexity

In restructuring assets, we might say that actors are 'identifying' new resources, but this would suggest that the resource was simply hidden or under-utilized and only needed to be uncovered. In fact, before recombining resources, they must first redefine them. We call this ability to recognize the properties of persons and things *organizational reflexivity*. It cannot be derived from the ambiguity of property claims but is a function instead of the ambiguity of organizing principles. The key to adaptability in this view is not simply the diversity of types of organization but the possibilities for cross-fertilization inside and across organizations where multiply operative legitimizing principles collide—or, in Harrison White's (1993) phrase, 'values mate to change'.[25]

Some might argue, of course, that multiple orders are fine—provided that each occupies a distinctly bounded domain. Such is the model of modernity in 'modernization' theory: through differentiation, each domain of society would develop as a separate autonomous subsystem with its own distinctive logic. Complexity in this view requires diversity but only as the juxtaposition of clearly bounded rationalities. Marxism, of course, has its own conception of complexity: the temporary overlap of mutually contradictory principles. Both modernization theory and Marxism are deeply grounded in the transition problematic. The noisy clash of orders is only temporary: the revolutionary moment for one, the passage to differentiated domains in the other.

If we break with this transition problem, we can escape from the impoverished conceptions of complexity in both Marxism and modernization theory. In the alternative conception offered here, complexity is the interweaving of multiple justificatory principles on the same domain space. That view, of course, shares with modernization theory the notion of distinctive domains—relatively autonomous fields of action (Bourdieu 1990). And it shares with Marxism the notion of the collision of ordering principles. But unlike modernization theory, each domain is a site of heterogeneity; and unlike Marxism, that tension is not consolidated and then released in an all-encompassing revolutionary moment. The noisy clash of orders occurs throughout the social world, and it is not transient but ongoing—punctuated by relative, localized stabilizations but never equilibrium (Latour 1988).

Post-socialist societies are entering this discordant world. To still that noisy clash by the ascendancy of one accounting, with profitability as the sole metric and markets as the only co-ordinating mechanism, would be to duplicate the attempt of communism, with its imposition of a unitary justificatory principle, a strict hierarchy of property forms, and a single co-ordinating mechanism. To replicate the monochrome with a different colouring would be to destroy the heterogeneity of organizing principles that is the basis of adaptability.

As this account of recombinant property has demonstrated, post-socialist societies are not lacking in heterogeneous organizing principles. The problem therefore is not a simple lack of accountability but an over-abundance of accountability: an actor who, within the same domain space, is accountable to every principle is accountable to none. The adaptability of modern capitalisms rests not simply in the diversity of organizations but in the organization of diversity: enough overlap of legitimizing principles across domains to foster rivalry of competing accounts within domains and enough boundedness of rationalities to foster accountability. It is not in finding the right mix of public and private but in finding the right *organization of diversity* to yield both adaptability and accountability that post-socialist societies face their greatest challenge.

NOTES

Originally published in *The American Journal of Sociology*, vol. 101, no. 4, January 1996. Reprinted with kind permission from The University of Chicago Press. © 1996 by the University of Chicago. All rights reserved. Research for this paper was conducted while the author was a Visiting Fellow at the Institute for Advanced Study/Collegium Budapest and was supported by grants from the National Science Foundation and the Joint Committee on Eastern Europe of the American Council of Learned Societies/Social Science Research Council. My thanks to Luc Boltanski, Ronald Breiger, Rogers Brubaker, László Bruszt, Ellen Comisso, Paul DiMaggio, Neil Fligstein, Geoff Fougere, István Gábor, Gernot Grabher, Elisabeth Hagen, Szabolcs Kemény, János Kornai, János Lukács, Peter Murrell, László Neumann, Claus Offe, Jonas Pontusson, Ákos Róna-Tas, Ivan Szelenyi, Andrew Walder, and especially Monique Djokic Stark for their criticisms of an earlier draft.

1. The crumbling of the traditional structures, Durkheim wrote, had 'swept away all the older forms of organization. One after another, these have disappeared either through the slow usury of time or through great disturbances, but without being replaced' (Durkheim 1897: 446).
2. As such it shares many of the shortcomings of 'presentist' history—reading the past as approximations of later outcomes (Sewell, forthcoming; Somers and Gibson 1994). In a related critique in the sociology of science, Collins (1982), Latour (1988), and Pickering (1992) turn from outcomes to controversies.
3. Whereas Durkheim saw sociology as the science of morality that could guide society from the 'state of mental confusion' to a stable moral order (Wacquant 1993), today it is the science of choice that will guide the economies of Eastern Europe through the transition from socialism to capitalism. The difference between the transition that opened the century and the transition at its close is, of course, that this time, with almost a century of experience, we are no longer burdened by the ignorance of outcomes.

4. East European scholars have long argued that social change is a transformational reshaping of enduring structures exhibiting multiplicity rather than uniformity (Konrad and Szelényi 1979; Szücs 1985; Staniszkis 1993; Szelényi 1994).

5. See, by contrast, Burawoy and Krotov's account of change as retrogression: 'Our case study suggests that with the withering away of the party state the Soviet economy, far from collapsing or transforming itself, has assumed an exaggerated version of its former self' (1992: 34).

6. Szelényi (1978) argued that 'mixture' characterized both East and West: whereas a redistributive welfare state mitigates inequalities produced by markets under advanced capitalism, in state socialism subordinated market-like institutions mitigate inequalities produced by the dominant redistributive mechanism. Elsewhere (Stark 1986) I labelled this analytic method 'mirrored opposition' and used it to analyse differences between capitalist and socialist internal labour markets.

7. The essay's concluding paragraph, in a volume from a conference in 1986 well before the demise of socialism, articulated themes that continue to motivate the current study: 'Perhaps the distinctive contribution of the Hungarian experiment will be to demonstrate that the path to reforming a socialist economy lies less in promoting competition among firms than in fostering competition among organizational forms. . . . Collective intrapreneurial units and other mixed property forms will provoke ambivalence, and even paralysis, so long as an economy is justified on the basis of a single universalistic principle, be it market-defined "self interest" or bureaucratically-defined "societal interest". An alternative is to step unambiguously on the road to a mixed economy and to raise the plurality of property forms from the status of the contingent and ambiguous to one in which diversity is itself a principle of justification. Hungary might yet take such a step. As analysts, our next step is to accept the challenge of comparing mixed economies not on the basis of the relative weights of "capitalist" and "socialist" elements but on the basis of the complex combinations of diverse and internally heterogeneous organizational forms' (Stark 1989: 168).

8. In her analysis of 'political capitalism' in Poland, Staniszkis (1991) similarly identifies 'hybrid forms' of 'undefined dual status' in a variety of leasing forms and cost shifting arrangements through which nomenclatura companies enjoy the benefits of property transformation without privatization.

9. Three of these firms are among the twenty largest firms in Hungary and are at the core of Hungarian manufacturing in metallurgy, electronics, and rubber products. Three are small and medium-size firms in plastics, machining, and industrial engineering. This field research was conducted in collaboration with László Neumann, and involved longitudinal analysis of the same firms in which we had earlier studied an organizational innovation of internal subcontracting inside the socialist enterprise (Stark 1986, 1989, 1990; Neumann 1989).

10. These data were augmented by ownership data drawn from the files of some 800 firms under the portfolio management of the State Property Agency.

11. A partial list of interviewees includes: the former president of the National Bank; the former deputy minister of the Ministry of Finance; executives of the four largest commercial banks and two leading investment banks; the former president of the State Holding Corporation; directors, advisers, and officials of the State Property Agency; senior officials of the World Bank's Hungarian

Mission; the chief economic advisers of the two major liberal parties; the president of the Federation of Hungarian Trade Unions; and leading officials of the Hungarian Socialist Party (who later ascended to high-level positions in the new Socialist–Liberal coalition government).

12. Such data collection is not a simple matter where capital markets are poorly developed. There is no Hungarian *Moody's* and certainly no corporate directory equivalent to *Industrial Groupings in Japan* or *Keiretsu no Kenkyu* (see e.g. Gerlach and Lincoln 1992). The labour-intensive solution has been to gather that data directly from the Hungarian Courts of Registry. My thanks to Lajos Vékás, Professor of Law, ELTE, and Rector of the Institute for Advanced Study, Collegium Budapest, for his interventions to secure access to these data and to Szabolcs Kemény and Jonathan Uphoff for assistance in data collection.

13. This twenty-owner limitation is a convention adopted in research on inter-corporate ownership in East Asia (Gerlach and Lincoln 1992; Hoshi 1994). In the Hungarian economy, where only thirty-seven firms are traded on the Budapest stock exchange and where corporate shareholding is not widely dispersed among hundreds of small investors, the twenty-owner restriction allows us to account for at least 90 per cent of the shares held in virtually every company.

14. The total pattern of strong and weak ties will be examined in a later study using block-model analysis, testing for bank centrality, and assessing the relationship between ownership ties and director interlocks. The purpose of that study will be to identify the major corporate groupings in the Hungarian economy.

15. Many of these mid-level managers had experiences in the 1980s with an organizational precursor of the present recombinant forms—the intra-enterprise partnerships—in which semi-autonomous subcontracting units used enterprise equipment to produce goods or services during the 'off hours' (Stark 1986, 1989). Like second-economy producers who continued to hold a job in state enterprises, these intrapreneurial units were a widespread result of hedging strategies in the Hungarian economy. Some of these partnerships were scarcely disguised rent-seeking schemes that privatized profit streams and left expenses with the state-owned enterprise. Others creatively redeployed resources from diverse parts of the shop floor and regrouped, as well, the informal norms of reciprocity with the technical norms of the professionals.

16. The recombinet is not a simple summation of the set of horizontal and vertical ties: to label categorically the ties between a given KFT and a given Rt as 'vertical' would be to ignore the ways the KFTs are recombining properties. To the extent that genuinely network properties are emergent in the recombinet, the language of horizontal and vertical should give place to more appropriate descriptors such as extensivity, density, tight or loose coupling, strong or weak ties, structural holes, and the like (Breiger and Pattison 1986; Burt 1992).

17. To put these figures in perspective, for the United States the $105 billion savings and loan bail-out represents 1.6 per cent of GNP and 7 per cent of the projected 1995 federal budget. Venezuela's recent $6.1 billion bank bail-out is on a magnitude with the Hungarian programme representing 11 per cent of Venezuela's gross national product and 75 per cent of the government's 1994 national budget (Brooke 1994).

18. Those analysts who tend to focus on *strong ties* in an ideational network—that is, where the constituent idea-blocks of a form are tightly coupled and linked in dense patterns—call these forms 'ideologies' (for the classic statement, see Bendix 1956). Those analysts who emphasize the comprehensible, as opposed to comprehensive, quality of forms focus on the *weak ties* in an ideational network, as stressed in their employment of the term 'stories' and their attention to narrative structure (White 1992; Sabel and Zeitlin 1996). Ideologies are like road-maps, demonstrating the comprehensive connections; stories are like sketched pathways, telling how one got from there to here through a particular chain of connections.

19. See Padgett and Ansell (1993) for an analysis of such multivocality in another historical setting.

20. In a related path-dependent thought experiment: imagine two mixed economies each with half the firms fully public and half the firms fully private. The first arrived at that sectoral mix from a starting-point of only public firms, the other, from a starting-point of only private firms. Are their dynamics likely to be the same?

21. My argument, thus, bears no resemblance to 'third road' solutions (i.e. the mistaken notion that there could be some combination of the best features of capitalism with the best features of socialism), and it follows that I am not arguing that recombinant property is a 'best way'. As people living in East Central Europe have known for decades if not centuries, all the best roads to capitalism started somewhere else. I am reminded of the joke in which an Irishman in the far countryside is asked, 'What's the best way to get to Dublin?' He thinks for a minute, and responds, 'Don't start from here.'

22. Incongruity, in itself, neither ensures survival nor condemns an organizational form to an early death. Kim's (1991) discussion of the combinatory logic of the formation of the *chaebol* in Korea immediately following World War II invites comparison with the formation of recombinant structures during the contemporary period of East European reconstruction.

23. Stark and Bruszt (1995), for example, compare corporate networks in Hungary and the Czech Republic. They find that Hungarian networks are formed predominantly through enterprise to enterprise links, sometimes involving banks yet absent ties between banks and intermediate-level institutions such as investment companies. In the Czech Republic, by contrast, ownership networks are formed predominantly through ties at the meso-level in the cross-ownership of banks and large investment funds, but direct ownership connections among enterprises themselves are rare. Whereas Hungarian networks are tightly coupled at the level of enterprises but loosely coupled at the meso-level, Czech networks are loosely coupled at the level of enterprises and tightly coupled at the meso-level.

24. On strategic complementarities in the post-socialist economies, see esp. Litwack (1994). Hirschman (1958) provides the classic statement on low-level equilibrium traps and the importance of risk-spreading for economic development.

25. See esp. Grabher (1994) for a discussion of how rivalry of coexisting organizational forms contributes to reflexivity and adaptability. For related views on adaptability and complexity, see Landau (1969), Morin (1974), and Conrad (1983).

REFERENCES

AKERLOF, GEORGE A., and ROMER, PAUL M. (1993), 'Looting: The Economic Underworld of Bankruptcy for Profit', *Brookings Papers on Economic Activity*, 2: 1–73.

ALEXANDER, JEFFREY C. (1994), 'Modern, Anti, Post, and Neo: How Social Theories have Tried to Understand the "New World" of "Our Time"', *Zeitschrift für Soziologie*, 23: 165–97.

AMSDEN, ALICE (1994), 'Can Eastern Europe Compete by Getting the Prices Right? Contrast with East Asian Structural Reforms', in Andres Soimano, Osvaldo Sunkel, and Mario I. Blejer (eds.), *Rebuilding Capitalism: Alternative Roads after Socialism and Dirigisme* (Ann Arbor: University of Michigan Press), 81–107.

BENDIX, REINHARD (1956), *Work and Authority in Industry: Ideologies of Management in the Course of Industrialization* (Berkeley: University of California Press).

BLANCHARD, OLIVER JEAN, FOOT, KENNETH A., and SACHS, JEFFREY D. (1994), Introduction, in Oliver Jean Blanchard, Kenneth A. Foot, and Jeffrey D. Sachs (eds.), *The Transition in Eastern Europe* (Chicago: University of Chicago Press), ii.

BOKROS, LAJOS (1994), 'Privatization and the Banking System in Hungary', in László Samuely (ed.), *Privatization in the Transition Process: Recent Experiences in Eastern Europe* (Geneva: United Nations Conference on Trade and Development and KOPINT-DATORG), 305–20.

BOLTANSKI, LUC, and THÉVENOT, LAURENT (1991), *De la justification: Les économies de la grandeur* (Paris: Gallimard).

BOURDIEU, PIERRE (1990), *The Logic of Practice*, trans. Richard Nice (Stanford, Calif.: Stanford University Press).

BOYER, ROBERT (1991), 'Markets within Alternative Coordinating Mechanisms: History, Theory, and Policy in the Light of the Nineties', Paper presented to the Conference on the Comparative Governance of Sectors, Bigorio, Switzerland, 1991.

BREIGER, RONALD L. (1995), 'Social Structure and the Phenomenology of Attainment', *Annual Review of Sociology*, 21: 115–36.

——and PATTISON, PHILIPPA E. (1986), 'Cumulated Social Roles: The Duality of Persons and their Algebras', *Social Networks*, 8/3: 215–56.

BRESSER PEREIRA, LUIZ CARLOS (1993), 'The Crisis of the State Approach to Latin America', Discussion paper no. 1, Instituto Sul-Norte, São Paolo.

BROOKE, JAMES (1994), 'Venezuela Banks: A "Catastrophe" Awaiting Rescue', *International Herald Tribune*, 17 May 1994, Business Section.

BRUSZT, LÁSZLÓ (1988), 'A centralizáció csapdája és a politikai rendszer reformalternatívái' (The Trap of Centralization and the Alternatives of Reforming the Political System), *Medvetánc*, 1: 171–97.

BUNCE, VALERIE, and CSANADI, MÁRIA (1993), 'Uncertainty in the Transition: Postcommunism in Hungary', *East European Politics and Societies*, 7/2: 240–75.

BURAWOY, MICHAEL, and KROTOV, PAVEL (1992), 'The Soviet Transition from Socialism to Capitalism: Worker Control and Economic Bargaining in the Wood Industry', *American Sociological Review*, 57: 16–38.

BURT, RONALD (1992), *Structural Holes* (Cambridge, Mass.: Harvard University Press).

COLLINS, HARRY M. (ed.) (1982), *Knowledge and Controversy: Studies of Modern Natural Science*, special issue of *Social Studies of Science*, 2/1.

COMISSO, ELLEN (1991), 'Property Rights, Liberalism, and the Transition from "Actually Existing" Socialism', *East European Politics and Societies*, 5/1: 162–88.

CONRAD, MICHAEL (1983), *Adaptability* (New York: Plenum Press).

CUI, ZHIYUAN (1994), 'Epilogue: A Schumpeterian Perspective and Beyond', in Yang Gan and Zhiyuan Cui (eds.), *China: A Reformable Socialism?* (Oxford: Oxford University Press).

——(forthcoming), 'Möbius-Strip Ownership and its Prototype in Chinese Rural Industry', *Economy and Society*.

DENTON, NICHOLAS (1993), 'Two Hungarian Banks Said to be Technically Insolvent', *Financial Times*, 20 May.

DURKHEIM, ÉMILE (1897), *Le Suicide: Étude de sociologie* (Paris: Presses Universitaires de France).

EVANS, PETER (1992), 'The State as Problem and as Solution', in Stephan Haggard and Robert Kaufman (eds.), *The Politics of Economic Adjustment* (Princeton, NJ: Princeton University Press), 139–81.

Figyelö (1993), *Top 200: A legnagyobb vállalkozások* (The Top 200 Largest Enterprises), *Figyelö* (special issue).

GÁBOR, ISTVÁN (1979), 'The Second (Secondary) Economy', *Acta Oeconomica*, 22/3–4: 91–311.

——(1986), 'Reformok második gazdaság, államszocializmus. A 80- as évek tapasztalatainak feljödéstani és összehasonlító gazdaságtani tanulságairól' (Reforms, Second Economy, State Socialism: Speculation on the Evolutionary and Comparative Economic Lessons of the Hungarian Eighties), *Valóság*, 6: 32–48.

——(1994), 'Modernity of a New Type of Duality? The Second Economy Today', in János Mátyás Kovács (ed.), *Transition to Capitalism? The Legacy of Communism in Eastern Europe* (New Brunswick, NJ: Transaction Books), 3–21.

GEREFFI, GARY (1994), 'The Organization of Buyer-Driven Global Commodity Chains: How US Retailers Shape Overseas Production Networks', in Gary Gereffi and Miguel Kornzeniewicz (eds.), *Commodity Chains and Global Capitalism* (Westport, Conn.: Praeger), 95–122.

GERLACH, MICHAEL L., and LINCOLN, JAMES R. (1992), 'The Organization of Business Networks in the United States and Japan', in Nitin Nohria and Robert G. Eccles (eds.), *Networks and Organizations* (Cambridge, Mass.: Harvard Business School Press), 491–520.

GRABHER, GERNOT (1994), *Lob der Verschwendung. Redundant in der Regionalentwicklung* (Berlin: edition sigma).

GRANOVETTER, MARK (1985), 'Economic Action, Social Structure, and Embeddedness', *American Journal of Sociology*, 91: 481–510.

——(1995), 'Coase Revisited: Business Groups in the Modern Economy', *Industrial and Corporate Change*, 4/1: 93–130.

GREY, THOMAS (1980), 'The Disintegration of Property', in J. Rolland Pennock and John W. Chapman (eds.), *Property* (New York: New York University Press), 69–85.

HAMILTON, GARY G., and FEENSTRA, ROBERT C. (1995), 'Varieties of Hierarchies and Markets: An Introduction', *Industrial and Corporate Change*, 4/1: 51–91.

——ZEILE, WILLIAM, and KIM, WAN-JIN (1990), 'The Network Structures of East

Asian Economies', in S. R. Clegg and S. G. Redding (eds.), *Capitalism in Contrasting Cultures* (Berlin: de Gruyter).

HANNAN, MICHAEL T. (1986), 'Uncertainty, Diversity, and Organizational Change', in *Behavioral and Social Science: Fifty Years of Discovery* (Washington: National Academy Press), 73–94.

HART, OLIVER (1988), 'Incomplete Contracts and the Theory of the Firm', *Journal of Law, Economics and Organization*, 4/1: 119–39.

HIRSCHMAN, ALBERT (1958), *The Strategy of Economic Development* (New Haven, Conn.: Yale University Press).

HOSHI, TAKEO (1994), 'The Economic Role of Corporate Grouping and the Main Bank System', in Masahiko Aoki and Ronald Dore (eds.), *The Japanese Firm: The Sources of Competitive Strength* (London: Oxford University Press), 285–309.

HUNGARIAN CENTRAL STATISTICAL OFFICE (1994), *Monthly Bulletin of Statistics*, no. 5.

KIM, EUN MEE (1991), 'The Industrial Organization and Growth of the Korean *Chaebol*: Integrating Development and Organizational Theories', in Gary Hamilton (ed.), *Business Networks and Economic Development in East and Southeast Asia* (Hong Kong: University of Hong Kong, Centre of Asian Studies), 272–99.

KOGUT, BRUCE, and ZANDER, UDO (1992), 'Knowledge of the Firm, Combinative Capabilities, and the Replication of Technology', *Organization Science*, 3/3: 383–97.

——SHAN, WEIJAN, and WALKER, GORDON (1992), 'The Make-or-Cooperate Decision in the Context of an Industry Network', in Nitin Nohria and Robert G. Eccles (eds.), *Networks and Organizations* (Cambridge, Mass.: Harvard Business School Press), 348–65.

KONRAD, GEORGE, and SZELÉNYI, IVÁN (1979), *Intellectuals on the Road to Class Power* (New York: Harcourt Brace Jovanovich).

KORNAI, JÁNOS (1980), *The Economics of Shortage* (Amsterdam: North-Holland).

——(1992), 'The Post-socialist Transition and the State: Reflections in the Light of Hungarian Fiscal Problems', *American Economic Review*, 82/2: 1–21.

——(1993a), 'The Evolution of Financial Discipline under the Postsocialist System', *Kyklos*, 46: 315–36.

——(1993b), *Transitional Recession*, Discussion papers series (Budapest: Collegium Budapest, Institute for Advanced Study).

LAKY, TERÉZ (1992), *Small and Medium-Sized Enterprises in Hungary*, Report for the European Commission (Budapest: Institute for Labour Studies).

LANDAU, MARTIN (1969), 'Redundancy, Rationality, and the Problem of Duplication and Overlap', *Public Administration Review*, 29/4: 346–58.

LATOUR, BRUNO (1988), *The Pasteurization of France* (Cambridge, Mass.: Harvard University Press).

LIPSET, SEYMOUR MARTIN (1990), 'The Death of the Third Way', *The National Interest*, 20: 25–37.

LITWACK, JOHN (1994), *Strategic Complementarities and Economic Transition*, Discussion paper series (Budapest: Collegium Budapest, Institute for Advanced Study).

MELLÁR, TAMÁS (1992), 'Two Years of Privatization', *Népszabadság*, 22 May.

MORIN, EDGAR (1974), 'Complexity', *International Social Science Journal*, 26/4: 555–82.

MURRELL, PETER (1990), 'Big Bang versus Evolution: Eastern European Economic

Reforms in the Light of Recent Evolutionary History', *PlanEcon Report*, 6/26: 29.

NATIONAL BANK OF HUNGARY (1992), *Annual Report* (Budapest).

——(1994), *Monthly Report*, no. 2.

NEE, VICTOR (1989), 'A Theory of Market Transition', *American Sociological Review*, 4/5: 663–81.

——(1992), 'Organizational Dynamics of Market Transition: Hybrid Forms, Property Rights, and Mixed Economy in China', *Administrative Science Quarterly*, 37: 1–27.

NELSON, RICHARD R., and WINTER, SIDNEY G. (1982), *An Evolutionary Theory of Economic Change* (Cambridge: Cambridge University Press).

NEUMANN, LÁSZLÓ (1989), 'Market Relations in Intra-enterprise Wage Bargaining?' *Acta Oeconomica*, 40: 319–38.

NUMAZAKI, ICHIRO (1991), 'The Role of Personal Networks in the Making of Taiwan's *Guanxiquiye* (Related Enterprises)', in Gary Hamilton (ed.), *Business Networks and Economic Development in East and Southeast Asia* (Hong Kong: Centre of Asian Studies, University of Hong Kong), 77–93.

OI, JEAN C. (1992), 'Fiscal Reform and the Economic Foundations of Local State Corporatism in China', *World Politics*, 45: 99–126.

ORRU, MARCO, WOOLSEY BIGGART, NICOLE, and HAMILTON, GARY G. (1991), 'Organizational Isomorphism in East Asia', in Powell and DiMaggio (1991: 361–89).

PADGETT, JOHN F., and ANSELL, CHRISTOPHER K. (1993), 'Robust Action and the Rise of the Medici, 1400–1434', *American Journal of Sociology*, 98/6: 1259–1319.

PICKERING, ANDREW (ed.) (1992), *Science as Culture and Practice* (Chicago: University of Chicago Press).

PISTOR, KATHARINA, and TURKEWITZ, JOEL (1994), 'Coping with Hydra State Ownership after Privatization: A Comparative Study of Hungary, Russia, and the Czech Republic', Paper presented to the Conference on Corporate Governance in Central Europe and Russia, World Bank, Washington, Dec. 1994.

POWELL, WALTER, and DIMAGGIO, PAUL (eds.) (1991), *The New Institutionalism in Organizational Analysis* (Chicago: University of Chicago Press).

RÓNA-TAS, AKOS (1994), 'The First shall be Last? Entrepreneurship and Communist Cadres in the Transition from Socialism', *American Journal of Sociology*, 100: 40–69.

SABEL, CHARLES (1990), 'Möbius-Strip Organizations and Open Labor Markets: Some Consequences of the Reintegration of Conception and Execution in a Volatile Economy', in Pierre Bourdieu and James Coleman (eds.), *Social Theory for a Changing Society* (Boulder, Colo.: Westview Press and Russell Sage Foundation), 23–54.

——and PROKOP, JANE E. (1996), 'Stabilization through Reorganization? Some Preliminary Implications of Russia's Entry into World Markets in the Age of Discursive Quality Standards', in Roman Frydman, Cheryl Gray, and Andrzej Rapaczynski *Corporate Governance in Central Europe and Russia*, Vol. II: *Insiders and the State* (Budapest: Central European University Press) 151–91.

——and STARK, DAVID (1982), 'Planning, Politics, and Shop-Floor Power: Hidden Forms of Bargaining in Soviet-Imposed State-Socialist Societies', *Politics and Society*, 11: 439–75.

——and ZEITLIN, JONATHAN (1996), 'Stories, Strategies, Structures: Rethinking Historical Alternatives to Mass Production', in Charles Sabel and Jonathan Zeitlin (eds.), *Worlds of Possibility: Flexibility and Mass Production in Western Industrialization* (Cambridge: Cambridge University Press).

SCHMITTER, PHILIPPE (1988), 'Modes of Governance of Economic Sectors', MS, Stanford University.

SCHUMPETER, JOSEPH A. (1934), *The Theory of Economic Development* (Cambridge, Mass.: Harvard University Press).

SEWELL, WILLIAM H., Jr. (forthcoming), 'Three Temporalities: Toward a Sociology of the Event', in Terrence J. McDonald (ed.), *The Historic Turn in the Human Sciences* (Ann Arbor, Mich.: University of Michigan Press).

SÍK, ENDRE (1992), 'From Second Economy to Informal Economy', *Journal of Public Policy*, 12/2: 153–75.

SOMERS, MARGARET R., and GIBSON, GLORIA D. (1994), 'Reclaiming the Epistemological "Other": Narrative and the Social Constitution of Identity', in Craig Calhoun (ed.), *Social Theory and the Politics of Identity* (Oxford: Blackwell), 37–99.

STANISZKIS, JADWIGA (1991), ' "Political Capitalism" in Poland', *East European Politics and Societies*, 5: 127–41.

——(1993), *Ontology, Context and Chance: Three Exit Routes from Communism*, Program on Central and Eastern Europe Working Papers no. 31 (Cambridge, Mass.: Harvard University, Center for European Studies).

STARK, DAVID (1986), 'Rethinking Internal Labor Markets: New Insights from a Comparative Perspective', *American Sociological Review*, 51: 492–504.

——(1989), 'Coexisting Organizational Forms in Hungary's Emerging Mixed Economy', in Victor Nee and David Stark (eds.), *Remaking the Economic Institutions of Socialism: China and Eastern Europe* (Stanford, Calif.: Stanford University Press), 137–68.

——(1990), 'La Valeur du travail et sa rétribution en Hongrie', *Actes de la Recherche en Sciences Sociales* (Paris), 85: 3–19; trans. as 'Work, Work, and Justice', Program on Central and Eastern Europe Working Papers no. 5 (Cambridge, Mass.: Harvard University, Center for European Studies).

——(1992), 'Path Dependence and Privatization Strategies in East Central Europe', *East European Politics and Societies*, 6: 17–51.

——and BRUSZT, LÁSZLÓ (1995), *Restructuring Networks in Post-socialist Economic Transformation*, Cornell Working Papers on Transitions from State Socialism, no. 95.4 (Ithaca, NY: Cornell University).

——and NEE, VICTOR (1989), 'Toward an Institutional Analysis of State Socialism', in Victor Nee and David Stark (eds.), *Remaking the Economic Institutions of Socialism: China and Eastern Europe* (Stanford, Calif.: Stanford University Press), 1–31.

SZELÉNYI, IVÁN (1978), 'Social Inequalities in State Socialist Redistributive Economies', *Theory and Society*, 1–2: 63–87.

——(1988), *Socialist Entrepreneurs* (Madison: University of Wisconsin Press).

——(1994), *Socialist Entrepreneurs—Revisited*, Working papers, no. 4 (Ann Arbor: University of Michigan, International Institute).

SZÜCS, JENÖ (1985), *Les Trois Europes* (Paris: Harmattan).

THÉVENOT, LAURENT (1985), 'Rules and Implements: Investment in Forms', *Social Science Information*, 23/1: 1–45.

VOSZKA, ÉVA (1991), 'Homályból homályba. A tulajdonosi szerkezet a nagyiparban' (From Twilight to Twilight: Property Changes in Large Industry), *Társadalmi Szemle*, 5: 3–12.

——(1992), 'Escaping from the State, Escaping to the State', Paper presented to the Arne Ryde Symposium on the Transition Problem, Rungsted, Denmark, June 1992.

WACQUANT, LOIC J. D. (1993), 'Solidarity, Morality, and Sociology: Durkheim and the Crisis of European Society', *Journal of the Society for Social Research*, 1: 1–7.

WALDER, ANDREW (1994), 'Corporate Organization and Local Government Property Rights in China', in Vedat Milor (ed.), *Changing Political Economies: Privatization in Post-communist and Reforming Communist States* (Boulder, Colo.: Rienner), 53–66.

WEBSTER, LEILA (1992), *Private Sector Manufacturing in Hungary: A Survey of Firms* (Washington: Industry Development Division, World Bank).

WHITE, HARRISON C. (1992), *Identity and Control: A Structural Theory of Social Action* (Princeton, NJ: Princeton University Press).

——(1993), 'Values Come in Styles, which Mate to Change', in Michael Hechter, Lynn Nadel, and Richard E. Michod (eds.), *The Origins of Values* (New York: Aldine de Gruyter), 63–91.

WORLD BANK (1993), *The East Asian Miracle: Economic Growth and Public Policy* (Oxford: Oxford University Press).

3

Renegotiating the Ties that Bind:
The Limits of Privatization in the Czech Republic

GERALD A. MCDERMOTT

INTRODUCTION

Many analysts and policy-makers have concluded that industrial restructuring in East Central Europe is most effective when the full set of control rights and liabilities of firms assets are held by unitary actors, who interact through arm's-length relationships mediated by price alone. This belief has played a central role in the two-track economic reform strategies in the region: 'getting the prices right' and 'getting the institutions right'. The first part concerns macroeconomic stabilization and price and trade liberalization coupled with tight fiscal and monetary policies. Since state firms could not be relied upon to adjust employment, wages, and investment decisions to the market, stabilization had to be rapidly followed by privatization (the second piece of the puzzle). Clearly defining property rights and laws for bankruptcy and stock trading allows actors to minimize hold-ups and risks to firm restructuring by liquidating irresponsible firms and by exchanging control rights over assets for the formation of consolidated ownership structures.

The Czech government has pursued such a neo-liberal policy probably more forcefully than any other in the region. There were two basic steps toward restructuring industries. First, a market for the purchase of shares was spontaneously created as citizens, alone or through investment funds, could buy shares of firms with vouchers, distributed by the government for a nominal fee. Second, the government privatized the few commercial and savings banks and created a strict bankruptcy law and legal framework for financial markets. The assumed results were that once owners were in place, a board of directors could discipline managers and strategically reorganize the firm, while watchful investors could punish or reward a firm through equity trading and replacing directors. At the same time, once armed with a bankruptcy law, banks and supplying firms could initiate the closing of unprofitable firms, in turn freeing up financial and material resources for more beneficial investments. However, the results thus far have not been promising: a fall in industrial production by over 30 per cent since 1989 and in the critical engineering industry by over 50 per cent; virtually no bankruptcies, despite the highest insolvency rates in the region; and the continued inability of investors and banks to define a new set of governance rules and institutions, to gain access to market and resource information, and to evaluate assets.

This chapter is about the reconfiguration of Czech industrial manufacturing firms during the current period of radical privatization and market liberalization. It seeks to explain how the reform of property rights and financial institutions has given rise to an alarming liquidity crisis and the preservation of large industrial manufacturing organizations, yet with a diffusion of the very authority that privatization advocates argue must be concentrated and sovereign.

The next section, 'Reconsidering Property Rights and Restructuring', discusses two central theoretical issues: the relationship between property rights and the reorganization of firms, and the way property rights and institutions of economic governance get defined. First, mainstream views rest on the strong claims of property rights theory that once property rights are delineated and a legal order for market exchange is established, potential hold-ups[1] to restructuring can be resolved either by fusion—an exchange of control rights for the creation of a hierarchy—or by punishment—switching suppliers or customers or forcing the closure of debtors. Second, mainstream methods share the view that the state can unilaterally define and transfer to individuals property rights and the rules of economic governance.

These views are based on the assumptions that economic actors can consistently and clearly define their own self-interest and that the state already possesses the necessary set of control rights and authority over assets and market institutions. These assumptions are misguided for two reasons. First, the inherited tight economic and social interdependencies between suppliers and customers, firms and banks, as well as firms and their localities conflate an actor's definition of self-interest and limit one's discretion for unilateral action. Second, since the newly distributed rights allow only limited discretion and sovereignty, then one must recognize that the *de facto* control rights and social foundations of economic co-ordination continue to lie largely outside the domain of the central state and new owners.

The argument of this chapter is twofold. (1) Due to the peculiarities of Czech industrialization—the devolution of control rights within industrial associations and the increasing autarky of industrial communities—firm and local level actors formed alliances to gain privileges from the centre and created informal compacts of economic co-ordination to limit the uncertainties of the shortage environment, which became more or less institutionalized frameworks to define and renegotiate claims to assets and production flows. (2) Firms remain embedded in these social relationships, which underpin the flow of needed material, financial, and human resources and the definition of mutual responsibilities and obligations for transactions. The simultaneous restructuring of firms and the reformulation of decision-making rights and claims to assets is less about the simple transfer of ownership from state to private hands, and more about the political deliberations among stakeholders over how the risks and responsibilities will be borne.

The section 'Unresolved Rigidities: Czech Privatization' analyses how privatization, particularly the voucher programme, has more or less allowed the tight economic and social relations among firms in the concentrated industries and between firms and their communities to reproduce themselves, while the social distance and information asymmetries between the peak-level institutions, i.e. the government and outside investors, and firm and local actors has yet to be bridged.

The next section, 'Bank Reform and Bankruptcy', examines the reform of financial institutions, which are characterized by a few banks holding the majority of firm debt. The financial and production interdependencies among firms and units precluded firms from initiating liquidations, allowed them to utilize inter-firm debt to float one another, and caused banks to forgo debt–equity swaps since the interdependencies implied taking strategic responsibility for the restructuring of whole regions and industries.

The section entitled 'Industrial Reorganization' studies how pre-existing financial and technical links and informal contracting institutions within and among industrial firms provide the building-blocks as well as the political and economic constraints for the reorganization of production and the renegotiation of the control rights and obligations. The impact of these economic and social interdependencies is demonstrated through analysis of how firm and local actors deal with such issues as lay-offs, product development, and autonomy for firm divisions and how these issues affect the formation of joint ventures with foreign partners, the principal conduit for foreign investment and know-how. This empirical analysis draws on recent firm and industry surveys in the Czech Republic and cases of leading firms in the engineering and steel industries. By 1990 engineering and steel accounted for, respectively, 24 per cent and 8 per cent of Czech industrial production, 30 and 7 per cent of industrial employment, and 32 and 9 per cent of industrial value-added (OECD Industry Division 1992). The chapter concludes with a discussion of the main issues I have raised here and their implications for the future of economic reconstruction in the Czech Republic.

RECONSIDERING PROPERTY RIGHTS AND RESTRUCTURING

Rapid privatization has been an unspoken assumption, since most reformers and analysts conceptualize the socialist economy as one large hierarchy where the owner, the state, is unable to co-ordinate, monitor, and discipline the indivdual units (the firms). As long as the paternalistic state owned firms and was susceptible to bargaining and information distortions, soft budget constraints would prevail, as managers were responsible essentially to no one (Blanchard *et al.* 1990; Kornai 1990*b*; Lipton and Sachs 1991). If the triumph of capitalism has taught us anything, so the argument goes, it is that firms each need a strong principal to discipline managers and cut costs, a capital market to evaluate progress, and an open goods market to find the cheapest and most reliable inputs.

The only issue that has concerned reformers has been the mode and speed of privatization. But despite their differences, the main methods share common views about the relationship between property rights and the reorganization of firms, and about the way property rights and institutions of economic governance get defined. First, these methods rest on the strong claims of property rights theory that once the legal order for market exchange, corporate boards, and financial institutions has been established and property rights delineated, outside investors and banks could discipline managers or directors through trading shares on the stock market and foreclosing on outstanding debts (Frydman *et al.* 1993; Kornai 1990*a,b*; Lipton and Sachs 1991). The theory argues that when property rights are poorly defined, as in East Central Europe, no agent has unambiguous control over assets (Hart 1988; Hart and Moore 1986). There are no clearly defined rules about who has the authority over asset use. Subsequently, theft and asset-stripping becomes prominent and hold-ups abound, causing the assets to sit idle. Only when property rights are clearly defined can actors make *ex ante* asset-specific investments to integrate highly complementary assets to minimize *ex post* bargaining, concentrating control rights in a unitary owner, i.e. a board of directors representing shareholders. Thus, if managers, workers, or key suppliers can potentially block restructuring, a hierarchy can be created by an exchange of property rights. Schleifer and Vishny (1992), for instance, argue that firm or local actors can simply be bought out by giving them cash-flow rights or a minority percentage of shares in return for some of their control and decision-making rights. Advocates of a mass distribution of shares, such as in the Czech Republic (Tříska 1990), similarly argue that investment funds or foreign investors can buy out and merge complementary firms or firm 'pieces', so that the owner can then order subordinates in fused firms to co-ordinate execution of investment projects.[2] Banks would initiate debt–equity swaps to limit the fear that equity-holders and managers would gamble away unsecured debt on overly risky projects.

The counterpart to clearly defined property rights is the establishment of financial institutions and a legal code to enforce contracts and bankruptcies.[3] The process of economic Darwinism cannot fully function without, on the one hand, a capital market, where watchful investors can reward or punish directors or management (i.e. to maximize profit) by replacing board members, selling stock and driving down equity value, waging proxy fights, or renegotiating security provisions. On the other hand, market responsiveness will continue to be dulled without, for example, customers being able to switch suppliers or banks and firms to foreclose on outstanding debts and force liquidation.

Second, these methods share the view that the state can define property rights and the rules of market institutions and then simply withdraw itself from participation in industrial reorganization. As the sole owner of the complete set of property and control rights over assets, the state can unilaterally reassert its right to transfer assets to individuals and to define the rules of firm governance. The speed of the transfer becomes critical in order to neutralize firm actors so that they cannot block or alter state centred schemes of privatization and restructuring. Once it has politically redefined property and control rights, the state can let the 'selection' process of the market close inefficient firms, a process for which the state would lack not only the necessary information and know-how but also the legitimacy and will during troubled times.

While these views sound plausible, they have some serious limitations. First, the economistic theories believe that once equipped with the legal provisions of asset use and financial institutions, individuals will maximize their clearly defined self-interest to enforce contracts, and, if necessary, switch suppliers or force bankruptcies on irresponsible customers and debtors. For instance, owners will force the compliance of management or terminate their employment; banks and suppliers will avoid further lending to risky customers or force liquidation. This is true as well for firms or investors to merge complementary assets or banks to swap debt for equity in order to avoid potential hold-ups. The problem is that these views underestimate the inertia of two critical legacies of CPEs—the information asymmetries between firms and outside actors and the tight economic and social links between suppliers and customers, firms and banks, as well as firms and their localities. Take the problem of information asymmetries. The economistic view assumes that investors and/or banks can value firms according to their assets in order to merge complementary assets under a hierarchy to minimize hold-up possibilities. But that is exactly what banks and investors have been unable to do, since the potential value of the firm lies less in the physical assets and more in the knowledge embedded in the production networks which have grown up around assets. Indeed, recent analysis of the Czech privatization process shows that managers were able to control the flow of information in government review of privatization projects and that investment funds found financial and performance data worthless to 'buy' shares. Fund leaders also admit that they can not easily force the hand of management since the funds are dependent on them for necessary information and contacts to form reorganization strategies. A main reason why banks have not forced bankruptcies or initiated swaps is that they can not evaluate individual units or firms since the books and production programmes of establishments are so intertwined with one another.

The tight economic and social relationships among actors present an even greater problem since the resulting interdependencies conflate the definitions of actors' self-interest in a highly uncertain environment. For instance, concentration levels are so high and production programmes so interlinked that indidvual firms cannot easily change suppliers or customers, nor can firms foreclose on debts since a supplier or customer is often one of the only sources of certain inputs, parts, or sales. The inherited interdependency between a locality and firm or plant precludes managers or outsiders from laying off workers or shutting down plants since it can easily disrupt the fragile social peace among managers, workers, and local governments. The few Czech banks are so tied to the economic well-being of firms that they are reluctant to force liquidation. Apparent in the low number of foreign buy-outs or swaps, both investors and banks are averse to scooping up whole firms or groups of smaller, interlinked firms since the *ex post* financial and social costs and responsibilities would prove too costly a venture.

Taken together, the information asymmetries and the tight economic and social links among economic actors limit the discretion each has in forcing the hand of their counterparts, but also cause the risks to be too great to warrant the complete take-over or fusion of firms in order to break the stalemate and minimize future hold-up problems. It is thus unclear whether market development and firm restructuring is underpinned by necessity and feasibility of unitary actors holding the full risk and benefits of assets and interacting simply at arm's length.

This criticism questions not only the notion that clearly defining property rights and the rules of financial institutions is sufficient for industrial restructuring, but also reformers' second claim that the state by itself can define and rapidly transfer to private hands the rights and rules of asset use.[4] The assumption here is that the state already possesses the necessary set of control rights and authority over assets and market institutions. However, if these newly distributed rights allow only limited discretion and sovereignty for actors, then one must consider that the *de facto* control rights and social foundations of economic co-ordination continue to lie largely outside the domain of both the central state and new owners and are in fact only partially defined. One of the increasingly evident legacies of socialist economies is that while industrial concentration rigidified the economic and technical links among, say, customers and suppliers, the increasing self-co-ordination and autarky among interlinked firms within industrial associations allowed for the development of complex informal vertical and horizontal alliances among economic actors and localities. In Czechoslovakia during the 1970s and 1980s, under the umbrella of an association, constituent suppliers and customers, managers and workers, state bank branches, firms, and local Communist Party and council officials formed alliances to gain privileges from the centre and created informal compacts of economic co-ordination to limit and adjust to the uncertainties of 'shortage'—unreliable quantities and qualities of inputs and parts. Over time these informal relationships became institutionalized, though not necessarily legally recognized, and became the frameworks to define and renegotiate claims to assets and production flows.

The policy then of the state simply trying to end-run the potential hold-up powers of local and firm actors (i.e. through rapid privatization) is one-legged since the discretion and the necessary knowledge to reorganize production, which embody control and contracting rights, are bound up in these relationships. That is, the process of redefining the rules of economic governance is part and parcel of the actual reorganization of the economic and social relationships among constituent firms, banks, and localities. The combination of the tight financial and technical links and the embedded social relationships are sources of mutual hold-up power among actors as well as conduits for the flow of parts, credit, and knowledge. The production programmes among distinct groups of firms or divisions, the credit links among the few main commercial banks and major industrial firms, and the economic and social health of a locality and a group of plants have all become so intertwined that resolving debt burdens, breaking up firms, and reorganizing production are no longer bilateral or sovereign issues. Rather they are ones of collective action among actors, whose individual strategies must take into account the needs and concerns of the other constituent parties to assets. The problem is that in the face of new economic and social uncertainties and the lack of needed resources due to strict monetarist policies and the voucher scheme, these relations can very well end up in a stalemate, as is evident in the current liquidity crisis and the failure of several major joint-venture deals with foreign partners in the Czech Republic. The realization is that the simultaneous restructuring of firms and reformulation of property and contracting rights may have less to do with the simple transfer of ownership from the state to private unitary actors than with the political deliberations about how risks and responsibilities will be borne by the actors, institutions, and social relationships that have grown up around the assets into an economic whole.

Structure and Contours of the Existing Social and Economic Relationships

The devolution of control and decision-making rights from the state centre to the firm and local level can be characterized by three simultaneous processes in the industrial organization of Czechoslovakia: (1) the increased responsibilities of industrial associations (*Vyrobní hospodařské jednotky*, or VHJs); (2) the increasing tightness of financial and technical links among firms within VHJs; and (3) the emergence of informal, yet durable, institutions of economic co-ordination within and among firms and between firms and local officials.

Two principal industrial policies of communist Czechoslovakia were the vigorous rationalization of industries and the clustering of new interrelated plants in rural communities throughout the country (Myant 1992). In order to facilitate central administration of industries, authorities consistently decreased the number of firms while increasing their size (Zemplinerová 1989*a*). By 1988 there were effectively 1,604 manufacturing firms with an average size of 3,400 employees and ten units.[5] A key part of this programme was the increased guidance of production and contracting by VHJs—associations of firms within a single branch and clustered often in distinct geographic localities.[6] VHJs acted as middle-level management, creating a network to translate basic indices from the centre into detailed directives for firms within their branch and to control the distribution of resources. Concentration as well as the administrative, economic, and technical monopoly of VHJs grew. In 1958, 383 VHJs were created, which controlled 929 firms. By 1980 the number of VHJs was reduced to 101 but they controlled 1,050 firms (Gregus and Kalisova 1991).

Once labour shortages developed in traditional regions of industrial manufacturing, the government could tap into excess rural labour by grouping plants around small, isolated communities. This was particularly possible with geographically mobile engineering, electronics, and motor industries. Subsequently, communities became dependent on these firms or plants for employment and economic resources as well as increasingly isolated from one another, even within the same VHJ.

The combination of the monopolistic environment, the insulation of firms within VHJs, and the geographic dispersion of industrial communities allowed for increased autonomy for firms and their communities from the centre and the formation of alliances between functionally interdependent firms within the VHJs. First, partial structural and decision-making reform experiments culminated at the end of the 1970s in industry-wide revisions of the administrative system. State branch management bodies were abolished, leaving only broader industrial ministries and their branch directorates to focus mainly on long-run planning, broad production targets, and integration into Comecon. VHJs were fully responsible for elaborating and executing all their own technical, economic, and social functions in the annual plans, revising the five-year plans, managing a central VHJ budget, and co-ordinating operations among their member firms.[7] VHJ 'trusts' (accounting for 75 per cent of all VHJ firms) and the failed administrative centralization of VHJ 'concerns' and gave firms further formal and informal independence in co-ordinating production with constituent members. The centre became increasingly removed from developments within VHJs yet remained dependent upon them for the provision of goods and services and the information by which to evaluate plans.

Second, the dispersion of geographically concentrated VHJs and plants led to the fragmentation of the economy into autarkic industrial communities. The supply uncertainties of the shortage environment forced firms to produce as much needed parts and inputs as possible. For instance, several Czech scholars have reported that both the autonomy of 'trusts' and the tight integration between suppliers and customers within them increased (Illner 1992*b*; Myant 1992; Remeš 1984; Smrčka 1988). External supply relations grew increasingly unreliable, and the firms narrowed the assortment of production. Hence, the tightly integrated production lines and the shortage uncertainties reinforced the interdependence between customers and suppliers, managers and workers, and managers and local officials. Within a VHJ or locality constituent actors forged informal compacts to bargain with the centre and to compensate supply failures and facilitate the flow of goods (Čákrt 1991; Hrnčíř 1990; Illner 1992*b*; Premúsová 1989). Faced with continual interruptions in production due to problems of machinery maintenance and forced substitution, managers had to develop informal agreements with work groups, with one another, and with local bank and council officials to adapt shop-floor, inter-unit, and investment procedures. Strong informal groups provided resources for internal crisis management (the exchange of service, tools, labour, and information) and reliable channels for negotiations (Čákrt 1991; Illner 1992*b*; Stark 1986). Informal co-operation agreements evolved from being stopgap measures to institutionalized features of the firm. These compacts could circumvent the rigidities of the bureaucratically imposed procedures as well as become the framework of norms and obligations to define and renegotiate claims to assets and contracting rights (Hrnčíř 1990).

The burgeoning Czech sociological literature on the links between industrial firms and local communities shows how the interdependence between local firms and councils (*narodni vybory*) led to the formation of strong relationships between managers and council members to protect themselves from the interventionist centre and to co-ordinate services and the flow of goods within and between communities (Illner 1992*b*; Premúsová 1989; Vavřiková 1987). Just as the community depended on the firms or plants for providing resources and facilities for local social services and employment, so too did managers depend on the local council leaders to run these services, to arbitrate disputes among local plants, and to help obtain needed components and material inputs from distant industrial communities. Informal relations were reinforced as local units and council shared employees. For instance, in her study of communities in northern

Bohemia, Premúsová (1989) reports that over 60 per cent of council employees were former or current firm employees. These relationships became further institutionalized as communities created organs to co-ordinate the pooling of financial and material resources and their bargaining with the centre, be it through the industrial or territorial administrative channels.

The persistent strength of these alliances in Czechoslovakia was proved when the government attempted, in 1988, to break up the VHJs and make the individual firm the primary economic unit. The associations would have suffered from the greater independence given to the enterprises and the increased direct scrutiny of large, inefficient firms and units by the centre. Alliances of VHJ directors, certain ministry officials, and local Communist Party authorities fought to limit the changes as far as possible. They argued that many associations with a genuine economic justification could themselves become enterprises and continue as before (Myant 1989, ch. 10), and an additional decree in July 1989 allowed state enterprise to create (voluntary) associations while maintaining their legal status. This loophole allowed the VHJ structure and the existing alliances to continue to constitute informally the norms of economic co-ordination and production. The total number of firms increased from 1,714 to only 2,246, with only a handful of these new firms in the industrial sector (Gregus and Kaliśová 1991). The combination of compromise pacts and tight technical and financial links within VHJs and their localities provided actors with certain control and decision-making rights as well as a framework within which to renegotiate these rights. Firms are embedded in these social relations, which are sources of the skills and knowledge necessary for production adjustment, of reliable conduits for parts and credit, and of mutual responsibilities and obligations for transactions.

These relationships have several implications for analysis of the current restructuring of Czech industries. On the one hand, the resolution of potential hold-ups (i.e. high asset complementarity) through the merging of assets can prove costly for firms or investors under present uncertainties. On the other hand, the closing of apparently inefficient firms or plants either by directors or by bankruptcy proceedings is limited, since the lack of clear alternative sources of sales and inputs or parts and local autarky causes firms to take into account the concerns of their locality as well as their suppliers and customers. Unilateral action can disrupt not only the social peace in a region but also the social capital needed to keep key work groups, to maintain the flow of goods, to develop new products, and to search for new markets.[8] The notion that simply defining ownership rights and imposing new economic rules from above can lead to rapid economic reorganization is undermined since the assumed sovereignty and definition of self-interest is inherently constrained and intertwined with the concerns of fellow firms, plants, workers, and local officials. Rather, the reorganization of production and control rights is essentially a political process whereby constituent parties to assets renegotiate these inherited relationships.

UNSOLVED RIGIDITIES: CZECH PRIVATIZATION

This section gives an overview of the Czech privatization process and how the voucher programme has left the industry and equity markets rigid and concentrated, lacking financial resources and preserving information asymmetries. The preoccupation with speed and vouchers appears to have reinforced the social and economic interdependencies between the firm and locality as well as local cynicism toward the centre, in turn politically constraining firm restructuring.

The centre-piece of 'large' privatization, which concerns the great majority of firm assets, was the voucher programme.[9] Prior to the opening of the voucher market, the government evaluated privatization projects for each firm to be privatized. A project contains the technical, organizational, and financial characteristics of the existing firm, the strategy of restructuring, and the combination of methods of privatization (i.e. vouchers, direct sale, public auction, legal tender, and foreign participation). While the management of each firm had six months to submit a basic project for the whole firm, any citizen or group of citizens could also submit competing projects for the whole or parts of a firm. Privatization projects were reviewed by the privatization ministries of each republic, often in consultation with the ministries of industry and local privatization councils. The deadline was 20 January 1992, and bidding on the voucher market for the first of two waves of privatization lasted from 17 May 1992 to 22 December 1992. The stock market opened in June 1993.

The first wave of privatization included 2,776 Czech firms, for which 11,000 projects were submitted (8,065 were competing projects).[10] About 5.95 million Czechs (most of the eligible population) registered to partake in the voucher method, over 70 per cent of whom have allowed their portfolio of vouchers and shares to be managed by one of the 260 newly created domestic investment funds (IPFs). An investment company can not control over 20 per cent of the shares of any one firm (Burger and Mejstřík 1992).

The government has used the voucher method to privatize a substantial amount of firm assets. In the first wave, converting firms into joint-stock companies for the voucher method accounted for 89.3 per cent of asset value. Of these 948 firms, 836 firms had over 50 per cent of their shares in the voucher method and only sixteen had less than 25 per cent (Charap and Zemplinerová 1993, tables 2–5). Indeed, recent evidence shows that almost 80 per cent of the value of Czech industrial and manufacturing firms was allotted to vouchers (Buchtíková *et al.* 1992). These firms comprise the bulk of assets in the first wave and in the republic (Burger and Mejstřík 1992).

Reformers argued that the state could not get bogged down in breaking up or restructuring industries prior to privatization since the combination of investing and control over firms by IPFs, dynamic equity trading, and foreign buy-outs would do that more effectively. However, vouchers have left questionable results. First, privatization of larger entities facilitated administrative ease and speed, since the separate units of a firm often had no individual accounting records (Hlavacek and Mejstřík 1991). Consequently, the highly concentrated industrial structure has remained. For instance, between January 1990 and June 1991 the number of firms in the critical engineering sector increased from 475 to only 514, and 50 per cent of the firms still had over 1,000 employees.[11] Analysis of the current industrial structure shows very high two- and four-firm sales concentration ratios at the three-digit SIC level (Zemplinerová and Stibal 1993).[12]

Second, the persistence of information asymmetries can be seen in the weak competition among privatization projects and the random investment of vouchers. Although incumbent managers' basic projects accounted for only 25 per cent of all projects submitted in the first wave, they accounted for over 81 per cent of those approved, indicating management's effective control of vital information and knowledge of firms.[13] Švejnar and Singer (1992) show that both IPFs and administrators of voucher-bidding respectively invested vouchers and adjusted share prices between rounds based on *ad hoc* rules of thumb and not on typical financial or performance data.

Third, it appears that IPFs are reluctant to promote a lively equity market and hold strategic authority over firms. The equity market has become quite concentrated with 80 per cent of IPF shares held by nine investment companies, seven of which are owned by banks and one is the Czech Insurance Company.[14] Recent interviews with major IPF managers indicate that funds will try to sit on their equity and limit fluctuations in trading through co-operation among themselves and their parent banks. Most IPFs are strapped for cash, and the market is so thin that divestments would lead to big losses and a precipitous drop in equity value, destabilizing both the funds and the banks.[15] Moreover, fund managers openly admit that since they lack the manpower and information to effectively monitor firms and can not easily replace management, they give managers considerable discretion to develop restructuring and joint-venture strategies.

Fourth, although the government estimated that restructuring of Czechoslovak industry would need $US2–3 billion direct foreign investment per year from 1991 to 2000, by October 1992 foreigners had invested only $1.6 billion, and operating equity joint ventures involve only 288 firms (Kolanda 1992: 79–82; OECD Industry Division 1992: 54–7). Most projects are in services and real estate and located in the Prague region, only a few large projects with the best Czech firms account for most of the invested capital.

Investors are reluctant to purchase whole firms or divisions for three reasons: vouchers allow for no immediately clear domestic partner with capital;
investment prior to voucher completion causes capital to go directly into
state coffers and not into the firm; and, as discussed in greater detail below,
the tight links between firms and divisions imply restructuring responsibilities beyond the actual unit.[16]

The upshot is that the three-year voucher experiment has left both the
industrial and equity markets considerably rigid and concentrated, lacking
much-needed investment capital and information flows between firms and
outsiders. Indeed, the voucher process and the consequent occupational
and economic uncertainties may have actually reinforced the protective
instincts of managers and local actors towards their firm and community
(Buchtíková and Capek 1993; Mejstřík *et al.* 1992; Vláčil and Horniák 1992).
First, a 1991–2 survey of managers in fifty-nine major manufacturing firms
indicates that despite their scepticism about the economic benefits of the
voucher programme, managers did believe that vouchers would actually
allow them to maintain effective control of their domain.[17] Lacking any
credible sources for financing, sales, equipment, and supplies beyond the
following six to twelve months, only 6.5 per cent and 8 per cent believed
that vouchers would, respectively, improve the production and financial
health of the firm and help generate investment capital. Of the managers
surveyed 50 per cent asserted that their primary interest was to maintain or
increase their independence and decision-making rights over wages and
disposal of assets *vis-à-vis* the centre. Only 10 per cent believed that privatization, particularly vouchers, would allow 'the influence and interests of
new outside owners to be felt'. Managers recognized that they are not easily
replaceable because of their particular knowledge and experience of the
firm's operations and IPFs' lack of strategic information. Evidence of their
perceived necessity can also be seen in the fact that after many directors of
state firms were removed in 1990, they were replaced by middle-level
managers of the same firm (Brom and Orenstein 1993).

Second, as managers reasserted their control over firms, they and local
citizens found themselves in an uncomfortable but unavoidable marriage to
protect themselves from the perceived social instability and another form of
central intervention. On the one hand, given the lack of alternative local
manufacturing employment and weak labour unions, coupled with loyalties
divided between their firm and region and the union and low public legitimacy, workers had little overt leverage and exit options *vis-à-vis* management (Myant 1993). Indeed, from 1989 to 1993 real wage-rates declined
faster than productivity rates, and workers took a back seat to managers in
restructuring programmes (Buchtíková and Flek 1992, 1993; Spurný 1993;
Vláčil and Horniák 1992). With the rapid fall in transfers from the state
budget and the fragmentation of territorial administrations after 1989, local
governments have become dependent on the economic survival of the

entrenched state firms for maintaining employment, generating tax revenues, and feeding start-ups and spin-offs.[18]

On the other hand, management does realize their dependency on the local work-force and local officials for production and for promoting their restructuring and privatization plans. Recent data indicate that the decreases in employment in the engineering sectors since 1989 have not compensated sufficiently for the simultaneous fall in output and revenues and that hidden unemployment is between 10 and 20 per cent (Ham *et al.* 1993; Hawker 1993*a*; Kadlecová and Holman 1993). Managers recognize that the local work-force is not easily replaceable—not only is labour mobility low, but current work groups are the very ones who know the firm's problems and opportunities and with whom management has negotiated compromises in the past. Recent studies indicate that work-group cohesion and skill levels are quite high, and that managers are willing to limit lay-offs and set up semi-autonomous conversion units with excess facilities. Managers prefer to keep work groups for current reorganization, for expected production increases, and for maintaining the social peace vital to negotiations with creditors and local and national governments over proposed restructuring and privatization plans. This latter point becomes apparent through the inherited regional autarky, the re-emergence of local political identities, and the gradual down-sizing of firms, as is discussed in 'Industrial Reorganization' (Bohatá 1993; Čákrt 1991; OECD Industry Division 1992; Valenta 1992; Večerník 1992).[19]

Vouchers left restructuring options quite constrained by a concentrated industry, ineffective IPFs and equity markets, low foreign investment, and local social malaise. The disjunction between peak and firm- and local-level perceptions about restructuring uncertainties and possibilities becomes more transparent when one analyses the failed reform of financial institutions and the way firms have tried to reorganize themselves within the inherited social and economic links.

BANK REFORM AND BANKRUPTCY

A counterpart to privatization was reform of the commercial bank system and the establishment of a bankruptcy law. The plan was relatively simple.[20] First, the plan was to allow for new private banks to open, to privatize up to 50 per cent of shares of commercial and savings banks through vouchers, and to establish a state clearing-house, Consolidation Bank, to relieve some of the burden of inherited non-performing loans. Reformers wanted to limit the equity activities of banks, since assumptions underpinning the voucher method and the primacy of open equity markets implied a certain degree of separation between investment and commercial banking operations. Banks are prohibited from holding equity directly in any financial institution, and can not exceed equity stakes of 10 per cent in a non-financial firm or a total equity volume of 25 per cent of the bank's capital and reserves without the consent of the Central Bank. Second, the plan was to create a bankruptcy law to allow all creditors to enforce payment of debts with the threat of direct liquidation. Once armed with the law, supplying firms could initiate legal proceedings against debtors, and banks could cut off the free flow of investment funds, close firms, and redistribute the resources to more productive uses. However, the bankruptcy law, as theoretically strict as it could be, did contain contradictory principles, which together neglected the concept of voluntary strategic bankruptcies as a prime conduit for reorganizing firms.

The law was conceptualized to punish debtors and force involuntary bankruptcy. That is, bankruptcy meant simply realizing all creditors' claims on a debtor through liquidation of assets. Yet, if a creditor or supplier wanted to initiate bankruptcy proceedings on a debtor, it had to do so through the debtor's founding ministry (e.g. the Ministry of Industry), which could extend the proceedings for a year. The law established two classes of bankruptcy: primary insolvency was defined as the outright inability to sell goods, indicated by total debts exceeding receivables; secondary insolvency was defined as the inability to pay outstanding debts.[21] A firm could only be closed when it reached primary insolvency. These drawbacks, combined with a highly concentrated commercial banking sector with tight links to a concentrated industrial sector, were to result in the liquidity and domestic debt crisis.

On the one hand, there were large disincentives for the creditor to initiate bankrupty proceedings—the process was long and arduous and liquidation of a closely linked supplier or customer, as most were, could severely damage production, research and development, and sales (Hlaváček and Tuma 1993). Firms could effectively avoid proceedings by balancing their receivables and debts in conjunction with their suppliers and customers.

On the other hand, there are effectively seven main banks in both republics and three that concerned Czech industry, notably Komercni Banka and Investicni Banka.[22] These seven accounted for 99.5 per cent of total loans in Czechoslovakia in December 1990 and 80.1 per cent in July 1992, with the difference accounted largely by transfers of some of the inherited non-performing 'perpetual inventory' loans to Consolidation Bank. By June 1992 loans to the private sector accounted for only about 13 per cent of total loans in the system. By early 1993, 97 per cent of Komercni Banka's loan's and 55 per cent of Investicni Banka's loan's were to state firms. As of July 1992 the seven banks also held 92.8 per cent of all deposits in Czechoslovakia, 74 per cent of which were household savings. The bulk of savings in the Czech Republic is in the Ceska Sporitelna (Czech Savings Bank).

Outstanding inter-firm debt and bank loans for both republics rose by 250 per cent in 1991 and about 100 per cent in 1992 (Dyba and Švejnar 1992;

Hrnčíř 1993). The OECD estimated that Czechoslovak debt to banks in 1991 totalled 66 per cent of GDP. (For Hungary and Poland, it was 46 per cent and 30 per cent respectively; OECD Industry Division 1992.) It is estimated that over 30 per cent of all loans to the industrial sector were non-performing. Recent analysis also indicated that the machinery and elec-tronic engineering sectors accounted for 50 per cent of inter-firm debt, with liquidity ratios far below world standards.[23] The Czech Union of Industry estimated that about 80 per cent of Czech manufacturing firms were unable to pay their bills (Doleckova 1993). To understand why insolvency has increased so much and without bankruptcies, let us analyse the motivations at both the firm and bank levels.

First, firms faced a rapid decline in financial resources and rising interest rates. Although the rigid production structure limited their ability to change products or markets, firms were able to use these links to avoid primary insolvency. Because of inflationary expectations associated with the price liberalization in January 1991, firms used most of their liquid assets to increase greatly their input inventories.[24] Yet, the change in the size and structure of demand, noted by the collapse of the communist foreign trade regime, CMEA, and the sharp fall in domestic production, caused input inventories to be shifted to large inventories of semi-finished and finished goods, implying a greater demand for financing. State subsidies, previously 79 per cent of firm disposable income, dried up rapidly in 1990 (Holman 1991). Interest rates on perpetual inventory loans, transferred to the Con-solidation Bank, jumped from 6 per cent to 13 per cent, with firms meeting less than a third of mandated instalment payments. Despite an increase in the money supply to ease credit after mid-1991, indebtedness continued to rise. Real interest rates remained extremely high, since the oligopolistic banks with their low capital levels had little incentive to decrease lending-rates. Firms wanted to sustain employment (and thus as much production as possible) to maintain local social peace and keep workers for expected increases in future demand, although the tight links between suppliers and customers restricted their ability to find new markets. Firms could actually use their recognized interdepencies to maintain employment and avoid primary insolvency, and thus bankruptcy, by continuing to sell to one an-other through agreed levels of inter-firm credit. As long as everyone within production networks played the game, firms could avoid external interven-tions and float themselves through inter-firm debt and short-term credit.

Why then did the banks not begin to foreclose on outstanding loans? The answer is twofold: banks had a disincentive to call loans and cancel debts, and an incentive to maintain restricted lending. On the one hand, virtually all bank capital was already invested in industrial firms, and bankruptcies threatened the existence of the banks themselves. As noted above, loans to transforming state firms accounted for the large majority of total loans in the two main commercial banks, and the savings bank, with the only real source of liquidity, had begun to underwrite the loans from the other two commercial banks. With their limited loan-loss provisions and substandard capital–asset ratios, banks were unwilling to risk large losses by foreclosing, and were apparently dependent on the survival of most of these large firms. Since household savings are the primary source of financing bank credits, the government has been resistant to cancelling firm debt outright or allowing significant foreclosures. Moreover, the networks of inter-firm debt and the existence of large firms with several divisions makes the financial situation of firms much less transparent. This is evident in the continued rise of short-term lending and debt, despite the government's efforts in April 1992 to shore up banks by increasing write-off provisions by 22 per cent and bank capital by 7.8 per cent.

On the other hand, banks enjoy a seven point spread between credit and debit rates, giving them a prime source of financing to strengthen their capital base. As the government increasingly stepped in to guarantee short-term bail-out loans for the most insolvent firms in 1991–2, banks could simply sit on their loans and tally expected profits. Given their dependency on the survival of industrial firms and their guaranteed high rates of return, banks substantially increased short-term loans with only marginal increases in medium- and long-term loans.

Under pressure from the banks and leading firms, the government suspended the bankruptcy law in spring 1992 for a year to reform it. First, because of the existing structure of geographically dispersed industrial communities and the tight links among the limited number of customers and suppliers, closure or rapid down-sizing of firms could cause large pockets of unemployment and a downward economic spiral in the many localities and a domino effect of bankruptcies throughout regions. With the rise of local political groups, such as in the Silesian–Moravian region, the government feared such actions could result in a severe political backlash against both itself and economic reform. Similarly, a closure of large debtors could threaten the solvency of the banks, with or without a domino effect. Komercni Banka, for instance, had estimated that selling debts on the secondary market would bring returns of much less than 50 per cent of the nominal value. Second, banks were adverse to the notion of debt–equity swaps since bank managers recognized the interdependencies among firms and refused to take responsibility for the restructuring of whole regions or industries. Recent interviews reveal that banks lack the personnel to undertake strategic industrial reorganizations in any substantial manner, and that the complications following the small swap at the engineering company Škoda Plzeň in 1992 by Komercni Banka and Investicni Banka, arranged at a discount by the government, had left banks wary of any unilateral ventures into ownership responsibilities. Third, by the end of 1992 over 88 per cent of expenses of the Fund for National Property, the government's main source of liquidity, had gone towards the financial relief of banks and the

Fund did not expect substantial increases in revenues. Small privatization was almost concluded; vouchers and joint ventures, the main form of foreign investment, did not allow for much sales revenues; and the Fund would not receive payments for ten years on the bank bonds it bought to finance the Consolidation Bank's write-offs for bad bank loans (Klcacova 1993). During 1992 a series of well-publicized bankruptcies of large manufacturing holding companies—Zetor, Svit, Poldi Steel, Škoda Plzeň, Aero, ČKD Praha, Tatra Koprivnice—increasingly forced the government to bail out firms. In these cases, the loop of inter-firm credits had been broken by the refusal of large customers, notably former export partners in Russia and Africa and the Czech transportation and energy utilities, to make any payments on oustanding debts. The trade unions, the banks, and the Union of Industry demanded that the government provide guarantees for further short-term loans to keep the firms afloat, or risk large-scale unemployment, bankruptcies, and financial instability.

These events brought to light the need for a fundamental change in the role of the goverment in restructuring and the limits of the privatization programme in facilitating the reorganization of industries. The next section analyses how manufacturing firms began to reorganize and protect themselves over the past three years. Given the lack of financial resources and the concentrated industrial structure, the discretion of firms and divisions to switch production processes, change suppliers and customers, or close units is greatly constrained. In turn, actors have to renegotiate the pre-existing social relations without disrupting the social peace as well as the acquisition of needed parts and credit.

INDUSTRIAL REORGANIZATION

Reformers have more or less attributed the insolvency crisis to managers attempting to maintain their jobs and obstruct restructuring through lowering the value of assets by increasing debt and minimizing lay-offs and through keeping an oligopolistic market structure to increase their bargaining leverage and maintain their old product base. The general solution, reformers argued, was for the state to break up large firms and create independent, sovereign hierarchies, which could more easily switch suppliers or customers, be evaluated by outsiders, and be closed without risk of a landslide of bankruptcies. Such advances were soon halted. IPFs complained that since the state was no longer the sole or majority owner, it could not intervene alone; and if it was so difficult to value units, how could one divide shares of whole companies across various divisions. Similarly, banks and managers complained that the tight production and financial links among subsidiaries or units precluded any mechanical way of clarifying the currently blurred boundaries.

Although there may be some truth to the notion that managers had an interest in lowering the asset value of firms to avoid liquidation, the reformers' view misses the mark. First, given the interdependencies between, say, suppliers and customers or the firm and locality, single-handed actions or assertions of sovereignty could destabilize the pre-existing social peace among actors, in turn threatening the economic health of the firm. While the tight social and economic links could constrain an actor's new opportunities, these relationships were the foundations to assuring the flow of needed material, financial, and human resources. In turn, any formulation and execution of restructuring is intimately tied up with renegotiating the different rights and responsibilities of the relevant parties. Second, these relationships shape the production possibilities and financial strength of firms, since the needed parts of another unit or needed financial protection from a holding company comes at a price of limited autonomy. As we shall see, a relatively profitable firm can easily go bankrupt when it extracts itself quickly from the protection of the holding; investors interested in a joint venture with a certain unit must find a way to aid the development of a key supplier who wants to increase production of other parts that help cash-flow.

The next section analyses how firms have been able to contend with the pre-existing tight links among themselves and their localities through establishing self-co-ordinating units within a company or business group. The analysis then turns to how these developments are affecting the formation of joint ventures, the main method of gaining foreign partners and restructuring capital.

Reassessing Production and Financial Constraints in Firms

Given the limited alternatives for new sources of sales, inputs, equipment, parts, and financing, firms and divisions must often pool common resources and collaborate with principal suppliers and customers to reconstruct their production processes and product mixes. For instance, 85 per cent of the firms in the above-mentioned 1991–2 survey continued to produce only for their past few customers, and 25 per cent of firms devoted all of their production to a single customer. In addition, 80 per cent of the firms had almost fully internalized research and development, input and parts production, and distribution and marketing activities, but could no longer support such integration; 70 per cent said that the only alternative was to co-operate with their past customers to develop new processes and products. However, such collaboration constrains the discretion and autonomy of individual firms and production units to generate alternative production modes. On the one hand, production units have become responsible for their own financing and finding new suppliers and customers to develop new product lines; the central office is viewed as a holding company. On the other hand, units continue to depend largely on pre-existing networks and co-units within the firm for the following:[25]

- the firm, with an internal bank, is still the main conduit of financing, as units alone are finding it difficult to borrow the capital needed for restructuring;
- units pool material and labour resources, share production facilities, and co-operate on developing new products and processes since their production is interconnected due to previous local and firm autarky;
- each unit has often been the main supplier or customer of the other, making it difficult to find significant external contacts;
- since exporting had been conducted through state foreign trade syndicates, the units lack foreign contacts and export experience;
- firms or units mutually subsidize one another through purchases on credit and the holding bank for product development.

The following cases show how firms deal with such issues as streamlining operations, product development, and financial constraints through increasing autonomy and self co-ordination yet under the umbrella of the holding company. The economic and technical relations between firms and between units within them limit the available options but also become the building-blocks for restructuring and surviving.

A principal problem for firms is allowing individual units to increase in financial and sales independence for acquisition of new knowledge of certain technologies while maintaining the supply of critical parts or equipment for other units. Simply spinning off integrated units could damage supply lines with such a concentrated market and relatively unaffordable imports and possibly lead to the closing of the newly independent firm–unit in an illiquid setting. In turn, many firms have tried to develop 'internal markets' within a firm, while units gradually increase sales and purchases with companies outside the umbrella. Consider the case of ČKD Praha, which has eighteen subsidiaries.[26] First, it has grouped those units with similar product lines and who have shared parts production into four self-co-ordinating production groups–profit centres: transport (locomotives, trams); large engine production (diesel, electric, and combustion); compressors, hydraulics, and machinery; and cast-iron plates and models. Second, constituent units utilize existing and new product lines for direct sales outside the firm. Indeed, since 1990 outside sales account for up to 35 per cent of most units' production. However, transforming these groups or units into independent firms outside the holding is not possible at this time. Not only do groups and units depend on the head office for sales contacts (particularly in exports), but also the main product programmes—rail transport, engines, compressor and cooling systems, and electronic transformers—create a high degree of cross-fertilization and technical synergies across product groups. For instance, locomotive and tram production depend on semi-finished products from all other groups; motor and compressor production share component production (see Fig. 3.1).

Škoda Plzeň, with its thirty-five subsidiaries, has four main product groups: energy, transport, electrotechnical, and machinery. The ties across these groups is best demonstrated in the complications with its joint-venture projects (see below). Aero, an aircraft producer, has eleven subsidiaries and two main production groups: military and civilian aircraft production.[27] These production groups differ from those of Škoda and ČKD in that these groups focus on separate product programmes. First, in military aircraft, Vodochody is the final producer, with Letov and Technometra Radotín providing specialized engines and components; in civilian aircraft, Let Kunovice is the final producer, Motorlet, Moravan, Technometra Semily, and Mesit as principal suppliers. Although the product interdependence within these groups is very high, most of the supplying units between groups continue to collaborate on engine and component production, since not only are there great synergies across the two groups, but also group production has not filled capacity for well-developed component product lines, due to the recent loss of some domestic and CMEA markets. By sharing development cost and knowledge for new and upgraded products, units have been able to develop export and service contracts in Western Europe and Russia. Second, since aircraft production requires a great amount of operating and development investment, production cycles of the different programmes alternate. While the constituent units of one programme are not in full cycle, they can use idle capacity by collaborating in the other production programme. Third, three other subsidiaries have diversified generic activities and provide research and development, electronic components, and hydraulic parts and equipment to both product groups. Thus, the production and design interdependencies between both groups through these three units further constrain a rapid break-up of Aero, yet each gain in the sharing of costs and knowledge.

Firms face as well the necessity of down-sizing operations through lay-offs and closing or selling unneeded or financially unsustainable facilities without the sudden loss of key parts supplies or social dislocation. This issue has meant the sharing of operating and wage cost by firms, the local governments, and the Ministry of Labour for the support of side units with excess labour, which can be spun off in the future, and the support of regional subcontractors.

Poldi Steel, which was previously at the top of the list for closures, has taken significant steps to streamline operations, decreasing direct employment by 6,000 since 1990.[28] Poldi and the government have subsidized the formation of 'conversion units' from unused facilities and fifteen subsidiaries that provide machinery, transport, power, and spare parts, and computer programming. While many of the 6,000 have found employment nearby in Prague, the conversion units and the subsidiaries account for several thou-

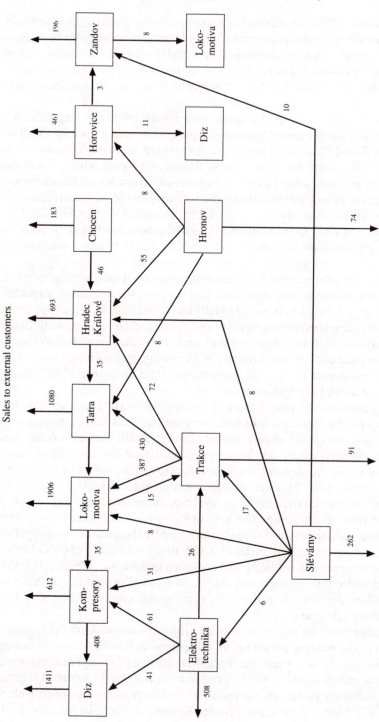

Fig. 3.1. Internal production and supply links among subsidiaries of ČKD Praha, 1990 (sales data in million kčs). Arrows between subsidiaries connote intersubsidiary sales; arrows pointing to outside of large box connote sales to external customers. Source: Internal analysis of ČKD Praha by AT Kearney, 1992

sand employees. The conversion units are headed by highly skilled workers, who have a strong technical knowledge and contacts throughout the manufacturing sectors. Most of these units have fully spun off into independent subcontractors, while the subsidiaries should be fully or partially sold by the end of 1993 (i.e. Poldi will have a minority stake in the two machinery plants).

Tatra Kopřivnice, one of the main truck producers in the Republic, is a primary purchaser for about 500 private and transforming state subcontractors in the Republic, most of whom are in northern Moravia.[29] Owing to low liquidity from a sharp fall in exports to Russia and North Africa, Tatra has had uneven purchases and payments to subcontractors, which has disrupted its production as well as threatened the solvency of the subcontractors. At the behest of the Association of Northern Moravian–Upper Silesian Municipalities and KOVO trade union, the government has begun to collaborate with the regional councils, Tatra, and the banks to share the costs of maintaining some of the more strategic contractors.

Aero has one of the more elaborate projects to limit local unemployment, develop new products and processes, and support its main subcontractors. The subsidiary Letov has used side facilities to establish a technology park, where subcontractors rent equipment and space and collaborate with Letov and Aero's research and development unit to produce new body components. The local council, the Ministry of Economy, and a French consulting company co-operate in the park to subsidize start-up costs and infrastructure as well as find foreign investors.

As suggested above, one of the key binding forces of large and medium-sized firms has been the poor financial strength of their units, coupled with a lack of alternatives for generating investment, credit, and export income. Units or subsidiaries do not have the capital base for leveraging loans because of either the size or the collateralization of the assets by the parent for loans in the past. This practice has skewed the accounts of individual units, putting productive assets at the risk of immediate bankruptcy if separated from the holding. The sale of property or side facilities is also constrained since these assets are often shared by the local community. For instance, in desperate need of cash, ČKD Tatra, a subsidiary of ČKD Praha, tried to sell unneeded property and facilities in Smichov, Prague, but this was blocked by the local council, which demanded provisions in the contract to allow the council to maintain some social services there. The deal subsequently fell apart.

Full autonomy for a unit in such an environment and without the financial umbrella of the holding puts interlinked units as well as the newly liberated one at risk. On the one hand, the immediate closing of insolvent units could lead to the dissolution of whole production progammes which integrate separate subsidiaries. Recall, for instance, the integrated horizontal production of ČKD Praha. Trakce and Hradec Kralove are both in primary insolvency. If the holding does not at least keep them afloat for the time being, both transport and engine production could shut down and further the distress of many other subsidiaries.

On the other hand, even the most profitable and modernized units find it difficult to survive under current conditions. The case of Jihlavan Jihlava, Jihostroj, and Mikrotechna is illustrative. These were three of the best divisions in Aero, manufacturing hydraulic, engine, and electronic components, respectively, which decided to become fully independent firms in 1990 with prospective foreign joint-venture partners. Perceiving that these three put the future financial and production stability at risk, Aero subsidiaries soon halted purchases and held up parts supplies for the three. The new firms also found it very difficult to raise the credit for operations and product developed. All three have subsequently lost their foreign partners, who viewed them as too great a production and financial risk, and are bankrupt. Mikrotechna returned to the holding in early 1992; Jihlavan and Jihostroj are requesting to be reabsorbed, but Aero subsidiaries have been able to collaborate to produce the engine and hydraulic components themselves. A similar story can be told about Slany and Naftove Motory, previous subsidiaries of ČKD Praha.

Although the cross-subsidization within or between firms may not create the most transparent situation, the financial and production links create enough interdependencies to make bankrupting one unit or firm, breaking up holdings, or developing new product lines alone appear largely untenable at this stage. Rather, increasing production and financial independence becomes a negotiated process over the decision-making rights and obligations of collaboration among the constituent units, head offices, local councils, and government ministries. While the cases above show how firms and their constituent units have attempted to balance independence and collaboration, they are by no means without conflict. Yet because of the binding force of these inherited relationships, production possibilities and economic sustainability become underlined by the ebb and flow of renegotiating the links and prerogatives of interdependent parties. The following analysis of recent trends in joint ventures attempts to demonstrate how these negotiations over the inherited links become a critical problem for the injection of much-needed foreign capital and know-how.

Joint Ventures: Searching for Investment, Markets, and Technology

Joint ventures, as opposed to complete acquisitions or mergers, have become the main conduit for foreign investment and partnerships for three interrelated reasons.

First, creating a joint venture after the conversion of a firm into a joint-stock company allows the capital to stay within the unit firm, while a buy-out allows the capital to go directly into coffers of the state or new owners.

Second, investors have been averse to scooping up whole firms or divisions since the excess capacity of firms and the implied responsibilities for other interlinked units pose substantial financial and social burdens of *ex post* restructuring. A less risky approach has been to take a partial stake in a division or single smaller firm within a business group, ceding a certain degree of control and decision-making rights to other investors in related units and to Czech managers, but tapping into the necessary local knowledge, be it about specific products or the possibilities to execute reorganization strategies. Recent interviews with foreign consultants and at the Ministry of Privatization reveal that foreign investors continually propose a joint venture with a single division or subsidiary and try to co-ordinate partnerships between remaining critical units and familiar investors. Managers are attracted to this approach since the particular unit gains essential investment capital and foreign knowledge without ceding complete control of the firm.

Third, joint ventures are convenient ways to tap into foreign export markets while regulating the fluctuation of sales and hedging the changing product specifications of purchasers. This aspect of joint ventures helps Czech firms find new Western markets as well as maintain productive relationships in the former USSR, which is a prime attraction for Western investors. Indeed, most Czech engineering firms, such as ČKD, Škoda, Tatra, Avia, Liaz, and Aero, have lost considerable income since the breakup of the CMEA and the liquidity crises in Russia and the Ukraine. Joint ventures allow Czech firms to use non-price mechanisms, such as barter and purchase-investment incentives, to guarantee sales and establish a network of local customers while minimizing the financial costs of building on pre-existing relationships.

However, as we shall see below, because these arrangements diffuse authority, be it between *de jure* partners and firm units or among interdependent units and firms, the co-ordination of production programmes and the recirculation of information is embedded in the resolution of possible conflicts and hold-ups. For instance, the discretion of joint-venture partners is constrained by the production strategies and financial needs of a critical parts supplier, be it another firm or a subsidiary. The resolution of such problems, in turn, creates the need for non-market specific institutions. Often the government is called on to create a consortium of local banks to refinance outstanding debts of the particular or linked units, to support local infrastructure and domestic or export sales through subsidies or operating credit, and to provide indemnities against inherited environmental damage. The following cases were chosen for two interrelated reasons. First, besides the early foreign investment in a few Czech gems, the prospective agreements between foreign investors and the particular subsidiaries or divisions were considered the easiest to conclude since the Czech units had some of the better track records in Czech manufacturing. In turn, one should not view complications in the joint ventures arising simply from the poor quality of the assets or management. Second, as foreign consultants and officials at the Ministry of Privatization have indicated, both investors and Czech firms are closely following these cases as possible models to reorganize firms.

One of the most closely observed projects was the prospective joint venture between Mercedes and the Czech truck manufacturers Avia and Liaz.[30] Avia and Liaz had compatible production modes, and Mercedes proposed production of Czech and Mercedes light and heavy trucks. Production of light trucks would continue at Avia, but assembly of generic heavy trucks, based on Mercedes' design, would be at Liaz Jablonec. The problem was that Liaz had been a specialized truck manufacturer and had developed operations for manufacturing and fitting customized components. Liaz began to protest the venture provisions in 1992 owing to its fear of sacrificing these programmes and, in turn, risking the health of units not directly involved with the joint venture. Liaz argued that all assembly should be done at Avia to capture economies of scale, and that it did not want to have to orient all its main parts production toward standardized parts for Mercedes. Specialized component production centred at Jablonec, cutting across several plants, and brought in much-needed cash-flow and new information on technologies. Indeed, Liaz had developed lucrative contracts with Telefunken for specialized cables and was in the midst of joint-venture negotiations with Rockwell for production of axles at a plant closely linked to Jablonec. An added difficulty arose in early 1993, when the government refused to provide indemnities against environmental damage already underground at Avia and Liaz to Mercedes for the venture. The indemnities were to be provided only in the case of buy-outs. Since the legal joint-venture partners were the two Czech joint-stock companies, and not the state, such provisions had to be given by the firms, which naturally were unable to do so. With additional pressure from serious losses incurred in 1992, Mercedes could not wait for further delays in settling the joint venture and withdrew from negotiations.

At ČKD concerns about accumulated debt burdens and production links have complicated joint-venture negotiations. Deutsche Babcock-Borsig (DBB) and ČKD Kompressory have negotiated for over a year on a project for the production of machine compressors. ČKD had been one of the prime suppliers of the former Soviet Union. Resisting a buy-out for ČKD Kompressory, DBB was to acquire a majority stake in the joint venture in return for substantial investments over three to five years and the assumption of much of the subsidiary's debts. After initially accepting the terms, DBB reopened negotiations. It argued that ČKD Kompressory teeters on the edge of bankruptcy, even if the terms were met, and demanded that the government step in to provide guarantees against bankruptcy and indemnities against environmental damage. Subsequent talks produced possible agreements by the government and the lowering of DBB's share to a minority stake.

One of the biggest prospective joint ventures for ČKD is between AEG and ČKD Transport group. AEG had originally wanted a venture with ČKD Tatra to produce tram and metro cars, but the tight production links with ČKD Trakce and ČKD Lokomotiva forced considerations of their inclusion. Although there have been some disagreements about the continuation of profitable side production in Trakce, the biggest concern has been the solvency of Trakce and Lokomotiva, which are saddled with large debts and the collapse of the Soviet market. These problems have necessitated government co-ordination of bank refinancing of debts, underwriting of exports to Russia, and clearer agreements for sales of metro and tram cars to Czech municipalities.

Škoda Plzeň's problem came to a head in 1992 when CSD, the state railway company, reneged on the purchase order it had made in 1990 for sixty locomotives.[31] Having finished the locomotives and incurred substantial debts for their production, Škoda was forced to close operations for a month and call on the government for a bail-out. Škoda's new director and the government agreed to the government's absorption of certain debts, underwriting of a bond issue, and financing of CSD leasing of the sixty locomotives in exchange for specific restructuring steps. Soon afterwards, the Finance Ministry refused the leasing provision, arguing that this was unwarranted government paternalism. The subsequent decline of trust between the government and Škoda would put Škoda in a catch-22 situation: the resulting financial instability increased the need to conclude several joint-venture negotiations, but also complicated them as foreign investors regarded the government's participation as essential. Most directly affected were joint-venture discussions involving Škoda subsidiaries in the transport and energy programmes.

Concern about whether the government and CSD would ever be dependable customers was only one aspect of broader issues that complicated joint-venture discussions between Siemens and certain units within Škoda Energo and Transport. First, Škoda Energo and Transport groups had collaborated on several projects, creating interdependencies on component production as well as sharing of debts and profits. If Siemens wanted to take a majority stake in a joint venture with Energo, it had then to take over many of Energo's old production and financial obligations towards other susidiaries and cover the difference between expected profit and sales income for in-progress production. Otherwise, Energo and other units involved in the production would face increased financial problems. Siemens had refused this, assuming the government would cover the obligations Škoda incurred as a state-owned firm. This disagreement led both the unions and the Škoda director to declare their reservations about ceding significant control and stakes to any foreign partner for fear that giving it discretion not to respect the continuing obligations between subsidiaries and to the government could threaten the economic health of other units as well as the holding. The director added that ceding full control to Siemens of operations that generated substantial liquidity through exports restricted the cross-subsidization between units necessary at this time.

Second, if Škoda Transport was to maintain important relations in the Ukraine and Russia, it had to develop and diversify its locomotive and related component production, which generated good cash-flow. In 1992–3 Škoda Transport strengthened these relations by using third-party finance and barter deals for locomotive sales. These were critical steps towards establishing joint ventures in Kiev and Moscow for further sales of locomotives and parts. (Russia alone had already over 2,000 Škoda locomotives in use.) Siemens, however, had wanted to orient Škoda Transport only towards wagon production.

Third, government refusal to assume certain obligations for current and future environmental damage further dampened talks with Siemens.

In July 1992 Škoda Blovice and Secheron established a joint venture for the production of electronic equipment for locomotives and trolleybuses. One of the main attractions of Blovice was its development of parts for the former Soviet Union, which operated at temperatures at $-50°C$. Secheron had stopped its agreed investments into Škoda Blovice for several reasons. First, Blovice sales were partially dependent on the development of Škoda Transport, particularly its operations in Russia. The complications between Škoda Transport, Siemens, and the government, in turn, threatened Blovice's liquidity, debt burdens, and development of new technologies. Second, prior to Secheron's entrance, part of a Blovice plant had been restituted to a Czech citizen. While the government decides whether it can force the restituent to accept money for the facilities, the citizen rents for free the facilities and has established a profitable firm producing components compatible with those of Blovice. Secheron does not want break the venture, since it would lose patent and technology sharing rights for the specialized components. However, if the property is given to the restituent, then Škoda's share of the venture would decline. This decline, Secheron fears, would decrease Škoda's share of Blovice's debts and temporary losses, which may be partially covered by the government. Secheron's financial responsibilities would thus be increased.

CONCLUDING REMARKS

The focus on rapid privatization in East Central Europe as the elixir to the renovation of industries has been based on the belief that firm restructuring is most effective when private, unitary actors bear the full risks and benefits of asset use and interact through arm's-length relationships mediated by price alone. The implementation of the voucher programme and a bank-ruptcy law designed to punish debtors followed this reasoning to the fore. Once property rights were delineated, boards of directors established, and creditors armed with the bankruptcy law, production or financial hold-ups could be resolved by the simple exchange of control rights for the creation of a hierarchy, or firms could be broken up and units closed, with suppliers finding new customers (or vice versa).

However, the above cases and the failed reform of financial institutions indicate that the existing information asymmetries and tight economic and social links constrain and blur the discretion and self-interest of actors. IPFs are unable to concentrate authority, but must cede strategic decision-making rights to managers. Banks are reluctant to foreclose debts of inter-linked firms for fear of incurring unsustainable losses. Managers of firms and units are precluded from closing units or initiating large lay-offs as such actions can easily disrupt the local social peace. They are also restrained from taking unilateral action over forcing the payments of debts, breaking up firms, or extracting a unit from a holding: in the Czech context of inherited regional autarky and tight financial and production inter-dependencies, such action can quickly result in the loss of one of the only partners, with whom a firm or unit can acquire critical parts, develop new production modes or products, and share financial burdens.

These constraints on the discretion of actors are not, however, unresolvable. The above cases demonstrate that in order to reorganize production modes and tap into strategic information, actors must renegoti-ate their claims to autonomy and responsibilities towards the needs of other constituents of the assets in question. For instance, units or subsidiaries must agree to the continued supply of certain components or provisional pooling of human and financial resources if they are to gain the independ-ence to develop alternative products or joint ventures and receive the benefits of financial aid and research and development of the holding. Firms must find new ways of down-sizing operations in return for the support and assistance of the local council or certain work groups. Investors must cede certain control rights if they are to gain critical knowledge and co-operation from managers and linked units.

However, such steps towards diffusing authority and reaching workable, lasting compromises amongst the interested parties are fragile at this time. The multilateral nature of discussions is particularly susceptible to the pressures of the current uncertainties of low liquidity and the absence of a mechanism for deliberation. The central problem for the renovation of industries is not, as is typically argued, how to assign rights so as to avoid conflicts of interest and the deceptions and compromises to which they give rise, but rather how to distribute rights amongst the interested groups and create institutions for the consultation among them to mediate conflicts and reach compromises that facilitate the reorganization of production.[32] The recent government steps towards institutionalizing strategic bankruptcies and work-outs, co-ordinating the cancellation of circles of inter-firm debt, and providing capital to shore up a new secondary market for the trading of debts are in the right direction but not sufficient. Indeed, by the end of 1993 few bankruptcies had been initiated, and government-sponsored netting out of inter-firm debts had resolved only 10–15 per cent of these debts (Sabela 1993). Simply allowing negotiated restructuring of debts or aiding decreases in debt burdens does not mean that possible conflicts will be resolved or creditors will not be constrained to initiate proceedings.

Reformers must recognize that the government is an active constituent itself to the reorganization of firms. This does not mean assuming the complete responsibilities and authority to managing assets or bailing out firms whenever needed. One of the lessons of the past forty years and the current period is that central imposition of rules and rights only exacerbates the political and social distance between peak and firm–local-level actors and the fragmentation of the economy into isolated industrial communities. It means, further, that the government, as a participant in aiding firms, investors, and localities in balancing the costs and benefits of non-market, non-hierarchical institutions of economic governance, must help arbitrate conflicts over the development of new and existing production modes and the down-sizing of firms; provide the needed capital to support networks of suppliers, conversion units, the development of new technologies, and on-site retraining; and provide necessary indemnities although it is not the full owner. The year 1993 may have marked the beginning of a new definition of the boundaries for the government and the firm in the Czech Republic, as the state began frequent negotiations with banks and holdings to help finance their restructuring. These deliberations have concerned the defining of each party's responsibilities toward inherited debts, the reorganization of production, and the monitoring of one another. But then the questions arise: Who is the principle and who is the agent? What differentiates the private from the public domain? For answers to these questions, the powers that be have us write dissertations, so stay tuned.

NOTES

I would like to thank the editors and participants at the WZB conference in September 1993 for their comments on the first draft. I also benefited from discussions with Suzanne Berger, Zhiyuan Cui, Tony Frost, Steve Grand, John Griffin, Tony Levitas, Richard Locke, Ivana Mazalkova, and Charles Sabel; all errors are, of course, my own. Special thanks go to Sandra Adair for her patience, support, and inspiration. Generous financial support during the writing of the chapter came from the American Council of Learned Societies and the International Research and Exchange Board.

1. A hold-up in this context is defined as the ability of one party to block the action of another party. The second party—e.g. a critical work group, supplier, or debtor—controls certain resources, influence, information, or supplies, causing the first party to be dependent on the second party's co-operation or conformity (Hart 1989).

2. Several of the theoretical points in this and the next paragraph are drawn from John Griffin. For an insightful discussion of these issues, particularly regarding the role of banks and capital markets, see Griffin (1993).

3. See again Griffin (1993). Griffin elaborates his view of economic Darwinism with the specific focus on corporate finance. My purpose here is simply to present, and subsequently criticize, the view that the rapid clarification of ownership and legal codes should resolve hold-ups and allow apparently inefficient producers to be punished.

4. For more on this point in Poland's attempt to privatize, see Dabrowski *et al.* (1991).

5. Note that this number does not include energy-producing firms or small local manufacturing firms and co-operatives. Altogether the total is 1,511. Of engineering firms 88 per cent had more than 1,000 employees and over 60 per cent had more than 2,000 (Bohatá 1991; Zemplinerová 1989b).

6. There were mainly two types of VHJs: the 'concern' consisted of a large branch enterprise to which smaller ones were attached; and the increasingly common 'trust' was an association of firms with comparable size and production programmes. Trusts accounted for 75 per cent of all VHJs (Rychetnik 1992; Smrčka 1988).

7. For a detailed discussion of the changes in VHJ structures and procedures, see Rychetnik (1981, 1992).

8. For an original and insightful analysis of the social capital constitutive of the formation of horizontal relationships, see Stark (1986).

9. For a basic outline of Czechoslovak privatization, see Mejstřík and Burger (1992).

10. The data from the first wave of privatization are adapted from Burger and Mejstřík (1992).

11. Also, the number of industrial firms has increased from 1,509 to only 1,664, and average firm size has declined from 1,771 to only 1,395 (Bohatá *et al.* 1991).

12. Moreover, post-privatization deconcentration is uncertain, because the further sale and restructuring of parts of firms will not be rapid due to the low level of domestic capital and the problems of asset evaluation (Hlavacek and Mejstřík 1991).

13. Moreover, in only 249 cases were two different projects competing with one another for the same property (Buchtíková and Capek 1993).

14. The fifteen funds, which hold the 80 per cent, are owned by the nine companies; 200 funds share the remaining 20 per cent (Hawker 1993b; Hrnčíř 1993).

15. Many funds, including all the leading ones, are expected to face additional financial constraints due to their guarantees to pay shareholders in funds over 1,000 per cent return within a year. For a comprehensive overview of the challenges that the IPFs face, see Vojtěch and Machaček (1993).

16. These points are nothing new. The Czech Minister of Industry from 1990 to 1992, Jan Vrba, had published several detailed analyses of various industries indicating the amount of needed foreign investment and how vouchers were severely hindering this. For an overview of his argument on these points, see Vrba (1991).

17. The survey included firms from machinery and electronics to chemicals and paper (Mihola and Havlin 1992; Mihola *et al.* 1991).

18. Owing to pent-up aspirations for local autonomy, the number of municipalities in the Czech Republic increased by 50 per cent from 1990 to 1992, yet the state eliminated the five regional administrations through which the former local councils and managers co-ordinated economic and social matters between different industrial communities (Illner 1992*b*; McDermott and Mejstřík 1992).

19. It is noteworthy that firm–local council relations have been able to reproduce themselves as local identities have strengthened. For instance, managers have transferred free of charge over 11 per cent of total assets to the local governments and helped in administrating the services which these facilities occupy. Analysis of local politics note that independents, former communists, and current communists often formed election coalitions and that many council members are managers of the local state firms or divisions. The fact that about 50 per cent of those elected to municipal councils in 1990, 1992, and 1993 were independents, communists, and former communists indicates, among other things, that local constituencies see these actors as relatively reliable protectors of their immediate concerns and future prospects for development against meddling by the centre, even with new reformist parties at the helm (Charap and Zemplinerová 1993; Herzmann 1992; Illner 1992*a*; Janyska 1990). In municipal elections for 375 communities and city districts in the Czech Republic on 29 Feb. 1992, the two main reform parties, the Civic Democratic Party and Civic Movement, won only 2.3 per cent of the seats (Foreign Information Broadcast Service, 15 Mar. 1992).

20. Two comprehensive discussions on bank reform can be found in Hrnčíř (1992) and Mejstřík and Burger (1992*a*).

21. In theory, the idea was that a firm suffering from secondary insolvency was able to produce marketable goods, but was not fully responsible for the inability of customers to pay outstanding debts.

22. Although there were forty-four new banks by the end of 1992, these have had little participation in manufacturing sectors (Hrnčíř 1993).

23. For an analysis of firm debt and bank liquidity, see Krauseová (1993) and Vintrová (1993).

24. The average increase in input inventories was 155 per cent and for industrial firms 140 per cent (Holman 1991; Horčicová and Vašková 1992).

25. These observations are based on analyses of the firms discussed below (see also Mihola *et al.* 1991).

26. The evidence from ČKD Praha a.s. is compiled from Bautzová and Adámková (1993); *Hospodářské novíny* (1993*a,b,c*); Ministry of Industry and Trade CR (1992*a*); and internal analysis of ČKD by AT Kearney.

27. Evidence from Aero was compiled from Adámková (1992, 1993*a,c*); Kubes (1993*a,b*); and interviews at Aero Holding, Feb.–Mar. 1993.

28. The evidence on Poldi was compiled from author's interviews at Poldi and the

Department of Steel at the Ministry of Industry and Trade CR, Feb.–Mar. 1993; Lukavská (1992).
29. Evidence on Tatra Kopřivnice was compiled from Bautzová (1992); Ministry of Industry and Trade CR (1992*b*).
30. Evidence from Avia and Liaz was compiled from interviews and internal documents at the Ministry of Privatization CR, Feb.–Mar. 1993.
31. Evidence from Škoda Plzeň was compiled from interviews at the Department of Investment Engineering of the Ministry of Industry and Trade CR, Feb.–Mar. 1993; Adámková 1993*b*; Prokoš 1993*a,b,c,d,e*).
32. I owe this insight to Charles Sabel.

REFERENCES

Adámková, A. (1992), 'Konverze bez cizí pomoci' (Conversion without Outside Help), *Ekonom*, 44: 41.
——(1993*a*), 'Diky bance nové šance?' (Thanks to the Banks, a New Chance?), *Ekonom*, 26: 41–2.
——(1993*b*), 'Lecba se protáhuje' (Treatment is Protracted), *Ekonom*, 9: 30–3.
——(1993*c*), 'Tradice závázuje' (The Obligations of Tradition), *Ekonom*, 7: 33–4.
Bautzová, L. (1992), 'Tatra Kopřivnice–zrcadlo doby' (Tatra Kopřivnice—A Mirror of Time), *Ekonom*, 49: 30–3.
——and Adámková, A. (1993), '(Nejen) Tramváj pro Manilu' ((Not Only) Trams for Manila), *Ekonom*, 14: 36–8.
Blanchard, O., Dornbusch, R., Krugman, P., Layard, R., and Summers, L. (1990), 'Reforms in Eastern Europe', MS, WIDER, Helsinki.
Bohatá, M. (1991), 'Pohled na výkonnost některých dnešních průmyslových podniků' (A Perspective on the Performance of Some Current Industrial Firms), *Politicka ekonomie*, 1: 27–41.
——(1993), 'Sector of Optical, Measuring, and Medical Instruments', MS, Ace Project, Prague.
——*et al.* (1991), *Analytika východiska tvorby průmyslové politiky v transformacnim obdobi* (An Analysis towards the formation of an Industrial Policy in the Period of Transformation), Working paper no. 2461/91 (Ústředni ústav narodohospodářského výzkumu, Nov.).
Brom, C., and Orenstein, M. (1993), *Restructuring and Corporate Governance in the Czech Republic*, IEWS Working paper, Prague.
Buchtíková, A., and Capek, A. (1993), 'Privatization in the Czech Republic: Privatization Strategies and Priorities', MS, Institute of Economics of the Czech National Bank, Prague.
——and Flek, V. (1992), *Wage Determination in Czechoslovakia: Government Power versus Trade Union Power* (Prague: Institut Ekonomie Statni Banka Ceskoslovenske).
————(1993), 'Income Policy and Wage Development in the Czech Republic', MS.
——Capek, A., and Macourkova, E. (1992), *Statistical Analysis of the Privatization Projects*, Studies no. 19 (Prague: Institute of Economics).

BURGER, J., and MEJSTŘÍK, M. (1992), 'Vouchers, Buyouts, and Auctions: The Battle for Privatization in Czechoslovakia', Paper presented at the Center for European Studies, Harvard University, 15 Dec. 1992.

ČÁKRT, M. (1991), 'Sociální klima v rizení průmyslého podniku' (Social Climate in the Management of the Industrial Firm), *Sociologický časopis*, 27: 469–82.

CHARAP, J., and ZEMPLINEROVÁ, A. (1993), 'Management Buyouts in the Privatization Programme of the Czech Republic', Paper presented to the 3rd Plenary Session of the OECD Advisory Group on Privatization, Budapest, 31 Mar.–2 Apr. 1993.

DABROWSKI, J., FEDEROWICZ, M., and LEVITAS, A. (1991), 'Polish State Enterprises and the Properties of Performance: Stabilization, Marketization, Privatization', *Politics and Society*, 19/4: 403–37.

DOLECKOVA, M. (1993), 'Sváz Průmyslu: Chceme stabilitu; Sdružení Podnikatelů: Chceme zvyhodnit' (Union of Industry: We Want Stability; Association of Entrepreneurs: We Want Preferential Treatment), *Hospodářské noviny*, 22 Feb. 1993.

DYBA, K., and SVEJNAR, J. (1992), 'Stabilization and Transition in Czechoslovakia', Paper presented to the NBER Conference on Eastern Europe, 26–19 Feb. 1992.

FRYDMAN, R., RAPACZYNSKI, A., and EARLE, J. (1993), *The Privatization Process in Central Europe* (London: Central European University Press).

GREGUS, M., and KALIŠOVÁ, L. (1991), *Economic Reforms and Enterprise Behavior*, Working paper (Prague: CEU).

GRIFFIN, J. (1993), 'Privatization and Financial Capitalism in East Germany', Paper presented to the Conference Rethinking Western Europe, Columbia University, 25–7 Mar. 1993.

HAM, J., SVEJNAR, J., and TERRELL, K. (1993), 'The Czech and Slovak Labor Markets during Transition', Paper presented to the World Bank Conference on Labor Markets in Transitional Economies, Washington, Sept. 1993.

HART, O. (1988), 'Incomplete Contracts and the Theory of the Firm', *Journal of Law, Economics, and Organization*, 4/1: 119–39.

——(1989), 'An Economist's Perspective on the Theory of the Firm', *Columbia Law Review*, 89: 1757–74.

—— and MOORE, J. (1986), 'Property Rights and the Nature of the Firm', *Journal of Political Economy*, 98: 1119–58.

HAWKER, A. (1993a), 'Low Unemployment Rate Perplexes Officials', *Prague Post*, 24 July.

——(1993b), 'Small Funds Face Crunch', *Prague Post*, 17 July.

HERZMANN, J. (1992), 'Volby v kontextu veřejného minění, 1989–1991' (Elections in the Context of Public Opinion, 1989–1991), *Sociologický časopis*, 28: 165–83.

HLAVÁČEK, J., and MEJSTŘÍK, M. (1991), *Preconditions for Privatization in Czechoslovakia in 1991*, Working paper (Prague: CEU).

—— and TUMA, Z. (1993), 'Bankruptcy in the Czech Republic', Mimeo, Faculty of Social Sciences, Charles University, Prague.

HOLMAN, R. (1991), *Insolvency of State Enterprise, 1990–1991*, Working paper (Prague: CEU).

HORČICOVÁ, M., and VAŠKOVÁ, D. (1992), 'Insolvency in the Transformation Period of the Czechoslovak Economy', *Eastern European Economics*, 30: 5–24.

Hospodářské noviny (1993a), 'Podmíněně záruky' (Conditional Guarantees), 25 Feb.

Hospodářské noviny (1993*b*), 'Borsig nesplnil své sliby' (Borsig does not Fulfil its Promises), 4 Apr.

——(1993*c*), 'Babcock–Borsig měl velké oči' (Babcock–Borsig had Big Expectations), 20 Apr.

HRNČÍŘ , M. (1990), 'From Traditional to Reformed Planned Economy: The Case of Czechoslovakia', *Czechoslovak Economic Papers*, 28: 25–45.

——(1992), 'Financial Institutions and Monetary Policies in Czechoslovakia', MS, Institute of Economics of the Czech National Bank, Prague.

——(1993), 'Financial Institutions and Monetary Policies in Czechoslovakia', MS, Institute of Economics of the Czech National Bank, Prague.

ILLNER, M. (1992*a*), 'Continuity and Discontinuity: Political Change in a Czech Village after 1989', *Sociological Review*, 18: 79–91.

——(1992*b*), 'K sociologickým otázkám mistní samosprávy' (A Sociological Approach towards Local Self-Government), *Sociologický časopis*, 28: 480–92.

JANYSKA, P. (1990), 'Co řekly volby' (What the Elections Said), *Respekt*, 39: 4–5.

KADLECOVÁ, I., and HOLMAN, J. (1993), 'Structurální aspekty vývoje zaměstnánosti' (Structural Aspects in the Development of Unemployment), *Ekonom*, 25.

KLVACOVA, E. (1993), 'The Role of the Fund of National Property in the Privatization Process', *Privatization Newsletter of the Czech Republic and Slovakia* (Apr.).

KOLÁNDA, M. (1992), 'Cs. průmysl a jeho narodohospodářské okolí v první etápě reformy, 1991–1992' (Czechoslovak Industry and its National Economic Setting in the First Stage of Reform, 1991–1992), MS, Prognosticky ustav, Prague.

KORNAI, J. (1990*a*), 'The Affinity between Ownership Forms and Co-ordination Mechanisms: The Common Experience of Reform in Socialist Countries', *Journal of Economic Perspectives*, 4: 403–37.

——(1990*b*), *The Road to a Free Economy* (New York: Norton).

KRAUSEOVÁ, J. (1993), 'Likvidita českých podniků na počátku renesance tržní ekonomíky' (The Liquidity of Czech Firms in the Beginning of the Renaissance of the Market Economy), *Finance a úvěr*, 43/1: 27–37.

KUBEŠ, T. (1993*a*), 'Partneři zakánznaci požaduji vic než podnikové záruky' (Partners of Customers Demand more than Company Guarantees), *Hospodářské noviny*, 6 May.

——(1993*b*), 'Porsche zřejmě odjde z Českého Krumlova' (Porsche Naturally Leaves Česky Krumlov), *Hospodářské noviny*, 7 May.

LIPTON, D., and SACHS, J. (1991), 'Privatization in Eastern Europe: The Case of Poland', *Brookings Papers on Economic Activity*, no. 1 (Spring).

LUKAVSKÁ, L. (1992), 'Poldi si nechce kleknout' (Poldi does not Want to Give Up), *Hospodářské noviny*, 17 Feb.

MCDERMOTT, G. A., and MEJSTŘÍK, M. (1992), 'The Role of Small Firms in the Transformation of Czechoslovakia', *Small Business Economics*, 4 (Sept.), 179–200.

MEJSTŘÍK, M., and BURGER, J. (1992*a*), 'Banking Center Reform in the CSFR', Paper for the Reform Round Table, CERGE, Prague, June 1992.

————(1992*b*), 'The Flood of Privatization Projects in the Czech Republic', *Privatization Newsletter of Czechoslovakia* (Feb.).

——KYN, O., BLAHA, Z., and MLADEK, J. (1992), 'Three Knots of Voucher Privatization', *Respekt*, 5.

MIHOLA, J., and HAVLIN, V. (1992), 'Volné ruce pro rozhodnování' (A free Hand to

Decide), *Hospodářské noviny*, 31 Jan.

————and SKALA, M. (1991), 'Adaptace podniku v prvnich mesicich transformace cs. ekonomiky' (Firm Adjustment in the First Months of the Transformation of the CSFR Economy), Mimeo Ústředni ústav narodohospodářského výzkumu, Prague.

MINISTRY OF INDUSTRY AND TRADE CR (1992a), *Současná situace ČKD Praha a navrhy vedení holdingu na její řešení* (Current Situation in ČKD Praha and Proposals to Lead the Holding towards its Resolution), C. 179/92 (Prague).

——(1992b), *Zprava o situaci v a.s. Tatra Kopřivnice a navrhy na jeji reseni*, C. 200/29 (Prague).

MYANT, M. (1989), *The Czechoslovak Economy, 1948–1988: The Battle for Economic Reform* (Cambridge: Cambridge University Press).

——(1992), 'Center Periphery Relations in Czechoslovakia', *Journal of Interdisciplinary Economics*, 4: 269–80.

——(1993), 'Trade Unions in Czechoslovakia', MS, Department of Economics and Business, Universities of Paisley.

OECD INDUSTRY DIVISION (1992), 'Industry Review of Czechoslovakia', MS, Paris.

PREMÚSOVÁ, J. (1989), 'Vázby mezi podniky a uzemním v lokalním ramci' (Links between firms and the Local Region), *Sociologický časopis*, 25: 171–82.

PROKOŠ, VACLAV (1993a), 'Škoda Ostrov pracuje sámostatně' (Skoda Ostrov Works Independently), *Hospodářské noviny*, 15 Feb.

——(1993b), 'Škoda a Dorries konečně svoji' (Škoda and Dornier Finally Connect), *Hospodářské noviny*, 19 Feb.

——(1993c), 'Joint Venture Skoda–Secheron neziskový' (Skoda–Secheron Joint Venture Unprofitable), *Hospodářské noviny*, 13 Mar.

——(1993d), 'Škoda Plzeň miři do Ruska' (Škoda Plzeň Aims at Russia), *Hospodářské noviny*, 19 Apr.

——(1993e), 'Uspora energie zatim není argument' (Cutting Energy meanwhile is not an Argument), *Hospodářské noviny*, 12 May.

REMEŠ, A. (1984), 'Funkce drobných podniků v moderním průmyslu' (The Function of Small Firms in Modern Industry), *Politicka ekonomie*, 32: 476–90.

RYCHETNIK, L. (1981), 'The Industrial Enterprise in Czechoslovakia', in I. Jeffries (ed.), *The Industrial Enterprise in Eastern Europe* (New York: Praeger), 114–28.

——(1992), 'Industrial Reform in Czechoslovakia', in I. Jeffries (ed.), *Industrial Reforms in Socialist Countries* (Elgar), 111–28.

SABELA, A. (1993), 'Má datí, dal: k výsledkúm započtové operace' (Have Data, Next: On the Results of Mutual Deduction of Claims and Liabilities), *Ekonom*, 53: 20–2.

SCHLEIFER, A., and VISHNY, R. (1992), 'Privatization in Russia: The First Steps', MS, National Bureau of Economic Research, Cambridge, Mass.

SMRČKA, J. (1988), 'The Prospects of Development of Organization Structures of the Enterprises', *Czechoslovak Economic Papers*, 26: 27–39.

SPURNÝ, J. (1993), 'Odbory se boji nezamestnanosti' (Labour Unions fear Unemployment), *Respekt*, 5–18 Mar., 15.

STARK, D. (1986), 'Rethinking Internal Labor Markets: New Insights from a Comparative Perspective', *American Sociological Review*, 51: 492–504.

ŠVEJNAR, J., and SINGER, M. (1992), *The Czechoslovak Voucher Privatization: An Assessment of Results*, Working paper (Prague: CERGE).

Tříska, D. (1990), 'Dočasná správá a denacionálizace narodního majetku' (Current Administration and the Denationalization of National Property), MS, Czechoslovak Ministry of Finance, Prague.

Valenta, F. (1992), 'Akciové spolecnosti v první vlně kuponové privatizace' (Joint-Stock Companies in the First Wave of Coupon Privatization), MS, Ekonomicky ústav, Prague.

Vavřiková, J. (1987), 'Některé aspekty spolůpráce oblástních a odvětvových orgánu' (Some Aspects of the Co-operation between District and Industrial Organs), *Planovane hospodářstvi*, no. 8: 87–90.

Večerník, J. (1992), 'Trh práce: problemy a perspektivy' (The Labour Market: Problems and Perspectives), *Sociologický časopis*, 28: 319–36.

Vintrová, R. (1993), 'The General Recession and the Structural Adaptation Crisis', *Eastern European Economics*, 31: 78–94.

Vláčil, J., and Horniák, V. (1992), 'Velká privatizace: Sociální konflikt a konsensus v pluralitě podnikatelských organizací' (Large Privatization: Social Conflict and Consensus in the Plurality of Business Organizations), MS, Sociologicky ustav, Prague.

Vojtěch, O., and Machaček, J. (1993), 'Investiční fondy: jak si stoji nejmocnější hráci na ekonomické šachovnice' (Investment Funds: How the Most Powerful Players Stand on the Chess-Board), *Respekt*, 19–25 Apr., 8–9.

Vrba, J. (1991), 'Comments on Privatization in Czechoslovakia', MS, Czech Ministry of Industry, Prague.

Zemplinerová, A. (1989*a*), 'Monopolization of the Czechoslovak Economy', Paper presented to the EARIE Conference, Budapest, Aug. 1989.

——(1989*b*), *Monopoly in a Centrally Planned Economy*, Research paper no. 333 (Prague: Institute of Economics).

——and Stíbal, J. (1993), 'Transition and the Problem of Monopoly', Paper presented to the Ford Foundation Conference, CERGE, Prague, 14–15 Dec. 1993.

4

Adaptation at the Cost of Adaptability? Restructuring the Eastern German Regional Economy

GERNOT GRABHER

REDUCING TRANSFORMATION TO PRIVATIZATION: THE CENTRAL IMPORTANCE OF WESTERN INVESTMENT IN GERMAN UNIFICATION

In an ironic way, Chancellor Kohl's prediction of 'flourishing landscapes' in eastern Germany is apparently turning out to be true. The shut-down of numerous combines has resulted in the deindustrialization of entire regions. The reduction of industrial employment from 3 million people to roughly 750,000 has in many places left hardly more than 'flourishing landscapes'. This disastrous economic consequence of German unification was inevitable given the radical German approach to privatization. In a sense, that approach mirrors the fatal misunderstanding of Soviet-type socialism. For just as the 'socialization of the means of production' was confounded with a once-and-for-all act of nationalization, so has privatization been reduced to a once-and-for-all transition, with productive assets being transferred from a sphere of what is allegedly public control to a sphere of what is allegedly private control. This transfer to private—mainly western German—control was predicated on a thorough break-up of the combines into separate plants. This dissolution of the combines was expected to enhance the attractiveness of eastern German plants for Western investors.

Discussion in this chapter is focused, first, on the motives of Western corporations investing in eastern Germany. I demonstrate how the initial expectations for economic development in eastern Germany and in Eastern Europe have been sorely disappointed. Almost as soon as the anticipation of growing markets in the East faded, labour costs rose. Second, I reconstruct the strategies adopted by Western corporations to cope with these unforeseen challenges of their investment in eastern Germany. Lastly, I evaluate the impacts that those strategies have had on regional development in eastern Germany. The main argument here is that whereas globally integrated strategies have culminated in the construction of cathedrals in the desert, multi-domestic strategies have favoured the emergence of locally integrated production networks. This evaluation of regional impacts, however, requires a brief glance backward at the spatial and organizational features of the former German Democratic Republic (GDR) that constitute the 'genetic material' for future development in the economy.

THE LEGACIES OF THE COMBINE-BASED ECONOMY: CORPORATE AND REGIONAL ORGANIZATION OF PRODUCTION IN THE GDR

Autarkic Mass Producers: Corporate Legacies

Despite the rhetoric of the dichotomous, opposed logics of market and planned economies, the post-war organization of production in Western and Eastern European economies followed, at least for a considerable time, a similar basic principle—the model of industrial mass production. In the GDR, central planning aimed at achieving higher levels of efficiency by means of 'concentration and specialization'. Within the GDR no single product was to be produced simultaneously by two different firms. This orientation implied a thorough reorganization of the traditional regional and sectorial production patterns, which were still largely dominated by rather small-scale craft production.

The history of the transformation of these traditional patterns of small-scale craft production culminated in the formation of the combines. The first wave of combine formation, which took place in the late 1960s and early 1970s, embraced about one-third of the GDR's total industrial employment. This model was generalized in a second, all-encompassing wave at the end of the 1970s. Under Erich Honecker, the giant corporation, economies of scale, and technological progress became joint guarantors of economic growth. In 1989 the GDR industry consisted of 126 centrally co-ordinated combines, each with twenty to forty plants and an average of more than 20,000 employees. Additionally, the plants co-ordinated at the district level, as was the case in the construction and food-processing industries, were integrated into ninety-five combines, each employing 2,000 employees on average (IAW 1990, table 4.16).

The combines were the institutional manifestation of 'reproductive self-containment' (*reproduktive Geschlossenheit*). The principle of integrating the main suppliers and basic auxiliary and maintenance functions served to enhance co-ordination and control of the various steps of production. To be sure, the concept of the combines cannot simply be reduced to vertical integration pushed to its organizational and technical limits. The combines also assumed municipal tasks, provided basic infrastructural services, and constituted the central locus of social integration. In other words, they organized not only work but education, recreation, cultural affairs, and social welfare as well.

However, behind the façade of hegemonic, large centrally co-ordinated combines was anything but the 'precision, promptness, clearness, continuity, discretion, uniformity, strict subordination, savings on frictions, material and personal costs' for which Weber (1922/1978: 561) bureaucratic mechanisms had celebrated. The East German economy corresponded to textbook models of bureaucratic planned economies about as closely as Western European economies corresponded to textbook models of market economies (Grabher 1993). In the GDR, as in other Eastern European countries (Neumann 1993), resources were by no means exclusively allocated by the central planning authorities. In addition, informal networks played a key role in compensating for the country's chronic shortages of raw materials, spare parts, and equipment. Particularly in the highly centralized planned economies of the GDR and CSSR, these informal networks provided a widespread infrastructure for barter (Heidenreich 1993: 7).

This sort of compensatory barter was governed by the principle of reciprocity. Reciprocity is a more general pattern than equivalence, which is said to govern market transactions. Contributions are not expected to balance out in every single exchange act but rather over the entire exchange relation (Grabher 1993: 8). For example, if member A of such an informal network received spare parts or other equipment from member B of the network, member A was not obliged to return a service immediately. However, the receiver was expected to assist other members of the network in a similar situation. This assistance included not only the supply of raw materials or spare parts. Members of the networks were also able to 'pay' with labour or accommodation contingents in the vacation homes owned by the combine. Although most of this exchange took place in the grey area of a personal network reinforced by mutual obligations, some combines turned this informal expedient into an auxiliary organizational device. Within the different production sites of the combines, there circulated special lists (*Pendellisten*) of resources and capacities that were idle and could be used as a kind of buffer inventory to cope with unforeseeable shortages.

These informal compensatory mechanisms between the combines were complemented by the formalized function of the maintenance, tool, and machine-building departments within the combines. In the late 1980s these departments, for which the GDR authorities had invented the term *Rationalisierungsmittelbau*, provided roughly 25 per cent of all investments in equipment and employed more than 70,000 workers (Haase 1990: 351) possessing an extraordinary level of craft skills and 'chaos qualification' (Marz 1992: 9), that is, rich experience in the development of *ad hoc* solutions. However, although the maintenance, tool, and machine-building departments of combines were central assets in day-to-day muddling through, this resulted in macro-economic irrationalities. The relative autonomy of the individual combine encouraged a bizarre dissipation of resources. Whereas, for example, the machine-building combines produced in exceptionally large batch sizes, their input was largely dependent on machines and equipment that they themselves produced. In 1987 about 700 plants were engaged in the production of robots. Their output per year amounted to fewer than seven robots on average (Voskamp and Wittke 1990: 18).

The Deregionalized Production System: Spatial Legacies

The concentration of production in increasingly large and autarkic combines was paralleled by a spatial concentration of planning, balance-sheet, price-setting, and trading functions in the central administrations at their headquarters and core plants (*Stammbetriebe*). Because of the strategic (and political) importance of these core plants, few financial and technical resources were ever allocated to the other plants of the combines. Although the formation of the combines initially increased the productivity of the GDR's industry, it culminated in an 'interindustrial organization of the productive system' (Quevit *et al.* 1992: 1).

The inter-industrial organization of the production system had—at least from a contemporary perspective—two disastrous consequences for the regions. First, this model of economic development based on autarkic large mass producers undoubtedly raised the level of industrialization in the lagging northern and eastern regions of the GDR, thereby narrowing the traditional north–south divide. However, this model also gave rise to new regional monostructures and deepened existing ones. In no fewer than fifty-four of the 189 districts of East Germany, the leading industry thus accounted for 40 to 60 per cent of total employment (Maretzke and Möller 1992: 156). Among the most prominent regional concentrations were the chemical triangle described by Halle, Bitterfeld, and Merseburg, a space that accounted for more than one-third of all chemical production in the GDR; the textile district of Cottbus, which accounted for roughly 50 per cent of the GDR's textile output; and the local concentration of steel production within a few large 'single-factory towns' such as Eisenhüttenstadt, Hettstedt, and Riesa (Heinzmann 1991: 102; Heise and Ziegler 1992: 548). The highly selective investment policy of the GDR, which favoured mainly a few ambitious projects in the electronics and data-processing industries and in the military sector, concentrated investment in roughly 20 per cent of the country's combines and, hence, exacerbated regional disparities in growth and productivity (Heinzmann 1991: 101).

Second, owing to the internalization of economic transactions, the notion of the region had no longer any economic meaning. Despite the utilization of the local labour force, the individual plants of the combines had no economic relation with the region in which they were located. The pre-existing intra-regional forward and backward linkages were severed and superseded by inter-regional linkages within the combines. Thus, the base for regional multiplier effects had been destroyed. Through the internalization of all economic interactions, that is, from the raw materials to the final product, the regions were deprived of agglomeration economies, economies that arise from a diversified regional economic structure and that are essential for the long-term adaptability of regions. In other words, the rationalization of production within the combines and across regional boundaries was a thorough attempt to increase the efficiency of production at the cost of demand flexibility. This flexibility was also provided by the craft-based localized production clusters that were deliberately destroyed as the combines were formed.

THE GERMAN APPROACH TO COPING WITH LEGACIES:
PRIVATIZATION AND DISSOLUTION OF COMBINES BY THE
TREUHAND

The 'deregionalization' of production was not simply reversed by the privatization and dissolution of the combines, executed by the Treuhandanstalt, the government holding company set up by the Federal Republic of Germany to sell off or liquidate the state-owned business and property of the former GDR. This decomposition typically occurred as an abrupt separation of the individual plants of the combines and a radical down-scaling or shut-down of those departments whose future returns were difficult, if not impossible, to calculate but that were crucial for long-term adaptability. To what extent future economic potential was sacrificed for the sake of rapid privatization may be seen from the wanton destruction of the research and development facilities. Between the end of 1989 and the autumn of 1992 the number of researchers in eastern German industry fell from 75,000 to roughly 15,000. Particularly pronounced were the reductions in the industrial core sectors of the GDR's industry. Electrical engineering lost 90.8 per cent of its research and development capacity; the chemical industry, 83.8 per cent; and the machine-building industry, 77.7 per cent (IWH 1992: 6–8).

This sort of short-term cost reduction pursued by the Treuhand was aimed at improving the micro-economic efficiency of individual plants. It was part and parcel of a strategy to isolate individual production plants by paralysing economic and social linkages with the pre-existing production system. This strategy was expected to facilitate the privatization of the GDR economy by enhancing the attractiveness of the plants for Western investors. In mere quantitative terms, the Treuhand's approach seems to have proved right. By 1 June 1993 the Treuhand had privatized 85.5 per cent of its 12,952 firms. The investors who took over these firms committed

themselves to investing DM 148.9 billion in the following years and to
providing 1,456,859 jobs.

Within eastern Germany two regions in particular share in these job and
investment commitments of Western investors (see Table 4.1). First, East
Berlin and the surrounding federal state of Brandenburg seems to be the
most attractive region for Western investors (if their commitments are
weighted by the number of inhabitants of the regions). This premier rank-
ing of the Berlin–Brandenburg region results mainly from two types of
investment project. One is in the core area of East Berlin, which will
constitute the new (old) centre of Berlin and has attracted huge investment
in real-estate development. These projects include the reconstruction of
luxury shopping areas and the erection of trade centres and office buildings,
the latter of which initially have been extremely scarce in Berlin. The
predominance of trade and services in the privatization of industry in East
Berlin is also reflected in the extraordinary labour intensity of investment in
terms of job commitments per privatization. The second type of project
making Berlin–Brandenburg attractive to Western investors focuses on a
variety of industries—food, beverages, and tobacco; construction; chemicals; and electrical engineering—which constitute the so-called *Speckgürtel*
('bacon belt') along the motorways around Berlin (Ministerium für
Wirtschaft, Mittelstand und Technologie 1992; see Table 4.2). The greater
Berlin area is one of the preferred locations for non-German investors, not
least because of the nearby market of approximately 5 million inhabitants,
the central location of Berlin within eastern Germany, and a relatively
advanced traffic and communication infrastructure.

Besides the unique position of the central Berlin–Brandenburg region,
investment activities in eastern Germany seem to duplicate the north–south
divide of western Germany and, hence, to revive the traditional spatial
pattern of industrial development in Germany. With a long tradition in
localized small-firm networks, the southern federal state of Saxony is one of
the leading regions in Germany's industrial take-off and represents the
second centre of new economic activity in eastern Germany. Mirroring the
industrial origins in Saxony, investment is concentrated in the machine-
building and electrical engineering industries. However, the construction
industry and the food, beverage, and tobacco industries are also strongly
represented in Saxony. In contrast to the Berlin–Brandenburg region,
Saxony is a place where non-German investors play a rather minor role.
Only 6.2 per cent of the investment commitments have been made by non-
German investors. This extraordinarily low share of foreign investment also

TABLE 4.1. *Investors' job and investment commitments in the federal states of eastern Germany*

	East Berlin	Brandenburg	Mecklenburg–West Pomerania	Saxony–Anhalt	Saxony	Thuringia	Eastern Germany
No. of inhabitants	1,284,535	2,611,816	1,945,447	2,992,032	4,841,613	2,653,797	16,259,240
Privatizations:							
No. of privatizations	853	2,017	1,586	1,926	3,575	2,320	12,360
Privatization rate (%)[a]	80.3	86.2	86.9	84.1	86.6	84.5	85.5
Proportion of management buy-outs in privatizations (%)	16.9	18.4	24.1	20.1	17.7	17.9	18.9
Job commitments:							
Total no.	246,567	284,818	126,550	183,534	415,731	192,514	1,456,859
Per 100 inhabitants	19.2	10.9	6.5	6.2	8.6	7.2	8.9
Per privatization	289.0	141.2	79.8	95.3	116.3	82.9	117.9
Percentage of foreign investors	10.1	15.1	6.1	9.7	6.2	7.2	9.1
Investment commitments							
Total (DM bn.)	24.3	31.5	11.6	20.4	44.0	12.9	148.9[b]
Per 100 inhabitants (DM m.)	1.9	1.2	0.6	0.7	0.9	0.5	0.9
Per privatization (DM m.)	28.5	15.6	7.3	10.6	12.3	5.5	12.0
Percentage of foreign investors	8.6	15.2	12.1	20.1	6.1	22.4	12.1
Plant shut-downs							
Jobs affected							
Total	26,348	39,799	20,375	32,621	115,488	62,858	303,671
Per 100 inhabitants	2.0	1.2	1.0	1.1	2.4	2.4	1.8
Assumed percentage of jobs saved	24.3	38.8	36.7	27.6	22.8	26.8	26.8
Unemployment rate[c]	13.7	15.1	16.9	16.1	13.8	16.0	15.1

[a] Proportion of privatized firms in the total number of firms handled by the Treuhandanstalt.

[b] Incl. investment commitments of DM 4.2bn. (sale of agricultural acreage and non-productive company real estate) not attributed to the new federal states.

[c] Data: as per end of May 1993.

Source: Calculations based on the Treuhandanstalt's monthly Information Bulletin; *IAB Report*, no. 12 (15 Feb. 1993) (Nuremberg: Institut für Arbeits- und Berufsforschung).

TABLE 4.2. *Regional structure of investment in selected industries* (in percentages)

	East Berlin	Brandenburg	Mecklenburg–West Pomerania	Saxony–Anhalt	Saxony	Thuringia	Total
Machines	5.5	5.5	3.6	23.6	56.4	5.5	100
Electrical engineering	16.7	1.7	8.3	18.3	31.7	23.3	100
Chemicals	13.6	13.6	—	40.9	27.3	4.5	100
Vehicles	8.7	8.7	13.0	—	26.1	43.5	100
Food, beverage, and tobacco	13.3	11.7	16.7	15.0	30.0	13.3	100
Construction	2.0	8.0	10.0	22.0	40.0	18.0	100

Note: Because of rounding, certain series of percentages may not sum to 100.

Source: IW (1991, no. 3, B-9).

reflects Saxony's strong industrial tradition. Soon after the unification, many firms in Saxony were taken over by western German firms that had previously run branch plants or that had even emerged from plants of this region's small-firm economies.

Similarly, investment in Thuringia mirrors the region's past strengths. However, whereas investment in Saxony is by and large a matter of 'German unification', 22.4 per cent of the investment in Thuringia has been committed by foreigners. The lion's share of this investment has been attracted by the automotive industry. Smaller investment projects have been launched in the tool and machine-building industries and the food, beverage, and tobacco industries. As in Saxony, privatization and investment in Thuringia have resulted in a relatively high number of plant shutdowns and lay-offs. In neither Saxony nor in Thuringia is the destructive dimension of this 'creative destruction' offset by the creative dimension. However, the overall balance of investment and shut-downs and, hence, the contribution of investment to regional structural change appears to be more favourable in Saxony.

Much as development in Thuringia is dominated by the automotive sector, investment in Saxony–Anhalt is largely determined by two closely interrelated industries that have dominated the area's economic development over the last forty years (IW 1991). Because only about 3 per cent of Germany's brown coal mining was located in eastern Germany before World War II, the government of the GDR resolutely developed this basic industry, making eastern Germany the most mining-intense country in Europe (Häußermann 1992: 11). Consequently, the basic chemical industry, which processes coal, was also concentrated in Saxony–Anhalt. The resulting industrial monostructure caused not only economic but also massive ecological problems that initially discouraged Western corporations from investing after Germany was united. However, the extensive subsidies from the Treuhand have facilitated a few large investment projects, such as a DM 6 billion undertaking that a French joint venture has entered upon in one of the chemical complexes of Saxony–Anhalt in order to gain access to the gas station network of the former GDR monopoly.

The situation in the most northern and geographically largest federal state, Mecklenburg–West Pomerania, seems even more dramatic than in Saxony–Anhalt. This region also demonstrates that resolute privatization is by no means enough to ensure investment and rapid structural change. Although privatization in Mecklenburg–West Pomerania has forged ahead rapidly, results have been poor. Investment as well as job commitments lie far below the eastern German average. Whereas, for example, the invest-ment commitments per privatized firm have amounted to DM 28.5 million in East Berlin, the respective commitments in Mecklenburg–West Pomerania total a modest DM 7.3 million. This rather poor outcome of privatization reflects the traditional industrial structure of Mecklenburg–West Pomerania. Aside from the drastically reduced ship-building industry on the Baltic Sea, the economic development of Mecklenburg–West Pomerania is largely determined by agriculture and the tourist trade. The low levels of barriers to entry in both these industries also explain the extraordinarily high share of management buy-outs (24.1 per cent) in the total number of privatizations. However, this statistic should not be misinterpreted as a promising indication that a small-firm economy is emerging. It is rather an unequivocal sign that Western companies are only moderately interested in investing in this peripheral region.

HIGH EXPECTATIONS—LOW RISKS: MOTIVES FOR INVESTMENT AND MODES OF CORPORATE INTEGRATION IN THE INITIAL STAGE

To be sure, this roughly sketched map of investment in eastern Germany largely reflects the spatial structure of investment plans that were laid down in the initial phase of the transformation process. At that time, the Wall was not only conceived as a restriction of basic human rights but also as a major barrier to trade. In this economic perspective, the events of 1989 also promised to open access to capacious markets. Hence, it does not come as a surprise that access to the eastern German market was the single most important motive for western German and foreign investors to become involved in eastern Germany (see Table 4.3). This investment motive was, and still is, particularly important in the industries of food, beverages, and tobacco; wood-processing; earth and stone; and the consumer-oriented sec-tors of the chemical industry (DIW 1992: 478).

Access to the eastern German market has rather different implications for investors, depending on the country they come from. Whereas western

TABLE 4.3. *Motives for investing in eastern Germany*

Motive for investing	Percentage of firms citing the given motive	
	Western German	Foreign
Access to eastern German market	71	50
Scarcity of firm's capacities	32	8
Availability of plants and labour	10	21
Low cost of labour	10	19
Access to EC market	—	41

Source: *DIW Wochenbericht*, no. 24 (1991), 331, as at April 1991.

German investors initially expected simply to extend their production capacities and markets proportionally and to establish a bridgehead to Eastern European markets, French and British investors were mainly motivated by the prospects of improving their market positions (*Wirtschaftswoche* 1992*a*: 132). To Swiss and Austrian investors, eastern Germany appeared to be a promising opportunity for getting a foot in the door to the EC market. The ratio of job commitments relative to investment commitments indicates that (probably smaller) Swiss and Austrian firms in labour-intensive industries took advantage of entering the EC market via its eastern back door. By contrast, American and Canadian investors represented rather large corporations intent on improving their positions in the enlarged EC market and on securing access to Eastern European markets by taking over an eastern German firm (see Table 4.4).

The high priority placed on gaining access to the market, as opposed to attempting to benefit from cost differentials, is also reflected in the prevalent modes of corporate integration (see Table 4.5). Across all industries, the predominant form of corporate integration was the founding of new firms, but only 7.3 per cent of those newly founded firms are geared to production. In 78.7 per cent the founding of a new firm has implied the establishment of a branch plant with exclusively distributive or representative functions. The other forms of corporate integration that were important in the first stage of investment in eastern Germany also reflect a rather cautious approach that contrasts somewhat with the rhetoric of the pioneering role that risk-taking capitalists have. 'Co-operative agreements' in most cases include a sort of risk-minimizing outsourcing based on short-term wage contracts. Accounting for 37.2 per cent of all forms of corporate integration other than the founding of firms, this contemporary version of the putting-out system represents the preferred form in the manufacturing industries. And even in those cases in which Western corporations committed rather large, long-term investment, the high priority of rapid privatization allowed them to shift risks and costs of the initial stage of their projects

TABLE 4.4. *Foreign direct investment in eastern Germany*

	Investment commitments (DM m.)	Job commitments	No. of firms
France	4,800	21,039	1,182
Switzerland	1,101	17,477	447
Great Britain	1,692	16,439	782
United States	2,746	11,952	419
Austria	693	13,717	276
Netherlands	962	8,263	247
Italy	649	4,956	303
Canada	1,848	16,708	34
Denmark	544	3,158	331
Luxembourg	399	2,000	275
Others	2,602	16,518	306
TOTAL	18,036	132,227	4,602

Source: *THA-Privatisierungsbericht*, no. 5 (1993), 16, as at end of May 1993.

TABLE 4.5. *Mode of corporate integration in Eastern Germany (in percentages)*

	Manufacturing	Trade	Traffic and communications	Services	Total
Joint corporations	18.5	15.5	44.0	12.3	17.5
Founding of new firms	28.5	44.0	28.0	62.1	37.1
Independent subsidiaries	4.3	5.9	4.0	7.0	5.2
Branch plants	24.2	38.1	24.0	55.1	31.9
Productive	4.1	—	—	—	2.7
Distributive	13.5	23.9	4.0	29.2	17.5
Representative	6.6	14.3	20.0	25.9	11.7
Co-operative agreements	37.2	32.1	28.0	13.2	31.2
Shareholding	15.4	4.8	—	9.9	13.1
Others	0.4	3.6	—	2.4	1.0

Source: IW (1991, no. 3, B-6).

to the Treuhand. Most of these large investment projects—and 18.5 per cent of the total investment in the manufacturing industries—were based on the establishment of a 'joint corporation' of which the Western investors held 12.5 per cent of the shares. Although the Treuhand consequently held

87.5 per cent of the shares, a syndicate contract assured that the Western investor controlled the management of the joint corporation. Since the property relations within the joint corporation also determined the cost-sharing, the Treuhand had to cover the bulk of the costs of preparing production in the new plants of the Western investors. These costs included, above all, the costs of removing ecological damages and selecting and qualifying a work-force for the new plants. The Western investor did not take over the entire joint corporation, including all costs and risks, until this transition stage had been completed.

BIG DISILLUSIONS—SMALL PROFITS: WITHDRAWALS AND STRETCHING OF INVESTMENT IN THE SECOND STAGE

Although the risks and costs of this initial transition and investment stage lay largely with the Treuhand, economic developments in both Western and Eastern Europe increasingly challenged the foundations on which those investments had been built. First, the expectation for the eastern German as well as the Eastern European markets have been sorely disappointed. Western investors were caught in the collapse of the eastern German productive system, a demise that they had unintentionally accelerated. In paralysing pre-existing social and economic relations, they also destroyed the informal networks within and between the combines. Those networks had been essential in compensating for the chronic shortages of raw materials and spare parts and in developing *ad hoc* solutions to production breakdowns. Together with the introduction of the Deutschmark the destruction of these networks that 'got the jobs done' triggered the implosion of the old combine-based economy. Hence, capital-goods projects that aimed at supplying the GDR industry no longer had an economic base.

The expectations that Western investors had for the development of the Eastern European markets were also thwarted. After 1 January 1991, by which time the account system in foreign trade was based on convertible currency, trade with Eastern Europe collapsed. The volume of exports from eastern Germany plummeted from 28.9 billion in 1989 to less than one-quarter of that amount in 1992. Trade with the former Soviet Union, the former Czechoslovakia, and Poland declined by 70 to 80 per cent and vanished almost completely with Hungary, Romania, and Bulgaria (see Table 4.6). Although the share of eastern German exports to Eastern Europe was still at 58 per cent in 1992, its dramatic decline (down from 71 per cent in 1989) jeopardized the strategies of Western investors to establish bridgeheads to Eastern European markets (*Sozialpolitische Umschau* 1992).

The costs of labour in eastern Germany increased almost as fast as the expectations for Eastern markets faded (Table 4.7). Eastern Germany lost

TABLE 4.6. *Eastern German exports to Eastern European countries (DM m.)*

	1989	1992	1992 as percentage of 1989
CIS	16,576	5,543	33.4
Ex-CSFR	3,814	789	20.7
Poland	3,116	524	16.8
Hungary	2,597	179	6.9
Romania	1,428	77	5.4
Bulgaria	1,361	67	4.9

Source: German Federal Statistical Office; Institut der Deutschen Wirtschaft, Cologne.

TABLE 4.7. *Contractual wage level in eastern Germany as a percentage of western Germany, by industry*

Industry	Percentage	Adjustment agreements	
		Year	Percentage
Construction (E. Berlin)	100	1992	100
Retail	79	1993	85
Construction (other *Länder*)	77	—	—
Private insurance	75	1994	100
Private banking	71	1994	90
Iron and steel	70	1994	100
Printing	70	1995	100
Public sector	70	1993	80
Footwear	70	—	—
Energy and power utilities	68	1993	77
Metal and electricity	67	1994	100
Lignite and gas	61	—	—
Textiles	61	—	—
Chemicals	60	1993	68
Clothing	58	1993	69

Source: Data from the Collective Wage Agreement Archive of the German Federation of Trade Unions (Deutscher Gewerkschaftsbund), as at 30 June 1992.

its economic attractiveness for at least 19 per cent of the foreign investors and 10 per cent of the western German investors (see Table 4.3). Although considerable increases in eastern German labour costs had been foreseen, the gradual adjustment of eastern German wage levels to western ones was obviously out of step with the expectations of Western investors. The disappointing development of Eastern European markets apparently jeopardized investment projects in Eastern Europe in general. None the less, the rapid increase in labour costs presumably did not call into question investment in Eastern Europe *per se*, just investment in eastern Germany. About one-third of the corporations in which high labour costs are regarded as a major obstacle for investing in eastern Germany have preferred locations in the Czech Republic, Hungary, or Poland because of their 'more attractive cost structures' (IHK and DIHT 1993: 59). Audi, for example, finally decided to establish its new engine plant in Hungary rather than Saxony–Anhalt, 'because the wages in Hungary amount to just 10 per cent of the wages in eastern Germany' (*Der Tagesspiegel* 1992: 23). To be sure, the attractiveness of these countries lies also in the opportunity for at least large investors to influence national trade policies in order to protect national markets from other foreign competitors. A case in point were the plans of Mercedes-Benz to take over the Czech truck manufacturers Avia and Liaz, which were subject to a subsequent raising of import tariffs and the introduction of import quotas for trucks (*Der Spiegel* 1992: 86).

More recently investment projects in eastern Germany have been challenged not only by the socio-economic contingencies in eastern Germany and Eastern Europe, but also by Western European recessionary tendencies that were aggravated in late 1993. This additional threat to investment in eastern Germany hit the western German investors especially hard. For more than 30 per cent of them, lack of their own capacities was a major motive for investment in eastern Germany (see Table 4.3). The recession, however, rendered a further expansion of capacities superfluous. To be sure, the crisis in western Germany did not result in an immediate interruption of investment activities and did not affect all eastern German sectors in the same way. Nevertheless, the recession in western Germany significantly slowed investment dynamics in the producing sector. Whereas western German corporations increased their investment in the producing sector by 73.4 per cent between 1991 and 1992, the growth-rate fell to 24.3 per cent in the subsequent year. Even more marked was the slow-down in investment dynamics in the manufacturing industries. After a boost of 87.5 per cent between 1991 and 1992, investment increased by only 10 per cent between 1992 and 1993 (IFO 1993: 3). In 1994 investment dynamics stagnated (see Table 4.8).

This stagnation of western German investment dynamics contrasted sharply with the Treuhand's statistics on investment commitments. According to those statistics, western German investors initially planned a further, considerable intensification of their investment activities in 1994. The obvious discrepancy between initial commitments and actual investment activities stemmed from the complete withdrawal of investors from eastern Germany and the stretching of large investment projects. Taken together, the withdrawal of investors and the stretching of investment projects re-

TABLE 4.8. *Western German investment in eastern Germany (DM bn.)*

	1991	1992	1993	1994
Total	25.95	41.76	48.65	49.46
Producing industries	12.31	21.54	27.69	27.69
of which manufacturing industries	7.69	15.38	16.15	13.85
Trade, traffic, and communication				
industries	10.77	16.15	16.92	17.69

Source: IFO Investorenrechnung Ost, as at Apr. 1993.

duced investment by approximately DM 5 billion in 1993 (IFO 1993: 3). Most pronounced were the reductions in the core industries of the German economy, the automotive and the machine-building industry.

A first disastrous and highly visible signal was the withdrawal of Mercedes-Benz, which had committed itself to invest DM 1 billion to build the 'most advanced truck assembly plant in Europe' and to create 4,000 jobs near Berlin (see Table 4.9). Mercedes-Benz set a precedent by breaking its commitments with the Treuhand in order to secure capacity utilization in the West instead of capacity expansion in the East. Soon after this shock over the 'fall of an industrial beacon' (*Frankfurter Rundschau* 1993: 9), Volkswagen announced it would extend the expansion of its new plant in Saxony over several years. Initially, Volkswagen had committed itself to invest approximately DM 4 billion in the construction of new plants in which 6,800 employees were to assemble 1,200 Golfs (type 3) daily from 1994 on. Given its heavy losses in 1992, however, Volkswagen had decided to postpone the completion of its initial plans to 1996–7 and to confine its investment, for the time being, to DM 1.7 billion. The company's ambitious production plans were reduced to 350 to 400 cars, to be assembled by 2,600 employees (*Süddeutsche Zeitung* 1993: 18).

These considerable reductions of the projects of major investors triggered set-backs in the supplier sector in its most volatile development phase. For example, more than sixty small firms had been founded or had moved close to the Mercedes-Benz site, 'most of which now find themselves in a serious crisis even before they could really could start business' (*Wirtschaftswoche* 1992b: 99). As regards Volkswagen's local supplier base, Rockwell-Golde, for example, a supplier of sliding roofs, indefinitely postponed its project to build a new plant near Volkswagen. These withdrawals are not confined to the automotive industry. In the steel industry, Krupp cancelled its investment of DM 1.1 billion (see Table 4.9), deciding to concentrate all its effort on consolidating its Western plants. In the metalworking and machine-building industries, firms such as FAG Kugelfischer and Heidelberger Druckmaschinen have been similarly affected by the

TABLE 4.9. *Selected withdrawals of Western investors in 1992 and 1993*

Corporation	Industry	Investment commitments (DM m.)	Job commitments
Mercedes-Benz AG	Vehicles	1,000	4,000
E. Holtzmann & Co. AG	Paper	800	800
Alcor Chemie AG	Chemicals	100	1,700
Krupp Stahl AG	Steel	1,100	2,800
McCain GmbH	Food	200	n.a.
Rockwell Golde GmbH	Vehicle parts	5	50
Allmetall BV	Metal	5	700
Pfersee Kolbermoor AG	Textiles	30	750

n.a. = not available.

Source: *Wirtschaftswoche* (1992*b*).

crisis of the Western economies and have scaled down their investment projects considerably.

Although these withdrawals and reductions of investment projects are significant on the whole and add to the exceedingly disappointing record of the 'upswing East', Western investment constitutes *the* basic element of the eastern German economy. The long-term development of the eastern German economy, however, will largely depend on the nature and intensity of the linkages between these Western investment projects on the one hand, and the regional economy and these investments on the other. The answer to the question of the 'regional embeddedness' of Western investment seems, at least at first glance, greatly determined by the general corporate strategy underlying investment in eastern Germany—the distinction between a multi-domestic, nationally responsive strategy and a globally integrated one (Quevit *et al.* 1992).

SHAPING THE FUTURE MAP OF EASTERN GERMANY:
REGIONAL IMPACTS OF CURRENT CORPORATE STRATEGIES

The Multi-domestic Approach: Local Integration

So far, nationally responsive—or, closer to the point, regionally responsive—strategies have appeared to be less affected by the foregoing challenges to Western investment than globally integrated strategies and have prevented an even more severe set-back in production and employment than has already been experienced in eastern Germany. For technological and product-related reasons two sectors were more successful than others of the eastern German economy in attracting investors and consolidating production. On the one hand, the eastern German construction industry attracted Western investors whose location decisions are largely influenced by high transport costs and the need for prompt delivery. In general, the vast public investment programmes dedicated to the improvement of the public infrastructure (DM 24 billion in 1992), the federal railways (DM 10 billion), and housing construction (DM 5 billion) was decisive for the take-over plans of Western investors (DIW 1992: 144).

Among the more important engagements of Western corporations in the construction industry of eastern Germany are the RMC Group (UK) and Lafarge Coppée (France), which plan to invest DM 470 million and DM 350 million, respectively, to modernize cement plants and establish networks of delivery plants for ready-made concrete (Morgan 1992: 4). In the early 1990s the Austrian Maculan Holding AG founded six largely independent regional subsidiaries and rose, behind the five leading western German corporations, to become the sixth largest construction enterprise in eastern Germany (*Wirtschaftswoche* 1993: 112). Because the plants of these corporations have to serve local markets, they enjoy a relatively high degree of local autonomy. At least they are equipped with basic managerial functions and sales and purchase departments. For technological reasons their regional forward as well as regional backward linkages are relatively strong, for the weight–price relation of the basic input materials of the construction industry does not allow for long transport distances. Some of the investors even acquired shares of firms that supplied their construction plants with raw materials such as gypsum and gravel. This strategy, not too far from the logic of the combine-based organization, was aimed at ensuring the survival of suppliers whose economic situation and perspectives as Treuhand firms were rather precarious. It may also explain why a rather large share of investment was dedicated to the earth and stone industry, especially in the first stages of the unification process. In 1991 western German corporations alone invested approximately DM 2 billion in this basic goods industry (IFO 1992*a*: 9).

A similar pattern of rather loose corporate integration and comparatively strong regional embeddedness characterizes investment projects in the food, beverage, and tobacco industries, which currently play a key role in eastern Germany. After investments of DM 1.8 billion in 1991 and of DM 3 billion in 1992, the investments (of western German corporations) amounted to 3.3 billion in 1993 (IFO 1993: 3). These investments are significant, for in the food, beverage, and tobacco industries, as in the earth and stone industry, the relation between investments in eastern Germany and in western Germany lies considerably above the average of the manufacturing industries as a whole. To be sure, the development of the food, beverage, and tobacco industries has to be seen in close connection with the strategies of the major retail chains. The breath-takingly quick and nearly complete take-over of the eastern German retail and distribution sector by the major western German corporations Metro AG, Spar AG, Tengelmann Group, and REWE AG led to an equally breath-taking collapse in the eastern German food, beverage, and tobacco industries. In the second half of 1990, for example, production in the eastern Berlin food, beverage, and tobacco industries dropped by 71.3 per cent (IFO 1991: 43). Since the Western retail chains maintained relations with their Western suppliers, eastern German producers initially had no chance to get on to the order lists of the retail stores. This circumstance also reflected the sudden stigmatization of Eastern products by eastern German consumers, who preferred Western products regardless of quality and price. Just as abruptly, however, the attitudes of eastern Germans changed again. First, the escalation of the unemployment problem turned consumer preferences into a political issue. 'Buying East' became more and more a demonstration of the disillusion with the unfulfilled promises of Western capitalism. Second, eastern Germans rediscovered, after a short period of experimentation with Western products, the merits, or at least customary pecularities, of eastern German products, particularly of regional fresh products and traditional GDR brands (IFO 1992b: 20).

The large Western investors in the food, beverage, and tobacco industries—Coca Cola (USA), which committed investments of DM 700 million, Unilever (UK, DM 100 million), Philip Morris (USA, DM 60 million), and EAC (Denmark, DM 40 million)—tried to adapt with a two-way strategy. First, they met the demand for popular Western products by acquiring additional production facilities in eastern Germany. In a few spectacular cases, these corporations decided to establish new green-field plants whose purpose, as so-called Euro plants, is to supply the EC market with a few European-wide brands (*Handelsblatt* 1991c: 19). Second, and partially responding to the limits of the Europeanization of brands and the changing preferences of eastern German consumers, they continued producing traditional GDR brands. A prominent victim of these limits of Europeanization and changing consumer preferences was the largest western German cigarette producer, Reemtsma, which spectacularly failed to penetrate the eastern German market with Western brands. By contrast, Philip Morris rather successfully pursued a strategy of what it called 'regionalization' by relaunching the most popular eastern German cigarette f6 with minimal modifications in the design and material of the cigarette box (*Handelsblatt* 1991b: 15). Imitating this strategy of regionalization, Reemtsma finally decided to relaunch the eastern German brands Cabinet and Juno, leaving their matchless taste untouched. In the food industry, too, popular eastern German brands are celebrating a spectacular come-back. A handful of eastern German products, such as Nordhäuser Korn, a rather tough-grain gin, was even promoted to the status of German market leader by its western German parent firm. In the largest Western retail chain Metro AG, eastern German products accounted for 10 per cent of total turnover in eastern Germany in 1991. However, this share, as well as the number of eastern German products that are offered in the Western retail stores are expected to grow (*Handelsblatt* 1992: 11).

From a regional point of view, this two-way strategy has had important implications. As in the construction industry, the need to monitor the local markets calls for at least some local autonomy and marketing capacities of the branch plants. This circumstance implies the need for at least a minimum number of middle-management and qualified white-collar positions within rural labour markets, which suffer from extraordinarily high levels of unemployment and massive deskilling of the remaining labour force. Additionally, Western investors have been trying to benefit from inputs that, especially in the agricultural sector, are still cheaper in product areas where transport costs and the need for rapid delivery favour local suppliers. Indeed, the relatively high amount of local content in meat, grain, and vegetable production may prevent the complete collapse of eastern German agriculture. Obviously, however, even rather intense regional backward linkages of the food industry to the agricultural sector cannot stave off the massive loss of production capacities and skills in the industrial sector.

Globally Integrated Approaches: Modernizing the Past and Experimenting with the Future

In contrast to these regionally integrated strategies in the construction and the food, beverage, and tobacco industries, the predominant approaches in the automotive, metal-working, electrical engineering, chemical, textile, and clothing industries have been seriously challenged by the socio-economic developments of the early 1990s. The strategies of establishing bridgeheads to East European markets and the attempts to economize on wage differentials did not satisfy initial expectations. Furthermore, the 1993 recession in western Germany forced considerable revision of the optimistic plans simply to extend Western capacities to serve the enlarged German market. Western investors tried to cope with these unforeseen challenges to their eastern German engagement by pursuing strategies that resulted in an unprecedented coexistence of 'modernizing-the-past' and 'experimenting-with-the-future' approaches. More specifically, branch plants in which the Fordist logic of mass assembly is pushed to its organizational and technical limits now stand side by side with branch plants in which the new post-Fordist orthodoxy of lean production is being pioneered. Both approaches require that pre-existing formal and informal networks be largely paralysed. The resulting *tabula rasa* facilitates a smooth implementation of the organizational and technical pre-conditions of these approaches.

Beyond this fundamental similarity in the vigorous demolition of the old *social* web and *cultural* standards and aspirations, Western investors differ in their attitude toward the *industrial* tradition of eastern Germany, the tradition of having a relatively well-qualified labour force. The modernizing-the-past approach aims at massive deskilling of the labour force in order to combine the benefits of imposed social backwardness *and* imposed economic backwardness. Unlike this classical approach to peripheries, the experimenting-with-the-future approach implies a paradoxical combination of social backwardness *and* industrial tradition, in other words, of social and cultural atomization *and* high qualification.

Modernizing the Past: Cathedrals in the Eastern German Deserts

The strategy of combining modern mass-production technology with rather cheap and narrowly qualified or unskilled labour that is placed under the technologically and organizationally most advanced means of corporate control seems just as important in the chemical, electrical engineering, metal-working, textile, and clothing industries. An example is the take-over of the Falkensee plant of the combine called Outer Wear Berlin, a change being executed by Helsa, a western German textile producer. As the disappointing development of the Eastern markets eroded the strategy to establish a bridgehead to Eastern Europe, the Western investor integrated its eastern German plant rather tightly into its European network of production plants. After the former facilities for production of outer wear had been closed down, they were modernized and streamlined for mass production of a rather simple textile component for outer wear. (Ironically, the textile components produced in Falkensee reflect the current mood in eastern Germany: shoulder-pads.) Whereas the production of these components for men's outer wear remains in the Western plants, the eastern German plant produces components exclusively for women's wear, which is much more contingent on seasonal and fashion cycles. Because the eastern German plant is restricted to a rather narrow production step and draws all its input materials from the Western plants, to which they are returned after processing, all the managerial functions have been dissolved in the eastern German plant. Since the transition, which was managed largely by Western managers, a foreman has been in charge of ensuring that the Eastern plant correctly meets the requests and orders from the Western headquarters, which are transmitted daily by Datex-p exchange.

Although real wages in eastern Germany are still lower than those in western Germany because of dissimilar social regulations (Bispinck 1991: 22), the strategy exemplified by Helsa revolves around persisting cost differentials that result from the further fragmentation of the production process. This means reaping the benefits of the technologically most advanced application of the Babbage principle, that is, to benefit from the deskilling and the concomitant wage-reducing effects of the further fragmentation of the production process. This further fragmentation also allows some investors to escape from the highly regulated institutional environment of their employers' association. The integrated production plants of the French Rhône–Poulenc group in western Germany, for example, are members of the employers' association of the chemical industry. The further fragmentation of the production process allowed Rhône-Poulenc to use eastern Germany as the site for a few simple processing procedures that were ascribed to the employers' association of the textile industry. Regardless of development in the wage differential between eastern and western Germany, this manœuvre guarantees continuous cost savings of 15 to 20 per cent because of the different tariff wage levels in the chemical and textile industries.

The regional impacts of the eastern German plants that are integrated into the Western corporate hierarchy basically according to the suggestions of Babbage (1835/1971) are almost negligible. They probably remain cathedrals in the desert. Because eastern German plants are vertically integrated into the production chain of their Western corporations, they create no regional supply opportunities and thus reduce the potential for establishing firms in the region. Moreover, regional linkages, particularly backward linkages, are the most important channel through which technological and organizational change is transmitted. In the Cottbus plant of ABB, for example, approximately 80 per cent of the inputs are supplied by Western plants of the corporation. It is exclusively in the area of construction and maintenance services that ABB's eastern German electrical engineering plant draws material and services from local suppliers. Undoubtedly, the eastern plants of ABB, Rhône-Poulenc, and Helsa employ the most advanced production technologies and stringent quality control systems. However, without business linkages that favour some sort of transfer or demonstration effects, regional firms will hardly be stimulated or encouraged to raise their technological level and improve their organization (Dicken 1990). Moreover, the truncated functional repertoire of the cathedrals in the desert, that is, the lack of decision-making functions, not only fails to provide 'seed-beds' for entrepreneurs but also hinders the development of a significant regional middle class and the culture and society associated with this strata (Massey 1983: 86).

Experimenting with the Future: Eastern Pioneers of Lean Production?

Whereas these cathedrals in the desert seem to be simply an eastern German version of the classical branch-plant syndrome in peripheral regions, the attempts to implement lean production aim at a more subtle combination of the benefits of imposed social backwardness and economic development. Although the complete withdrawal of Mercedes-Benz and the considerable down-scaling of Volkswagen's investment plans reduce the relative importance of this approach, the large automobile manufacturers play a pioneering role in experimentation with this new production concept.

These corporations quickly abandoned their initial intention to continue at least a small share of the production of GDR passenger cars for the Eastern European market, for the Treuhand finally refused to cover the difference between production costs and sales price. The annual subsidies for the production of the Wartburg alone would have amounted to approximately DM 100 million (*Frankfurter Rundschau* 1991: 11). Initially, Volkswagen also intended to shift part of the assembly of its smallest car, the Polo, from its Spanish plant in Pamplona to the eastern German plant. However, as it became ever clearer that the rise of eastern German wage levels would soon make the assembly of small cars in Spain more profitable again, Volkswagen decided to develop its eastern German branch into a major assembly plant for its compact car, the Golf. With the collapse of the market for Eastern products and the prospect of diminishing wage differentials between eastern and western Germany, both Volkswagen and GM proclaimed their eastern German plants 'future-oriented models' for the organization of automobile production (Heidenreich 1992: 350).

Even more pronounced than Volkswagen, GM, largely inspired by the crusade-like anti-Japanese campaigns of its American headquarters, confesses to the topical management fetish of lean production. Although the rhetoric varies from corporation to corporation (Mickler and Walker 1992: 30), they all seem to adhere to the key elements of Toyota's corporate organization, a model that obviously should be beaten with its own weapons. That arsenal includes decentralization of competencies and responsibilities; the introduction of market elements within the corporate organization; reduction of the ratio of in-house production to the generalization of just-in-time supplier networks; the integration of production, maintenance, and quality control; and all the other notoriously repeated new dogmas of automotive production (Womack *et al.* 1990).

For Western investors, eastern Germany appears as an almost perfect location for implementing this new 'one best way'. First, the vague prospect of getting a job in a prestigious Western corporation helps paralyse preexisting social and economic relations and helps demolish the old economic and cultural standards and aspirations regarding such aspects as job security, frequency of changes in work organization, and work intensity. Western managers revel in the opportunities to experiment, opportunities opened up by what one has called the 'salutary culture shock' to which eastern Germans have been exposed. This salutary culture shock allows Western managers to introduce forms of work organization that, under the conditions of the highly institutionalized system of industrial relations and the 'saturated mentality' in western Germany, would otherwise be much more troublesome to implement. This, in the perspective of Western investors, beneficial impact of the social *tabula rasa*, however, has not to be dearly paid for with economic backwardness in terms of qualifications and the wider infrastructure. Instead, establishing a joint corporation would make it possible to create hand-picked 'olympic teams' of highly skilled workers (*Die Zeit* 1992) and a tailor-made transport and communicational infrastructure—at the Treuhand's expense.

The regional impacts of these strategies are rather ambivalent. First, the implementation of new organizational and managerial practices à la Toyota implies decentralized managerial competence at the operative level. The GM engine plant, for example, will be managed decentrally as a profit centre. However, all these plants will be integrated within the European corporate networks, with both their headquarters and the central developmental departments being located outside eastern Germany (Mickler and Walker 1992: 42). Second, a key element of lean production is the reduction of the ratio of in-house production. Volkswagen, for example, intends to keep in-house production to between 25 and 30 per cent in its Saxony plant as compared to 43 per cent in its Western plant (Wolfsburg) (*Handelsblatt* 1991*a*: 13). In order to encourage the development of a competitive regional supplier infrastructure and to guarantee itself quality standards, Volkswagen has also organized 'supplier conferences' to bring together pairs of eastern and western German producers of the same component. These conferences have resulted in approximately forty takeovers and licence agreements that have been approved by Volkswagen. The respective firms can act as suppliers when assembly of the Golf commences (*Industriemagazin* 1991: 37). Although some of these agreements have been jeopardized by the crisis at Volkswagen, this strategy will allow the costs of monitoring and upgrading potential Eastern suppliers to be shifted to the company's Western suppliers. Most probably, the Eastern branches of the Western suppliers will be integrated as second-tier suppliers within the supply pyramid controlled by large Western first-tier suppliers (Doleschal 1991: 49). In any case, the Eastern branch plants of Western suppliers are not equipped with their own research and development facilities. At best, they are provided with small engineering departments for customizing their products and developing special tools for the production process (Lungwitz and Kreißig 1992: 5). In the final analysis, this experimenting-with-the-future approach most probably leads to tightly integrated production complexes that resemble the transplants of Japanese automobile producers in the United States. The extraordinary productivity and quality of these just-in-time integrated networks must be paid for by an equally extraordinary dependence on the destiny of a single corporation.

THE FUTURE OF INSTANT CAPITALISM: EFFICIENCY AT THE COST OF ADAPTABILITY?

So far, the brief history of Western investment in eastern Germany is a history of attempts to cope with unforeseen and rapidly changing circumstances of the transformation process. Almost as soon as expectations for growing markets in the East faded, labour costs rose. On top of that, the 1993 recession in core sectors of the western German economy triggered a considerable withdrawal and temporal stretching of investment projects.

The coping strategies of Western investors resulted in three different patterns of corporate integration and regional embeddedness of their Eastern branch plants. First, regionally responsive strategies in the food, beverage, and tobacco industries and the construction industry, which, by definition, are less vulnerable to external contingencies, favour loose forms of corporate integration combined with regional embeddedness. Because plants in these industries must monitor and serve regional markets, they enjoy at least a minimum degree of local managerial autonomy; for product-related reasons they establish not only regional forward but also regional backward linkages. In a sense, these industries, which at present are among the major investors in eastern Germany, constitute a comparatively stable element in their regional host economies. However, this stability is associated with a rather low degree of organizational and technological dynamism, particularly in the construction industry, and its contribution to the modernization of the industrial structure of the eastern German regional economies is severely limited. The demand for low-qualified labour and for construction materials can neither compensate for the massive loss of industrial skills and industrial production capacities nor stimulate the development of advanced service and manufacturing industries as a core of crystallization.

Second, globally integrated strategies, which are of particular importance in the automotive, electrical engineering, chemical, and textile industries, are resulting in an unprecendented coexistence of modernizing-the-past and experimenting-with-the-future approaches. Branch plants in which the Fordist logic of mass assembly is pushed to its organizational and technical limits are being established side by side with branch plants in which the new post-Fordist orthodoxy of lean production is being pioneered. The modernizing-the-past approach culminates in the construction of regionally isolated cathedrals in the desert, whereas the experimenting-with-the-future approach most probably leads to tightly integrated local production complexes.

The 'proper' implementation of both these approaches not only presupposes a far-reaching paralysis of pre-existing formal economic relations and informal networks, it also inevitably results in a depreciation of the chaos qualifications (Marz 1992) and network capital (Sík 1994) that have accrued in these compensatory social and economic ties. Undoubtedly, these approaches, which aim at benefiting from the so-called salutary culture shock, will, in the final analysis, yield high levels of micro-economic efficiency. In particular, the experiments with a 'lean future' are expected to end up with productivity levels that appeared unattainable in the highly regulated corporatist institutional context and the 'saturated mentality' of western Germany.

However, the price of these gains in micro-economic efficiency probably will have to be a rather limited adaptability of the eastern German economy. First, although the concept of lean production was initially confined to a blueprint for efficient automobile production, it has already been translated into a universally valid catechism that inexorably calls for all sorts of 'organizational slack' (Cyert and March 1963) to be eradicated. Adherence to this canon of the new orthodoxy typically reduces all those 'redundant resources', such as research and development, whose future returns cannot easily be calculated but that are essential for the long-term adaptability of firms. This stubborn reduction of industrial reorganization to cost-cutting measures is currently compounded by the proposals of the federal government to ensure the competitiveness of Germany as a production site.

Second, the long-term adaptability of the eastern German region probably might be restricted not only by the low adaptability of individual firms but also by the nature and intensity of linkages between them. Admittedly, Western investment has led to an increasing diversity of organizational forms in which specific bundles of routines are embedded (Stark 1992, 1993). However, this increase in organizational diversity *per se* does not necessarily enlarge the repertoire of organized solutions to problems of collective action. In an evolutionary perspective, organizational diversity engenders new organizational solutions to new problems only when those different forms of organization are linked and when they then exchange resources and information. In a sense, this exchange between different forms of organization allows for a blurring of boundaries and, hence, provides for a larger 'genetic pool' for the evolution of new organizational mutations that might be more appropriate for coping with new challenges (Grabher 1994).

The current fragmentation of the eastern German economy, however, does not seem very conducive to a blurring of boundaries between different forms of organization. On the contrary, the crisis in western Germany has probably led to a tighter integration of the Eastern branch plants. It might thus even have aggravated the fragmentation of the eastern German economy. Although organizational diversity has increased, its potential is 'frozen' in dissimilar, regionally isolated ways of organizing production. This fragmentation at least partially mirrors the deregionalized production pattern of the old economy based on combines.

NOTE

This chapter is based on approximately seventy interviews with managers and union representatives in the chemical, food, drink and tobacco, metal, textile, and clothing industries in the eastern German federal state of Brandenburg. These interviews are part of the research project 'Decomposition and Privatization of Combines and Regional Development in Eastern Germany' which the author conducted at the Wissenschaftszentrum Berlin für Sozialforschung. The author is grateful to colleagues in working groups 1 and 2 of the European Science Foundation RURE for stimulating discussions of earlier versions of this chapter, which was originally published in the *Netherlands Geographical Studies*, no. 181 (1994), 109–31.

REFERENCES

BABBAGE, C. (1835/1971), *On the Economy of Machinery and Manufactures* (New York: Kelley).

BISPINCK, R. (1991), 'Collective Bargaining in East Germany: Between Economic Restraints and Political Regulation', Paper presented to the 13th Annual Conference of the International Working Party on Labour Market Segmentation, Bremen, July 1991.

CYERT, R., and MARCH, J. G. (1963), *A Behavioural Theory of the Firm* (Englewood Cliffs, NJ: Prentice-Hall).

DICKEN, P. (1990), 'Transnational Corporations and the Spatial Organisation of Production: Some Theoretical and Empirical Issues', in A. Shachar and S. Öberg (eds.), *The World Economy and the Spatial Organisation of Power* (Aldershot: Avebury).

DIW (Deutsches Institut für Wirtschaftsforschung) (1992), *Gesamtwirtschaftliche und unternehmerische Anpassungsprozesse in Ostdeutschland, 5th Report*, DIW-Wochenbericht 12–13 (Berlin: DIW).

DOLESCHAL, R. (1991), 'Daten und Trends der bundesdeutschen Automobilzulieferindustrie', in G. H. Mendius and U. Wendeling-Schröder (eds.), *Zulieferer im Netz zwischen Abhängigkeit und Partnerschaft* (Cologne: Bund).

Frankfurter Rundschau (1991), 'Aus für Wartburg Produktion', 23 Mar., 11.

——(1993), 'Rezession im Westen treibt gefährliche Krisenspirale in Ostdeutschland an', 3 Apr., 9.

GRABHER, G. (1993), *The Embedded Firm: On the Socioeconomics of Industrial Networks* (London: Routledge).

——(1994), *Lob der Verschwendung. Redundanz in der Regionalentwicklung* (Berlin: edition sigma).

HAASE, H.-E. (1990), *Das Wirtschaftssystem der DDR* (Berlin: Berlin Verlag).

Handelsblatt (1991*a*), 'Volkswagen AG: Die ehemaligen Trabi-Werker finden wenig Geschmack an Golf-Montage', 26 Aug., 13.

——(1991*b*), 'Philip Morris GmbH: Die ostdeutsche Marke "f6" ist jetzt die drittgrößte deutsche Zigarettenmarke', 4 Dec., 15.

——(1991*c*), 'Ernährungsindustrie: Die Strategien der Großkonzerne zielen über den Euro-Binnenmarkt hinaus', 31 Dec., 19.

——(1992), 'Ostprodukte: Zaghafter Vorstoß in westdeutsche Ladenregale', 2 Feb., 11.

HÄUßERMANN, H. (1992), 'Regional Perspectives of East Germany after Unification of the Two Germanies', Paper presented to the Conference on 'A New Urban Hierarchy?', University of California, Los Angeles, Apr. 1992.

HEIDENREICH, M. (1992), 'Ostdeutsche Industriebetriebe zwischen Deindustrialisierung und Modernisierung', in M. Heidenreich (ed.), *Krisen, Kader, Kombinate. Kontinuität und Wandel in ostdeutschen Betrieben* (Berlin: edition sigma), 335–64.

——(1993), 'Netzwerke im Transformationsprozeß. Zur Umbildung industrieller Strukturen in Ostdeutschland und Mitteleuropa', MS, University of Bielefeld.

HEINZMANN, J. (1991), 'Strukturwandel altindustrialisierter Regionen in den neuen Bundesländern. Bedingungen und Probleme', *Raumforschung und Raumordnung*, 2–3: 100–6.

HEISE, A., and ZIEGLER, A. (1992), 'Struktur- und Industriepolitik in den ostdeutschen Bundesländern', *WSI-Mitteilungen*, 9: 545–54.

IAW (Institut für angewandte Wirtschaftsforschung) (1990), *Wirtschaftsreport* (Berlin).

IFO (Institut für Wirtschaftsforschung) (1991), *IFO-Schnelldienst*, 16–17.

——(1992*a*), *IFO Schnelldienst*, 6.

——(1992*b*), *IFO Schnelldienst*, 33.

——(1993), *IFO Schnelldienst*, 11–12.

IHK (Industrie- und Handelskammer) and DIHT (Deutscher Industrie- und Handelstag) (1993), 'Wirtschaftslage und Erwartungen. Ergebnisse der DIHT-Umfrage bei den Industrie- und Handelskammern', Bonn, Feb.

Industriemagazin (1991), 'DDR-Autozulieferindustrie: Rette sich wer kann', 5 Oct.

IW (Institut der Deutschen Wirtschaft) (1991), *IW-Trends* (June).

IWH (Institut für Wirtschaftsforschung Halle) (1992), *IWH-Kurzinformation*, 7–8: 6–8.

LUNGWITZ, R., and KREIßIG, V. (1992), 'Sozialer und wirtschaftlicher Wandel in der Automobilindustrie der neuen Bundesländer', in M. Heidenreich (ed.), *Krisen, Kader, Kombinate. Kontinuität und Wandel in ostdeutschen Betrieben* (Berlin: edition sigma), 173–87.

MARETZKE, S., and MÖLLER, F.-O. (1992), 'Wirtschaftlicher Strukturwandel und regionale Strukturprobleme', *Geographische Rundschau*, 44/3: 154–9.

MARZ, L. (1992), 'Dispositionskosten des Transformationsprozesses. Werden mentale Orientierungsnöte zum wirtschaftlichen Problem?', *Aus Politik und Zeitgeschichte*, 24: 3–14.

MASSEY, D. (1983), 'Industrial Restructuring as Class Restructuring: Productive Decentralisation and Local Uniqueness', *Regional Studies*, 17: 73–89.

MICKLER, O., and WALKER, B. (1992), 'Die ostdeutsche Automobilindustrie im Prozeß der Modernisierung und personellen Anpassung', in M. Heidenreich (ed.), *Krisen, Kader, Kombinate. Kontinuität und Wandel in ostdeutschen Betrieben* (Berlin: edition sigma), 29–44.

MINISTERIUM FÜR WIRTSCHAFT, MITTELSTAND UND TECHNOLOGIE (1992), *Jahreswirtschaftsbericht Brandenburg 92* (Potsdam).

MORGAN, J. P. (1992), *Investing in Eastern Germany: The Second Year of Unification* (Frankfurt: Morgan).

NEUMANN, L. (1993), 'Decentralization and Privatization in Hungary: Towards

Supplier Networks?', in G. Grabher (ed.), *The Embedded Firm: On the Socio-economics of Industrial Networks* (London: Routledge), 179–201.

QUEVIT, M., DESTERBECQ, H., and NAUWELAERS, C. (1992), 'General Theoretical Framework for Mastering the Interaction between TNC's Strategic Behaviour and Regional Restructuring in Europe', MS, Université Catholique de Louvain.

SÍK, E. (1994), 'Network Capital in Capitalist, Communist and Post-communist Societies', *International Contributions to Labour Studies*, 4: 73–93.

Sozialpolitische Umschau (1992), 'Wegbruch des Osthandels', 9 Nov.

Der Spiegel (1992), 'Autoindustrie: Ganz andere Töne', 2 Feb., 86.

STARK, D. (1992), 'From System Identity to Organizational Diversity', *Contemporary Sociology*, 21/3: 299–304.

——(1993), *Recombinant Property in East European Capitalism*, Discussion paper no. FS I 93-103, Forschungsschwerpunkt Arbeitsmarkt und Beschäftigung (Berlin: Wissenschaftszentrum Berlin für Sozialforschung).

Süddeutsche Zeitung (1993), 'Auf niedrigen Touren über die Durststrecke', 23 Feb., 18.

Der Tagesspiegel (1992), 'Audi wechselt nach Ungarn', 26 Nov., 23.

VOSKAMP, V., and WITTKE, V. (1990), 'Aus Modernisierungsblockaden werden Abwärtsspiralen—zur Reorganisation von Betrieben und Kombinaten der ehemaligen DDR', *SOFI-Mitteilungen*, 18: 12–30.

WEBER, M. (1922/1978), *Economy and Society: An Outline of Interpretive Sociology*, ed. G. Roth and C. Wittch, trans. E. Fischhoff *et al.*, 2 vols. (Berkeley: University of California Press).

Wirtschaftswoche (1992a), 'Napoleonische Attacken. Ostdeutschland—Sprungbrett für ausländische Konzerne', 22 May, 132–5.

——(1992b), 'Ostdeutschland: Mit Vollgas zurück', 20 Nov., 99.

——(1993), 'Bauindustrie Ost: Versierte Sanierer', 9 Apr., 112–13

WOMACK, J. P., JONES, D. T., and ROSS, D. (1990), *The Machine that Changed the World* (New York: HarperPerennial).

Die Zeit (1992), 'Schlank und Rank—Deutsche Industrielle übernehmen die Methoden der Japaner', 14 Feb., 42.

II

ENTREPRENEURIAL NETWORKS:

New Firm Formation

5

Network Dynamics of New Firm Formation: *Developing Russian Commodity Markets*

JUDITH B. SEDAITIS

INTRODUCTION

The foundings of new market organizations in formerly command economies has proven to be a complex institutional process. In Russia particularly, the state has continued to dominate economic activity and most new
market organizations have been spin-off firms hived from state institutions
(Joskow *et al.* 1993). At the same time, new start-up firms were created by
a growing number of endogenous, new Russian entrepreneurs. In either
case, new, private firms depended on state organizations to provide important financial, logistical, and political support (Johnson and Kroll 1991:
303). New start-ups, therefore, faced clear institutional disadvantages to
state-embedded spin-offs, but were also not without particular advantages.
This chapter contrasts the founding process of start-ups with spin-offs using
the development of post-Soviet commodity exchange markets as an illustration. By focusing on the extensiveness of ties among founders, it suggests
that social ties are key to organizational outcomes of new firms in two
primary respects. Firstly, the social structure of founding networks regulate
the scope of individual action as the stronger the ties among actors, the
more narrow their latitude for autonomous action (Burt 1983; Granovetter
1985). The more tight-knit or dense the ties in a network, the greater
autonomy and freedom of individual action is constrained. Secondly, the
diversity of founders' ties shape the institutional embeddedness of the new
firm they create. As new organizations emerge, they draw on the legacy of
founders' institutional ties as their initial source of links to the external
environment (Stinchcombe 1965; Wiewel and Hunter 1985). Thus, the social network density of founders shapes both internal organizational processes as well as external, inter-firm ties. As a result, structural differences in
founding processes run deep throughout the early period of organizational
development to shape the way new organizations fit into the overall process
of market transformation.

Following a brief overview of the emergence of new firms in Russia, the model of founding network density and its effects on performance is elaborated. The development of post-Soviet markets is used to illustrate how structural imperatives make the benefits of high- versus low-density networks mutually exclusive. A trade-off is suggested, therefore, between the advantages of new firms, hived-off state agencies, and those initiated outside the dominant structure of state authority. In contrast to the negative popular image of new entrepreneurs as glorified crooks, this research finds that the sparse and flexible embedding of newcomers actually enables them to provide better opportunities to the dominant, value-adding state sector.

THE EMERGENCE OF NEW MARKET ORGANIZATION IN RUSSIA

The Soviet political élite itself introduced the first alternative to complete state ownership in the organizational form of semi-private 'co-operative' ventures. While they provided a realm of relative freedom from stringent state regulations, the overall economy was still dominated by state 'orders' and centralized control. As a result, the majority of technically 'semi-private' co-operatives were created by state enterprises as fully integrated units within the state command system (Jones and Moskoff 1991). More autonomous organizations began to emerge only in April 1990 as smaller spin-offs from large state enterprises in response to a series of decrees that offered tax holidays to new or small-scale organizations (Simon and Kroll 1991). In addition, a revised law on state enterprises was passed in 1990 that allowed state enterprises to form new joint-stock companies and gave them more freedom and control over their finances and outputs.

Combined with an official policy to undermine the traditional planning authorities, legislative reforms prompted a wave of spontaneous privatization in which workers and managers simply used state funds to create new private ventures at low prices or as interest-free loans (World Bank 1992: 85). The number of 'privately' employed persons began to increase dramatically in Russia, from 0.2 per cent of the working population in September 1990 to 1.2 per cent one year later (*Ekonomika i zhizn* 1992). Privatization efforts increased further in 1991 when the first series of decrees on privatization were released in December to regulate and *de facto* legitimize the growing transfer of state assets into private hands. By 1992, 23 per cent of all Russian employees worked in the non-state sector and about 80,000 new businesses were registered. In particular, industries that dealt in highly divisible or substitutable goods privatized themselves (Sapir 1994). By mid-1992, key, 36 per cent of enterprises in construction and 40 per cent of enterprises in light industry had restructured themselves into joint-stock companies (Joskow *et al.* 1993).

For a number of reasons, the only areas in which new organizational forms appeared in any significant number in Russia were the service and trading sectors. As such, some observers refer to the transition period as one of 'mercantile capitalism' in which trade and arbitrage are the only kinds of economic activity that could flourish (Ardishvili and Cardozo 1993; Burawoy and Krotkov 1992). They argue that in the absence of an asset-holding middle-class, the interest and ability to move from fluid and high-risk venture lacks institutional support. With no investment banking system to provide venture capital or state policies committed to private sector development, potential entrepreneurs lacked access to financial credits and the cash-flow necessary to meet high start-up costs of productive ventures (Gibb 1993; Murrell 1992*a*). In addition, the fear of competition among politically powerful state industries often resulted in administrative barriers to entry against new organizational forms in the industrial sectors (Boycko *et al.* 1993). Finally, two aspects of the early reform period in particular made trading popular: the two-tiered pricing structure of gradual price liberation, and the breakdown of established inter-republican trade.

In early 1991 Gorbachev initiated a cautious reform policy that gradually lifted price ceilings on state-made goods while allowing free prices on goods made in the 'private' sphere. As a result, a two-tiered market emerged of low, regulated state prices alongside the higher, 'free' prices and offered great profits to sellers at the margin. Smaller and less state-embedded new firms could more easily circumvent laws to the contrary and engage in lucrative arbitrage with little fear of official retribution.

Since the barrier intended to separate economic activities between state and non-state spheres proved largely porous, prices began to escalate sharply. By the end of 1992 wholesale prices increased thirty-four times, while retail prices went up twenty-five times (*Ekonomika i zhizn*, 4 January 1993: 13–15). In response to escalating prices, the state continued to save ailing enterprises by printing more money. It fuelled a spiralling inflation that generally made the local currency an increasingly less attractive medium of exchange while promoting bartered exchanges. It also inhibited capital investment in long-term production-oriented activity. Soviet domestic production began to suffer a steep decline and by 1992 had dropped by roughly 35 per cent.[1]

To deal with growing shortages, separate regional jurisdictions such as republics, regions, and even large cities engaged in a 'war of sovereignty' by erecting customs posts or limiting the sale of products to non-residents. These new, regional trade barriers were especially detrimental to union-wide industrial production since they disrupted established supply lines of the old system. As a result, small pockets of isolated and specific shortages developed that trading companies could best exploit. In turn, commodity exchange markets provided an efficient arena for traders to meet and was one of the most popular new market forms to appear in the wake of economic reform.

NETWORK DYNAMICS OF NEW FIRM FOUNDINGS

Two modes of thought on the foundings of new market organizations figure in the current debate on market transitions. Murrell and others promote new start-up firms by newcomers to management on the grounds that new entrepreneurs provide a more promising organizational 'fresh start' than former state managers, who are ostensibly steeped in dysfunctional Soviet-era practices (Gibb 1993; Murrell 1992*a,b*). In contrast, others suggest that slower adaptation by former state officials includes key benefits of established trust and trading patterns that in fact are especially valuable to new firms under the highly unstable conditions of market transition (Solinger 1991). This debate, however, misses two important points: firstly, the economic focus on individuals eschews a social analysis of new firm creation. Secondly, its focus on the relative benefits and constraints of individual state actors is misplaced since state actors under socialism were ubiquitous.

A social analysis of foundings shows that the founders of spin-offs generally constitute a different social group from those new entrepreneurs that created start-up firms. Spin-offs from state structures were particularly prevalent among top-level administrative or planning offices. Unlike production or banking administrators, spin-off founders had less access to fungible goods that could retain value in the radically shifting economy. Their strongest asset was their network capital in terms of their established relationships with people in positions of power. As ministries and planning agencies ostensibly disappeared, therefore, their internal structures resurfaced in new organizations. Thus, state administrators drew on their experience and strengths by preserving old ties through dense founding networks. In addition to the pull of capitalizing on their strengths, planning officials were also pushed into action by the fact that many of their agencies were already earmarked for collapse under Gorbachev.

The institutional domains of planners and most top-level administrators provided services that are obsolete in a market-oriented economy. By leaving a sinking ship *en masse*, they could extend the life and value of their experience, norms, and practices even as their formal institutional context disintegrated. From the rubble of the industrial branch ministries, for instance, private trade associations and other 'private' organizations emerged that usually included all or most of the former ministries' constituent state enterprises (Joskow *et al.* 1993). The Construction Materials Association, for instance, included 90 per cent of all the enterprises that formerly belonged to the Ministry of Construction Materials (Kroll 1991). Similarly, whole departments throughout Gossnab, the huge state supply structure, formally left the collapsing organization to resurface together as managers and founders of the new commodity exchange markets in their regions (Sedaitis 1994).

Administrators also figured prominently in the founding networks of start-up firms, especially young former activists from the Communist Youth League. In addition, however, survey research paints a profile of new entrepreneurs as largely former academics and researchers (Grischenko *et al.* 1992). The state budgetary crisis cut deeply into the Russian scientific community and by 1993 the decreasing support for research, sinking salaries, and the persistence of bureaucratic meddling sent over 30 per cent of the science and research community out of state service to work abroad or in the private sector (*Ekonomika i zhizn*, no. 18, 1993: 1). New careers as brokers or distributors in particular attracted opportunity-seeking career-changers (Sterlin and Kozlov 1993; Kolobanov 1991). The overwhelming majority of brokers surveyed had been working in the private sector for less than six months as at October 1991, while only 1 per cent had commercial experience before the onset of market reforms. The majority were over 30 years of age and 89 per cent had a college education. Thus, contrary to the popular image of shady young speculators and former black-marketeers, new Russian entrepreneurs were generally well-educated opportunity-seekers new to commercial activity.

The second deficiency in the dominant perspective comes from pitting state actors against new entrepreneurs. In socialist economies that were dominated by the state sector, almost everyone was a state actor of some kind. In addition, former top state officials did not resist reform but spearheaded the privatization process across the Eastern bloc (Staniszkis 1991; Stark 1992), taking a leading role in exploiting market opportunities for which others argue they were uniquely well suited (Nee and Lian 1992: 13). A key factor in the potential of new market organizations is not the extent to which it was founded by former state managers, therefore, but the process by which founders came together.

Emerging new entrepreneurs could not find adequate financial, material, or political support in the fledgling Russian private sector alone. To succeed under conditions of high political uncertainty, new entrepreneurs needed to reach widely and establish relations with powerful actors and resource-rich institutions in order to supplement the limited resources of their own circle of co-workers and colleagues. While most start-up initiatives were sparked from outside positions of state authority, therefore, they still needed connections to those positions (Nee 1992). The exceptions were 'Mom and Pop' family businesses that generally operated in a lost-cost niche bounded by the confines of close and affective ties (Kozminski 1993), but even these required implicit state approval. While a core group of colleagues, friends, or family members were usually responsible for germinating the initial project, competitive new start-up founders balanced their strong ties to one another by reaching out to new actors for a founding network of overall low social density but great diversity of individual and institutional ties. In turn, their aggressive outreach strategy attracted other opportunity-seeking actors (Burt 1992*a*). Thus, low-density funding networks of necessity created low-density market organization if they hoped to compete with more state-embarked firms.

Because most managers were initially strangers to one another, the breadth and quality of their skills were unknown. This newness necessarily makes the low-density organization a *self*-defining institution (Eccles and Crane 1988) in which members initially set the style, pace, and parameters of action themselves. Their internal structure allows and facilitates aggressive strategies that seek out the greatest opportunities unencumbered by prior institutional obligations. For the same reason, however, no one founder is obligated to them and they do not have the luxury of passive dependence but are constrained to pursue resources actively. As a result, low-density founding networks tend to make for organizations with flat and flexible internal structures that are embedded in wide and shallow institutional ties. With minimal constraints both internally and externally, they are relatively free to pursue market opportunities in a manner some have labelled as 'shark' behaviour (Kozminski 1993). As the case-study on commodity markets shows, however, market development overall is actually furthered by the creative destruction of aggressive strategies and rent-seeking behaviour that low-density founding networks facilitate.

Dense founding networks were informed by a completely different rationale. In contrast to the active, future-oriented rationale of low-density networks, high-density founding networks emerged from a process rooted in tradition, loyalty, and the memory of past accomplishments and processes.

The social denseness of ties in networks of spin-off founders captures the process by which they adapt their old set of professional ties to a new institutional context. Because they tend to know the same people from the same professional backgrounds that they shared in common, high-density network founders choose new personnel from an initially narrow and constrained institutional range. As a result, their founding process yields new firms that tend to prolong old trading patterns since they inherit the strong ties and institutional embedding of their parent organizations. Western research suggests that prior experience working together makes for less conflict among the managers of spin-off firms (Eisenhardt and Bourgeois 1988). However, prolonged tenure together can promote a false sense of the viability of shared past practices that forestalls openness to new opportunities.

In both models of the founding process, the founding network reproduces itself in the organization it creates, facilitating a different type of organizational structure and strategy. In both cases, the social structures that result let actors draw on their strengths. The dynamics of low-density

TABLE 5.1. *Trade-off benefits between high- and low-density foundings*

	Founding network density	
Organization traits	High	Low
Internal		
Range of talent	Limited	Diverse
Internal complicance	High	Low
Creative capacity	Low	High
Decision-making style	Controlled	Flexible
Rationale	Tradition	Profit
Institutional		
Degree of reliability	High	Low
Access of resources	Narrow	Diverse
Legitimacy	High	Low
Institutional relations	Habitual	Competitive
Manoeuvrability	Encumbered	Facile

foundings provide profit-seekers with the freedom and flexibility to respond quickly and innovatively in pursuit of shifting opportunities. In contrast, high-density networks facilitate a steadier and less opportunistic approach that helps professional networks retain power while slowly integrating their resources into the transformation process. In fact, the strength of one approach defines the weaknesses of the other and suggests a trade-off between the value of each of the kind summarized in Table 5.1. Thus, sparsely embedded, low-density organizations enjoy greater immediate returns on investments from their manœuvrability and more varied access to resources. At the same time, their diversity in turn provides little basis for social cohesion and trust to stem the risks of opportunism. They trade internal controls and reliable inter-firm relations for maximum profitability. High-density networks, on the other hand, inherit institutional legitimacy as they help maintain the viability of past institutional arrangements but suffer a constricted range of talent and limited profitability. They make less money initially, not because of any personal lack in the individuals involved, but because the initial structure of their founding facilitated a less aggressive strategy and diverse embedding than the structure of low-density firm-founding.

A STRUCTURAL MODEL OF MUTUALLY EXCLUSIVE BENEFITS AND CONSTRAINTS

The Advantages and Disadvantages of Low-Density Forms

Unencumbered by specific inputs, obligations, or production needs of key state founders, low-density new firms were flexible enough to move goods and change strategies quickly, an essential trait to economic survival under market transitions (Hisrich and Grachev 1993). Barter as the preferred mode of exchange disadvantaged firms locked upstream in the production flow. The asset-specific and often antiquated domestic industrial inputs they produced for founding state enterprises were of little interest to anyone else (Hendley 1992). In contrast, firms unburdened by production obligations could more freely pursue access to the most tradable items, such as popular retail goods or valuable natural resources. Holdover restrictions on foreign trade hampered the initial ability of state institutions to deal directly with exporters, while non-state firms could contract with foreigners from the very onset of reforms and establish joint-venture companies. As a result, they also had better access to the more tradable Western imports and technologies. It was perhaps ironic, then, that sparsely embedded firms could more directly serve market demand and best exploit the lucrative opportunities in the disruption of established distribution patterns than state-embedded agencies and their dependent spin-offs.

The disadvantages of the low-density form centre on issues of control. The high autonomy of individual managers made commitment to their firm hard to enforce, especially in light of the shifting opportunities in the unstable environment of market transformation. Firms born of low-density managerial networks, therefore, were more vulnerable to internal opportunism, malfeasance, and high turnover as individuals used their networks to further individual self-interest. In the absence of strong ties and the trust and co-operation they engender, low-density firms were less protected by the high uncertainty of their environment. It also left them bereft of political sponsorship that was more readily available to state-embedded firms.

Typical of most modern states, the post-Soviet governments formally did not let firms exist without their assent, even in the turbulence of market reforms. The process of registration often posed barriers to entry for outsider new private or co-operative firms (Jones and Moskoff 1991) whose need for legitimacy was heightened by the break-up of the Soviet empire. Newly empowered jurisdictions generated new and disparate import–export policies, tariffs, and customs all requiring some official sanctions. In addition, the lack of developed legal frameworks of property rights and contract law left private ventures under the constant risk of non-compliance and even state appropriation with little access to formal arbitration or grievance procedures (Gibb 1993; Hendley 1992b). Thus, outsider, entrepreneurial firms needed at least benign state approval even to formally begin the founding process. State assistance was also usually required in some form to meet extensive start-up costs such as procuring facilities, equipment, lines of communication, and other vital services that state-embedded firms could access more easily.

The Advantages and Disadvantages of the High-Density Model

The strongest advantage of high-density new firms sprang from the social capital they were created to preserve. Subsequent to break-up of the Soviet Union, formal state structures began to dissolve seriously or disappear completely. Although formal institutions were collapsing, however, the ties between former colleagues remained and gave high-density ventures access to the same goods and service their members and founders controlled in the former economy. The legacy of old ties served to funnel extensive and important logistical support systems such as state banking, transportation, and storage that were vital to serious commerce or any trade that involved any great distance or volume. In the absence of a new, co-ordinated banking system, for example, inter-republican balance of payments was difficult to maintain (Panagariya 1993). Many former republics adopted different and non-convertible currencies that Russian banks often did not accept. In lieu of access to rouble credit, new firms outside the Russian Republic would have to go to great lengths and risks in order to make payment, such as smuggling in their own roubles to conclude a trade and risking the confiscation of their funds. State-embedded new firms could inherit the trading pathways, service providers, and high-placed trouble-shooters that gave them an advantage in negotiating the many logistical obstacles of business in the early reform period.

While the commonality of shared social ties provides many benefits, however, it also creates an insular system of accepted routines that limits openness and awareness of new ideas and possibilities (Granovetter 1973). Even firms that were technically competitive are often unable to engage in an aggressive strategy to make the most of their potential. Where the routines of the command economy are preserved by the transfer of an intact management team, a passive attitude dependent on outside aid or assistance often prevails (Kozminski 1993; Murrell 1992*a*). Kozminski found that it came as a great shock to many former managers of state enterprises that they could and should seek out new clients, target a market, and actively strategize to achieve and maintain a market position. In turn, the dense structure of state-embedded firms makes relearning more difficult.

Actors in high-density ventures know of each other's professional expertise and were often brought into the new firm to provide the same services they performed in their old settings. In this manner, shared past histories constrained the range of future possibilities. By providing high job definition, old ties limit organizational flexibility and maintain a 'segmented' system of circumscribed action and responsibility that limits the potential of management to respond creatively to the new environment and the problems it poses (Kanter 1983). Industrial ministry administrators, for example, retained control over their constituent enterprises in part by promising that as members of the new trade association, they would reap the benefits of

newly devised policies for integrated investment and technological development in addition to the continuation of old services. However, the new
policies never materialized (Joskow *et al.* 1993). However daunting the task
of innovative responses to systemic change, it was not facilitated by the
highly dense network of former administrators that founded the new trade
associations. In turn, the narrow range of inter-firm ties typical of high-
density firms also restricts openness and freedom.

The greater dependency of high-density networks on a narrow band of
resource-holders limits both the technical and normative options available
to them. The diversity of material inputs available to dependent new institutions is generally limited to those commodities readily accessible to their
founders, such as goods that founders either administered or produced
themselves. Material dependence also makes it difficult for them to disre-
gard the needs and norms of their key resource-holders. Burawoy shows,
for example, the reluctance of spin-off new timber firms to shift to more
competitive but unstable new private suppliers. By doing so they would
have risked alienating their still-powerful former ministry structure on
which the firms depended for a steady stream of lumber. In turn, however,
the former ministry demanded compliance to its own needs (Burawoy and
Krotov 1992). While state structures were formally destroyed, they still
stood in the centre of inter-firm relations and could dictate terms that
limited the potential of spin-off ventures too dependent to venture out on
their own. Thus, the high-density model enjoys important and tangible
benefits of state patronage at the risk of forgoing larger and more profitable
markets. As such, their more freely roaming low-density counterparts could
more directly facilitate the emergence of a market economy overall, as the
case-study of commodity markets helps to illustrate.

AN ILLUSTRATION: THE CASE-STUDY OF DEVELOPING
RUSSIAN COMMODITY MARKETS

The commodity exchange market was a popular new organizational form
particularly well suited to the peculiarities of early market reform. Commodity markets provided a open arena in which buyers could meet sellers
and begin to remedy the isolation of state managers whose range of trading
partners was narrowly restricted in the command economy. More importantly, commodity markets also provided the opportunity to channel state
assets into private wealth (Yakovlev 1991). Soon they began to mushroom
across the whole Soviet Union. The first market appeared in Moscow in
October 1989. By January 1991, ninety-five markets were registered in the
Russian Republic alone. By January 1992 the number of Russian markets
doubled to 201. However, as the turbulent period of partial reform began to
stabilize in 1992,[2] arbitrage was no longer as lucrative as it had been. Also,

the market form was a victim of its own success. Traders circumvented the markets that first brought them together and market sales suffered a 50 per cent drop by the end of 1992. Finally, the emergence of *ex post* regulations forced many new markets either to disappear or to transform themselves into different organizational forms. The case-study of commodity markets, therefore, can illustrate how different types of foundings weather the full cycle of new firm foundings, development, and decline.

At the onset, the typical Russian commodity exchange, or *birzha*, had little in common with its Western counterpart. The commodities initially traded in Russia and in other former republics fluctuated wildly both in kind and in quality. Although managers of commodity exchanges tried to organize trade mostly in traditional commodities such as grains, metals, and oil, by the end of 1990 still only 20 per cent of all the goods traded were of the traditional commodities traded. Instead, traders in the first two years of market operation could find different products on different days ranging from flour and honey to women's blouses, screwdrivers, aeroplanes, and even whole factories.

With no standardized product list, let alone a system of delivery or quality control, the level of uncertainty in contracting at the new commodity markets was extremely high. The same commodity was often listed for days only to disappear once a buyer was finally found. Some exchanges used the old Soviet planners' code to classify and list the various commodities and a few adopted an international system of coding. The large majority of exchanges, however, used no classification system at all, leaving brokers to best describe their products in as few words as possible. In addition, exchange managers had no way of monitoring behaviour or of contracting compliance. In order to mediate trade and collect its fees, the exchange organization relied on brokers to report the deals they concluded, but had few ways of ensuring compliance. Thus, the typical new exchange reflected the wild or 'frontier' capitalism that defined the new private sphere and initially resembled more a bazaar or farmer's market than the Chicago Board of Trade. Despite the general lack of standardization, however, palpable differences in the operation of different markets emerged at the onset. Some markets were beehives of communication and energy while others were models of quiet and order only occasionally punctuated by flurries of activity. To uncover the root of clear differences, the structural characteristics of twelve founding networks were examined.

When the density among founders is high, fewer of them are needed to act as contact people to the world outside their organization. Since everybody knows everyone else, their connections are redundant and increasing the number of contacts does not bring in any more new resources or people to the market. In low-density networks, on the other hand, network members are relative strangers who can each link their new firm to different resources. There is generally an inverse relationship, therefore, between the

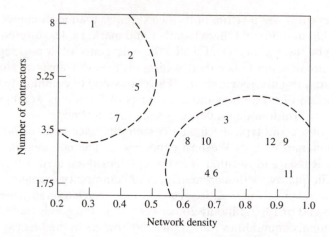

FIG. 5.1. Founding network density and contractors. Plot = exchange market code ($n = 12$). Under appropriate sampling conditions, the network density correlation would be -0.78; $p = 0.003$. These and further statistics are given as points of reference only

density of a network and its openness to the outside environment, which is reproduced in Fig. 5.1 by the twelve markets surveyed.

As indicated in Figure 5.1, founding networks clustered at each end of network density. We distinguish the clusters into the two analytically distinct models of the founding process. The upper left-hand cluster is made up of markets with loosely connected and resourceful organizers which are characteristic of 'entrepreneurial' networks (Burt 1992b). The clusters in the bottom right are more 'bureaucratic': they feature more closely knit organizers who engaged less actively in the development of their commodity exchange. The structure of the founding network shaped both the internal characteristics and their external, institutional embeddings of new markets that diverged radically in how they participated in the overall process of market transformation.

Internal Processes: The Organizational Risks of Diversity and Structural Autonomy

Consistent with the logic of sparse, competitive networks, the founders in sparse networks came from more diverse functional backgrounds than the individual founders in dense networks. As Table 5.2 indicates, more than half the dense founders were trained in various Soviet management institutes and over a quarter had received largely technical vocational training. In contrast, the organizers of sparse exchange organizers were academically more accomplished: almost all those surveyed (90 per cent) were college-

TABLE 5.2. *Educational background of market founders* (n = 110)

Education	Entrepreneurial market	Bureaucratic market
Management (institution)	4	26
Engineering (university)	5	9
Economics	4	7
Computer science	5	0
Social science	6	0
Humanities	2	0
Technical high school	6	7
Theoretical physics–mathematics	9	1
TOTAL	41	50
Missing	15	3

educated and many had advanced degrees. Their backgrounds spanned a range of professions from art teacher to computer programmer with some predominance of researchers in theoretical physics (23 per cent).

Many of the founders in sparse networks had already diversified their experience earlier in their careers by shifting to the co-operative sector, which was the only non-state arena in the very beginning of reform. This connection was the first experience of most of the sparsely linked founders with commerce and the business world and allowed them the opportunity to begin accumulating the capital they would need as founders of commodity markets. An early founder of the second largest Moscow commodity market, for example, was first drawn into commercial activity while he was employed as a history teacher by the owner of a small co-operative. The owner was eventually arrested for his gold-mining activities but the commodity organizer went on to build a small construction empire before turning to the project of building a commodity exchange. Another entrepreneurial exchange organizer from a sparse market in Kaliningrad started a co-operative venture 'on the side' with his students from the local university where he taught physics. They amassed substantial capital and attracted the interest of other local co-operateurs by selling his patented hydraulic gauge. Officially a science lecturer, he launched a parallel career as a co-op owner that left him well positioned to initiate the development of a local commodity market.[3]

The more diverse founders in low-density networks drew in equally diverse managers to create flexible organizational structures that bore the strains of loosely controlled organizations: particularly in terms of management instability and general non-compliance. Two years after the emergence of the first exchange markets, the leading figures at all four entrepreneurial, low-density markets had left their exchanges for new projects. In different ways, they explained impatience with the prognosis for Russian commodity markets and readily acknowledged that their markets were initially created to access 'a good opportunity to make a lot of money quickly'. In light of shifting opportunities, two of the chief executive officers left their markets to create other private firms and two went on to pursue careers in politics. In contrast, the chief executive officers at the dense, bureaucratic markets were still at their posts at the end of 1992.

Denser networks were linked with better compliance both in terms of broker observance of market procedures and in terms of the ability of brokers and their clients to follow through on the contracts made. Informally, brokers at entrepreneurial markets suggested that as much as 50 to 70 per cent of their trading went unreported to market managers in order to avoid paying them and heavy state taxes, which was consistent with the data collected from market managers. In contrast, brokers registered 75–80 per cent of the deals they made at dense, bureaucratic markets. Other, more anecdotal, evidence elaborates on the fact that compliance was a bigger problem at sparse markets.

By early 1992 the dwindling clientele and impending loss of investment opportunities demanded by new laws heightened the financial cost of unreported trading. In response, the larger and centrally located markets, of both dense and sparse networks, changed their membership format. All the sparse, entrepreneurial markets dropped the Western style of selling brokers' seats and instituted a fee system that required no monitoring. Instead, brokers paid the market organization an average 25,500 roubles per month simply for access to commodity listings and 'market prices'. The dense markets, however, instituted this change later and charged traders a nominal fee roughly six times less than sparse markets required.

One difference in the operating procedures at markets observed anecdotally might account for the greater compliance at dense markets, in which generally greater intervention and rule-setting was observed. During interviews at one bureaucratic market in Moscow, for instance, managers explained that they 'monitored brokers' trading patterns to ensure a balance between buying and selling'. If a brokerage firm continued to buy and not sell products (which was by far the most common 'imbalance'), it was barred from trading activity for a month. At another dense Moscow market, brokers reported that they 'constantly turn to management for help' in procuring necessary documents, credit, or other logistical issues important for the success of a transaction. The bureaucratic markets surveyed had special access to necessary official support and documentation, such as licences needed to export natural resources and other valuable goods. For example, one of the bureaucratic markets sampled was the first and only exchange to establish an official clearing-house backed by the Central Bank of Russia (*Kommersant*, 9 (1992)). Similarly, both Moscow state-made markets in the survey were promised exclusive rights to auction the quota for certain natural resources that other, less well-connected market organizations would then compete for.

External Links: The Constraints of State-Embeddedness

Founders in more homogeneous networks tended to have fewer and stronger ties to founding institutions. As Table 5.3 indicates, a majority (68 per cent) of primary institutional ties in dense networks linked them to state planning or administrative agencies. While ties in non-state commercial activity provided common ground for entrepreneurial organizers, the institutional embedding of their markets was less concentrated. A small majority (37.5 per cent) of primary ties linked low-density founders' co-operative ventures which they usually owned. Initial institutional links also included ties to research institutions (18 per cent), government organs (8 per cent), commercial banks (8 per cent), or manufacturing enterprises (8 per cent).

As a result of their relatively more concentrated institutional embedding, high-density markets were also more dependent on a smaller group of resource-holders than low-density markets. This dependence was reflected in the range and types of goods they generally featured. Overall, they offered fewer commodities and less variety than goods brought to sparse, low-density markets. Daily transactions involved roughly 426 different commodities each month at the low-density markets analysed, where no particular good constituted more than roughly 6 per cent of the total market trade. In comparison, the high-density markets traded a monthly average of only 193 different commodities, which were dominated by a narrow and specific repertoire of goods that reflected the depth of dependence on the light industrial hardware controlled by their state founding organizations.

The lion's share traded at high-density markets consisted of assorted light

TABLE 5.3. *Institutional embeddedness of commodity exchange markets*

Source of organizers	Entrepreneurial market	Bureaucratic market
Government organs	5	12
State wholesale	2	25
Service ministries	4	5
Manufacturing sector	5	0
Official youth organs	4	2
Research institutions	10	5
Co-operative sector	21	3
Banking sector	5	0
TOTAL	56	52
Missing data	0	2

equipment and consumer goods, which together constituted over 50 per cent of all the goods traded at the dense markets. The category of light equipment refers to nuts and bolts, tools, parts, housewares, and light equipment such as hand drills and saws that state enterprises could trade at the local level and that constituted the bulk of decentralized supplies controlled by the parent founding organizations of these bureaucratic markets. In contrast, the entrepreneurial markets featured a greater variety of consumer goods that also included imported clothing, state-of-the-art technology, Western cigarettes, and other popular goods.

Despite the fact that most natural resources were closely monitored by the state for their strategic importance, the entrepreneurial markets traded twice the proportion of metal products and over three times more energy-rich materials, such as coal, oil, and gas, than did their bureaucratic counterparts. They also sold many more cars and more 'high-tech' electronic equipment such as personal computers and copying and facsimile machines. The bureaucratic, high-density markets, on the other hand, sold no computers at all; their electronics category consisted primarily in domestic audio equipment. Not surprisingly, the array of high-ticket, popular goods at low-density markets made them much more profitable. More surprising perhaps were the clientele they served and the overall role in the process of creating a new economic system.

Market Performance and Clientele

Not surprisingly, low-density, entrepreneurial exchange markets were commercially much more successful than their high-density counterparts. They drew more brokers and more marketable commodities; hence, entrepreneurial markets concluded twice the number of deals during their first two years of operation of bureaucratic markets. The marked success of entrepreneurial markets in their first year of operation was compounded by the fact that they also traded at higher prices. Thus, low-density markets spun new ties widely to successfully pursue their goal of profitability. Their commercial success supports the popular imagination of new Russian entrepreneurs as little better than criminal 'sharks'. However, these data show that it was the low-density entrepreneurial markets that were more useful to state managers trying to fulfil the official obligations in the dominant economy.

A survey of the ownership status of market clients suggests that entrepreneurial markets served more state enterprises as clients than did the state-embedded dense markets. Large state enterprises, together with state administrative and service agencies, constituted about 44 per cent of clients at the low-density markets surveyed. These state clients were generally interested more in buying than selling goods and cited the need to supply state enterprises as their main motivation for doing so. Contrary to public expectations, therefore, the opportunity-seeking activity of low-density founders was compatible with the needs of major players in the former economy while their networking patterns helped address the changing needs of emerging markets.

In contrast, high-density markets were dominated by private clients such as small-scale firms and traders (68 per cent). As such, their clients were interested mostly in buying commodities and cited their lack of direct contacts with producers as their main motivation for trading on the exchange. This trend was especially pronounced among the 'private' and co-op clients, who could then act as distributors in their own right and resell the goods they bought at artificially low prices at their state-created markets. Basically in the privatizing local units of the former state supply system, these traders were relating to the new commodity exchange market in much the same way as they had to the state: as the fount of low-cost goods that they would distribute. While they privatized their assets, however, their opaque trading behaviour undermined the creation of open competition and the process of creating market-clearing prices on which private enterprise depends. While high-density networks prolonged old pathways and habits that may eventually help state-embedded actors shift gears (Solinger 1991), this research suggests that old pathways may be simply prolonged and exploited while real change or adaptation is made more difficult.

SUMMARY AND DISCUSSION

By engaging in network-level analysis of several small groups that founded commodity exchange markets, a new type of market organization, this research extends structural analysis to the problem of new organizational forms under market transition. It focused on the extensiveness of ties between market founders as the key element in the development of this new organizational form and to that end created a dichotomy of high-versus low-density founding networks. As the different markets began to operate, the autonomy of low-density networks facilitated a wide and loose institutional embedding that differentiates their markets as more integrated in the evolving process of creating an endogenous market system.

There are two primary aspects of these initial findings. First, they show that the extensiveness of ties among founders had real impact on both the founders' network and the organizational characteristics of their new markets. These findings therefore suggest that neither inertia nor change is the property of formal organizations, but of the structure of ties that link organizational actors. As such, the process of systemic change is illuminated as a complex of shifting and recombining social and institutional ties (Stark 1994; Murrell 1992*a*) in which the larger social chunks of past institutional arrangements are slower to rearrange their past practices and inter-firm ties.

At the same time, the data also suggest that a real trade-off exists in terms of the benefits of each density type. Although the close ties of the high-density model constrain the discovery of newer, more profitable trading relationships, they help maintain greater compliance and institutional support and lower transaction costs. Especially to the extent that major resource holdings and services are slow to change hands, the strong institutional links of high-density firms can help promote slow but steady growth as long as they do not stop the momentum of transformation altogether. Such a scenario is favoured by the perspective of population ecology which underscores the value of advantages of established forms during turbulent conditions.

Brittain and Freeman (1980) proposed a formal, untested model in which risk-taking organizations become the 'first movers' in exploiting new markets on the basis of their highly manœuvrable and light, inexpensive structures. As more new organizations enter the field, however, new, risk-taking organizations will ostensibly need to become more efficient to keep up with more resourceful hold-overs from the earlier period. Similar to extant organizations, high-density new firms have more established ties and greater access to resources and capital, which they can refine to ultimately overtake newly created organizational forms.

A different scenario emerges from the perspective of evolutionary economics. Murrell and others have argued for start-ups on the grounds that they are the source of variation in the economic environment that is especially needed in times of radical change to shift resources away from inefficient old forms (Murrell 1992b: 39). Extant state enterprise are incapable of such innovation and creative change, argues Murrell, because they are limited by inertia that binds them to the routines, habits, and norms of the old command economy that are dysfunctional in the new environment. This research shows that in fact inertia is a product of social ties and so can constrain even newly created organizations if they emerge from a highly dense network of founders. Thus, low-density start-up firms are specifically those forms most capable of uncovering new opportunities, exploiting turbulence, and moving the project of market transformation forward. As such, they enjoy greater returns on investment, but are institutionally less stable and non-compliant. While economically driven perspectives pit the innovativeness of new start-up firms against the stability and resources of spin-off forms, this research illuminates how each approach is viable, but at a cost.

NOTES

1. A Soviet economist, Grigori Khanin, believes the official figures mask the depth of decline, which he places close to a 50–60 per cent drop in production from 1989 to mid-1992 (Khanin 1992).

2. Based on data gathered and tabulated by the official Committee on Statistics of the Russian Republic (*Roskomstat*) (Mar. 1992).
3. Personal interview, Nov. 1991, Kaliningrad. Also see *Kommersant*, 35/85 (1991), 2, or *Königsberg Courier*, 8 (1991), 5.

REFERENCES

ARDISHVILI, ALEXANDER A., and CARDOZO, RICHARD N. (1993), 'Socio-political Structure of a Society as a Determinant of Entrepreneurial Behavior: The Case of Post-communist Russia', 3rd Global Conference on Entrepreneurship Research, 1993.

BOYCKO, MAXIM, SHLEIFER, ANDREI, and VISHNY, ROBERT W. (1993), 'Privatizing Russia', *Brookings Papers on Economic Activity*, 2: 139–92.

BRITTAIN, JACK W., and FREEMAN, JOHN (1980), 'Organizational Proliferation and Density-Dependent Selection', in J. R. Kimberley and R. H. Miles (eds.), *Organizational Life Cycles* (San Francisco: Jossey-Bass).

BURAWOY, MICHAEL, and KROTOV, PETER (1992), 'The Soviet Transition from Socialism to Capitalism: Worker Control and Economic Bargaining in the Wood Industry', *American Sociological Review*, 57: 16–38.

BURT, RONALD S. (1980), 'Autonomy in a Social Typology', *American Journal of Sociology*, 85: 892–925.

——(1983), *Corporate Profits and Cooptation* (New York: Acadenui Press).

——(1992a), *Structural Holes: The Social Structure of Competition* (Cambridge, Mass.: Harvard University Press).

——(1992b), 'The Social Structure of Competition', in N. Nohria and R. G. Eccles (eds.), *Networks and Organizations: Structure, Form and Action* (Boston: Harvard Business School Press), 57–91.

ECCLES, ROBERT G., and CRANE, DWIGHT B. (1988), *Doing Deals: Investment Banks at Work* (Boston: Harvard Business School Press).

EISENHARDT, KATHLEEN M., and BOURGEOIS, L. J. (1988), 'Politics of Strategic Decision Making: Towards a Mid-Range Theory', *Academy of Management Journal*, 31: 737–70.

Ekonomika i zhizn (1992), 'Predprinimatel Na Rasput'e' (The Entrepreneur at the Crossroads), 2: 1, 8.

GIBB, ALLAN A. (1993), 'Small Business Development in Central and Eastern Europe—Opportunity for a Rethink?' *Journal of Business Venturing*, 8: 461–86.

GRANOVETTER, MARK S. (1973), 'The Strength of Weak Ties', *American Journal of Sociology*, 78: 1360–80.

——(1985), 'Economic Action and Social Structure: The Problem of Embeddedness', *American Journal of Sociology*, 91: 481–510.

GRISCHENKO, Z., NOVIKOVA, L., and LAPSHA, I. (1992), 'Social Portrait of an Entrepreneur', *Sociologicheskiye Issledovaniya*, 10.

HENDLEY, KATHRYN (1992), 'Legal Development and Privatization in Russia: A Case Study', *Soviet Economy*, 2: 130–57.

HISRICH, ROBERT D., and GRACHEV, MIKHAIL V. (1993), 'The Russian Entrepreneur', *Journal of Business Venturing*, 8: 487–97.

JOHNSON, SIMON, and KROLL, HEIDI (1991), 'Managerial Strategies for Spontaneous Privatization', *Soviet Economy*, 7/4: 281–316.

JONES, ANTHONY, and MOSKOFF, WILLIAM (1991), *Koops: The Rebirth of Entrepreneurship in the Soviet Union* (Bloomington: Indiana University Press).

JOSKOW, PAUL K., SCHMALENSEE, RICHARD, and TSUKANOVA, NATASHA (1993), *Competition Policy in Russia during and after Privatization*, Brookings Panel on Economic Activity (Dec.).

KANTER, ROSABETH M. (1983), *The Change Masters* (New York: Simon & Schuster).

KHANIN, GRIGORI (1992), 'The First Quarter of 1992: Russia's Economic Results', *EKO*, 6–7.

KOLOBANOV, SERGEI (1991), *A Survey of Russian Brokers* (Moscow: Institute of Sociology).

KOZMINSKI, ANDRZEJ K. (1993), *Catching Up? Organizational and Management Change in the Ex-socialist Block* (Albany: State University of New York Press).

KROLL, HEIDI (1992), 'Monopoly and Transition to the Market', *Soviet Economy*, 7: 143–74.

MURRELL, PETER (1992a), 'Privatization Complicates the Fresh Start', *Orbis*, 3: 333–48.

——(1992b), 'Evolution in Economics and in the Economic Reform of the Centrally Planned Economies', in C. Clague and G. Rausser (eds.), *The Emergence of Market Economies in Eastern Europe* (Cambridge, Mass.: Blackwell).

NEE, VICTOR (1992), 'Organizational Dynamics of Market Transition: Hybrid Forms, Property Rights, and Mixed Economy in China', *Administrative Science Quarterly* (Mar.), 1–27.

——and LIAN, N. (1992), *Sleeping with the Enemy: Why Communists Love the Market* (New York: Cornell University, Center for International Studies).

PANAGARIYA, ARVIND (1993), *In Memoriam: A Eulogy to the Payments for the Former Soviet Republics*, World Bank draft (Jan.).

PIORE, MICHAEL J., and SABEL, CHARLES F. (1984), *The Second Industrial Divide* (New York: Basic Books).

SAPIR, JACQUES (1994), 'Conversion of Russian Defense Industries: A Macroeconomic and Regional Perspective', in Michael McFaul and Tova Perlmutter (eds.), *Privatization, Conversion, and Enterprise Reform in Russia* (Stanford, Calif.: Stanford University, CISAC).

SEDAITIS, JUDITH B. (1994), 'Spin-offs versus Start-ups under Market Transitions: The Development of Post-Soviet Commodity Markets', Diss., Columbia University.

SOLINGER, DOROTHY (1991), 'Urban Reform and Relational Contracting in Post-Mao China: An Interpretation of the Transition from Plan to Market', in Richard Baum (ed.), *Reform and Reaction in Post-Mao China* (New York: Routledge), 105–23.

STANISKIS, JADWIGA (1991), '"Political Capitalism" in Poland', *East European Politics and Society*, 5: 1.

STARK, DAVID (1991), 'Privatization in Hungary: From Plan to Market or from Plan to Clan?', *East European Politics and Societies*, 4/3: 351–92.

——(1994), 'Recombinant Property in East European Capitalism', MS.

STERLIN, ANDREI, and KOZLOV, VASSILY (1993), 'Emerging Entrepreneurship in Russia: Entrepreneurs' Perceptions of their Social and Economic Function', 3rd Global Conference on Entrepreneurship Research, 1993.

STINCHCOMBE, ARTHUR (1965), 'Social Structure and Organizations', in J. G. March (ed.), *Handbook of Organizations* (Chicago: Rand McNally).

WIEWEL, WIM, and HUNTER, ALBERT (1985), 'The Interorganizational Network as a Resource: A Comparative Case Study on Organizational Genesis', *Administrative Science Quarterly*, 30: 482–96.

WORLD BANK (1992), *Russian Economic Reform: Crossing the Threshold of Structural Change* (Washington: World Bank).

YAKOVLEV, A. A. (1991), *Birzhi v. SSSR: Pervii god raboti* (Moscow: Institute for the Study of Organized Markets).

6

Too Many, too Small: *Small Entrepreneurship in Hungary— Ailing or Prospering?*

ISTVÁN R. GÁBOR

What sets us against one another is not our aims—they all come to the same thing—but our methods.

(Antoine de Saint-Exupéry)

INTRODUCTION

As a result of exceedingly rapid expansion of self-employment in sectors other than agriculture, it already accounts for more than one-fifth of all non-agricultural employment in Hungary, a high ratio by international standards. However welcome this may be among professionals, it may well be an indication that the small-business sector in Hungary is becoming over-populated and over-fragmented, a process that may endanger the success of the country's economic transformation.

In the mid-1970s, when I started to study the Hungarian small private business of the time, or the second economy as I called it, I regarded this peculiar private economy as an organic part of the state-socialist order rather than as a mere vestige of the capitalist past or as some sort of an anomalous outgrowth of socialism (Gábor 1979). My main concern was to clarify the inherently conflictual, partly competitive and partly complementary, relation that existed between the second economy and the first and to form an idea of that relation's probable long-term outcome.

Until the early 1980s my views on this long-term outcome were based on the anticipation of successful reforms that would soon make market mechanisms the dominant mode of co-ordination in the first economy, gradually obscuring the boundary between it and the second economy (Gábor 1989a). By the mid-1980s the apparent failure of reformists to place the first economy on a market footing without altering the predominance of state ownership led me, however, to expect any future evolution of the system to occur through the expansion of the second economy rather than through further reforms within the state sector (Gábor 1986, 1989*b*). From then on, it was from this expansion that I expected the attributes of a market economy to gain prominence.

Toward the end of the 1980s, when the transformation into a capitalist market economy became the order of the day, I had again to reconsider my view on the potentially evolutionary role of the second economy (Gábor 1990). This shift put me at odds with the general view at that time, according to which, on the eve of a radical systemic change, small businesses were evolving from the second economy as vehicles or catalysts for transition to a market economy.

True, I myself was expecting a rapid spread of small businesses. Nevertheless, I thought it unlikely that the multitude of semi-wage workers—semi-entrepreneurs who had been brought up under state socialism—would now quickly and eagerly adjust their economic mentality to the requirements of a market economy. I feared that their inherited mentality would mark the course of development of small entrepreneurial activity for a long time to come.

Experience during the first two years of transformation confirmed and increased my fears. I came to realize that the development of small businesses had been hampered not only by the historical heritage but also by the context of the transformational crisis itself.[1] I saw mass and chronic unemployment in particular as a contextual factor thwarting the emergence of an efficient and dynamic small-business sector (Gábor 1992).

After attempts to transform the system since 1990, it is now time to re-evaluate the developmental trends and future prospects of small entrepreneurship in contemporary Hungary. In doing so, I have in mind primarily the so-called 'individual small undertakings', whose working owners constitute the largest segment of the self-employed category in numerical terms. In identifying this segment, I make allowances for the fact that unpaid family helpers, members of production co-operatives, and working owners of what in Hungarian phraseology are called 'joint undertakings without legal entity' are also treated in international statistics as self-employed (ILO 1990).

Adopting a macro-level economic approach to assess whether small entrepreneurship in Hungary is ailing or prospering, I concentrate on the effects of narrowly economic determinants as observed in larger aggregates of self-employment. Starting from the experience of established market economies as a comparative standard of measure, I argue that small entrepreneurship in Hungary is exhibiting a syndrome that might be characterized as 'too many, too small'. In conclusion, I suggest some of the implications that this syndrome has for economic policy.

SMALL ENTREPRENEURSHIP IN CONTEMPORARY
MARKET ECONOMIES

Three sets of research findings on small entrepreneurship in market economies are especially relevant for establishing an objective comparative measure: (1) secular trends and cross-national variations, (2) short-term cyclical fluctuations, and (3) intranational spatial variations in the proportions of self-employment.

Secular Trends and Cross-national Variations

Data series gathered for today's advanced market economies document a secular decline in self-employment until the 1970s. This trend cannot simply be interpreted as a by-product of the shrinking share of employment in agriculture, with its traditionally high rate of self-employment, for the same decline can be observed within non-agricultural employment. Therefore, it must be rooted in developmental tendencies more or less common to all sectors, most probably in a steady increase in economies of scale.

One might speculate whether the unexpected reversal of this declining trend in the 1970s can be attributed to particular developments in the world economy, such as the rise of energy prices and the resulting stagflation, or to country-specific government policies, such as the granting of greater benefits to the self-employed as a way of countering unemployment on the European continent, or the raising of marginal tax-rates on higher incomes in the United States (Blau 1987; Bögenhold and Staber 1991). More fundamentally, one may question whether an episodic deviation from the earlier historical trend is involved or, as is implied by Piore and Sabel (1984), the emergence of a new course of development.

The latter possibility is supported by strong arguments. As Sengenberger (1988) points out, some authors stress the importance of the revolutionary penetration of computers into industrial production, leading to radical cuts in economies of scale. Others focus upon the growing instability of the modern world market, which they claim undermines the viability of traditional mass production, given its specialized manufacturing equipment. However promising these arguments may be, the recent expansion of self-employment is still both too short and too modest to warrant the conclusion that it marks an epochal change in the earlier declining trends.

Until at least the 1970s, time-series studies indicate an unambiguously negative impact of economic development on the rate of self-employment. International comparisons are less clear, however. Though the negative effect of economic development on self-employment seems evident when considering group averages of countries sharing similar levels of economic development, too many individual countries diverge for economic development to stand as a sufficient explanatory factor.

In order to identify additional factors that might contribute to cross-national variations in self-employment, I conducted multi-variable regression analyses, taking self-employment rates among eighteen OECD countries as a dependent variable and the level of economic development (as measured by per capita income), the rate of unemployment, and an index of labour market corporativity as independent variables.[2] The choice of economic development and unemployment as independent variables is self-evident. The inclusion of labour market corporativity, that is, the role of macro-level negotiations between organizations representative of collective interests, as the third independent variable was motivated by the conjecture that corporativity, to the extent that it modifies employment conditions, may also influence the choice of self-employment. In addition, corporativity of the labour market may be construed as a proxy for economic actors' disposition for corporative government. For that reason alone, it may be more or less characteristic of the entire economic system, including the small-business sector.

Contrary to a common-sense expectation that higher or increasing unemployment rates generate higher rates of self-employment, my preliminary analysis suggests no such positive correlation. One should not conclude from this statistical finding, however, that self-employment bears no relation to the rate of unemployment. The counter-intuitive coincidence of a relatively high rate of self-employment and a relatively low rate of unemployment in a particular country at a particular time might as well indicate that, for instance, an earlier rise in the rate of self-employment has lowered the unemployment rate (cf. Meager 1992; Rasin 1990).

Beside this negative lesson, the cross-national regression analysis yielded a positive result. The level of economic development and the level of corporativity combine to account, with a high degree of significance despite the small number of countries included in the analysis, for about one-half of the cross-national variation of self-employment rates in both the industrial and service sectors.[3]

Here, the 'outlying' cases are also instructive. For example, Italy and Japan both have strikingly high non-agricultural self-employment rates compared to the predicted values of the regression equations. These two countries exemplify, though in radically different ways, the close integration of small businesses. Italy is known, particularly after the so-called industrial districts in the north, as a classical case of horizontal integration of small businesses, where micro-enterprises are linked typically on a basis of flexible specialization. Japan typifies the close vertical, or pyramidal, integration of small businesses into large enterprises. Generalizing from these two outlying cases, one may venture the proposition that the economic role of self-employment depends in no small measure on the degree of economic integration of small businesses, that is, on the existence of a kind of support network that nevertheless does not deprive the self-employed of independence. This hypothesis could be supported by the example of those Latin American countries that are struggling hard to escape their state of underdevelopment. Characterized by a peripheral position in the world economy, a dual economic structure with a proliferating informal economy, and high rates of urban unemployment, these countries also exhibit extensive self-employment. But with integration of small businesses virtually absent, high rates of self-employment in Latin American countries, in contrast to the Japanese and Italian cases just discussed, represent over-populated and stagnating small-business sectors (Soto 1988).

Before proceeding to the discussion of short-term fluctuations, I close this section on the long-term trends and cross-national variations of self-employment rates by advancing two more hypotheses on the importance that the degree of economic integration of small businesses has for the rate of self-employment.

According to the first hypothesis, both the horizontal and vertical integration of small businesses would increase self-employment partly by widening the domain of economic activities in which small businesses can meet the requirements of economies of scale. It is this integration that may account in part for the strikingly high rates of self-employment in Italy and Japan. But whereas horizontal integration of small businesses may simultaneously reduce the number of other economic organizations, for horizontally integrated small businesses are capable of replacing economic organizations with a large work-force, vertical integration may tend to reduce not the number but the staff size of other economic organizations, for vertically integrated small businesses are capable of replacing production and employment inside the factory gates of large integrating firms.

According to the second hypothesis, which complements rather than precludes the first one, the positive effect that the degree of integration of small businesses has on the rate of self-employment stems from the fact that it lessens the dependence of the self-employed on household needs in their business behaviour. A slackening of such dependence fosters longer-term business rationality as opposed to the short-term consumption orientation of households, thereby working towards greater economic efficiency. Perhaps this hypothesis, again, may help explain the positive relation that the Italian and Japanese examples show to exist between the degree of integration of small businesses and the rate of self-employment. It may also help throw light on what may be a root cause of the low economic efficiency of self-employment in Latin America.

Short-Term Fluctuations of Self-Employment

Any relevant econometric study must start from the assumption that individuals switch from wage employment to self-employment and vice versa as a response to shifts in the expected (risk-adjusted) relative returns of self-employment versus wage employment (an assumption that originated from the influential early work by Knight 1921).[4] According to the 'push' hypothesis, inflow into self-employment will thus fluctuate counter-cyclically, that is, parallel to unemployment, because rising unemployment will lower the expected returns to wage employment. According to the 'pull' hypothesis, however, with profitability of self-employment moving as it does parallel to the business cycle, short-term fluctuations of new entries into self-employment may also exhibit a pro-cyclical pattern. Whether the result of such push and pull forces has a positive or a negative sign is a priori impossible to determine.

Business fluctuations may also have a contradictory effect on the gross inflow into self-employment via variations in the constraints on this inflow. In times of recession it becomes easier to achieve an independent status, provided that more frequent set-backs in production and plant closures increase the supply of second-hand machinery, business premises out of use, and so forth. These changes may encourage a higher rate of inflow into self-employment. At the same time, however, greater uncertainties in recessionary periods tend to increase the concern of banks and investors about financing new business start-ups.

The direction of the net effect that business fluctuations have on outflows from self-employment is similarly uncertain. Booms exert a pull effect on influx into the labour market, thus inducing outflow from self-employment. Yet at the same time they restrain outflows because of the greater profitability of self-employment under such circumstances.

Not surprisingly, econometric studies that try to relate short-term fluctuations of self-employment to cyclical effects by reflecting the net result of changes in inflows and outflows utterly fail to reach clear conclusions. Besides, international comparability of their findings would call for the adoption of some rate-type self-employment indicator as a variable to be explained, such as the ratio of the self-employed to total employment or to the labour force. Such a rate-type indicator, however, may vary over time with employment (the denominator), decreasing at times of stagnation and increasing in times of revival even without any change in the number of the self-employed (the numerator).

Intranational Regional Dispersion of Self-Employment

Unlike the cross-national comparisons and time-series analyses just reviewed, which usually reveal no close and clear relation between unemployment and self-employment, such relations are strongly negative in cross-regional comparisons within countries. Characteristically, the rate of self-employment is relatively low in regions coping with depression and is high in prosperous regions.[5] In other words, rather than serving to decrease unemployment in regions afflicted by depression, self-employment is itself a victim of local depression. This tendency cannot be counteracted even by government incentives for the unemployed to become self-employed, presumably because such benefits can be used to best advantage by the jobless in regions least affected by depression. For that matter, the positive effect expected from the various government measures encouraging self-employment cannot be verified at the macro level either, probably because the undertakings thus established are either ephemeral or, if they do become steady, displace small undertakings that already exist.[6]

ENCOUNTERING THE SYNDROME OF 'TOO MANY, TOO SMALL'

During the rapid, almost abrupt, proliferation of small businesses in Hungary from 1990 through 1994, the number of registered non-agricultural individual small entrepreneurs rose from little more than 400,000 to over 750,000. At the beginning of 1995 self-employment in Hungary accounted for more than one-fifth of employment in non-agricultural sectors.[7] High by international standards, this ratio is roughly twice the average for OECD countries (11 per cent). It vastly exceeds the average for North Africa and the Middle East (15 per cent) and is only slightly lower than the average for Latin America (26 per cent) and the Asian region (27 per cent). In five groups of countries selected according to per capita income, Hungary ranks between the second-to-last group (25 per cent) and the middle group (18 per cent), which have per capita annual incomes ranging from $US500 to $2,000 and $2,000 to $6,000, respectively. This ratio drops to 13 per cent in the group of countries with per capita annual income ranging from $6,000 to $12,000 and is as low as 6 per cent for countries whose per capita annual income exceeds $12,000 (ILO 1990).

Considering also the large dispersion of self-employment rates across countries in the same group (those having roughly similar levels of economic development), the probable causes of which have already been suggested, Hungary is nevertheless not the only country with a high self-employment rate related to the level of development. By contrast, aside from the former socialist countries of the region, so rapid a spread of self-employment is indeed extremely unusual.[8] With economic decline and rising unemployment, not even a modest rate of expansion of self-employment is a general rule in the more advanced parts of the world, as was indicated in the previous section.

At the same time, the expansion of self-employment in Hungary has not helped much to curb unemployment and the decline in employment. Despite an addition of some 350,000 to the total number of individual undertakings over five years, the number of active earners in such undertakings has increased by less than 100,000 while employment has declined by about 1,500,000 and unemployment has risen by over 500,000.

This paradox results from a relative decline in the number of full-time individual undertakings and a falling number of full-time employees in such undertakings. Even in the last two years (1993–4), two-thirds of the sizeable net gain of some 160,000 individual undertakings came from an increase in the number of part-time entrepreneurs, that is, entrepreneurs who conducted their business on the side or in their retirement. Owing to the declining share of full-time entrepreneurs and a contraction in the average number of full-time employees of these entrepreneurs, the number of undertakings with at least nine employees and family members remained as low as 1,000. This proliferation and fragmentation of individual undertakings is coupled for the sector as a whole with a tendency towards 'over-tertialization', meaning that entrepreneurs in this sector are increasingly turning away from productive lines of business with a higher investment intensity.

Meanwhile, small units—those with a staff of not more than ten—are multiplying. The same is true among joint undertakings without legal entity, with a sharp decrease in the number of such undertakings with a staff of more than twenty. Even among economic organizations possessing legal entity, spectacular increases cannot be found, except in the number of organizations in the smallest size category. The number of such businesses with a staff of eleven to twenty is diminishing rapidly, and the increment in the next size group of such businesses—those with a staff of twenty-one to fifty—is marginal. In all likelihood that increment results from the separation of formerly larger companies into smaller units rather than from the establishment of genuinely new firms or from the transformation into companies of individual or joint undertakings without legal entity. This interpretation is suggested by the steadily declining number of firms in the largest size group. An overwhelming majority of new companies with a foreign interest may also probably be found in the smallest size categories, as is suggested by the fact that the initial assets of as many as two-thirds of the new companies established with foreign participation in 1994 and 1993 did not exceed 1 million forints (about $10,000), the minimum required by law.

Taken together, these facts show it highly unlikely that transformation either into joint undertakings without legal entity or into limited liability companies currently represents a significant way of increasing the size of individual undertakings. Indeed, it may even be supposed that the excessive spread and fragmentation of undertakings is peculiar not only to individual undertakings but also to joint undertakings and even to firms with legal personality.[9]

There is little question that these adverse characteristics of small-business development in Hungary are related in part to the inertia of the economic mentality inherited from the second economy of the past regime. The factors likely to have worked in this direction include the one-sided consumption orientation of households and their strong feeling against longer-term business investment and risk-taking, the accustomed leisurely pace of work in full-time employment, the low appreciation of free time compared to income, and the poor tax morale. At the same time, their negative influence has been accentuated by the transformational crisis it-self, especially the pressure for households to make short-term adjustments to rising unemployment and falling real wages. Yet these factors alone cannot explain the excessive numerical growth and fragmentation of under-takings I have outlined.

Obviously contributing to this process of proliferation and fragmentation has been, first, the exaggerated and one-sided propaganda campaign adver-tising entrepreneurship as a wide and preferable alternative path to success in life. It disregarded international experience with the 'normal' economic significance of self-employment and sought to create an inferiority complex in people shy of establishing a business. This overtly aggressive propaganda accentuated, willingly or unwillingly, the spontaneous mechanism under which more and more people probably embarked on a business solely because they had naïvely judged business prospects by the proliferation of undertakings. Indeed, Hungary's ratio of prospective entrepreneurs to adults in the national population was one of the world's highest, peaking at well over 40 per cent in 1990, according to the Hungarian Household Panel Survey (Lengyel and Tóth 1993).

The rapid erosion of business contacts previously established between the second economy and large enterprises may have been a second factor contributing to the proliferation and fragmentation of businesses in Hun-gary. Responding to the pressure of their economic difficulties, large enter-prises cut their ties to small-business partners first (Bagó 1991). Although it was possible to foresee this process and its unfavourable effect on small-business development, the government, in the course of its passionate propaganda drive for the foundation of undertakings, hardly even tried to intervene by stimulating the integrative efforts of large enterprises or by facilitating local-sectoral co-operative schemes between small entrepreneurs.

Finally, the growing weight of other than full-time employment and its preponderance in individual undertakings direct attention to the extreme rigidity of the Hungarian labour market, to which the government was virtually resigned. In a market economy, it is for the most part both ven-tures other than full-time business undertakings and second jobs that fall victim to slumps, whereas employment may even grow with the rise in unemployment, provided that the population of working age expands for demographic reasons. By contrast, falling demand for labour in Hungary, which followed upon the crisis, caused a dramatic decline in employment without substantially diminishing the insider power (job security and bar-gaining power at the workplace) of those people whose jobs did not fall victim to closures. They only lost opportunities for extra earnings (over-time, bonuses, and so forth) at the place of employment. It was these employees who, keeping their primary jobs, constituted the major source of recruitment for the growing mass of entrepreneurs working on the side, and it was mainly the growing mass of people displaced from the labour market who, with little chance of being rehired later, swelled the ranks of working owners of over-fragmented undertakings or joined the ranks of employees working for small undertakings—typically under irregular and substandard employment conditions. It is little surprise, then, when only a minority in public opinion polls agree that unemployment helps improve work discipline in Hungary (Lengyel and Tóth 1993).

The deleterious effects of inherited mentalities and of the circumstances surrounding the transformational crises may also have been coupled with self-generating processes within the small-business sector.[10] Paralleling the proliferation and shrinkage of undertakings, economic inefficiency became an ever less effective barrier to entry. Second, as the undertakings grew in number and shrank in size, it became easier for them to conceal income, a change that provided them a source of protection against larger competitors, which are less able to conceal incomes. Third, the more fragmented small businesses became, the less they could afford with their diminished incomes, and the less they found it worth while, given the crowded market, to attempt business expansion even though crowding may also have discouraged financially stronger firms from entering the market as potential rivals.

Given these self-reinforcing patterns, the specific too-many-too-small syndrome experienced among small undertakings in Hungary today will not necessarily and automatically change when the original causes disappear. Unless effective remedy can be found, it may grow into a self-sustaining phenomenon, a kind of low-equilibrium trap that would constrain economic transformation perhaps for a long time to come.

COUNTERING THE SYNDROME: SUMMARY AND CONCLUSIONS

As noted in the introduction, most economists in Hungary, caught up in the euphoria of the systemic change in the making, expected that liberalization of private business would rapidly release enormous business energies accumulated in the so-called second economy. That heightened expectation came about, however, because the positive aspects of the second economy heritage were overestimated and its negative aspects underestimated.

Even today many economists would see their earlier, optimistic expectations justified by the burst of self-employment. Still more might be dissatisfied with the present record of small-business development but would none the less consider the small-business sector to be a relatively successful part of Hungary's present economy and regard its development prospects as promising. I, however, interpret this proliferation in another light—as indicating the over-population and over-fragmentation of small businesses, a process threatening the Hungarian economy with a new type of dualization that endangers the longer-term prospects of economic transformation. My assessment that the small-business sector is indeed being marginalized stems partly from findings reported above:

1. A much-expected business expansion of small undertakings has failed to materialize.[11]
2. Part-time businesses are not on the wane but, in fact, are now preponderant in this sector.
3. Hidden and unregistered small-business activities show no signs of retreat.[12]

The danger of dualization, which I attribute partly to the inherited economic mentality of state socialism and partly to the contextual effects of the transformational crisis, suggests to me a possibility that small businesses might become a burden on the economy instead of acting as an agent of economic growth. In this situation I think it naïve to expect a decisive improvement from a reduction of high tax-rates, from tax relief for business investments, from lower interest rates, from more favourable credit repayment terms, and from similar financial and tax incentives. These are carrot-dangling policies that, coupled with other means of alleviating recession, could at best effectively stimulate small-business expansion in the downturn of the business cycle in an otherwise stable market environment.

Given the currently precarious situation of the budget and of commercial banks, Hungary scarcely has resources to throw in such a direction. Should any government still insist on doing so, one should expect nothing more than marginal improvements. And even where such incentive measures are complemented by a get-tough policy against the hidden economy, as some advocate, an end to widespread tax violation should not be expected. More energetic big sticks are not likely to have far-reaching effects when concealment of income is prevalent.

But if similar measures cannot effectively combat the too-many-too-small syndrome and the trend towards a new type of dualization of the Hungarian economy, is there any hope that this syndrome can be eliminated? I trust this task is not impossible, but in order to manage it one must sensibly take into account the historical and contextual determinism of small-business development in this country.

In my view, this effort would call for a pronounced shift in policy on small businesses, a new government strategy with three main thrusts: (1) promotion of sectoral–regional integration of small businesses, (2) reduction of unemployment and elimination of excessive job-rationing on the labour market,[13] and (3) abatement of the rush to found small businesses.

Promoting Integration

I do not have in mind another office of small-business administration, as if entrepreneurship could be established by government tutelage or state largesse. The less efficient such offices are, the more superfluous they are, too. And in so far as some are more efficient in the short term, they are more dangerous in the long run because they are all the more likely to stifle the spontaneous self-organization so vital to the small-business sector.[14]

Dissemination and popularization of, and support for, incipient self-organizations and provision of services to aid them are more suitable means of promoting concerted action by small entrepreneurs *vis-à-vis* banks as creditors and *vis-à-vis* larger firms as suppliers or buyers. The task is not to persuade banks to be more generous in granting credit to small businesses. Nor, as some advocate, should new institutions for venture capital be artificially stimulated by state funds or government pressure on the banks. As illustrated by my earlier conclusions drawn from the Italian, Japanese, and Latin American examples, the only viable path in the long run is for small businesses to increase their horizontal and vertical integration and to embark on a course of expansion.

Reducing Unemployment and Curbing Excessive Job-Rationing on the Labour Market

As indicated, total job security for some on the one hand and virtually endless unemployment of those displaced from jobs on the other hand (which together perpetuate strong inflationary pressure on wages despite a high rate of unemployment) generate the current trend towards dualization. These two situations contribute to making small entrepreneurial status a blind alley, a ghetto-like enclosure, a special space of socialization from which there is ever less chance of return to regular employment.[15]

I grant that our high rate of unemployment is largely a natural concomitant of the protracted transformational crises, although I think it would have been somewhat lower if Hungarian firms and trade unions had shown more wage restraint. I also acknowledge that Hungary's extraordinary job security at places of employment with continuing stability has roots in general problems well known in the literature on labour economics. Notably, these problems are difficulty in assessing actual skills when screening job applicants, costs of work-force replacements, and other sources of insider bargaining power. Yet acceptance of these partial causes does not justify inaction in the present on the basis of false expectations of the job-creating effects of an imminent economic revival.

In fact, if wage inflation remains unconstrained, and if the various factors contributing to insider power are left unchanged, there are good reasons to expect that the higher labour demand that accompanies growth will fuel wage inflation rather than immediately create new jobs. Alongside a more proportional distribution of the burdens of unemployment and efforts to preserve the value of human capital embodied in the jobless, the plausibility of such a scenario is additional justification for policy measures that check wage inflation and spur two-way flows between the working population and the jobless with the aim of mitigating the causes of economic dualization.

In light of a two-digit unemployment rate, it may sound odd to warn about a danger of wage inflation. But under the conditions just described— and given the experience in 1993, when wage inflation exceeded, and continues to exceed, price inflation despite an additional reduction of employment by 250,000—I still hope that such a proposal will meet with a more sympathetic response in Hungary this time.

Slowing the Rush to Found Small Businesses

By contrast, I cannot be optimistic in the least about the probable response to the third element of the strategy I am proposing, the institutionalization of some sort of 'birth control' for undertakings. I am even prepared to be accused of the ultimate sin of rejecting the principle of free entry into the market as a fundamental value of a market economy.

To be sure, I have in mind no bureaucratic constraints, no restoration of the right of administrative review of applications for an entrepreneur's licence, or even a fixed number of permits like the medallions issued by Western cities to prevent an undue rise in the number of taxi-drivers. I do not believe that the desirable rate of small-business density could be decided by administrative discretion, except in some special fields of activity. What I have in mind is an institutional increase in the costs of establishing a new undertaking. Instead of 'free entry', I propose an 'entry fee', which might even be combined, for a short transitional period at least, with an 'exit premium' set at a fraction of the entrance fee and payable to entrepreneurs going out of business.

Such an entrance fee would not only reduce the gross inflow, it would also improve the quality of new entrants by filtering out people liable to go into a venture on a momentary impulse without thinking through the means and ends. By screening out people attracted to an 'entrepreneurship' without investment or risk, it would also shift the composition of new business entrants towards those more capital-intensive fields of activity for which the entrance fee is a comparatively insignificant item in the total volume of start-up capital.

My proposal is not based on a supposition of some positive relation between the ability to pay an entrance fee and the possession of entrepreneurial capability. Instead, I would suggest two alternative, complementary rationales that are less in conflict with current concepts of social justice, economic efficiency, and desirable state involvement in a market economy.

According to the first rationale, the entrance fee may be seen as a special 'environmental pollution tax' serving to internalize the negative external effect of a growing crowd of new entrants. If my central thesis of overcrowding in the small-business sector is accepted, it seems reasonable that each entrant should pay for the total damage to society from the growth of overcrowding that he or she causes.

The second rationale starts from the observed asymmetry in which insider employees are, as pointed out earlier, protected from outside competition to the detriment of the self-employed. Raising the costs of entering into self-employment can also be considered a way of offsetting this unjust asymmetry by providing similar protection to the insider self-employed. If the entrance fee is justified (and made necessary) in part by the existence of insider power on the labour market, it follows that the entrance fee should (and could) be reduced in proportion to the opening of the labour market and finally abolished with the elimination of the asymmetry.

The receipts from entrance fees, augmented by some reasonable normative support from the budget, should, of course, flow back in full to the small-business sector. Entrance fees could thus promote elimination of the too-many-too-small syndrome not only by checking inflow into self-employment but also by providing additional resources for the expansion of small businesses.

A final component of the proposal is that entrance fees will be set (and their utilization determined) by organizations representing the self-employed, thereby promoting the self-organization of this economic sector, an aspect also stressed as a main strand of my proposed strategy. This arrangement would at the same time provide a mechanism for sensitively adjusting entrance fees to the density of small businesses varying in time and space, for small entrepreneurs' interests in setting high entrance fees intended to exclude entry (even at the price of no receipts) might be offset by their interests in maximizing receipts (from higher numbers of entrants). These conflicting interests would provide a good basis for reaching consensus on a fee close to some optimum from the perspective of development in the small-business sector.

These receipts from fees, together with the described mechanism of collective decision-making, enhances the likelihood that the proposed entrance fee would function as a positive screener in yet another respect. The longer the period that someone anticipates remaining an entrepreneur when considering entry, the greater that person's hopes of recovering the entrance fee from the fees that he or she helps set for later entrants. It would pay less to base an undertaking on a plan to make the most of only momentary possibilities. Consequently, the entrance fee could give an

added impulse to self-employment embarking on a new course of development. It would retard the excessive proliferation of small businesses in
Hungary and remove the acute danger of economic dualization.

NOTES

An earlier version of this chapter was prepared during the author's fellowship at the
Collegium Budapest, Institute for Advanced Studies, in the 1993–4 academic year.
The author owes thanks to his colleagues at the Collegium and to Monique Djokic
for their helpful comments and advice. He is also grateful to David R. Antal, the
technical editor of this volume, for his competent and devoted assistance in improving the text.

1. For the general causes and symptoms of what is termed from here on as
   transformational crisis, see Kornai (1993).
2. Figures for the first three variables were taken in these calculations from ILO
   (1990); for the extent of labour market corporativity, from Calmfors and Driffill
   (1988).
3. Having the estimation function leave out the rate of unemployment as a factor
   of insignificant explanatory power, I found that the proportion of the explained
   part of the cross-national variation of self-employment rates (adjusted R^2) was,
   in one specification, 55.9 per cent across all non-agricultural sectors; 54.1 per
   cent for the industrial sectors; and 56.3 per cent for the service sector. The
   parameter values were all highly significant for both dependent variables (with
   their respective p-values ranging from 0.028 to 0.048 and from 0.0024 to 0.0045).
4. On the subject of this section, see esp. Meager (1992) and Storey (1991).
5. This observation may appear to contradict my earlier claims, which are based
   on the inspection of secular trends and cross-national variations of self-
   employment rates, about the negative impact that the level of economic development has on the rate of self-employment. For a theoretical attempt to resolve
   this apparent paradox, see Hamilton (1989).
6. The futility of adopting general incentives for the unemployed to become self-
   employed in depressed regions is empirically illustrated in Rasin (1990).
7. Hungarian self-employment and small-business figures cited herefrom are
   based on the registry of APEH (Tax Collection and Audit Bureau) and KSH
   (Central Statistical Bureau). The author owes thanks to Mrs József Féli, head of
   the Economic Organizations Registration Department at KSH, for letting him
   examine and draw on unpublished figures calculated from this pooled data base.
8. Except perhaps for short periods of post-war recovery, during which destroyed
   large-scale production capacities are recovered, thereby restoring wage employment to its previous, pre-war role as a means of living.
9. A similar assessment was drawn by Végvári (1993) from a preliminary comparison of the overall number of firms per capita in Hungary, Germany, and Austria. Or, as Laki (1993: 8) points out, 'the founding capital of new companies has
   considerably decreased in the past one-and-a-half years. . . . [F]or joint ven-

tures ... the average founding capital of HUF 52.2 million in 1991 had decreased to HUF 17.2 million by 1992. This year [1993] two thirds of all joint ventures have been founded with the required minimum capital.' For further evidence on the excessive fragmentation of firms in Hungary, see also Lukács (1994).

10. By self-generating processes I mean positive feedback mechanisms similar to what Litwack (1994) claimed to have discovered in studying various aspects of the economic transition in Eastern Europe. Exploiting my demographic metaphor of over-population a little further, one may even associate these mechanisms with what some economic demographers (such as Dasgupta 1993) claim to be responsible for the excessively high birth-rates in many Third World countries.

11. In a survey carried out in 1993 among several hundred small entrepreneurs (Sóvári 1993), only 15 per cent of the entrepreneurs answered in the affirmative to the question whether they had any intention to invest. Even among those respondents none was planning to invest more than a few hundred thousand forints (a few thousand US dollars). As for the expansion of employment, none of the respondents was planning more than two new hirings.

12. See Durst (1993), Árvay & Vértes (1994), and Lackó (1995) for factual evidence.

13. For an empirical analysis of the latest labour market developments in Hungary, one important aspect of which is referred to here as excessive job-rationing, see Köllő (1993). See also Fazekas (1993) for the impact that the geographical distribution of industrial and entrepreneurial capacities has on the dispersion of local unemployment rates.

14. Compare with what Soto (1988) labels (and warns about) in the Latin American context as new 'mercantilism'.

15. Parallel with the increasing overcrowdedness of Hungary's small-business sector, the rate of flow from full-time small entrepreneurs to employees has even declined in recent years from 20 per cent in 1989–91 to 17.5 per cent in 1992–4 (Sági 1994).

REFERENCES

Árvay, J., and Vértes, A. (1994), *A magánszektor és a rejtett gazdaság súlya Magyarországon, 1980–1992* (The Weight of the Private Sector and of the Hidden Economy in Hungary, 1980–1992) (Budapest: GKI, Institute for Economic Research).

Bagó, E. (1991), 'A nagy- és kisvállalatok kapcsolatai az iparban. Nemzetközi és hazai tendenciák' (Relationship between Large and Small Firms in Industry: International and Hungarian Tendencies), *Közgazdasági Szemle*, 23: 917–26.

Blau, D. (1987), 'A Time-Series Analysis of Self-Employment in the United States', *Journal of Political Economy*, 95: 445–67.

Bögenhold, D., and Staber, U. (1991), 'The Decline and Rise of Self-Employment', *Work, Employment and Society*, 5: 223–39.

CALMFORS, L., and DRIFFILL, J. (1988), 'Bargaining Structure, Corporatism and Macroeconomic Performance', *Economic Policy*, 6: 14–61.

DASGUPTA, P. (1993), 'Poverty, Resources and Fertility: The Household as a Reproductive Partnership', in A. B. Atkinson (ed.), *Alternatives to Capitalism: The Economics of Partnership* (New York: St Martin's Press–International Economic Association), 161–200.

DURST, J. (1993), 'Levezető szelep. Láthatatlan jövedelmek' (A Safety Valve: Invisible Incomes), *Figyelö*, 9 Sept., 18–19.

FAZEKAS, K. (1993), 'A munkanélküliség regionális különbségeinek okairól' (On the Causes of Interregional Differentials in Unemployment), *Közgazdasági Szemle*, 40: 694–712.

GÁBOR, I. R. (1979), 'The Second (Secondary) Economy: Earning Activity and Regrouping of Income outside the Socially Organized Production and Distribution', *Acta Oeconomica*, 22: 291–311.

——(1986), 'Market Reforms and the Second Economy in State Socialism: Speculation on the Evolutionary and Comparative Economic Lessons of the Hungarian 1980s', Paper prepared for the International Conference on Markets and Social Policy in Comparative Perspective, Santa Barbara, Calif., 8–11 May 1986.

——(1989a), 'Second Economy and Socialism: The Hungarian Experience', in L. F. Feige (ed.), *The Underground Economies: Tax Evasion and Information Distortion* (Cambridge: Cambridge University Press), 339–60.

——(1989b), 'Second Economy in State Socialism: Past Experience and Future Prospects: The Case of Hungary', *European Economic Review*, 33: 509–604.

——(1990), *On the Immediate Prospects for Private Entrepreneurship and Reembourgeoisement in Hungary*, Working Papers on Transitions from State Socialism no. 6 (Ithaca, NY: Cornell University, Center for International Studies).

——(1992), 'A második gazdaság ma—az átalakulás kérdőjelei' (The Second Economy Today: Queries on Transformation), *Közgazdasági Szemle*, 39: 946–53.

HAMILTON, R. T. (1989), 'Unemployment and Business Formation Rates: Reconciling Time-Series and Cross-section Evidence', *Environment and Planning*, 21: 249–55.

ILO (1990), *The Promotion of Self-Employment* (Geneva: International Labour Office).

KNIGHT, F. H. (1921), *Risk, Uncertainty and Profit* (New York: Houghton Mifflin).

KÖLLŐ, J. (1993), 'Unemployment and the Prospects for Employment Policy in Hungary', MS.

KORNAI, J. (1993), 'Transformational Recession: A General Phenomenon Examined through the Example of Hungary's Development', *Économie Appliquée*, 46: 181–227.

LACKÓ, M. (1995), 'Rejtett gazdaság nemzetközi összehasonlításban. Becslési módszer a háztartási villamosenergia-fogyasztás alapján' (Hidden Economy by International Comparison: A Method of Estimation Based on Household Energy Consumption), *Közgazdasági Szemle*, 42: 486–510.

LAKI, M. (1993), 'The Conditions for Enterprise in Hungary', in A. Patkós (ed.), *Private Sector Development and Local Government in Hungary* (Budapest: Public Policy Institute Foundation), 7–15.

LENGYEL, G., and TÓTH, I. J. (1993), 'Gazdasági attitűdök' (Economic Attitudes), in

E. Sík and I. G. Tóth (eds.), *Egy év után . . . jelentés a Magyar Háztartás Panel II. hullámának eredményeiről* (One Year Later . . . Report on the Results of the Second Wave of the Hungarian Household Panel Survey) (Budapest: Budapest University of Economic Sciences, Sociological Department, and TARKI (Social Research Information Association)), 113–28.

LITWACK, J. M. (1994), 'Strategic Complementarities and Economic Transition', MS, Fellow lecture, 20 May, Institute for Advanced Studies, Collegium Budapest.

LUKÁCS, É. (1994), 'Sok magáncég, kis tőkeerővel. Hiányzó középvállalatok' (Private Firms Large in Number, Small in Capital: Medium-Size Enterprises Absent), *Figyelö*, 4 Aug., 16.

MEAGER, N. (1992), 'Does Unemployment Lead to Self-Employment?' *Small Business Economics*, 4: 87–103.

PIORE, M., and SABEL, C. (1984), *The Second Industrial Divide: Possibilities for Prosperity* (New York: Basic Books).

RASIN, E. (1990), 'Spatial Variations in the Israeli Small Business Sector: Implications for Regional Development Policies', *Regional Studies*, 24: 149–62.

SÁGI, M. (1994), 'Karriermobilitás a rendszerváltás körül' (Career Mobility around the Systemic Transformation), in I. G. Tóth (ed.), *Társadalmi átalakulás, 1992– 1994. Jelentés a Magyar Háztartás Panel III. hullámának eredményeiről* (Social Transformation: Report on the Results of the Third Wave of the Hungarian Household Panel Survey) (Budapest: Budapest University of Economic Sciences, Sociological Department, and TARKI (Social Research Information Association)), 100–9.

SENGENBERGER, W. (1988), 'Economic and Social Perspectives of Small Enterprises', *Labor and Society*, 13: 249–59.

SOTO, H. DE (1988), *The Other Path: The Invisible Revolution in the Third World* (New York: Harper and Row).

SÓVÁRI, G. (1993), 'Comments in the General Discussion on Laki (1993)', in A. Patkós (ed.), *Private Sector Development and Local Government in Hungary* (Budapest: Public Policy Institute Foundation), 28–30.

STOREY, D. J. (1991), 'The Birth of New Firms: Does Unemployment Matter? A Review of the Evidence', *Small Business Economics*, 3: 167–78.

VÉGVÁRI, J. (1993), 'Magyarország a vállalkozók országa' (Hungary is a Country of Entrepreneurs)', *Bank és Tőzsde*, 8 Oct., 8.

7

Towards Industrial Districts? Small-Firm Networking in Hungary

TIBOR KUCZI and CSABA MAKÓ

INTRODUCTION

Since the late 1980s the number of entrepreneurs has increased rapidly in Hungary, nearly doubling, for example, from 197,000 in 1988 to 339,000 in 1990. The most rapid growth has been among private limited companies, whose number rose from 4,500 to 18,000 in 1989 alone (Laky 1994). The ensuing prosperity has generated a commensurate amount of capital, but not enough to meet demand in a relatively poor country such as Hungary. How can potential entrepreneurs acquire the capital they need? Privatization would be one of the most important sources for establishing new firms, but a recent survey of companies with fewer than fifty employees (Czakó *et al.* 1994) showed that privatization is not a serious factor. Only eighteen of the 1,700 firms in the sample had been established through privatization. For potential entrepreneurs to establish their own firms, it seems that they must rely mainly on themselves, their own savings, the assistance of their relatives and friends, and the knowledge that they have accumulated in their formal jobs.

Co-operation in a given village would be yet another form of the capital that could help a qualified person go into business (Beccatiniai and Giovanni 1992). In this chapter we report the findings of research conducted in a village near Budapest where we have found a type of economic organization corresponding in many respects to what is known as the industrial district phenomenon (Ganne 1989; Trigilia 1992). Our investigation has revealed that it is possible in Hungary, too, for relatively capital-rich members of an area (e.g. a village) to become entrepreneurs by collaborating rather than competing with one another. Co-operation allows an undertaking to involve even those individuals who could not otherwise satisfy all the conditions for operating an independent business (professional, financial and market expertise, contacts, and money) (Amiot 1991, 1992; Ricovery *et al.* 1990).

We conducted our survey in a settlement of 2,000 inhabitants near Pest. More than twenty joiners live there, although the village has no plant capable of employing so great a number of specialists at any time. The needs of the population could be met by a single joiner (as confirmed by a neighbouring settlement where one craftsman attends to all the tasks of his trade). At the time of the survey these twenty joiners were engaged in supplying 5 or 6 million forints' worth of carpentry work for the construction of a three-star hotel. Their partnership in this collective project, most of which took place in the spring of 1992, had two interesting features. First, the order, which had come from a contractor who had emigrated from their village, involved a volume of work far too large to have been manageable for an artisan working alone or with just one or two partners. Second, the contractor had intentionally placed the order not with an established specialized firm but with a group of independent craftsmen and a few limited liability companies, all organizationally unrelated yet acting as a structured group. Using this structure helped solve occupational and organizational problems, procure materials, and raise the necessary financing.

The participants in the project constituted three functionally distinct groups: home-working entrepreneurs, local entrepreneurs, and outside (nationwide) entrepreneurs. The first group manufactured assembly units, spare parts, and individual products for a larger economic unit. In the 1980s this work had been co-ordinated through industrial co-operatives and co-operative farms, which are now in the process of disintegration and transformation. Since the onset of the transition to the market economy in Hungary, the artisans have been working out of their own homes. They were characterized by a relative independence, often coupled with poor working conditions or rather unstable earnings. They performed partial tasks appropriate to the capacity of their workshops and machine tools. At the same time they did more than simple outwork, for they enjoyed a great measure of professional, as opposed to economic, independence.

Unlike the homeworkers, the local entrepreneurs involved in the project not only appeared on the market with independent products and services but also had an independent managerial structure and legal status. They have taken over the integrative function once performed by industrial co-operatives and co-operative farms. It is with the help of the local entrepreneurs that homeworkers are joining the mainstream of regional economies.

Lastly, the nationwide entrepreneurs in our study represented initiatives by which a firm acting independently on the domestic and international markets of a given sector tries to integrate, within the framework of a project, the networks of homeworkers and local entrepreneurs doing highly specialized tasks and operating in a particular region.

The group differences arising from the division of labour in the project were likewise of sociological relevance, for these groups differed in terms of workplace careers, professional and vocational skills, market expertise, and financial knowledge (Héthy and Makó 1972). The homeworking entrepreneurs, for example, had taken up work mainly in small co-operatives over the previous ten to fifteen years. They had always sought homeworker status of some sort because they aspired to independence (the goal being to work at home in their own workshops) while avoiding clear-cut market situations. Along with relative independence, their primary consideration was to achieve their professional ambitions, or at least maintain a harmonious attitude to their work. The emphasis was more on the latter, for what was involved was not a modern sense of vocation but a traditional attachment to a line of activity. Most of these entrepreneurs still seek to continue in this way. They are trying to preserve their status as homeworkers even though several of them have well-equipped workshops and even employees (which points to the existence of conditions for becoming fully independent entrepreneurs). They are reluctant to have managerial functions replace their familiar daily woodworking.

The workplace careers of the homeworking entrepreneurs had two essential elements:

1. The 'homeward trend'. Most of the entrepreneurs working out of their own homes had had their first workplace in Budapest and, aspiring to set up workshops in their homes to supplement their earnings by outwork, had moved closer to their place of residence with each change of workplace.

2. A strengthening of the homeward trend. Their choice of workplace had been motivated by an endeavour to widen their margins of independence. That is, they had tried to escape the constraints entailed by work at state enterprises. In essence, the general aspiration was to have a workshop and machinery enabling the owner to earn a living by working at home.

Working at home at one's own speed in one's own workshop was the greatest value in the eyes of homeworkers, who were even ready to make the professional sacrifice of accepting less qualified work for the sake of working at home. At the same time, the desire to eliminate constraints does not mean a desire for full economic independence. Homeworkers find it important to use their work time and available family help on their own, and to decide by themselves on the purchase of materials and on professional matters, but they seek no independent appearance on the market. The homeward trend was a step-by-step process that took place without severe shocks. The careers of the homeworking entrepreneurs we studied were characterized by continuity as well as by a slow and cautious accumulation of wealth.

The careers of the local entrepreneurs were characterized by a sense of duality regarding their place of residence and place of work. The homeward trend had no influence on their choice of workplace. The members of this group took up work where they could earn the highest income, but the contacts they had in their place of residence were extremely strong. Their choice of workplace and frequent changes in occupation were motivated by increases in pay. For instance, they had become actively involved in the second economy and had chosen full-time employment, often outside the field for which they had been trained. In doing so, they preferred places of work with work schedules like those in, say, the fire brigade or car salvage, which left room for regular work in the second economy.

For these reasons, the professional careers and the workplace careers of local entrepreneurs were typically fragmented by abrupt shifts, shocks, disciplinary dismissals, accidents, and frequent changes of workplace and occupation. The life path was winding even for one entrepreneur who happened to have spent a relatively long time at a place of work. He had been a Young Communist League secretary in the 1970s and had then become a groundsman while belonging to the highly paid inside contracting group at his workplace, which was organized basically along professional lines. In summary, nearly all the entrepreneurs in the village we surveyed had experienced some dramatic turning-point that had prompted them to rethink their past activities.

For all the discontinuity in professional and workplace careers, however, it was highly characteristic that the local entrepreneurs had maintained their contacts. Although they had frequently changed their activities and the places where they pursued them, the same actors had always been involved. These people have brought together the advantages offered by local contacts and a freer choice of employment outside the village (more favourable labour market), a combination that has also helped them ride out typical crises.

Those who had become local or nationwide entrepreneurs on a fairly large scale in the village made the most of the trades practised there, but did not necessarily belong to them. One of our interviewees had learned the joiner's trade rather late and under pressure. When he had started his business, none of the village's building contractors were in the bricklayer's trade, nor did they have any related experience. The local entrepreneurs were more at home at the social level, upon which they relied as a resource for running their businesses.

The nationwide entrepreneur whom we interviewed had made a career independent of his settlement's professional and human 'spaces'. He was making the most of the local system of contacts, but his career was independent of them. He was virtually outside the village hierarchy in terms of occupation, prestige, status, and even the economic and market context. However, because he had been born in the village and because his parents were still living there, his local orientation was good. In promoting his business, he was making rational use of his knowledge of local conditions and values.

The carpentry project for the construction of the three-star hotel had been launched by a nationwide entrepreneur who was the presiding manager of a small industrial building co-operative based in the capital city. In the early 1990s the firm ranked among the country's top 100 enterprises in terms of annual turnover. The local entrepreneur dealing with the purchase of materials and woodworking (Company *A*) received 70 per cent of the orders, whereas a second local entrepreneur (Company *B*) and three homeworking joiners shared the rest of the jobs. The nationwide entrepreneur concluded contracts with both companies and with the homeworkers on a free-lance basis. To smooth the utilization of the individual capacities combined under the project, the small co-operative and the companies *A* and *B* advanced the working capital and materials that the home-working entrepreneurs needed to begin production. The nationwide entrepreneur not only advanced the working capital indispensable for the participation of the homeworking entrepreneurs, who had little capital, but also provided them with broader support, a 'protective shield'. Speaking about the 'quasi' incubator role of his firm, the president of the small co-operative stated:

The small co-operative and I myself give a certain measure of protection to the start-up entrepreneurs. They have no experience because they have not been in a position to gain any, even though they already had their joinery shops and machinery in their own homes. One such entrepreneur, for instance, worked as a maintenance joiner in factory '*M*' and did a second job at home, making doors, windows, and panels.

The participants in the project were not linked to the nationwide entrepreneur by written employment contracts and agreements governing relations between them (see Fig. 7.1). However, this arrangement between the actors of the allocative market did not mean that relations between the entrepreneurs were unclear. They co-ordinated their activities precisely and operated as members of a collective work organization, as a group in the process of doing carpentry work for the hotel. The relations between individual entrepreneurs, and their behaviour as a group, were fundamentally regulated by the 'community market' (*mercato communitario*), reflecting a developed relationship of trust (Sabel 1992). In essence, the combined 'play' of market mechanisms and reciprocity that prevails among participants in economic transactions is capable of establishing and sustaining their co-operation with each other (Costa 1988; Makó and Simonyi 1992: 46).

CO-OPERATION AND CIVIL INITIATIVES

We shall now turn to the factors of the community market that admitted of long-term susceptibility to influence, integrated the participants into the project, and determined the substance of the special 'regulators of behaviour' governing their relationship under the project. Finally, mention will be

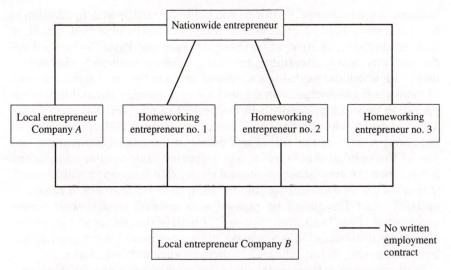

Fig. 7.1. The relationships between participants in the project

made of the local society's specific 'civil' initiatives, which sustain the values and relations of trust that give rise to the community market. In other words, we attempt to describe social institutions that integrate individual actions by agents of economic transactions.

As emphasized earlier, co-operation cannot be construed to mean mere exchange relations established between participants in transactions and based on calculations of economic gain. It is embedded in a set of economic and non-economic relations. Daily contact between participants is also regulated by non-economic values and institutions (Saglio 1991). In the course of our research, we found three values central to co-operation between entrepreneurs.

Professional Competence

The primary criterion of selection for involvement in the carpentry project we studied was professional competence, with work being given to those entrepreneurs who had solid professional reputations in the village. At the same time those concerned likewise interpreted their participation as a recognition of their skill and competence. As explained by the nationwide entrepreneur handling the project, '[a craftsman] wishing to take part in joint work is also kept on the right track by considering what the others will say if he doesn't work properly. I know that he won't be a poor hand. He will seek their opinion and advice if something seems amiss with his sample piece.'

Another point is that professional values strengthened integration by facilitating the exchange of information between participants. In addition to co-operation, a kind of professional competition was observed, which, in turn, made space for innovation (Sengenberger and Pyke 1992). Such endeavour was clearly discernible, for example, in the tools and other equipment with which the workshops were outfitted. On the other hand, the spell of innovation and competition seemed apt to jeopardize the stability of co-operation between participants in the project (Koike and Takenori 1990). The nationwide entrepreneur who was organizing the collective activity of the entrepreneurs in the village was aware of the risk of competition and was of the opinion that stability was a greater value at that stage of the project than the emergence of internal rivalry that innovation would entail. 'I don't want to overdevelop [the project], because that would lessen its visibility. And I wouldn't be pleased with internal rivalry, with people saying what "I am" and what "you are". I believe that things will go well if, at least until stabilization is achieved, people are proud that a product has been made here, in this village. Let there be such a driving force.'

Furthermore, a relatively definable community has emerged along professional values. The joiners of the village counted on one another and knew how large each workshop was, what equipment each had, and what quality of work could be expected of each other. When asked to 'classify' their fellows in the trade, each joiner mentioned, on the whole, the same eight to ten individuals as the best specialists. One might as well say that this 'group' functioned like an occupational organization, with clear conditions for joining and staying in the group. The advantages of belonging to the 'group' were similarly palpable because its members had easier access to orders. Under the project the allocation of jobs on the basis of trade and equipment was largely governed by the internal assessment system of this group.

Trust

Trust was another dominant value of integration shaping the group behaviour of the entrepreneurs participating in the project. A source of this trust was the fact that the social relations of the village were interwoven with ties of kinship and friendship. Nearly all the inhabitants were related, as was well illustrated by the remark of a homeworking entrepreneur: 'My brother-in-law works in the metropolitan small co-operative. So do his son-in-law and my sister. So when I went into business I spoke to the president of that small co-operative, asking him to give me a job when he had one. As a matter of fact, that is how I got involved in the project.'

Preference for kin was likewise manifest in the employment policy of local entrepreneurs. One of the most successful among them, for instance, recruited 90 per cent of his employees from among his relatives. Moreover, he employed no one but relatives in the business's central workshop. He described his 'family-centred' employment policy as follows:

Working for me are my two brothers, my sister's son, and my brother-in-law. If I pay someone, it must be deserved, for the pay is good. And we should take care who we give the money to. This policy is better than other lines of action. I feel that if you can't pay, you mustn't expect anything either. Once I found myself getting into deep water, when I left hospital, starting with a debt of hundreds of thousands of forints. It's true this is a story long past, but if I hadn't been helped out with money [from the family] there would have been no prosperity. I would certainly have gone under in Budapest. I could even have been written off on the face of it.

The intensity of family relationships, or kinship ties, constituted a source of trust among entrepreneurs. On occasion, however, trust and obedience happened to conflict.

One morning I sent my older brother home. 'Boy', I said, 'we start work at seven in the morning', but he came by bike five minutes late. You can't allow that. It happened again the next day. 'Well, boy, go home for a week on unpaid leave and think it over,' I said. If someone wants to work, he must be aware of the starting and finishing time of work. If not, he should come and pick up his cards. Not even my older brother is an exception. You either do that or get 'swallowed up'. We come across great problems of this sort. I don't do favours for anyone. He who works gets his money. But, of course, if you're running a firm, you can't let yourself be ruined.

Serious expectations about discipline in the workplace of family members employed in a business indicated that loyalty—toleration of one another's interests and endeavours—was but one component of trust. Loyalty was two-way, that is, family members also had to respect the organizational requirements for the long-term survival of a business. This mutual respect for one another's interests can be called 'moral competence'. Its abiding presence along with a second component—the partners' professional competence, including work discipline—guarantees the long-term advantages of trust relations (Héthy and Makó 1988; Makó and Simonyi 1992: 58–9). A third dimension of trust was time, which is, in effect, tantamount to testing the participants' moral and professional competence and is seen as a period in which relations based on mutual dependence, as opposed to unilateral dependence, either develop or become impossible.

In addition to kinship ties, trust relations were shaped by informal relations that had evolved between people in the shared past at the factory or through joint participation in the second economy before workmates had become entrepreneurs. For instance, readiness to co-operate and mutual respect for the individual interests of homeworking and local entrepreneurs collaborating under the project were attributable to having worked together at the factory. In return for working capital for materials needed for work under the project, one of the homeworking entrepreneurs was ceding some of the jobs (assembly of the wooden components he had made for French balconies) to Company *B*. In effect, he thereby obtained an interest-free loan of some 200,000 forints ($US200) and, through the order he received, involved the local entrepreneur in the project.

Trust relations impart increased dynamism to economic transactions, liberate participants from the risk avoidance and constraints of constant administration complicating economic transactions, accelerate the exchange of information, and create a kind of social control guaranteeing top-quality work. Generalizing from the observations in this study, one could thus cite two major advantages to trust between the partners in business, or any type of economic transaction: (1) the sharing of both economic gains and losses in order to secure the benefits of long-term co-operation; and (2) the predictability of the participants' behaviour. However, advantages offered by a developed pattern of trust may turn into a drawback if they spill over into unfounded good faith in outside partners. Such a case occurred with homeworking entrepreneurs who had formed a group under the project. They had performed various jobs in good faith—under verbal agreements and without journal entry—for other firms involved in the hotel construction, and they never received payment.

Thus, homeworkers collaborating under the project were linked by professional values and developed relations of trust that served to mobilize the ready forms of co-operation. Relations between the homeworkers and the local entrepreneurs were governed primarily by trust, with professional competence playing a subordinate role. For instance, local entrepreneurs gave homeworkers materials on credit and verbally agreed on deadlines and quality requirements. No complaint has been made about the quality of the work done or about compliance with schedules by homeworking entrepreneurs. Agreements governing the relations between homeworking, local, and nationwide entrepreneurs can best be likened to relational contracting (Dore 1987), which differs from the engineering and construction contracts common in market economies. The latter two types of contract specify in writing the obligations of participants in economic transactions concerning performance and payment. The stronger partners try to impose their will on the weaker ones, particularly under unfavourable economic circumstances. By contrast, the relational contracting that regulated the economic transactions of the participants in the project had the following features:

1. The stronger partner did not try to exploit his advantage over the weaker one, even under adverse economic circumstances. For instance, the local entrepreneurs assisted the homeworking entrepreneurs with interest-free working capital in an economic environment characterized by extremely high interest rates.

2. Business relations were 'interwoven' with special socio-cultural rela-

tions. They were organized between members of one and the same ethnic group.

3. There was an understanding of one another's interests and aspirations, mutual tolerance, and an attitude oriented to professional performance.

4. The special stability of relations lends perspective to thinking and action in such areas as business development and investment activities at a time when the macro-environment is unfavourable to such ventures.

5. The parties to economic transactions under the project took for granted the hierarchy prevailing in their relations (nationwide, local, and homeworking entrepreneurs).

Ethnicity

Ethnicity was the third integrative value that dominated co-operation between entrepreneurs in the project we studied. Embracing almost the entire village (80 per cent of whose inhabitants were of German origin), ethnicity was also the most general of the values. It incorporated the narrowest group—those integrated along the lines of professional competence—and the network of trust, which was wider in scope. If the first two conditions to which involvement in the project was subject were professional competence and trust, the third condition was thus residence in the village of '*I*'. In essence, the first was a subset of the second; the second, a subset of the third.

As an integrative value, membership in an ethnic group came to play an important role because that value had resulted from individual, but mainly collective, efforts that were significant in Hungary among people of German origin (e.g. fear of repatriation and confiscation of property). This largely explains why people in this village showed relatively strong mutual solidarity and why they are rather reclusive. Solidarity came into play even when serious risk was involved. In 1948, for example, the village notary, who had been protecting locals by not disclosing that they were threshing grain in *kaláka* (labour exchange among kin), was charged with having failed to report the fact to his superiors (Sík 1988; Asztalos and Brandtner 1991: 289). The attitude of local inhabitants, who had been under constant pressure to defend themselves, came to be characterized by duality. On the one hand, they helped and supported one another; on the other hand, they were introverted. 'This village is not very open,' said an interviewee. A highly respected cabinet-maker characterized the local population by saying: 'Local people work for the common cause and pool their efforts. They are made that way and are hard-working. Most of them are honest and ambitious.' This assessment, dating from the early 1990s, differs little from that of a former vicar of the village at the beginning of this century: 'The inhabitants of the village of "*I*" are honest, reliable, straightforward, industrious, and thrifty' (Asztalos and Brandtner 1991: 331).

OTHER INSTITUTIONS PROMOTING CO-OPERATION

Family, kinship, and neighbourhood are only some of the institutions regulating and providing a framework for co-operation between entrepreneurs
in the village of '*Γ*'. They are able to meet most of the needs of co-operation.
Their integrative function and their contribution to maintaining trust have
been discussed earlier. The village of '*Γ*', however, has seen the evolution of
a few institutions that not only draw on the existing local models of co-
operation and integration but also do much to sustain, develop, and enrich
them.

The Foundation

At a self-government meeting held in the spring of 1991, the establishment
of a foundation to create jobs, protect the environment, and improve the lot
of the aged and of minorities was proposed by the newly elected mayor of
the village and was seconded by two local entrepreneurs and a nationwide
entrepreneur. The village self-government has since contributed 1.5 million
forints ($15,000) in real estate and 100,000 forints ($1,000) in cash. The
total contributions by entrepreneurs have amounted to 350,000 ($3,500)
forints, thus augmenting the share of the business profits that the village has
been able to keep. The local entrepreneur who did much to establish the
foundation set out its plans and its economic and social along the following
lines:

Its purpose is to enable the village to retain taxes on business profits. If I, as an
entrepreneur, took out my share of profits from the company at the end of the year,
I would have to pay 40 out of every 100 forints to 'Uncle State'. I would rather pay
them here, not there. This is the crux of the whole thing. One may also consider
giving a particular job to entrepreneur *Z* in Budakeszi and telling him to pay a
certain amount to the foundation. If he refuses, we thank him very much and say,
'Well, pal, we lost on this job, but you won't get the next one.'

Then, in order to get it, he will see to it that the tax on his profits is paid into
the foundation. This can help the village prosper.

So far it has been impossible for the foundation to achieve its most
important goal, that of solving the unemployment problem, because the tax
office has refused to grant a tax allowance despite the avowed intention of
using the foundation's money for job creation. The initiators have not
abandoned their plan to help local unemployed (but mainly qualified)
workers who have been displaced from the labour market. They have set up
a village workshop financed by the foundation for the purpose not only of
alleviating employment problems but also of helping qualified, unemployed
persons without workshops of their own to go into business themselves.

The significance of the foundation is that it has raised conflict management from the individual to the community level, with local self-government and the village's new economic élite playing a major part (Ishikawa *et al.* 1993). A new type of institution capable of using rational financial procedures has thereby been added to the existing relations of trust and solidarity.

Sunday Conversations

The nationwide entrepreneur we interviewed spends every weekend in his native village and encourages entrepreneurs to exchange views on the premises of the local self-government. These conversations are unlike work conferences, for there is no agenda or range of participants. The encounters are informal, more like a news exchange, with people informing themselves about each other's professional problems and discussing tasks of village development. (The foundation itself was born in such conversations.)

Discussants belong to the network of professional and/or trust relations, or they are local inhabitants in the wider sense. At the same time their presence serves to maintain that network. The Sunday conversations symbolize a reinforcement of the sense of belonging to a 'group' and thereby exercise an important function that regulates and integrates action.

Leisure Club

One of the local entrepreneurs converted the basement of his family house into a body-building hall, which is operated as a club open to the public. The range of people actually making use of this facility can be defined easily. The club is a place of informal meetings mainly for entrepreneurs and people in that line of work. It is an important integrative institution, for it helps promote non-professional, non-economic cohesion between entrepreneurs (or people of higher social standing).

This institution fulfils three functions. First, it strengthens the network of trust, since the club functions in an open, unsupervised room, leaving it to everyone's conscience to take care of the equipment. Second, it sustains the unity or cohesion of the family, since entrepreneurs often take their families to the club. Third, the club provides facilities for the care of the body, a service indicating that a value cherished by 'high society' has also found its way into the village while performing a certain integrative function.

Entrepreneurs' Club

The entrepreneurs' club is an institution of information exchange initiated by five leading entrepreneurs of the village, owners of a company. It was not operating at the time of our survey, although the overwhelming majority of entrepreneurs at different levels sympathized with the initiative. Those concerned agreed on the need to have such an institution providing opportunities to exchange ideas and information. It is characteristic of the interest in the club that the first meeting was attended by nearly all the local entrepreneurs. It seems that the club will continue to function if it can draw up a programme addressing the concerns of different groups of entrepreneurs. It may also be able to help promote social integration in the village.

POSTSCRIPT

Since the onset of Hungary's transition to a market economy, the biggest question is whether the country's economy must follow the Western path. In this chapter we have tried to show that modern and traditional elements can be successfully combined to bring prosperity to a given district (Szelényi 1988). We have tried to convey the fact that in some districts in Hungary modernization has not destroyed the traditional ties and norms of society while building up-to-date knowledge. Of course, the case presented here does not describe the only way to make the transition from socialism to capitalism. But with capital to establish new firms often lacking in Hungary, people do have a chance to become entrepreneurs if they can use their social ties and rely on their social norms.

REFERENCES

AMIOT, M. (1991), *Les Misères du patronat: Le monde des petites et moyennes entreprises industrielles et leurs patrons* (The Misery of the Small Business Owners: The World of Small and Medium-Size Firms) (Paris: L'Harmattan).

——(1992), 'Kis- és Középvállalkozások Franciaországban' (Small and Medium-Sized Enterprises in France), *Társadalomkutatás*, 4: 68–75.

ASZTALOS, J., and BRANDTNER, P. (1991), *Iklad (Egy magyarországi német falu története)* (Iklad: History of a German Village in Hungary) (Iklad, Aszód: Petofi Múzeum, Iklad Község Önkormányzata).

BECCATINAI, G., and GIOVANNI, P. (1992), 'East-Central Europe and the Italian Entrepreneurial Model', Paper presented to the 6th International Meeting of the Italian Association of Sociology of Work, Bologna, Italy, Nov. 1992.

COSTA, C. (1988), 'Décentrage productif et diffusion industriel' (Industrial Decentralization and Industrial Diffusion), *Économie et Société* (special issue), 31: 24–32.

CZAKÓ, A., KUCZI, T., LENGYEL, G., and VAJDA, A. (1994), *A vállalkozók társadalmi összetétele* (The Social Composition of Entrepreneurs), MS, Central Statistical Office, Budapest University of Economic Sciences.

DORE, R. (1987), *Taking Japan Seriously* (Stanford, Calif.: Stanford University Press).

GANNE, B. (1989), 'PME et district industriel: Quelques réflexions critiques à propos "du modele italien" ' (PME and the Industrial District: Critical Reflections on 'the Italian Model'), *PME Revue Internationale*, 2–3.

HÉTHY, L., and MAKÓ, C. (1972), *Munkásmagatartások és a gazdasági szervezet* (Forms of Workers' Behaviour and Business Organization) (Budapest: Akadémiai Kiadó).

——(1988), *Worker's Behavior and Business Organization* (Budapest: Institute for Labour Research and Institute of Sociology).

ISHIKAWA, A., KAWASAKI, Y., and OKANO, H. (1993), *For Reorganization of Local Community in Hungary under Post-socialism*, Research report (Tokyo: Chuo University, Institute of Social Sciences).

KOIKE, K., and TAKENORI, I. (1990), *Skill Formation in Japan and South-East Asia* (Tokyo: University of Tokyo Press).

LAKY, T. (1994), *A vállalkozók és a vállalkozások a kilencvenes évek kezdetén* (Entrepreneurs and Enterprises in the Early Nineties), MS, Institute for Labour Research, Budapest.

MAKÓ, C., and SIMONYI, A. (1992), 'Social Spaces, Acting Society', in G. Széll (ed.), *Labour Relations in Transition in Eastern Europe* (New York: de Gruyter), 29–85.

RICOVERY, G., CILONA, O., and FOCKER, F. (1990), 'Labour and Social Conditions in Italian Industrial Districts', Paper no. 6 presented to the International Conference on Industrial District and Local Economic Regeneration, Geneva, Sept. 1990.

SABEL, C. F. (1992), 'Studies Trust: Building New Forms of Cooperation in a Volatile Economy', in W. Sengenberger and F. Pyke (eds.), *Industrial District and Local Economic Regeneration* (Geneva: International Labour Organization), 215–51.

SAGLIO, J. (1991), *Industrie locale et strategie des acteurs: Du peigne à la plasturgie dans la zone d'Oyonnax* (Local Industry and Strategy of Social Actors: From the Comb to the Plastics Industry) (Lyons: Groupe Lyonnais de Sociologie Industrielle).

SENGENBERGER, W., and PYKE, F. (1992), 'Industrial District and Local Economic Regeneration: Research and Policy Issues', in W. Sengenberger and F. Pyke (eds.), *Industrial District and Local Economic Regeneration* (Geneva: International Labour Organization), 3–29.

SÍK, E. (1988), *Az 'örök' kaláka* (The 'Eternal' *Kaláka*) (Budapest: Gondolat Könyvkiadó).

SZELÉNYI, I. (1988), *Socialist Entrepreneurs: Embourgeoisement in Rural Hungary* (Madison: Wisconsin University Press).

8

Regional and Local Factors in the Restructuring of South-Eastern Poland

JERZY HAUSNER, TADEUSZ KUDŁACZ, and JACEK SZLACHTA

INTRODUCTION

Regional Differentiation and Post-socialist Reforms

No matter how the progress of the transformation processes is evaluated, it seems obvious that the key issue in the economic policy of the state is now economic restructuring. In its absence, steady economic growth would be hardly possible, and the achievements in the field of systemic transformations since 1989 might be endangered. Among other things, this is due to the fact that the causes of inflation are increasingly linked to the faulty economic structure, ill-suited to the needs of market economy and international competition. This is true of the organizational, material, technological, and regional aspects of that structure. Even the best macro-economic policy will not be able to eliminate these problems. Their existence, however, constantly jeopardizes the relative economic equilibrium that has been reached. At the same time, the coexistence of economic structures formed under the conditions of socialism with adaptation mechanisms typical of a market economy leads to processes of rapid differentiation, the most important of which concern regional differences.

Measures intended to modify the economic system, and in particular labour and ownership relations, must be oriented towards the fundamental problem of economic development, i.e. industrial and regional restructuring. If no steps are taken or if they go in the wrong direction, the result may be an immediate regression of the ongoing transformation. A blocked or slowed-down restructuring process would profoundly affect the economic equilibrium, touching off hyperinflation again and posing a real threat to democratic government. Likewise, growing regional differentiation may endanger the systemic reforms that the market economy hinges upon. It follows that the problem of efficient restructuring of the economy lies at the heart of not only economic, but also political, development.

Under post-socialist conditions, the specificity of any economic strategy is determined at the outset by the state of profound economic imbalance and, on the other hand, by a systemic vacuum, i.e. the lack of a stable configuration of political and economic agents. This greatly complicates all kinds of measures aimed at restructuring, which form the backbone of every economic strategy. Accordingly, care must be taken to avoid increasing the imbalance, or at least to foster the restoration of equilibrium in a relatively short time. Unfortunately, restructuring efforts, even if oriented towards restoring current equilibrium, by their very nature tend to upset the balance at first. The lack of a stable agent structure, in turn, entails in practice the absence of certain types of actors, indispensable for the implementation of the adopted restructuring goals.

The OECD (1993) report on the problems of regional development policy in Poland points to the fundamental importance of 'structural mega-adjustments'. This is connected with the fact that superimposed on the regional adjustments known from OECD countries, there are adjustments connected with the transformation of the economic system which occur in all the regions. That is why the regional dimension of restructuring processes in the reforming countries is so important.

The level of susceptibility to structural change varies across regions in Poland. One can distinguish expansive and crisis-prone regional structures. Observation of the spatial characteristics of the transformation processes after 1989 confirms growing regional differentiation, and polarization of regions into transformation leaders and problem areas. This is corroborated by analysis of the spatial development of four processes crucial to the transformation: changes on the job market (including unemployment), privatization of the economy, foreign investment, and formation of an environment favourable for business and economic activity.

Even though positive structural adjustments dominate in Poland—the fastest transforming state in Central and Eastern Europe—there are regions of the country where negative adjustments occur as well. Consequently, regional structures become increasingly incoherent, which can pose a threat to the transformation at the economic as well as political level.

Regional restructuring in Poland has been profoundly influenced by local government reform. One of the fundamental post-1989 systemic changes was the formation of self-government at the local level. The establishment of local government marked a breakthrough in the construction of democratic state structures. Its emergence signified a break with the socialist doctrine of unity of the state and local administration, treating the local level as the bottom rung of central administration.

The systemic changes initiated in 1990 have been limited so far to the local level. This was first of all due to the fear that the simultaneous creation of a second level of self-government structures might restrict the capacity of the local level to act independently. Another cause was probably the desire to avoid dividing limited human resources between the two levels, which could hamper the entire undertaking. Finally, the restriction of the first stage of the reform to the basic level of local government structures was justified under the circumstances by the pioneering character of the task and the vast range of necessary legislative and organizational preparations.

Thus, the increasing role played by local self-government is not reflected at the regional level. This is an important factor which determines not only the situation in Poland after 1990, but also the directions that further reforms of the state should take. The lack of a supra-local self-government agent capable of solving problems common to the entire region is a powerful determinant of the regional policy of the state, including regional restructuring.

From Imperative Methods to Negotiated Strategies

We believe that a *negotiated strategy* has precisely those advantages that enable efficient restructuring of the economy. The reason is that this strategy, unlike strategies based on the imperative method, facilitates the integration of the technical–economic and socio-economic dimensions of policy. Such integration is a pre-condition for harmonizing restructuring and system-creating processes and maintaining current economic equilibrium, without which the post-socialist transformation cannot be completed.

The integration of restructuring and system-creating policies through the negotiated strategy should not be taken to mean that conflicting interests will be reconciled through negotiations between representatives of existing economic agents. Such an approach would lead to the petrifaction of the existing structure rather than its change. The point is that institutionalized negotiations over specific restructuring policies should lead to the formation of such economic agents that will carry out these policies and forge the new economic system in the process. This means that the negotiation strategy must consist not only in articulating and mobilizing certain interests, but also in a conscious effort to dearticulate and demobilize other interests, which in a given case cannot be reconciled with the restructuring policies. Of prime importance is the selection of partners at both the micro and meso levels and according to specific economic interests, rather than at the macro level, according to political and ideological criteria.

It clearly follows from the above that restructuring, especially industrial and regional, is of key importance for the implementation of the negotiated strategy. The crucial question here is: what should be the role of state (government) and other economic agents in precipitating and carrying through this process? So far two opposing viewpoints have been presented in the public debate: the first stresses the need to preserve the purely market-oriented character of restructuring, while the second underlines the need for an industrial policy consisting in structural reforms which are to be carried out chiefly by the state. In fact, the pendulum is swinging more and more towards the second option.

We believe that the dichotomy: *restructuring without state intervention* versus *restructuring controlled by the state* should be overcome and an approach based on *restructuring with the participation of the state* should be developed in a way that would be coherent with the principles of the negotiated strategy. The main tenets of this approach are as follows:

1. The state (government) must have a comprehensive, long-term programme of economic development that would include a specific vision of desired structural changes and their deadlines.
2. The state (government) carries out macro-economic policy whose aim is to maintain current economic equilibrium, while facilitating the implementation of the long-term programme, including the planned structural changes.
3. The state (government) undertakes policies (organizational, economic, legislative) to forge an infrastructure (technical, institutional, legal, social) for the operation of economic agents whose aim is to increase economic efficiency.
4. The state (government) possesses the means and instruments—as well as the ability to use them—to become involved in restructuring.
5. The state (government) participates in negotiations between various types of partners (local self-government, employee representatives, employer and business representatives, professional associations, economic agents, agencies and foundations of regional development, etc.) over specific programmes and restructuring measures in branch and/or regional structures.
6. The provision of resources by the state (government) for specific programmes and restructuring measures is the outcome of agreements and is conditional upon all the parties abiding by these agreements.

The corner-stone of the 'restructuring with the participation of the state' approach is the creation of institutions complementary to mechanisms of market and administrative co-ordination, at the same time ensuring social control over these mechanisms. The supply strategy oriented towards qualitative restructuring requires the state to design, protect, and stimulate certain institutions. In particular, it is vital that the local systems of economic regulation should be encouraged to take the role of independent, active agents.

The reason why it is so important to create appropriate institutions is that in this way social agents gain self-identity and thus help to lay the foundations for the economy's long-range goals. Since restructuring can only be undertaken and carried out by certain agents under the given conditions, to create institutions means to create a social fabric enabling restructuring and the resolution of specific problems, as well as the accumulation of experience and its application in other areas of social life. Thus, institutions also forge the rights and contract-making capabilities of the various agents, defining their role in the restructuring, as well as in finding solutions to more general problems.

The 'restructuring with the participation of the state' approach needs to be developed, and the political and institutional conditions under which the state (government) would perform the above-mentioned function should be specified. Of equal importance is a detailed classification and characterization of the means and instruments needed by the state to participate in industrial and regional restructuring; agents participating in restructuring programmes and undertakings should similarly be described and classified. This does not mean that an arbitrary selection of either the means or the partners should be made, but that in each given case such selection should be facilitated and at the same time infrastructural arrangements enabling certain means to be used and certain partners to act should be delineated.

Finally, one should add that it is not necessarily the government and its agencies that must initiate restructuring programmes and undertakings. Perhaps this is unavoidable in the initial stage of implementing the negotiated strategy, but its ultimate success will be measured by the growing initiative taken by other agents.

INSTITUTIONAL STRUCTURES AND REGIONAL DEVELOPMENT

Our investigation was carried out in the south-eastern part of Poland among nine provinces, which account for about 15 per cent of the country's area and about 18 per cent of its population. The nine provinces differ along a range of socio-economic variables,[1] but it is the major differences in institutional structures that we highlight here.

The Province of Bielsko-Biała

Bielsko-Biała province is notable for its economic and entrepreneurial dynamics. For one thing, it has a relatively large number of new private economic entities; for another, it surpasses other regions of the country in the scope and efficiency of the transformation of state-owned enterprises and their adaptation to the conditions of market economy. What is more, the existence of a broad range of industries is a structural feature of the province's economy, and many of the enterprises boast high technological standards. It is thus possible to speak of a symbiosis between the old and the new economic actors, which offers favourable prospects for further development and a chance to attract foreign capital and financial institutions.

Other important factors include the existence of several well-developed urban centres, the location of the province on the state border and along an important north–south route, and, finally, the existence of a local, albeit small, academic centre. It is difficult to given an unambiguous assessment of the impact of the organizations concerned with the region's development on the highly favourable tendencies in its economy. There must exist a correlation here, but it should not be overestimated, especially in view of the fact that these organizations have not developed a particularly extensive network of links. On the other hand, one must acknowledge the role of the Province Administrative Office, which prepared on time a strategy for the region's development and implemented it in co-operation with local partners and central authorities. This task was facilitated by the influential position and active involvement of some of the members of parliament from the region.

The Province of Kielce

The main economic problems of the Kielce district are connected with the difficult situation of many large, state-owned enterprises, particularly ones situated in the former Central Industrial Region and concerned with defence production. Their collapse is the main cause of the high unemployment in the area. There are two powerful centres of regional restructuring in the province: the larger one in Kielce and the smaller in Starachowice. A key role is played in both by agencies for regional development, which co-operate smoothly with the administration. In both centres strong ties have developed between the participating organizations (information flow, person-to-person contacts, capital links). The partners engage first of all in joint efforts to increase the volume of the region's exports. Not much attention, on the other hand, is given to other parts of the province, particularly some other large industrial towns (e.g. Jêdrzejów or Skarźysko-Kamienna). They show few signs of new institutional arrangements favourable to structural reform.

The Province of Kraków

The province of Kraków is characterized by high dynamics of economic growth and entrepreneurship. It is also notable for the particularly large number of organizations that actively participate in regional restructuring processes. These organizations represent the whole spectrum, comprising administrative structures, educational and advisory institutions, organizations for economic promotion, local-government structures, and enterprises. The high potential of Kraków as an academic centre provides the province with an adequate scientific and expert support. The organizations receive the active assistance of the Province Administrative Office and City Administrative Office. In particular, the former efficiently co-ordinates the functions of the organizations concerned with transformations in state-owned enterprises. This group of organizations includes, among others, some departments of the Province Administrative Office, the Regional Development Agency, and the local office of the Ministry of Ownership Transformations. Both the Province and the City Administrative Offices are attentive to the development of technological and transportation infrastructure in the region, with beneficial effects for business. Obviously, this is possible owing to the good financial standing of the local government, but this dependency in fact goes two ways: efforts of the local government bring in more income. On the other hand, one factor which is to some extent detrimental to regional restructuring processes is the intense rivalry between the structures of state and local-government administration.

The organizations active in the region do not form a visible hierarchy. There are strong interdependencies between them, in terms of both personal relationships and capital links, which facilitate co-operation. The impression is that almost all the participants form a single association with a high degree of mutual rivalry and control, but within a fixed institutional framework. This creates an atmosphere in which steps towards integration are readily accepted (for instance, the establishment of the Kraków Development Forum). It is an entirely different question whether such an arrangement will prove durable and efficient in the long run.

The Province of Krosno

Krosno is a province where organizations for regional development of any kind whatsoever are particularly scarce. Those which do exist are weak and unable to influence their environment in a significant way. One of the reasons is the low level of regional integration. The province has three relatively strong urban and industrial centres (Jasło, Krosno, Sanok), engaged in a permanent rivalry, while the remaining areas are of peripheral importance only. The Province Administrative Office is incapable of fulfilling its integrative function. It acts mainly as an intermediary between the central and local authorities. Therefore, the institutional configuration of the province is of an atomistic type, with severely underdeveloped network ties. Integration of the province's subregions is also very poor, resulting from the tensions and distrust that mark the relationship between the municipal authorities and the emerging business circles (particularly in Krosno and Sanok). To make things worse, the province suffers from a general lack of qualified personnel. A positive sign is the development of associations of communes (*gminy*), the lowest level of administrative units, as in the case of Brzozów and Ustrzyki Dolne.

The Province of Nowy Sącz

In the province of Nowy Sącz a rapid development of the private sector can be observed. This can hardly be attributed to institutional support, although the organizations for the support of entrepreneurship do exert some influence. The main factors, however, are local tradition and experience. An instructive example is provided by the towns of Nowy Targ and Gorlice. Both experienced a breakdown of the local labour market in the wake of the collapse of the dominating enterprise (NZPS Podhale in Nowy Targ and Glinik in Gorlice). In Nowy Targ, however, many new small firms have emerged and the unemployment rate is down to about 9 per cent, while the parallel tendency in Gorlice is much weaker, with an unemployment rate exceeding 17 per cent. Undoubtedly the favourable development in the Nowy Targ is a consequence of the long-standing tradition of small private enterprise (tanning, furriery, carpentry) non-existent in the latter.

A strong pro-enterprise centre has been formed in Nowy Sącz, mostly owing to the Nowy Sącz Chamber of Commerce and Industry. Its efficiency is largely due to good co-operation with the Province Administrative Office. The Chamber took the initiative by establishing the Regional Economic Council in 1993, which brings together the most active organizations of economic self-government. The other peculiarity of the institutional configuration of the province is the proliferation of commune-level associations, co-operating mainly in the field of tourism. Most of the communes participate in the Mountain Lands Alliance. These two structures play an increasingly important role in regional development, stimulating anti-recession activities and formulating plans for the future.

The Province of Przemyœl

There are few organizations for the support of regional restructuring in the province of Przemyœl, reflecting the general low level of economic activity in the region. The existing links between the organizations are of a formal and residual character. The organizations are aware of one another's existence, but not so much of the scope of activities that each of them undertakes. Besides, the administration often looks upon civic organizations and the local government as competitors rather than allies and potential partners, making them feel undervalued and disparaged. This syndrome is to some extent a consequence of personal and political animosities.

All in all, the province has not evolved an efficient mechanism of co-operation between organizations, which results in the weakness of its institutional system of economic restructuring. This is not compensated even by the active policy of some of the organizations, which undertake important initiatives that bring significant effects. The lack of an overal strategy for regional development, the formulation of which is also impeded by the low level of competence and qualifications of the province administration, leads to dissipation of the still rather meagre resources of the citizens' energy. The situation is further complicated by the fact that the economically active region of Jarosław has much stronger social and economic ties with the province of Rzeszów.

The Province of Rzeszów

Rzeszów province has a fairly large number of organizations that deal with structural reforms of the economy. There are some thirty organizations active in the field of economic education and consulting. Some of them have achieved a relatively high level. Two agencies for regional development function in the province, with good access to resources provided by foreign aid. However, these funds are used on a limited scale only and not always efficiently, with miscalculated projects. Besides, the multiplicity of organizations engenders conflicts of competence, which often occur in connection with the allocation of financial aid. Such a situation is a consequence partly of the lack of an overall development strategy for the province and its subregions, and partly of controversies of a personal and political nature.

Two strong centres of regional development have emerged in the province: Rzeszów and Mielec. The dominant position in Rzeszów is occupied by the Province Administrative Office and the Rzeszów Regional Development Agency, which is closely linked with the former. Those two agents are disinclined to co-operate with other organizations. In Mielec, the leading role is played by the Mielec Agency for Regional Development, which lends its support to other organizations established on its initiative. A lot of tension and disintegration in the subregion is due to the conflict between the Agency and the WSK enterprise—the dominant one in Mielec. The main issue in the controversy is the plan to establish a special economic zone in Mielec. Among other organizations should be acknowledged the important and highly constructive role of the local office of the Ministry of Ownership Transformations.

The Province of Tarnobrzeg

Two characteristic features of the province of Tarnobrzeg are the weakness and small number of its socio-economic organizations. Such a state of affairs is to be explained mainly by the slow development of private enterprise in the region, dominated by large, state-owned enterprises. Another factor is the relative weakness of informal networks in the province, which was established only in 1975. On the other hand, there is keen rivalry between the main towns of the province (Janów Lubelski, Sandomierz, Stalowa Wola, Tarnobrzeg). In the first years of the economic transformation, each of the economic agents acted on its own. A major qualitative change was brought about by the Province Administrative Office, which came up with an initiative to formulate a strategy for the economic development of the province and established the Tarnobrzeg Agency for Regional Development. These steps had a beneficial, stimulating impact and provided the local government with an example to follow. However, the matter of implementation of the strategy is far from obvious, in view of the weak system of institutional links and the low level of competence of the administrative personnel, especially at the town and commune levels. To complicate matters further, the prevailing conviction among the top-level executives in the province is that the chances of the region depend first of all on access to foreign aid. This contrasts sharply with the relatively moderate expectations for government aid. The situation is paradoxical, since, regardless of the role of small business, the economic prospects of the region are inseparable from the restructuring of large, state-owned enterprises. Under the circumstances, it seems highly appropriate that the tradition of the Central Industrial Region is now being invoked, although not yet as actively as it should. The development of the region should be based on the existing industrial potential and concentration of the available capital.

The Province of Tarnów

The institutional system of regional restructuring in the province of Tarnów comprises a relatively large number of entities, but their motto seems to be 'Each organization for itself'. Under the circumstances, the dominant role is played by the Province Administrative Office. Its contacts with other organizations are formal, pragmatically motivated, and treated by both sides as a necessary evil. Serious conflicts occur between the Province Administrative Office and administrative offices at the town and commune levels (particularly the City Administrative Office of Tarnów). This is largely a consequence of strong animosities of personal and political nature in the province, which have been observed for some time and have now gained intensity. The administrative personnel is poorly qualified. Civic organizations complain about being undervalued and disregarded by the state administration and local government alike. As a result, many apparently reasonable initiatives backfire, and many ideas are developed which are never put into practice. Despite some steps undertaken to establish a regional development agency, the idea was finally abandoned, while a Regional Council for Development was formally created, but never really started to function. The dominant feelings are those of apathy and stagnation. It appears to be the received wisdom that no initiative whatsoever makes sense, as it is always doomed to failure through the actions of certain people who will block and sabotage any project.

Four main configurations of institutional set-ups of regional restructuring emerge from the gathered data:

- *Atomistic* (Krosno, Przemyśl, Tarnów), where the organizations maintain strictly formal and statutory links, without engaging in real co-operation;
- *Bipolar* (Kielce, Rzeszów, Tarnobrzeg?), where the restructuring is organized around two centres, or poles, which have emerged within an atomistic organizational structure;
- *Hierarchic* (Bielsko-Biała, Nowy Sącz), where the capital of the province is the dominating centre, co-operating with a couple (sometimes a larger number) of smaller, regional centres;
- *Network* (Kraków), where there exist many different organizations, with tight network links between them.

In the case of the Tarnobrzeg province, the question mark indicates that this is a borderline case, which might also be classified within the atomistic type.

The following general remarks can be made in connection with the synthetic classification presented above:

- The character of a given institutional configuration is determined not by the number of organizations involved, but by the intensity and quality of links between them.
- In cases where there is an obvious shortage of organizations and their diversity is too low, their configuration will remain atomistic, despite all possible efforts to alter that situation.
- The development of the organizations depends, in general, on the development of entrepreneurial and economic activity, not the other way round. Where apathy and stagnation dominate, the organizations will not make any progress, and even external support will not allow them to become entrenched in the local structures.
- Only organizations which are fully entrenched in the local structures can efficiently support entrepreneurial and economic activity.
- The tradition and experience of small private business in a region have a beneficial influence on the entrepreneurial and economic activity.
- Another stimulating factor is the general level of education of the inhabitants and qualifications of the administrative personnel; these in turn depend on the level of schooling and the existence of an academic centre in the region.
- If favourable stimuli are lacking, even allocation of substantial funds will not solve the problem automatically. The only way to turn these funds to advantage is by using them efficiently to create the infrastructural conditions necessary to stimulate business activity in the region. This requires a good strategy and consistency in its implementation.

INSTITUTIONAL BARRIERS TO REGIONAL RESTRUCTURING

The data collected and analysed in the course of the survey allow us to enumerate the following main institutional barriers to regional restructuring:

- tensions between the central-level authorities and local-government structures, mounting since the 1993 parliamentary election, which makes the local agents increasingly distrustful of the province governors and province administrative offices. This phenomenon is reinforced by the practice of evaluating and replacing the governors on the basis of political criteria;
- general incompetence of the state and local-government administrative personnel, which results, among other things, from their relatively low wages (particularly in the case of state administration), and poor regional schooling systems at the levels of secondary, further, and higher education;
- sharp conflicts of a personal and/or political nature, either inherited from the past, or arising as a result of politicizing the local-government structures and the low level of political culture among the élites;
- lack of tradition and collective experience in the sphere of small business;
- a generally low level of socio-economic activity; disheartenment and apathy;
- unsettled ownership relations in the sphere of real property;
- the non-existence of a state treasury as a separate institution, which impedes rational management of state property;
- defective regulations pertaining to the transfer of property to communal owners, which impedes rational management of communal property;
- instability of regulations pertaining to economic activity, particularly in the sphere of taxation;
- the unsolved question of outstanding debts of state-owned enterprises, owed to suppliers, the state budget, and local budgets;
- the non-existence of specialized regional and local financial institutions that could provide capital for medium-size and small businesses, and handle the finances of local projects connected with infrastructure development;
- high levels of environmental pollution and high social costs of environmental protection, combined with a low level of ecological consciousness and pro-environment activity;
- the excessively centralized model of the state, particularly in the area of public finances; inconsistent regulations concerning the sources of revenue for local budgets;

- lack of a clear idea of the role of the state in the processes of regional restructuring, and of appropriate instruments to perform this role.

It is clear that the barriers are of a heterogeneous character. Some have a nationwide dimension, and so their removal will require central-level action, mostly in the form of legislative and systemic changes. This will in turn depend on the existence of a clear strategy for further transformation of the state and the economy, and the willingness and political ascendancy necessary to pursue it. Others, even if they are observed in all or nearly all of the provinces in question, are of a regional dimension and it is generally at this level that appropriate solutions are to be sought, although their implementation is also conditioned by the legislative and systemic measures indicated above.

Barriers of the second type, even if they are present in all or nearly all of the provinces, vary across the regions in the degree of their seriousness. This factor, combined with the high differentiation of regional conditions and determinants of growth, implies that it is an error to adopt a uniform approach to structural transformations in particular regions—a single strategy for all the provinces. Obviously, the structure of economic and social activity must differ between industrialized and agricultural provinces, and so the institutional framework for structural changes will also be different. Likewise, it is incorrect to assume that grass-root initiative is in principle better than measures introduced in a top-down fashion, or vice versa. After all, bottom-up activity often leads to petrifaction of the existing structures, instead of restructuring. The same may be the case with top-down action. Legitimacy of a grass-root initiative always depends on its objectives under the concrete circumstances, in just the same way as the efficiency of top-down measures depends on what exactly they trigger and what they block.

Characteristically, it is either in regions with the greatest potential, or in the most critically endangered areas, that external factors and resources interlock with internal ones (although for entirely different reasons and in different proportions), which is a pre-condition of structural transformations. In the high-potential regions, the mobilization of internal resources attracts external resources, while in the danger regions, external resources are allocated by way of political and administrative decisions. No such interlocking mechanisms are observed in stagnant regions. Those regions pose in fact the most difficult problem, which requires an individualized approach, tailored to the needs of every concrete case.

ASSESSMENT OF THE ROLE OF THE INSTITUTIONAL SET-UPS IN THE PROCESS OF REGIONAL RESTRUCTURING

The conclusions reached in the course of the survey justify the generalization that at the regional level, two types of institutions play a decisive role as stimulants of processes of structural change: regional development agencies (in those places where they exist), and regional policy departments of province administrative offices (although in some provinces they do not seem to show enough interest in structural transformations).

At the local level, the most important institution is the local government, particularly when it comes to handling social conflicts arising in connection with structural transformations.

Three significant observations can be made in connection with the matters in hand:

1. There is a conspicuous lack of institutions co-ordinating restructuring processes at the province level. This is the case even with provinces which do have strategies for economic development. It appears that the units of public administration best suited legally and instrumentally to perform this task are regional policy departments. Among non-government institutions, this role is best assigned to regional development agencies, and on the local level, to local-government structures.

2. The network of links between the institutions under investigation is underdeveloped. The task of crucial importance in this respect is, of course, co-operation in the pursuit of the adopted goals. Weakness of the network links is a consequence of a number of circumstances, not the least important of which is, unfortunately, competition (understood in negative terms) for domination in a given area of activity and the access to funds that such domination entails. The survey indicates that person-to-person contacts are the only significant form of links between organizations.

3. One observes an incompatibility of interests and incongruous perception of the arising problems within the configuration made up by the state administration, local-government administration and other institutions, either private, or public. Under the circumstances, it is becoming difficult to reach a consensus on the desired course of transformations and activate the factors that trigger the expected changes. In some cases, the efficiency of the institutional system is also adversely affected by the fact that major urban centres within a province refuse to co-operate on problems common to the entire region.

The impact of the institutional system on the processes of development and structural change at the province level should be seen in two dimensions. The first aspect is connected with the immediate effects of concrete measures, observable even over very brief time spans. For example, one can organize an event to promote the special qualities of the region, the directly measurable effect of which is the interest it has generated. Likewise, one can hold a seminar to instruct the interested actors about problems involved in undertaking economic activity.

The second dimension has to do with the expected effects, which are, to be sure, a consequence of the immediate effects, but neither their scale nor their timing can in fact be predicted. One could ask, for instance, to what extent the seminar proposed above will boost the entrepreneurial spirit in the region and when this effect is to be expected. It is easy to see that effects of this type are the main manifestation of the institutional influence on processes of province-level development and restructuring, but on the other hand, a temporal distance is required to observe them, as there exists an objective time lag between actions and their effects. To clarify this fundamental problem in an unequivocal way, one needs to observe the relationship between the functioning of the institutional system and the processes of development and structural change over a longer period. Unfortunately, no such observational data are available as yet in the case of most of the institutions in question. Therefore, in view of the incompleteness of the information, one should exercise utmost caution in formulating conclusions about the role of the institutional system in the restructuring processes.

The analysis leads to the following final conclusions:

1. There exists an observable correlation between the degree of advancement of restructuring processes at the province level and the development of the relevant institutional structures. This regularity holds regardless of how advanced a given entity is in terms of progress of the restructuring processes. It is, therefore, a plausible hypothesis that the institutional configuration is an important determinant of the restructuring processes at the province level.

This general conclusion can be supplemented with a number of detailed observations, such as:

- Provinces at a higher stage of development are characterized by a greater diversity of institutions.
- In provinces that rank higher on the development scale and, consequently, have reached a more advanced phase of the restructuring process, a rich institutional structure is the initiating element in the chain of dependencies shown above. It functions as an important stimulant of real-sphere processes in the regional economic system, which leads to a gradual modernization of its internal structure.
- The relationship in question takes a different form in economically poorly developed provinces, where structural transformations lag behind. The institutional configurations that exist there, on a limited scale, concentrate on defensive action, whose real aim (regardless of the statutory functions of the organizations) consists in: at best, prevention of negative structural changes—a task which is difficult to achieve, given the weak potential available; usually, preservation of the existing economic relationships, which leads directly to the retrogression of the economic structure in some provinces.
- These opposing tendencies result in mounting structural differences between provinces, which in turn increase the gap between provinces positively and negatively evaluated from the point of view of their economic structure.

- One should take notice of a certain inaccuracy in the assessment of the economic system of the Nowy Sącz province (concerning mainly its level of development, but also, indirectly, the potential for structural transformation), due to the considerable extra income, not reflected in the present survey, received by the inhabitants in the form of domestic and foreign transfers.

2. A high advancement level of the restructuring processes clearly correlates with the existence of a regional development agency in the given province. In more highly developed provinces, such agencies were usually established earlier and search for new areas of activity with greater energy.

3. The measures initiated by particular institutions at the moment allow observation only of their direct consequences. In the future, however, their indirect effects will affect the observable course of structural economic transformations in the provinces.

GENERAL CONCLUSIONS AND RECOMMENDATIONS FOR ECONOMIC POLICY

The analytical material presented in the report and the generalizations arrived at on its basis allow us to formulate the following conclusions and recommendations:

The transformation process presents tremendous challenges and problems for regional policy to cope with. It is a time when the differences between regions inevitably grow, while no adequate instruments and institutions exist for the neutralization of the negative consequences of that phenomenon. The complexity and importance of the problem have not as yet been handled appropriately at the conceptual level, either. Market transformations are an acid test of the value of various resources and skills that have been accumulated in particular regions during the process of economic adaptation to the conditions of a competitive market. Under the circumstances, those regions which lack adequate resources or the capability to utilize them generate bottom-up pressure to create and put into operation centralized mechanisms of inter-regional distribution. The adoption of such a philosophy of regional policy would in practice impede market transformations, favour economic étatism, and limit the room for self-government and entrepreneurship.

In view of this, we are very cautious about the idea of establishing at the central level a leading agent of regional policy. Instead, we suggest that it is necessary to develop a complex yet coherent system of agents involved in regional restructuring, which is especially needed at the intermediate, regional and local, levels. The system should include central institutions, too, but their main function should be to assist intermediate-level institutions, rather than to give them directions or take their place. In the future, problems of regional policy should be handled at the central level first of all by the Ministry of the Economy; they ought to be closely connected with the Ministry's regulatory functions oriented towards making the economy internationally competitive. As the economy becomes increasingly global in character, increasing the competitiveness of particular regions of Poland will be an important element of that task. The policy of the Ministry of the Economy in this field will have to be well co-ordinated with the ministries responsible for the environment, infrastructure, treasury, and public finance, and many other offices and agencies. Accordingly, we link the chances for an efficient regional policy with the reform of the economic centre of the government.

The second indispensable condition for the implementation of the idea of a regional policy outlined above is an appropriate administrative reform combined with a reform of public finance. The necessity for such a combination is obvious, if not always sufficiently emphasized, because in order to function as a genuinely independent agent, the local government needs not only to have a certain degree of authority delegated to it, but must also stand on a firm financial footing and enjoy financial autonomy.

It should, therefore, be stressed that sustained efforts are necessary to reinforce the autonomy of regional structures. The lack of regional self-government means that the public administration at that level is unable to perform efficiently the role of one of the main actors of regional restructuring. Owing to the non-existence of the institution of regional (province) budgets, most of the regional problems are addressed directly to the central agencies. And the lack of elective representative bodies at that level means that the regional communities cannot exercise sufficient control of the administration, which leads to alienation of the state administration system at province level.

The implementation of the systemic changes indicated above will create a suitable framework for regional and local agents to generate strategies of restructuring and economic development appropriate for their regions. Moreover, central-level agents will be able to concentrate on gradual removal of the general and specific barriers that impede restructuring (among others, those mentioned in the previous section). It goes without saying that such barriers can and should be eliminated even under the systemic arrangements currently in force.

The right course of action should therefore be to extricate regional policy from the redistributive scheme based on discretionary exemptions and allowances for selected economic units, combined with a limited decentralization of competence (or responsibility). The conception of 'restructuring with the participation of the state' developed in this chapter does not imply the state's passive role. Far from it. The state should acquire and develop the capacity to give positive support to regional restructuring processes in a way subordinated to the general economic strategy. The instruments of such a regional policy include, apart from appropriate systemic changes and macro-economic regulation, the organization of the national infrastructure (transportation network, border-crossings, principal power lines, etc.) and participation, in accordance with relevant agreements, in the implementation of regional restructuring programmes, understood as a means to organize the regional populations for constructive action, and not as lists of demands addressed to the central authorities.

Our analysis does not question the need and necessity of initiating mechanisms, including financial ones, for the support of restructuring processes utilizing public funds. However, the restructuring measures proposed in the regions under study are usually highly traditional and boil down to government investment. Only seldom is the possibility mentioned of joint financing of restructuring projects from various sources. Such overlooked opportunities include partnership between the public and private systems. Another factor which passes unnoticed is the importance of co-operation between the central, regional, and local systems.

The notion of joint financing has two crucial elements which should be brought to the fore. First of all, this is the right way to raise capital for institutions needed to implement the regional strategy, as it not only allows such institutions to be established, but also provides a credible mechanism for the control of their performance. This will ensure the fulfilment of their statutory functions and prevent them from becoming autonomous. Secondly, joint financing must also be used in the case of concrete projects that the institutions undertake. The point is to subordinate the projects to the objectives of the regional strategy, while simultaneously attracting new partners interested in the commercial aspects of the undertaking.

It is necessary to combine the liquidation–transformation approach and the development approach in processes of regional restructuring. Under the conditions of the transformation it is vital to reorganize the existing structure while simultaneously enriching it with new elements typical of the market economy. Maintaining a socially acceptable proportion between the two approaches is not always possible on the basis of the endogenous potential of economically weak regions.

Another necessary type of activity consists in fostering the formation and development of regional bodies (at the level of the province) in which all the institutions important for regional restructuring would be represented. The existence of such bodies significantly facilitates information exchange between particular actors and helps them reach a consensus about priorities. In many regions, forums of that type have already been established. In some provinces, however, internal conflicts within various groups effectively prevent their formation. Establishment of this kind of body should be a priority of the regional policy of the state.

It is necessary to vary the instruments of the state's regional policy. In regions which are at the forefront of systemic transformations, the rich network of institutions and the success of structural reforms mutually condition and reinforce each other. Unfortunately, in many regions negative structural adjustment takes place, which occurs within an atomistic institutional model. An additional problem stems from the clearly peripheral character of most of the border regions. Overcoming that syndrome will require the development of cross-border co-operation and of technical infrastructure, as well as state support for the formation of institutional infrastructure for regional restructuring in problem areas. Systemic reforms are threatened by the model of regional development observed in Third World countries, with sporadic islands of success in an otherwise stagnant or sagging economy.

The experience gained so far suggests that regional development agencies should be treated as the principal agent of regional restructuring and need, therefore, adequate financing from public funds so as to be able to perform efficiently their functions connected with the market transformation. In the first years of the reform, a large proportion of agencies, foundations, and other institutions stimulating business activity have taken advantage of financial aid as the principal source of funds. This means that many of them will be forced to discontinue or scale down their activities in the years to come as, in some cases, financial aid was provided only at the very outset and, in others, it is offered for a limited period only.

The establishment and development of institutions which create an economic environment favourable for business activity should be given constant support. In particular, this concerns specialized regional and local financial institutions which provide capital for small and medium-size businesses (also for increased-risk investments—so-called venture capital) and handle the financial side of local projects connected with the infrastructure. They are of special importance in problem regions, as the lack of such institutions hinders the expansion of small and medium-size business.

NOTE

1. For a detailed presentation of these variables, see Hausner *et al.* (1995).

REFERENCES

HAUSNER, J., KUDŁACZ, T., and SZLACHTA, J. (1995), *Regional and Local Factors in the Restructuring of Poland's Economy: The Case of South-Eastern Poland* (Kraków: Kraków Academy of Economics).
OECD (1993), *Problems of Regional Development Policy in Poland* (in Polish) (Warsaw).

9

Private Entrepreneurship and Small Businesses in the Transformation of the Czech Republic

VLADIMÍR BENÁČEK

The most important prerequisite for becoming an entrepreneur is the ownership of capital.

(M. Kalecki, in M. Kalecki (ed.), *Selected Essays on the Dynamics of the Capitalist Economy*)

INTRODUCTION

The impressive and spontaneous build-up of small and medium-sized private businesses in the Czech Republic from 1990 to 1993 coincided with similarly dramatic changes in the 'alternative' (shadow) economy. This is the reason why the size of the private sector is significantly statistically underestimated. The origins of the new private entrepreneurs can often be traced to communist times—to the *nomenklatura*[1] and illicit marketeers. The remaining part of society was partially handicapped in its entry into the new capitalist class because it was less endowed with various kinds of capital. Macro-economic and micro-economic policy was an important factor in promoting, redirecting, and checking the productive orientation of emerging businesses. The formation of capital and the institutional conditions influencing both the efficiency of local markets and the behavioural patterns of entrepreneurs seem to remain the core of problems affecting the development of the economy at large.

THE POSITION AND ROLE OF CZECH SMALL BUSINESSES

There are many studies describing the macro-economic performance of economies in transition from the command to the market system (see e.g. OECD 1994; EU 1995). There are also many analyses estimating the current and the expected financial standing of companies undergoing privatization (the journal *Comparative Economic Studies* is the best source for such papers). Yet surprisingly, there are only sporadic papers describing the environment from which indigenous entrepreneurship is borne and in which decisions are supposed to be made for it to survive or expand. Newly created small businesses, many of which have been established as start-ups on a green field, are especially vulnerable. The conditions they face are often very different from those of privatized state companies and corporations. This chapter attempts to unveil a part of that environment as observed from my own experience and from communication with various entrepreneurs who have become increasingly visible during the recent few years of the Czech transition to a market economy.

Non-corporate, small, and medium-sized enterprises (SMEs) play a distinctive and irreplaceable role in any transition to the market economy. At the beginning of 1993 there were approximately 1,700 industrial enterprises with over 100 employees in the Czech Republic (see Charap and Zemplinerová 1993). Most of them were toiling through (or even waiting for) the process of privatization or transformation into micro-economic units with market-consistent behaviour. By 31 December 1993, 1,262,264 licences to run small businesses or to act as entrepreneurial agents had been registered (data from the Ministry of Economics; see *Hospodářské noviny* 1994: 13). Many of these businesses were part-time sole proprietorships involving no capital, but there were also 15,451 private limited liability companies and approximately 5,500 joint ventures. According to the same source, 877,669 business entities (physical or legal persons) had been registered for trade activities operating outside corporate business at the end of 1993. The speed of development among SMEs was also staggering. In 1993 the number of such businesses increased by nearly 34 per cent, despite many exits. This figure also implies an amazing degree of real expansion in both output and employment.

The number of practising entrepreneurs in the country cannot be quantified directly from these figures, for more than one licence could be issued to the same entrepreneur, and some business entities could be represented by more than one entrepreneur. The Czech Business Register in January 1993 reported there were a total of 1,060,222 registered entrepreneurs, a number that would represent 22.5 per cent of the entire labour force of the Czech Republic. If the working family members and other employees are added in, then approximately one-third of the Czech labour force may be fully or partially associated with entrepreneurial activities in the generic private sector enjoying stabilized ownership and functional property rights. These estimates imply that the boom in the SMEs was the most dynamic economic factor behind the stormy changes in the new capitalist developments in Czechoslovakia, which were initiated practically from scratch in November 1989. The crucial aspect of this developement is that it evolved spontaneously from society's grass roots. Understanding the background of this fact and its effects on the economy as a whole is essential to gaining insight into the fundamentals of the Czech economic transformation, its successes, and its problems.

The following working hypothesis can now be formulated: even though the generic private sector (voucher privatization excluded) officially produced 21.5 per cent of the GDP[2] in 1992, its statistically unrecorded activities (including illegal or semi-legal activities) may have substantially compensated for the officially reported 27 per cent fall in total production from 1990 to 1993. Although factual effective Czech domestic production, even with this additional injection, experienced several severe structural shocks on the demand side from 1990 to 1993 followed by an intensive reallocative shake-out and falling output in many traditional industries, average household welfare remained essentially the same or even rose because product quality improved, the service sector expanded, and shortages and queues disappeared.

During the first four years of transition, the development of Czech household income was adversely affected by: (1) high uncertainty about its future flow, (2) the risk of lay-offs, (3) sharply rising inequality in the distribution of income, (4) stress about the need to acquire new skills, and (5) an intensification of effective work (except for some state companies and bureaucracy).

These negative externalities could have caused more dissatisfaction within the households about their 'way of living' than the presumed loss in official real income and the alleged decline in standards of consumption. How can the gap between reality and the official figures derived from the 'normal economy' be explained and quantitatively assessed? The problem lies in the size of the second economy. For better understanding, the second economy will be divided into the 'black' and the 'shadow' economies. Activities of the black economy include violent crime, drug-dealing, theft, extortion, smuggling, and some forms of prostitution and are explicitly prosecuted by law. The shadow economy has to do with the remaining, seemingly 'normal' economic activities concealed from official statistical recording. They vary from tax frauds to do-it-yourself activities.

The size of the Czechoslovak shadow and black economies can be very roughly estimated on the basis of several phenomena.

1. From 1990 through 1993 the Czech Statistical Office recorded that 678,000 people had quit work and that 205,000 people who had completed their schooling had entered the labour market. Of the people who had left the labour market, 308,000 had retired and 185,000 had registered as unemployed (see *Ekonom* 1994: 18). This means that the final classification of the remaining 390,000 people (i.e. approximately 8 per cent of the total Czech labour force) remains unknown. It is assumed that they 'disappeared' largely into the black and shadow economies. The OECD (1994: 15) estimates that 350,000 to 400,000 people of productive age may have been employed in the Czech shadow economy alone in 1992.

2. It is estimated that between 30 per cent and 60 per cent of the regis-

tered 'unemployed' may in fact have worked illegally in the private sector, generally as cheap (and insurance-free and tax-free) part-time workers. The number of unfilled vacancies remained large even though official statistics show that it slowly increased throughout 1993 and that it has declined again since 1994. In September 1993, for example, 1.8 unemployed people per vacancy were reported in Bohemia, whereas the figure was 7.4 in Moravia. The adjusted (i.e. slightly lower) real figures may still indicate that the labour market was very relaxed in most districts from 1990 through 1993.

3. A significant number of full-time employees have private 'parallel fringes' during their working hours, and second or temporary jobs abound. A large number of these fringes and jobs go unrecorded. In 1992 wages and salaries constituted only 49 per cent of all personal income. According to a 1993 micro-census, 29.8 per cent of all household revenues were collected from 'other economic activities', that is, second jobs, casual contracts, and capital gains (*Hospodářské noviny* 1994: 7). From 1991 to 1993 official aggregate domestic expenditure (including increasing savings) regularly exceeded aggregate disposable income by 20 billion to 35 billion kčs.

4. The estimates made at the Ministry of Economics concluded that receipts from tourism, as recorded in the balances of the Czech National Bank, were not consistent with the micro-census on tourist spending. The gap between the two sets of figures indicate that unrecorded earnings may be as high as 51 billion kčs.

5. Many managers of corporations undergoing privatization under the voucher scheme, or managers in restituted firms, have used the environment of weak ownership control to find themselves a safe niche allowing them to pursue their own shadow entrepreneurial activities by exploiting the resources of and abusing their power over the company that employs them (*Prague Post* 1994: 5).

6. The output and sales of many private companies is partly unrecorded and thus underestimated in official statistics, tax evasion being the main motive. The booming years for evading taxes on profits were 1991 and 1992. The introduction of VAT in January 1993 has checked its further growth. On the other hand, the new scheme's two-tier system of tax rates (23 per cent and 5 per cent) offers new opportunities. For example, an 18 per cent additional profit can be earned if some commodity can be easily declared for the lower 5 per cent rate while the sales price includes the 23 per cent rate. For example, retained VAT and excise taxes charged on 1993 sales of diesel oil declared as heating fuel were officially estimated at 5 billion kčs.[3]

7. The construction sector, which experienced one of the most dramatic changes during the transition, has many ambiguous features. On the one hand, it was privatized more quickly than any other sector of the economy. In 1993 private construction firms accounted for 73 per cent of the sector's output. State construction behemoths spontaneously disintegrated into small private working units based on intensive subcontracting. The nature

of their business makes the monitoring of taxes and employment very difficult. On the other hand, officially reported output in construction de-clined more than in other sectors. For example, its share of the Czechoslo-vak GDP declined from 8.7 per cent in 1989 to 6.6 per cent in 1992, whereas its share of total employment in the Czech Republic rose from 8.2 to 9.7 per cent. At the same time, wages in this sector steadily grew much faster than average after 1989, and its private firms were overloaded with contracts. One possible explanation of this phenomenon would be that the construc-tion sector is systematically under-reporting its activities.

8. A similar argument may pertain to the service sector. With its new booming private ventures and its share of total employment rising from 42 per cent in 1989 to 49 per cent in 1993, potential for under-reporting is even greater than in the construction sector.

9. With liberalized foreign trade and the rise in the number of joint ventures, the latitude for unreported activities and tax evasion has widened considerably. A country-by-country comparison of Czech foreign-trade statistics on the basis of data recorded in the neighbouring countries (for example, by comparing the Czech customs export database with the Eurostat import statistics) points to a systematic underestimation of Czech trade flows. From 1991 to 1992 the Czech figures for exports and imports were 4 per cent to 6 per cent lower.

10. The booming inward processing traffic (IPT) contracts, heavily used in many labour-intensive Czech manufacturing industries, may, because of its lenient customs regulations, underestimate the real contribution of some industries to the GDP. For example, in 1993 the Czech IPT re-exports of clothing fell short by 4.5 billion kčs, if compared with the Eurostat statistics.

11. The expansion of the Czechoslovak money supply in 1992 neither decreased the country's credit crunch (or lowered the interest rates) nor increased inflation. Money supply (M2) increased nominally by 27 per cent, while the inflation in 1992 stood at 11.5 per cent, and the reported real GDP fell by 7 per cent. The real increase in M1 was also positive (4.5 per cent). Presumably, the higher growth in the money supply was matched by hidden growth in the output of the shadow economy.

12. There was a preference of work over leisure. According to a January 1994 micro-census (ECOMA 1994), 32.9 per cent of Czechs did not go on holiday in 1993 (though they officially took leave) or used only a part of the annual paid leave to which they were entitled. This figure suggests that the trade-off between the official offer of leisure and work was biased towards work and that there were sufficient opportunities to engage in some sort of rewarding work.

13. There were 76,000 people registered for work abroad (e.g. for daily commuting to Germany) at the end of 1992. The real employment of Czech citizens abroad may be significantly above 100,000 jobs, with most of their relatively lucrative income being spent at home. The Bavarian Chamber of

Commerce estimates that Czech daily commuters alone take at least DM 300 million out of Bavaria per year (*Hospodářské noviny* 1993c: 6).

14. In June 1993 there was a community of 110,000 registered immigrants in the Czech Republic (coming mainly from Eastern Europe), 61,000 of them registered for long-term stays. They are often engaged in unrecorded temporary jobs and the second economy.

15. Private entrepreneurs account for a very small share of the aggregate profits in the private sector at large. In 1992 Czech limited liability companies reported 12.5 billion kčs in profits, whereas the 670,000 private entrepreneurs, registered as business entities, declared only 2.6 billion kčs (16 per cent of the total; see *Ekonom* 1994: 27).

16. From 1992 to 1993 inventories decreased by 73 billion kčs (measured in constant 1984 prices; see *PlanEcon* 1994: 16). A significant part of the 'useless' inventories that were sold were siphoned off by the managers in state enterprises to owners of aligned private firms, with the prices being negatively correlated to the affinity of shared vested interests in these links.

Assuming that unreported employment in the Czech economy was as productive as the reported employment, or adding the unreported revenue to the official figures, it can be roughly estimated from these facts that actual production must have been significantly higher than that officially reported. It can also be roughly estimated that at least 18 per cent of the labour force in the Czech Republic, but potentially up to 35 per cent, may be engaged in the shadow or the black economy (in a regular or temporary profession). If the corresponding income were to be added to the official figures of the GDP, which indicate a 27 per cent real fall in output from 1990 to 1993, the alleged dramatic decline in the standard of living over the last four years may *not* be a reality. The unrecorded activities of the second economy might significantly compensate for the fall in the officially reported decline in national income.

Apart from the second economy, there is another reason for an incomplete and unreliable statistics. The state system of statistics suffered a great deal from the breakdown of the hierarchical structure of central command, the proliferation of new firms, and changes of ownership. Many skilled statisticians moved to better-paid jobs in the private sector. Moreover, the whole system of statistical reporting was almost completely overhauled. The errors and omissions in reporting from all economic agents (both large and small) have increased sharply as the capacity to prosecute them has decreased. More important is that this situation has been widely expected, tolerated, and thus taken advantage of. Combined with the infant tax-enforcement institutions, the resulting bias leads to a one-way loss of information and the underestimation of income statistics. The distribution of undetected 'errors' has a natural tendency to be biased towards the negative tail of the sample, that is, in favour of the suppliers of information.

All this may explain certain Czech phenomena that are inconsistent with dramatic declines in disposable income:

1. No strikes.
2. No visible starvation or extensive pauperization.
3. The belief of the average Czech voter that lay-offs, unemployment, and bankruptcies should be expected to rise in the future and that they are a necessary condition for future prosperity.
4. Reversal of emigration. In 1992, for example, only 468 people emigrated from the Czech Lands to the West, whereas 7,332 people settled permanently in the country (*Hospodářské novíny* 1993a: 1). This development reverses the patterns of the period from 1968 through 1989, when average annual Czechoslovak emigration numbered 12,000 persons.
5. Increased propensity of households to save from their incomes. The behaviour changed dramatically from a steady average of +3.3 per cent during the 1980s and a rock bottom of −2 per cent in February 1991 to an average of 14 per cent from 1991 through 1992 and to 20.6 per cent in 1993 (CNB 1994).
6. General satisfaction of the population with the living standards. In March 1993, for example, 72 per cent of the Czech respondents in a public opinion poll declared that their standard of living was either higher (31 per cent) or the same (41 per cent) 'as in the past' (ECOMA 1994). Similar opinions were reported in January 1994 when three different and independent surveys revealed dissatisfaction by only 8 per cent, 23 per cent, and 36 per cent of the questioned households, respectively (*Hospodářské novíny* 1994: 7).
7. A high-level and steady increase in travel abroad, especially for summer vacations in Spain, Italy, Croatia, and Greece and for skiing in the Alps. In 1993 the expenditure on tourism recorded by the Ministry of Industry and Trade increased by 9.5 per cent to $505 million (approximately half of what is spent on foreign tourism by the average Spaniard).
8. Increased purchase of some high-cost durables. The sales of cars, most of which were imported from the West, increased from 137,000 in 1987 to 267,000 in 1992. A similar pattern was observed in Poland (see Winiecki 1993), where the majority of households significantly increased their wealth and the consumption of durables during the country's transition to a market economy.
9. Difficulties that businesses have in filling vacancies even in areas where official unemployment figures are high. The unemployed may often ask for wages that are well above the national average.

Of course, it cannot be assumed that the shadow and black economies were created *in toto* from 1990 to 1993 alone. What matters is the growth of that sector. A significant second economy existed in Czechoslovakia prior to 1990. Much of it (e.g. artisan moonlighting) was transformed into regular small businesses, some activities simply lost their purpose (e.g. hard currency dealing and the smuggling of standard consumer goods), and some lost intensity (e.g. the widespread do-it-yourself business). However, exits from the second economy were more than offset by entries of newcomers. The bulk of the second economy is made up of formally registered entrepreneurs who prefer not to report (and tax) the full extent of their activities. The Czech black and shadow economies of 1993 may thus be much greater than has been presumed. Their share of the GDP may range between that in the Mediterranean (20 to 30 per cent) and that in Belgium and Sweden (13 per cent) rather than approaching the German standard of 9 per cent (*Economist* 1993: 25).

If the reasoning in this chapter is correct, then effective Czech domestic product, income, and expenditure in 1993 may have been significantly higher than reported. As a working hypothesis, let it be assumed intuitively that the second economy (in its widest definition) might contribute an additional 18 to 28 per cent of the officially estimated GDP. Of course, the main engine of the hidden dynamics is not to be found in the big old corporate sector, where production was recorded quite reliably and where the development of the shadow economy was checked by other institutional barriers. The hypothesis that the corporate sector suffered a substantial real down-slide from 1990 to 1993 cannot be refuted here. The engine was effectively privatized businesses, which during that period were found preponderantly outside the corporate industrial sector; in other words, in the SMEs. In 1994 the share of SMEs (including unreported private activities), which represent the core of the overall private sector with clarified ownership, may thus comprise between 35 and 40 per cent of GDP. This still falls short of the potential 60 per cent that is normal in the developed market economies. By the same token, the non-state sector (including the firms subject to both voucher privatization schemes) may have accounted for more of the effective GDP than the 67 per cent officially estimated at the end of 1993.

It is the medium, small, and micro businesses and their hidden shadow parts that should be rated as one of the most important factors almost directly affecting the development in an economy undergoing the transformation from a command to a market system. One of many indications supporting this hypothesis is the Czech Republic's high negative correlation between the number of entrepreneurs in a district and the local unemployment rate. The second economy and the SMEs are also closely interlinked in their functioning, as expressed by their joint unprecedented expansion immediately after the liberalization of markets. They both rely on the strength of private ownership being closely related to managerial responsibilities and to the direct link between decision-making and ensuing profit or loss.

The important role of SMEs in the economic development has also been slowly discovered in the West since the oil shocks of the 1970s, and the discovery process is still continuing (see Jong-il You 1992). Besides directly contributing to the GDP, small-business development has several positive external effects that can be classified as the provision of public goods (see also McDermott and Mejstřík 1991).

1. It creates more competitive markets, improves information flows, and builds up the institutional environment.
2. It provides a source of self-sustained economic dynamism, autonomous innovation, and counter-cyclical growth.
3. It creates new jobs and high productivity standards.
4. It absorbs lay-offs from the ailing state and corporate sectors. (For example, these net reallocations to the private SMEs comprised approximately a quarter of the Czech labour force from 1990 to 1993.)
5. It provides training grounds for self-starting entrepreneurship and management.
6. It supports the capitalist ethic (e.g. the belief that one's own work, and not redistributional bargaining with bureaucracy, is the source of prosperity).
7. It creates a politically stable and strong middle class.

If these public goods are contrasted with potential 'public bads' of similar standing and with opposite influence, one could speak of the creation of institutions, pressure groups, and habits intended to create anarchy and general disobedience to the law. In fact, that is very close to what some people describe as the post-Soviet syndrome. Its correlation with the lack of space for spontaneous large-scale entrepreneurial expansion in these countries may be more than a coincidence.

If one accepts the reasoning that the SMEs as public goods provide external social benefits that cannot be commercially delivered by other autonomous business activities and that these benefits are of exceptional importance during times of transition, then the conditions for the development of the SMEs would be expected to become the focus of fundamental interest to the Czech government and other institutions representing the state and their economic policy. As the evidence shows, however, the conditions conducive to the development of SMEs has in many respects not attracted particular interest in either the Czech Lands or other transient economies. Is the argument about government failure in transition therefore well founded?

There are some views in the economic and business literature (Jong-il You 1992) that the small business revival of the 1970s and 1980s does not constitute a new historical breakthrough. If that opinion is true, then the

Schumpeterian concept of entrepreneurship is dead once and for all. It need not always imply that the corporate sector is all that matters. Some authors (e.g. Gábor 1994 as the most outspoken case) claim that the SMEs in Central Europe suffer from overcrowding and over-fragmentation. It is particularly so with the self-employed, allegedly lured into the business by naïveté, short-sighted governmental promotion, and the lack of employment alternatives. The emerging dualization of the economy can indeed become a problem for social and economic policy.

However, it is doubtful that this dualization will become a real barrier of growth, a trap for employment with no way out. Present Czech experience shows that the state or corporate sector can hardly cope with the well-known problems of agriculture—hidden unemployment, disintegration of large segments of society, subsidization, and an increase in inefficiency from anti-market intervention. The nature of small-business activities in emerging market economies is fundamentally different from that pattern. The SMEs are a result of a deliberate and flexible choice. Their activities do not downgrade skills, the capital involved is highly mobile, and they do not preclude the build-up of efficiency in big businesses. If an SME performs poorly, it becomes a burden to its practising protagonists long before it can become a burden to the government. The argument about the negative externalities of small businesses is thus untenable. As profitability declines and as the endless workload becomes unbearable, the owners of stricken ventures will move elsewhere—to alternative ventures or to the haven of a forty-hour working week in big businesses. If the latter are also in recession, one cannot blame small businesses and use the fact against them. The transition in the Czech Lands has indeed revived Schumpeterian entrepreneurial creativity. At this stage one cannot easily claim that it is a permanent phenomenon, but Schumpeterian spirit certainly helped substantially in making the transition so successful.

ORIGINS OF THE CZECHOSLOVAK ENTREPRENEURSHIP

Two legacies have moulded the massive rise of Czech (and Slovak) private economic activities since 1989: Czech capitalism and Czechoslovak totalitarian socialism.

The roots of Czech capitalism can be traced to the 1780s, when Czech Protestant inclinations began to be tolerated by Habsburg rule. The entire nineteenth century was thus marked by a Czech national revival (*vis-à-vis* Austro-German pre-eminence) that aimed more at national economic prosperity than at plain nationalism. The Czech political leaders of that period, such as F. Palacký (1798–1876) and K. Havlíček (1821–56), were typical liberal intellectuals with cosmopolitan backgrounds relying more on Czech bourgeois vitality than on local religious, nationalistic, or agricultural sentiments. In 1913 the Czech Lands were the most industrially developed part of the Habsburg Empire, competing technologically and commercially with the most advanced countries in Europe. This trend continued during the period of Czechoslovak independence from 1918 to 1938.

Czech society and economic development before 1938 was characterized by a number of principles[4] (see also de Ménil and Maurel 1993):

1. reliance on democracy;
2. a combination of market competition and foreign trade controls, cartels, and bureaucratic intervention;
3. restrictive monetary policy and convertibility;
4. enforcement of private property rights;
5. a liberal attitude towards religion and other nationalities;
6. competition between Czechs and the local German and Jewish minorities;
7. intensive free trade, mainly with the neighbouring countries to the west and south;
8. division of labour and specialization in labour-intensive and human-capital-intensive industries.

The Nazi occupation of Czechoslovakia from 1939 to 1945 severely suppressed practically all these factors. The short period of left-wing Czechoslovak capitalism from 1945 to 1948 was marked by extensive nationalization, confiscation of property, and proliferation of theories of central control. However, some features of small-scale entrepreneurship (such as the ethic of serving the consumer, esteem for the innovator and the hard worker, self-reliance, and the independence and sole responsibility of the decision-maker) were preserved from 1939 to 1948 and survived in a hidden form until the late 1960s, even though by 1964 practically all private property had been liquidated. These were the first roots of present Czechoslovak entrepreneurship, which originated in Czech capitalism. Even though post-war socialist developments may seem to have been more powerful, the long-term effects of Czech capitalism's legacy must be stressed. It became strikingly apparent in the contrast between districts with capitalist entrepreneurial traditions and industrial districts developed under socialism but void of this legacy. The Czecho-Slovak divorce can largely be explained by social and cultural conflicts emanating from different attitudes to the past and its meaning for the future.

From the mid-1960s Czechoslovakia evolved as a country with practically exclusive state ownership, which was almost completely controlled by state bureaucracy. Czechoslovak industrial production was organized into approximately 400 giant monopolies subject to hierarchical organization, a feature that was almost unparalleled in the planned socialist commonwealth. None of the major economic reforms (e.g. 1958, 1963, 1968, 1974, and 1987) changed these systematically evolving characteristics of the totalitarian state (Kysilka 1988).

The new Brezhnev style of political and economic management of these enterprises was introduced in 1970 in the aftermath of the Soviet invasion in 1968. It deepened everyone's formal hierarchical subordination to central controls, while informally the hierarchical superstructure received the first series of blows. What was innovative and quite substantial was that the managerial bureaucracy received more space for manœuvring in order to fulfil its planned production targets. As an option, there could either be an inward orientation towards innovation and efficiency or an outward orientation towards negotiations with higher-ranking bureaucracies. The former proved to be much more demanding (and thus less often used) than negotiations for, say, a softer plan, higher prices, pollution control exemptions, and increased quotas of labour, investments, energy, and raw material (see Quandt and Tříska 1990). With greater possibilities for the official accumulation of wealth, the first socialist millionaires were made in the 1970s. The inequitable distribution of income was also slowly increasing and probably became greater than in Sweden at that time. When the window-dressing of central planning and hierarchical subordination were finally abolished completely in 1990, the enterprises and the economy hardly recognized any change. The 'shadow management systems' (see Kysilka 1989) were already in full control of the economy at that time.

The Brezhnev style of management was in fact a silent revolution that introduced a new generation of socialist entrepreneurs into the ranks of bureaucracy. Even though they were definitely not the Marshall–Schumpeter brand of entrepreneurs, they significantly differed from the Stalinist bureaucrats who lacked education, followed dogmatic doctrines of communist orthodoxy, knew nothing of pragmatism, and relied on military subordination to implement decisions. Bureaucrats who fulfilled the targets in the plan (which were slack) and showed sufficient loyalty to superiors were given a free hand to exercise power over resources, staff policy, and bonus remuneration in the economic unit belonging to their respective rank in the hierarchy. The manager had powers to collude with other 'partners' of equal bureaucratic rank to form cartels, information asymmetries, and political coalitions that liquidated potential competition in production, distribution, or planning processes. In their relation to various superiors (at the level of state planning, district council supervision, and party subordination), bureaucrats had a wide range of alternatives for negotiations and vertical collusions to strengthen their strategic standing. In fact, the management of the monopolies or their main divisions was in control of both the micro and macro levels of the economy (see Mlčoch 1991).

Typically, career-building in socialist Czechoslovakia required the selected future élite to complete university, enter the petty functions in the party network, then work in the higher ranks of the administrative bureaucracy. Only after reaching maturity, approximately after the age of 50, could a member of this élite assume the lucrative and powerful job of a director of some corporation.

This is the second legacy of the Czechoslovak private entrepreneurship, which was so quickly and easily reintroduced within three years after 1989. The essential point here is that these two legacies originated from two incompatible and in many aspects antagonistic social groups. For the sake of orientation, let us call the one group *operators*; the other, *nomenklatura*. The following approximate list of occupational activities is offered to distinguish between the two groups.

Operators: Restaurant and hotel staff; cab-drivers (or drivers of any automobile); foreign-exchange touts; greengrocers; used-car dealers; repair workers; shop managers; shop assistants for personal sales; gas station operators; stock-keepers; popular entertainers; agents selling or buying scarce supplies; organizers and administrators of queues; bureaucrats issuing licences, certificates, and permits; artisans; tradesmen; and ringleaders of organized crime.

Nomenklatura: Directors of companies and their deputies; heads of divisions or financially independent units; paid party *apparatchiks*; high-ranking bureaucrats in ministries and district and municipal councils. This definition of *nomenklatura* covers groups extending beyond politicians of the Communist Party (CP), army officers, and police agents, as is sometimes implied, and does not include rank-and-file party members. When speaking about *nomenklatura*, one should distinguish between ranks (e.g. of those of the central, county, or district-committee levels).

Table 9.1 presents the most characteristic differences between these two entrepreneurially oriented groups. Conversely, some of their characteristics and values were similar:

1. Reliance on their own decision-making from a set of alternatives.
2. Collusion with bureaucratic networks.
3. Barriers against the entry from the group of outsiders.
4. Position of a social minority with class distinctions (e.g. I intuitively estimate that the operators may have accounted for 10 to 15 per cent of employment; the *nomenklatura*, for 4 to 8 per cent).
5. Wide involvement in money transfers with other economic agents.
6. Higher-than-average income, including unofficial and fringe incomes (in the late 1980s, for example, the annual income of operators may have been two to ten times higher than the national average; of *nomenklatura*, two to five times higher, with both estimates being intuitive).
7. Accumulation of money (cash, bank deposits, and convertible currency holdings) or wealth (real estate).
8. Feelings of being an overworked élite with natural privileges.
9. A high degree of pragmatism and adaptability and a propensity to tolerate or use unethical principles as their means.
10. Admiration of the Western (mainly lower-middle-class) life-style.

TABLE 9.1. *Characteristics of two types of entrepreneurship in Czechoslovakia*

Characteristics	Capitalist Roots (operators)	Socialist Roots (*nomenklatura*)
Type of market environment	Perfect competition	Imperfect competition
Attitude to market	Market development	Market suppression
Communist Party support	Negative	Positive
Size of activity	Small business	Corporations
Main fields activity	Small-scale services and exchange	Corporate sector, material production, banking
Contacts with state bureaucracy	Occasional (through bribing)	Daily (through subordination)
Original source of power	Bargaining skill	Politics, personal networks
Source of main income	Shadow or illegal	Official remuneration
Fringe benefits	None	Various(housing, car, travel, etc.)
Execution of power	Through skill and cash	Through bureaucracy, remuneration, and pull
Social prestige	Low	High
Risk-taking	High	Low
Level of education	Low	High

11. Persuasion that the state-owned physical and financial capital administered by them on an employee contract basis is identified so much with them that they can use it as their own property and appropriate a part of the accrued profits or wealth.

Without doubt, even though the vested interests of the two macro groups were of a conflicting nature, their mutual workaday dependence on liquid money, bureaucratic networks, and shadow markets, the availability of which was not uniformly distributed among them, pressed them into close collaboration, tolerance, and ultimate collusion in running business.

There is still one aspect that requires comment, the influence of foreign capital and foreign entrepreneurs on the local capitalistic scene. While foreign capital was officially barred from entering the small-scale privatization scheme, and foreign portfolio investments went beyond the foregoing definition of small and medium-sized business, a great deal of room remained. Foreigners could enter the local entrepreneurial class either by using fictitious domestic owners or, as with former Czech emigrants, by accepting back their Czech citizenship and permanent Czech residence in order to be eligible for the property restitution scheme. The high purchasing power of foreign capital became an immediate advantage hardly matched by local capital. The link between foreign capital and domestic entrepreneurs (real or fictitious) is thus very difficult to uncover, even though it may be quite strong. The evidence that only about a quarter of the transactions made through the small-scale privatization scheme were leveraged by bank loans may lead to the assumption that the share of the foreign capital behind it must have been significantly higher than officially recorded.

Let us now examine the remaining group of 'non-committed' citizens or workers, who fell into neither of the above categories. I shall call them *outsiders*. The basic question is whether this group was void of entrepreneurial or managerial talent. The outsiders are a very heterogeneous group whose core consists of people who never aspired to be leaders, innovators, or independent workers and who would enter the ranks of entrepreneurs only by mistake. Within the ranks of outsiders there is a large subgroup of professional workers of technical orientation (engineers, computer whiz kids, workers in applied sciences, etc.) whose ambitions to be independent can be strong. Another important subgroup is formed by low-ranking managers (e.g. supervisors, foremen, heads of small teams) whose 'higher' position in socialism was generally not associated with privileges. (It often implied more work for less pay.) Without doubt, these two subgroups have serious potential for the recruitment of entrepreneurs. Hence, the whole heterogeneous group of outsiders, which comprised more than three-quarters of the inhabitants, may contain at least as many potential entrepreneurs as the other (much less numerous) two groups. Why, then, have so few outsiders gone into business?

The mechanism of career-building under communism was such that only a fraction of the talent conceded—or was asked—to enter the ranks of the *nomenklatura*. Most of the eligible were either blankly refused or had ethical or aesthetic inhibitions that kept them from fighting for attention and had to satisfy themselves with staying with the crowd. Entrance to the group of operators was also limited in that it required a certain amount of capital and certain skills which, because of their low educational demands and slicker nature, were intellectually not very appealing. The entrepreneurially minded members of the subgroup of outsiders could satisfy their natural urge by organizing sports, arts, hobbies, holiday trips, children's camps, local trade union events, underground political dissent, and the like. Their entrepreneurial skills were largely frittered away in non-business-oriented activities, practised almost exclusively on an amateur, voluntary, and unpaid level, and were not rooted in any professional aspirations. Nevertheless, their skills were not completely wasted or forgotten, and their results were often internationally recognized (e.g. in sports or arts). It was these very people who were pressed to take the badly paid, low-ranking positions of team heads and assigned organizational responsibilities.

Even though some segments of the heterogeneous group of outsiders (e.g. among the intelligentsia or engineers) are endowed with a high level of human capital, it was the social capital (or, more specifically, the personal network capital), as a subset of human capital, that really mattered (Bourdieu 1986; Šík 1993).[5] They represent that part of human capital that includes interpersonal links in an exclusive coalition (a network of closed informal contacts), that is built for sharing (insider) information, favours, or privileges, and that has its implicit purpose in securing economic gains, namely, wealth and power. Unlike physical capital, the use of social (network) capital is oriented primarily to the redistribution of existing opportunities, not to the creation of new values. As a social phenomenon, network capital is not a complement to perfect market behaviour. In fact it relies heavily on the concept of 'voice' (see Cyert and March 1963) in the environment of market imperfections, market failures, and bureaucratic decision-making. Surprisingly, it was not a sunk capital when the transition began in 1990.

The speed of capital transferability in an economy under transition seems to be crucial to the success of going into business. Cash and social (network) capital are best suited to this purpose. The *nomenklatura* and especially the operators were practically the only domestic groups having available liquid financial capital. But since the total stock of asset money in all post-communist countries lagged far behind what was required for starting business transactions, the next capital available for relieving that constraint was social (network) capital. Unlike the development of financial capital, that of social (network) capital boomed during totalitarian socialism because that kind of capital was the essence of the local bureaucratic power game, the shadow management systems, and the parallel markets.

Because of the highly uneven distribution of transferable capital of all kinds at the end of 1989, some owners had an advantage in using it to start their own private businesses. Liquid financial assets were highly concentrated in the hands of operators and *nomenklatura*, the former most probably being more successful than the latter, whereas the distribution of social (network) capital favoured the *nomenklatura* over the operators. The outsiders trailed last in both cases. Their competitive position in technical or classical education, foreign languages, and cultural overview, though helpful in earning them the positions of new managers, administrators, or politicians, could not offset their disadvantages in the ownership of the liquid forms of capital that were the most important assets for acquiring private businesses and becoming higher-ranking entrepreneurs.

WHO ARE THE NEW 'BIG' CZECH ENTREPRENEURS?

According to an extensive sociological survey carried out at the Czech Academy of Sciences (Vítečková 1993), the structure of Czech private entrepreneurs in December 1992 had some interesting features. The study was limited to a widely distributed sample of 1,000 business people, trades people, and artisans, each of whom had registered as a firm with legal status and had hired a staff of employees. It excluded persons licensed for self-employed proprietorship. In 1992 the latter numbered over 1 million (out of 4.8 million full-time employed Czechs), whereas the number of private firms with registered legal status and relevant capital endowment did not exceed 80,000. Thus the number of 'big' Czech entrepreneurs with capitalistic businesses of their own, selected from the set of the existing one and a quarter million people with entrepreneurial aspirations, could be estimated at approximately 120,000.[6] The origins and mobility of Czech entrepreneurs are summed up in Table 9.2. If these estimates are correct[7] and reflect at least the basic structure of past Czech management and present private business, then a number of implications can be inferred:

1. There is a very strong link between the incidence of having been a communist bureaucrat in a top or middle managerial position and membership in an emerging class of private capitalist entrepreneurs. Given that the vast majority of communist 'executives' survived the shocks of the 'Velvet Revolution' (the reshuffling of positions was often sufficient mimicry) and that more than 80 per cent of the manufacturing output in 1992 was still produced in the non-private sector, practically all departures (forced or voluntary) must have been of people going into private businesses. (The politically minded reader is expressly warned that the aim of this chapter is *not* to make value judgements on the local socio-political scene!)

2. Since practically all top- and middle-ranking managers prior to 1990 were members of the CP, and since a high proportion of the low-ranking

TABLE 9.2. *Structure of Czech private entrepreneurs in 1989 and 1992 (stylized facts)*

Rank of management	Intuitively estimated employment, 1989 (A)	Number and highest pre-1990 rank of entrepreneurs who legally founded firms, 1990–1992[a] (B)	Percentage degree of transition from A to B (B/A)
Top	45,000	13,200 (11)	29
Middle	161,000 (3)	19,200 (16)	12
Low	806,000 (15)	52,800 (44)	7
No managerial rank	4,362,000 (81)	34,800 (29)	0.8
TOTAL	5,374,000 (100)	120,000 (100)	2.2

Note: Figure in parentheses represent percentages of the respective total.

[a] See Vitečková (1993).

managers also had to be party members, approximately half of the emerging Czech capitalist class were people chosen by the CP. However, if one enquires into the transition of real *nomenklatura* to private businesses and assumes that only the top communist management and middle-ranking management was associated with *nomenklatura*, then such people may have accounted for less than 27 per cent of the new private entrepreneurs, a figure far lower than that claimed in most public opinion polls. The correlation between the *nomenklatura* and capitalism in the Czech Republic seems to be strong, less because of its extent than because of its intensity. It should be remembered that the *nomenklatura* had other stakes to win, such as those in top management, in boards of directors of the new corporations privatized largely by the voucher scheme (banks, industrial firms), and in investment funds.

3. None of the above statements about the *nomenklatura* are meant as value judgements. What is important is their descriptive implications. Many Western observers of the transition make the mistake of tacitly assuming that Eastern totalitarian society was completely devoid of any entrepreneurship, organizational spirit, and rationality and that all these qualities thus have to be imported and introduced from abroad. The philosophy of the West's early approaches to German unification still has its heirs. The most assertive conclusion of that sort is the absurd recommendation to import entrepreneurial know-how exclusively from the more dynamic Far East. On the contrary, successful entrepreneurship is often found to be closely linked with domestic management, domestic traditions, and domestic resources—a fact that is often disregarded even by local insiders. The local *nomenklatura* must have some place in the process.

4. Generously speaking, it might be conceded that in the last twenty years of its rule the CP in Czechoslovakia developed an extremely enlightened and far-sighted personnel policy. (However, very few observers among the dissidents would have come to this surprising conclusion prior to 1990!) Less generously, one can see an updated version of Orwell's *Animal Farm*. The true evaluation lies somewhere in between. Admittedly, one of the main reasons for the collapse of communism was that it failed to offer the vast majority of people a free opportunity to fulfil their ambitions. Instead, it nurtured only a narrow, privileged élite organized in the upper levels of the party hierarchy. On the other hand, it required from that élite some degree of animal vitality and leadership, which have now proved to be viable skills in all circumstances. This assessment would fully fit Baumol's (1990) theory that entrepreneurship and its aim of profit or power is omnipresent in all societies. The problem lies in the question of which alternative economic fields (productive, unproductive, or destructive) and under what conditions and incentives entrepreneurship is allocated in a given period.

5. Had the party *nomenklatura* been subject to a certain degree of efficiency, competition, and meritocracy, its members could have had strong

motives to take part in the change of the inefficient system of planning, public property, bureaucracy, and political paternalism that limited their motives for wealth and power. In other words, the *nomenklatura* would not have minded velvet-type revolutions so much. More surprisingly, the opposite is also true. Thus, even the new political élite, recruited from the ranks of former dissidents, may have reasons for accepting their former oppressors as business allies.

6. The rate at which former low-ranking state managers and supervisors are making the transition to new private businesses seems to be quite high, accounting for 44 per cent of the total. (A large percentage of them may actually come from among the operators and the returned emigrants; it is now difficult to distinguish between these groups.) Lacking capital and bureaucratic connections, the former low-ranking managers found their most natural destiny in establishing their own small businesses, for which they had the experience and the human capital. It is probably in this subgroup of outsiders, who have not been able to exploit their potential fully until now, that future hard-working, talented entrepreneurs are hidden and from where they may be recruited.

7. The most interesting finding is that only a negligible fraction of people with no formal managerial position during the communist era had succeeded in entering private entrepreneurship by the end of 1993. In addition, a significant part of this group must have been former operators whose entry into the ranks of entrepreneurs was much easier. Unfortunately, the survey does not enable one to separate operators and outsiders from the statistical sample of 'no managerial rank'. If it did, then the 0.8 per cent degree of transition among those with no managerial rank (see the last column in Table 9.2) would imply that it was even more difficult for this significantly larger subgroup of employed persons—the rank-and-file wage-earners with neither communist managerial experience nor stakes in illicit marketeering—to enter the emerging capitalist élite of owners and entrepreneurs. Even if it is conceded that most outsiders were the less ambitious and the less motivated workers who can be considered entrepreneurial 'dead wood' in any case, one cannot exclude the existence of barriers to their outward mobility. That means one cannot deny that, during the communist period, some talented people found themselves in the non-managerial group of employees only because of prosecution, persecution, political discrimination, personal resistance to political powers, or commitment to ethical principles. Therefore, there must have been obstacles other than managerial incompetence preventing outsiders from entering business on a larger scale after 1989: lack of wealth, lack of appropriative access to public property, and lack of pull within the bureaucracy or old-boy network.[8]

The Czech government has opened extremely wide possibilities for the transfer of property because more than half of the national physical capital was privatized between 1991 and 1994. Unfortunately, this has not prevented an uneven distribution of opportunities in the majority of schemes that have favoured privileged social groups. Nor has there been perfect competition for property acquisitions among these privileged groups.

Very similar reasoning applies to conditions for creating new small businesses. The only exception was that start-ups had to acquire their property and physical capital on more competitive markets asking higher competitive prices. Consequently, their financial resources for required capital investment had to be correspondingly greater. Thus, internal net returns on capital (i.e. net profits after deduction of interest and instalments for credit disbursement) were lower for the start-ups. The start-ups should be distinguished from ventures established by taking advantage of softer approaches to privatization (restitution, direct transfer, non-competitive buy-out, or semi-legal appropriation). Having acquired their assets at a discount, ventures in the latter group could augment their annual net return by an addi-tional rent that made their further business activities more competitive.

Perhaps another classification is more important for long-run developments. Some people went into business on strong entrepreneurial impulses. In their life-long mission their profit margins, or the size of the firm they started with, do not matter. Under healthy capitalist conditions they will always be among the winners. On the other hand, there may be people who set up their own businesses just because their possible employers were completely incompetent or because they had a unique chance to privatize under advantageous conditions. As their industry recovers, they will once more return to being employees. Without doubt, a substantial percentage of the Czech entrepreneurs were people from the latter group. At some point, then, many SME exits and bankruptcies should be expected. If it is assumed that approximately 20 per cent of the whole labour force can find employment in business activities (in transition it could be even more), then economic policy should provide conditions for the unhampered entry of newcomers intent on replacing the exiting entrepreneurs. In the Czech Republic a substantial degree of mobility can be expected to continue over the next five to seven years among members of the entrepreneurial class, both within their hierarchy and in the interchange with the rest of the society. There are many frustrated outsiders waiting for opportunities, and many of them deserve a chance. It is a well-known fact that the barriers to entry are mounting as the transition proceeds.

It would be disturbing if, in emerging capitalism, it were found to be as hard to rise from the bottom as it was under communism. It may be that the process of rising is now slightly different and requires different techniques, but for those without the access to capital it remains difficult and humiliating.

THE PRESENT ENVIRONMENT OF THE SMALL BUSINESSES IN THE CZECH REPUBLIC

Let us now turn to the type of environment, procedures, and risks that challenged a standard entrant to a small or medium-sized Czech business from 1992 to 1994. One may assume that the 'standard entrant' commanded only the average stock of savings per capita (40,000 kčs = $1,300), possessed average wealth (owned real estate worth 300,000 kčs = $10,000), had no past career in the group of operators or *nomenklatura*, had significantly above-average entrepreneurial skills, was able to work fourteen hours a day and seven days a week, was determined to comply with tax laws and other legal regulations, and did not want to run a self-employed, one-person business with no legal status and little capital requirement.

Registration and Licensing for Entry

Formal entitlement to any new business entry started with registration and licensing for the given type of expected activity. The decision to issue the licence lay exclusively with the district council within whose jurisdiction the applicant lived. A licence was granted for each required activity from a list of approximately 300 classified entries, so a standard business had to apply for several of them. The fees were 2,000 kčs for each business activity and 1,000 kčs for each craft entry. To meet the requirements for each given activity, the applicant (not the employees) had to show proof of education, professional examination, and period of practice. The processing of business applications lasted one to four months, subject to difficulties of renegotiation. Even for fully qualified candidates, there was no guarantee that the registration would be successful within that period. A bribe proportional to the expected producer surplus could significantly shorten both the time and the uncertainty. The problems of registering limited liability companies were similar.

Availability of Capital

Czech entrepreneurs not lucky enough to have recovered property nationalized after 1948 (most of it was nationalized between 1945 and 1947) or to have recently inherited some property from abroad had to find their own way of financing the new business. The initial capital of $20,000 was supposed to be the minimum required for most ventures—an amount that had been impossible for an 'outsider' to amass legally during the communist period. It had been achievable for the *nomenklatura*, however, and had been routine for black-marketeering operators.

The demise of state control and the onset of devaluation, price liberalization, and loose enterprise discipline from 1990 to 1992, combined with a rise of private contracting, created lucrative opportunities for the private accumulation of capital. Some opportunities were legal (exports, imports, the sale of scarce stocks, and speculation), some were not (fraud, theft, insider trading, and so forth). Even this additional injection of private capital gains was far too little to cover the transaction costs of establishing private businesses and privatization on the scale prepared by the government from 1991 to 1993. Actually, the wild appropriation of property and capital in the Czech business environment was relatively small compared to that in other countries under similar circumstances. The traditional sense for financial discipline, functioning property registration and accounting, observance of the law, and the low rate of organized crime prevented spontaneous privatization from becoming a dominant way of enrichment.

Thus, in their search for capital, most future Czech entrepreneurs had to rely on the financial market, primarily on the availability of bank credits. This situation was significantly different from that in developed market economies, where retained profits and depreciation provide between 55 and 75 per cent of total investment resources. In 1993, after three years of unparalleled growth, the Czech banking sector had developed considerable size, density, and scope. The number of bank employees jumped from 8,000 in 1989 to 54,000 in 1994. Nevertheless, its efficiency was still low, and its functioning was subject to market imperfections. The real interest on deposits (the nominal rate ranged from 2 to 12 per cent) was generally negative, and the nominal interest rate on loans (15 to 20 per cent) still did not clear the market. The banks, like skilled profit-maximizing oligopolists, were limiting the supply of their services by universally refusing to finance 'risky ventures', that is, those without at least a 100 per cent mortgage or other secure collateral available. Hence, as confidential personal communication widely discloses, the entrepreneurs with highly promising projects but no property for collateral (say, for investing in inventories or paying for the lease of premises) were regularly refused credit unless a sufficient bribe (2 to 5 per cent of the loan) were paid. It even became routine to require a 2 per cent bribe for credits hedged by a mortgage—a rather unorthodox interpretation of both market clearing and corporate governance in the privatized Czech banks. It is the bribe that blurs the distinction between a loan for a serious investment project and a non-performing loan purposely acquired for capital-stripping and subsequent suicidal bankruptcy. Even though the latter type of non-performing credits have been on the decrease since 1993 (there were estimates that they constituted up to 30 per cent of loans from 1991 through 1992, whereas estimates for 1993 are 10 to 15 per cent), their role in spoiling financial-market ethics is substantial.

The rent-seeking of the bank agents, behaving like effective owners (without paying taxes and without feeding the appropriated economic rents back into the banking), is a sign of weak market rules and a failing financial market. It shows all the signs of moral hazard and incomplete contracts, with all the ensuing devastating externalities (see Eswaran and Kotwal 1989). The resulting losses due to inefficient allocation of capital, the insufficient formation of investment in the borrowing by private businesses, and the sustained concentration of capital in the hands of those who were lucky enough to come in during the early stages of Czech capitalism are also creating negative side-effects throughout society.

Acquisition of the Business Premises

Once the entrepreneurs succeeded in securing financial resources, the next stage was to acquire the business premises, a process also subject to official approval. A host of problems could be avoided if the entrepreneurs received a real-estate restitution or if they intended to run the business from their homes. Otherwise, they had to enter the real-estate market and lease the property (very often just for one year) or purchase it. The private property market quickly became quite competitive and efficient. The problem was, however, that its prices followed the housing shortages and the annual rents in towns could reach $350 to $700 per square meter. The payment often had to be disbursed before the premises were approved by the district council.

Acquiring the premises in an auction was a special case subject to the small privatization scheme. Auction prices could be much lower than competitive prices, especially if the information was incomplete or if the auction was rigged. That means that the success of the future entrepreneur depended on his or her capacity to comply with the illicit dealings. For example, the entrepreneur was forced to become involved in the 'protection' ring and pay for fending off competitors. But entrepreneurs were most likely to find themselves on the opposite side, as a target of racketeering and extortion intended to dissuade them from participating in the auction. Other privatization schemes available were public tenders (e.g. submitting a 'competing project' for privatization) or bids for a 'direct sale' (i.e. an exclusive right to purchase property for an administratively stipulated price). The decision made by a privatization commission was often subject to unexpected hazards such as luck, bureaucracy, insider trading, and corruption.

Green-field capital investments seemed to be even more dramatic events, as chronicled by an account in the local press of a Czech entrepreneur who successfully opened his brand-new glass factory employing seventy-five workers (*Profit* 1993: 4). The number of rubber stamps, permissions, and approvals that were needed totaled over 900. The building and refurbishing of the factory took ten months; the preparations and approvals took twenty-six months. The privatization of an already established and equipped company is a much simpler operation in both transaction cost and capital requirements. In the long run, however, it may not be the most efficient approach to market adjustment, restructuring, and use of resources.

Acquisition of Approval for Running the Premises

Approval for operating the business premises was granted by the district council within whose jurisdiction they were located. The application was placed through the district council within whose jurisdiction the applicant resided. Part of the procedure involved obtaining approval from the Commission for the Environment. It was irrelevant whether the premises in question were in the applicant's own home, whether the same activity had already been approved for and carried out by the previous owner (who, for example, had just gone bankrupt), or whether the business by its very nature could not damage the environment. The whole approval process could last from three to six months, with no certainty about success. This could become critical for those who had already had to pay for the premises and who could run the business immediately.

Often only a bribe (sometimes a substantial one) or an offer to share the property could accelerate the procedure. The exclusive administrative monopoly of the district council was the main source of its power. The complaints filed over the district council's bureaucracy, intentional procrastination, unfounded objections, or professional incompetence seldom received a positive response. Applicants generally avoided raising them for fear of retribution by the council, which could refuse approval or later order financial audits or inspections of hygiene, or simply harass the entrepreneur on endless (often fictitious) charges.

Hiring of Staff

The travails of entrepreneurs were not over once the business was permitted to open. One of the most damaging legacies of the communist past was, and still is, the devastation of the workers' morale. The continuing very low level of unemployment in the Czech Republic, sustained by the cautious bankruptcy policy of the government and commercial banks (see Hlaváček and Túma 1993) and by numerous schemes for resuscitating indebted corporations, has not been conducive to change in work discipline. For a country in intensive transition, the average unemployment rate of 3.14 per cent in May 1994 is tantamount to full employment. Much can be improved through remuneration incentives. Their impact on performance and discipline crucially depends on the strength of negative alternatives. That is, habits of accepting unemployment or seeking only transient employment should become a deterrent. As shown by Japan (where unemployment rates are below 2 per cent), the transaction cost of remunerative incentives should be significantly greater than zero for the employees as well.

Even though Czech wages still significantly lag behind the poorest countries in Western Europe, overall productivity is often proportionally lower. The problem is not so much that the workers expect a soft, regular, eight-hour shift and do their shopping or telephoning during work hours or that they lack the necessary education or skills. More damaging is the lack of identification with their job. They are not accustomed to co-operating professionally in an informal way, and they refuse to take risks, initiative, or personal responsibility in their work. But such co-operation, risk, initiative, and responsibility are essential elements of the environment required by the new post-Fordist organization of business (see Piore 1991). Customer-friendly behaviour, immediate response to demand, and loyalty to the firm are still considered alien and often judged as a 'disgusting hypocrisy'. Rises in pay that are 25 per cent to 30 per cent above average are not considered by the workers a sufficient incentive to change their performance. In fact, similar pay rises have been in effect since 1992, but they have only increased inflationary pressures, not increased productivity. Wage rises of more than 40 per cent (as introduced by some foreign companies and banks) would be prohibitively costly in most local firms and would deplete their falling profits even further, especially since the introduction of social security and the wage regulation. Profits in Czech industry fell by 28 per cent in 1992 (see Wörgötter 1994: 71), and the only cost item that increased in the industrial sector in 1992 was total wages, which rose by 5 per cent.

The bilking of the employer and the customers is quite frustrating. The firing of an employee and the hiring of a substitute is often a long and very costly process because of high transaction costs. The entrepreneur and his family are thus often the only people who can bear the strain of operating a small private business. Competition and the vision of future opportunities drive them to work shifts lasting from twelve to eighteen hours with no weekends off. These conditions are especially typical for entrepreneurs who used not to belong to the privileged classes, who started from scratch, and who are trying to earn their own capital for the next real start or to repay a loan.

TABLE 9.3. *Average annual gross wages in the Czech Republic, 1992 and 1993* ($US)

Year	Type of firm		
	Private	State	International
1992	2,025	2,062	2,423
1993	2,748	2,878	3,535

Source: CSU (1993, 1994).

Daily Business

The transition from a seller's market to a buyer's market, which took place mainly from September 1990 to June 1992 and for which the macro-economic changes orchestrated by the government were absolutely crucial, was the most significant condition for quickly consolidating private activities based on market competition. The nature of these productive entrepreneurial activities is clearly different from becoming rich through artificially contrived market failures (economic rent-seeking) or bureaucratic redistributive concessions. However, a transition from a seller's to a buyer's market had not been completed by the beginning of 1994. Some commodities in demand (often cheap domestic products, some of them piled up in factory inventories) were still missing from the market, or it took a great deal of time to discover who provided them. Among other ills, the price differentials were sometimes irrationally wide, the quality of the same product fluctuated and did not relate to the price, and the customers were cheated or rudely treated (see e.g. ECOMA 1994). On the other hand, some buyers exercised their power over suppliers by requiring a tacit personal commission for a contract or by demanding acceptance of cash payment with no invoice. These behavioural patterns signal that Czech market prices may not be perfect and that market clearing may be incomplete (Benáček 1993).

Because the discipline of suppliers significantly consolidated in 1992, the stocks necessary to secure the regular flow of business were much lower. The credibility of inter-firm payment discipline remained a critical problem, however. The processing of a bank transfer could take up to a month, so some recipient firms could not honour their other payments because they were often short of liquidity and the banks were reluctant to engage in short-term credit services. There was also a high risk of the customer's long-term default in payments because some firms took these payments as an opportunity to raise their capital. Hence, some firms refuse to accept anything but advance payments in cash, even for large contracts. Inter-firm indebtedness in 1993 was estimated by CNB (1994) to be around 160 billion kčs.[9] Legal action against payment defaults was not a credible threat because the whole state judiciary system was, and remains, in crisis.

The price that Eastern Europe must pay for its capitalist resurrection is an increased intensity of work, an escalation of general uncertainty, and the proliferation of crime.[10] Whereas the first two characteristics are natural and revitalizing necessary conditions, the last one is connected with a failure of public administration. Even though the development of modern public administration in the Czech Lands has been proceeding relatively rapidly since 1990, it has not kept pace with what is necessary. Public administration is one of the most expensive institutional social networks. It depends on long-term investments in human and physical capital, both of which are lacking in an economy in transition. At the same time, unfortunately, the demands on public administration during transition are much higher than in established market economies. Most laws must be rewritten; the new laws are too complicated to be absorbed into daily routines; their many loop-holes tempt too many people to circumvent the laws; and the shortage of qualified lawyers, judges, police, and administrators is often exacerbated by contrived scarcities. Naturally, the underground tries to fill the missing links in the 'markets' for these services and, hence, profit from the situation. Most entrepreneurs are at loggerheads over how to escape this maze in the rules of the game.

Financial Links with the State

There are two positive idiosyncrasies characteristic of traditional Czech society: abiding by fiscal obligations and saving. It came as a surprise that the budget revenues from the ill-prepared new VAT scheme of 1993 sur-passed all expectations. This scheme, which introduced a 5 per cent tax on food and a 23 per cent tax on most other products, became a nightmare for small entrepreneurs. The law was very complicated, was amended several times, and was badly advertised. The help offered to SMEs by the tax exemption option later proved disadvantageous, for it disorganized the pricing procedures and created the need for even the smallest businesses to search for professional accountants, who were very scarce.

The level of taxation in the Czech Republic has been high even by some West European socialist standards. The sceptics argue using Murphy's Law, which holds that once taxes are introduced they are never lowered and can only go higher. An income (profit) tax of 45 per cent, with practically no tax relief for heavily investing or newly founded enterprises, was a great disincentive to run one's own business. Many small firms were tempted to manipulate costs (e.g. of expensive furniture, electronics, cars, or travel) in order to arrive at a 'fair' level of taxation (Charap 1993). Another serious burden was the compulsory 49.5 per cent social and health insurance that has been levied on gross payroll since 1993 (of which 36 per cent was paid by the employer). In addition to the 13.5 per cent insurance contribution by the employee, personal income tax (15 to 47 per cent) must be also paid, so that the individual's net income in its upper brackets is only 48 per cent (or less) of the labour cost paid for them by the employer. For example, if the average gross wage in international firms at the end of June 1994 was 9,000 kčs per month, and if the 36 per cent insurance is added, the resulting labour payment averages 12,240 kčs per month, or $5,100 per year. It is definitely much more than what Table 9.3 might indicate. The net income after income tax and insurance is deducted comes to 6,650 kčs per month.

Some entrepreneurs admit that monitoring and adapting the new fiscal system was the most demanding challenge of the whole transition. It some-times took more decision-making time than all the other remaining prob-lems. On the other hand, some of the country's industrial-policy schemes that would have been far less bureaucratic and that would now promote the orientation to investment instead of consumption were not practically sup-ported. One of them may have been accelerated depreciation, that is, the use of an additional portion of gross profits for the partial repayment of the new investment goods during the first year after their purchase. Other schemes of tax relief for investment expenditures could also be considered.

Tax evasion has been a strong temptation for small businesses that sell directly to consumers or foreign firms. The net 'profit' can thereby be increased two- to threefold, with the risk of prosecution being negligible. The Ministry of Finance has estimated the arrears in tax payments alone to be more than 10 billion kčs in 1993 (including the corporate sector), while the SME support schemes (the vast majority relating to agriculture) com-prised 16 billion kčs. Tax evasion and tax arrears have thus become two of the most important instruments of capital accumulation by SMEs during the transition. Unfortunately, not everyone is able to use this instrument. As a result, this unofficial (but practically tolerated) 'scheme', which has far-reaching impacts on developments in small and medium-sized busi-nesses, punishes virtue and rewards vice, making it one of the least efficient schemes that could have been adopted.

CONCLUSION

Small and medium-sized private Czech businesses and their entrepreneur-ship expanded with unprecedented speed from 1990 to 1994. Even though official estimates confirm their booming development, a significant part of the private activities has not been recorded and has escaped the statistics. Cautiously stated, the share of the GDP accounted for by the effective private sector (the corporate sector excluded) may have already ranged between 35 and 40 per cent, far more than the official estimate of 26 to 30 per cent for 1993.

Even though much of this success must be attributed to the government's macro-economic and privatization policy, the essential element was the spontaneous motivation of members of the population to use their own capacity and resources in organizing their livelihoods. The legacy of past entrepreneurial animal vitality (both capitalist and socialist) played a key role in the revival of private business. At the beginning, its most important barrier was the lack of individual endowments of physical capital and diffi-cult access to financial capital. Because the emergence of the markets was not subject to industrial-policy schemes for the promotion of entrepreneurship, and because the capital—financial, physical, and social (network) capital—was unequally distributed, some social groups with privileged positions in the socialist economic system enjoyed superior initial conditions for establishing their own ventures. These groups were identified as the *nomenklatura* and the operators. The entrepreneurs from the remaining group, the outsiders, are only slowly gaining ground in their plight because of bureaucracy, lack of capital, bank rent-seeking, forced criminalization, overwork, and established competitors. Substantial mobility in the Czech Republic's entrepreneurial class can be expected over the next five to seven years, both within its hierarchy and in the interchange with the rest of the society. The natural development of this class in the Czech Republic requires conditions conducive to the extremely difficult mission and mobility of the entrepreneurs.

A distinction should be made between the government-devised conditions for the redistribution of wealth (i.e. privatization) and the conditions for the creation of wealth (i.e. the running of a business). The former received wide attention from 1990 through 1994, whereas the latter remained largely underdeveloped and neglected, especially where the promotion of new small businesses was concerned. Generalizing even further, one can say that the Czech economy is split into two sectors along lines of ownership: private businesses with stable ownership, and the sector wavering in the process of transient and uncertain governance. In 1994 these sectors were roughly the same size. Their functioning, internal problems, and decision-making may be so different that each of them may require different economic policy objectives and instruments. For example, the fiscal, monetary, exchange rate, and industrial policies aimed at stabilizing one of the two sectors may impair the development of the other. Flexible and innovative approaches to economic policy-making should be considered.

NOTES

Support from the TEMPUS Programme of the University of Cambridge, Department of Applied Economics, and Clare College is gratefully acknowledged. I would like to thank R. C. Matthews, S. Zamagni, B. Gui, Z. Túma, J. Cekota, A. Zemplinerová, G. McDermott, R. Filer, and G. Grabher for their comments and suggestions on the draft of this chapter.
  1. The spelling used here originates from the transcript of the Russian word adapted by Communist *apparatchiks* for the description of politically privileged and as elsewhere hierarchically ranked people.

2. There are many quantifying characteristics and data used throughout this chapter. To convert the Czech currency (kčs) into US dollars the fixed exchange rate of 28.50 kčs can be used for the period 1991–4. The nominal GDP in 1993 was 923 bn. kčs (approx. $3,100) per capita. The Czech Republic had 10.4 m. inhabitants in 1993 and 4.8 m. people were officially employed.

3. More speculative estimates inferred from the sudden drop in sales of diesel oil after the introduction of VAT and from tax frauds related to oil re-export calculate the potential tax loss at 20 bn. kčs (*Telegraf* 1994). Excise tax losses due to tobacco smuggling were estimated to be 2.5 bn. kčs in 1994. The smuggling of clothing is estimated to account for 30 per cent of sales in that sector, that is, at least 1.5 bn. kčs (*Profit* 1991: 4). Trafficking in antiquities and objects of art abroad is estimated at over 2 bn. kčs per year.

4. It is interesting to note how in just three years Czech society returned to these principles, which the external political forces had been trying to suppress systematically for fifty years. The recovery was sometimes radical. For example, the share of total Czech exports that goes to Germany increased from 8.3 per cent in 1989 to 33.3 per cent in 1992. The turnover with Germany increased from DM 6 bn. in 1990 to DM 15 bn. in 1993. The territorial structure of trade thereby closely approximated that of 1928.

5. The broader concept of capital is based on those stocks of assets that take a long time to accumulate, can be personally appropriated (owned and conserved), and bring certain returns (yields) to their owner, thus reproducing their wealth. In the case of the economic transformation, the essential property of the capital is its transferability (conversion) to alternative uses, that is, its independence from technological and institutional set-ups (Leamer 1993). If this condition is not satisfied we speak of 'sunk capital'.

6. Obviously, this intuitive approach does not represent an unimpeachable scientific method for making generalizations about reality. Unfortunately, data that would allow more objective and verifiable statements have not been made available. Perhaps it can be argued that the intuitive estimates made here about such sensitive matters as ethical classifications are no more biased than the notoriously subjective personal confessions required in surveys using questionnaires.

7. Naturally, the quantitative estimates in Table 9.2 cannot be taken strictly at face value. The error factor can be relatively large, and its size and alternative estimates are debatable. Nevertheless, the bias is unlikely to be serious enough to reverse the tenor of the conclusions reached in this chapter.

8. Recent quantitative empirical studies have concentrated on the classification, origins, and success of new Czech entrepreneurs. Matějú (1993*a*) comes to the conclusion that being a member of the *nomenklatura* results in 'far higher chances to enter the group of entrepreneurs' (p. 86), mainly due to the role of various social assets (e.g. the ability to mobilize informal contacts) that had been accumulated in one's past career. Another study (Matějú 1993*b*) aimed at explaining the level of success of the entrepreneurs (measured by their 1992 incomes, among other things) found a high statistical significance of such exogenous variables as income in 1989, property accumulated before 1990, and the importance of the person's position in the hierarchy of the *nomenklatura*. Nevertheless, the study also confirmed the significance of such factors as educa-

tion and professional commitment to the job, both of which testify that the outsiders could have certain opportunities to enter the ranks of entrepreneurs.

9. See also Charap and Zemplinerová (1993), Hlaváček and Túma (1993), and Hrnčíř (1993) for more detailed analysis of the debt problem.

10. The total number of investigated crimes in Czechoslovakia has increased from 94,000 in 1989 to 295,000 in 1992 (see *Hospodářské noviny* (1993b: 8) for statistics of the Public Prosecutor). Of this number, crimes against property rights (mainly theft) increased from 23,500 in 1989 (30.4 per cent solved) to 327,000 in 1993 (21 per cent solved). However, the number of 'other economic crimes' fell from 20,444 in 1989 to 1,788 in 1992. These include tax evasion (eighteen investigated cases in 1991 and only slightly more in 1992), crimes against business competition, fraud, insider trading, and corruption. It is not that the incidence of such crimes have been declining recently but simply that they have become less transparent and increasingly difficult to investigate in the new legal environment.

REFERENCES

BAUMOL, W. J. (1990), 'Entrepreneurship: Productive, Unproductive and Destructive', *Journal of Political Economy*, 98: 893–921.

BENÁČEK, V. (1993), 'The Market Failure versus the Government Failure: The Options of Emerging Market Economies', in M. Sojka and S. Zamagni (eds.), *What Markets can and cannot Do: The Problem of Transition in CEE Countries* (Rome: Nova Spes), 41–66.

BOURDIEU, P. (1986), 'The Forms of Capital', in J. G. Richardson (ed.), *Handbook of Theory and Research for the Sociology of Education* (New York: Greenwood Press), 141–58.

CHARAP, J. (1993), *Small and Intermediate Private Firms' Contribution to GDP* (Prague: Charles University, Institute of Economic Studies).

——and ZEMPLINEROVÁ, A. (1993), *Restructuring in the Czech Economy*, Working paper no. 2 (London: European Bank for Reconstruction and Development).

CNB (Czech National Bank) (1994), *Monthly Bulletin of Czech National Bank* (Prague: CNB).

CSU (Czech Statistical Office) (1993), *Statistické prehledy* (Statistical Reviews), no. 3 (Prague, CSU), 79.

——(1994), *Statistické prehledy*, no. 6 (Prague: CSU), 11.

CYERT, R. M., and MARCH, N. C. (1963), *A Behavioral Theory of the Firm* (Englewood Cliffs, NJ: Prentice-Hall).

ECOMA (1994), *Konjunkturní bulletin* (Business Cycle Bulletin) (Prague) (June).

ECONOMIST (1993), 14 Aug.

EKONOM (1994), no. 19.

ESWARAN, M., and KOTWAL, A. (1989), 'Why are Capitalists the Bosses?' *Economic Journal*, 99: 162–76.

EU (European Union) (1995), *The Czech Republic and its Integration with the European Union*, Doc. II/418/94 (Brussels: European Commission).

GÁBOR, I. R. (1994), 'Non-agricultural Small Entrepreneurship in Hungary—Ailing or Prospering?', mimeograph, Budapest.

HLAVÁČEK, J., and TÚMA, Z. (1993), *Bankruptcy in the Czech Economy*, Working Papers in Economics (Prague: Charles University).

Hospodářské noviny (1993a), 21 Apr.

——(1993b), 23 June.

——(1993c), 'Are the Eastern Investments Detrimental to the German Border Region?' 22 July.

——(1994), 'Living Standards of Employees', 16 Mar.

HRNČÍŘ, M. (1993), *Financial Intermediation in the Czech Republic: Lessons and Progress Evaluation*, Discussion Papers on Economic Transition no. DPET 9302 (Cambridge: Department of Applied Economics).

JONG-IL YOU (1992), *Small Firms in Economic Theory: A Survey*, Small Business Research Papers no. 17 (Cambridge: Cambridge University).

KYSILKA, P. (1988), *Strucna historie Ceskoslovenskych ekonomickych reforem* (The Brief History of the Czechoslovak Economic Reforms) (Prague: Institute of Economics).

——(1989), *Stinove ridici systemy a reforma* (Shadow Management Systems and the Reform) (Prague: Institute of Economics).

LEAMER, E. E. (1993), *Models of the Transition in Eastern Europe with Untransferable Eastern Capital*, Discussion paper (Vienna: Institute for Advanced Studies).

MCDERMOTT, G., and MEJSTŘÍK, M. (1991), *The Role of Small Firms in the Industrial Development and Transformation in Czechoslovakia*, Discussion paper (Prague: Charles University).

MATĚJÚ, P. (1993a), 'Revolution for Whom? Analysis of Intragenerational Mobility in 1989–1992', *Czech Sociological Review*, 1: 73–90.

——(1993b), *Determinants of Economic Success in the First Stage of the Post-communist Transformation: The Czech Republic 1989–1992*, Working paper (Prague: Institute of Sociology).

MÉNIL, G. DE, and MAUREL, M. (1993), *Trading with Neighbours in Turbulent Times: Lessons from the Break-up of the Austro-Hungarian Empire in 1919* (Paris: Delta).

MLČOCH, L. (1991), *The Behaviour of the Czechoslovak Enterprises* (Prague: Institute of Economics).

OECD (1994), *OECD Economic Surveys: The Czech and Slovak Republics* (Paris: OECD).

PIORE, M. J. (1991), *Eastern Europe: The Limits of the Free Market Solution* (Cambridge, Mass.: MIT).

PlanEcon (Czech Economic Monitor and Review) (1994), 9, Reports 46, 47, and 48.

Prague Post (1994), 'Shadow Economy is not Retreating', 23 Mar.

Profit (1991), 'We are Unique in Our Trade Liberation', 21 Nov.

——(1993), 'Black Economy—the Fiend', 22 Aug.

QUANDT, R. E., and TŘÍSKA, D. (eds.) (1990), *Optimal Decisions in Market and Planned Economies* (Boulder, Colo.: Westview).

SÍK, E. (1993), 'Network Capital in Capitalist, Communist and Post-communist Societies', in B. Wellman (ed.), *Networking in the Global Village* (Boulder, Colo.: Westview).

Telegraf (1994), 'Trafficking in Oil Flourishes Quietly', 28 Mar.

VÍTEČKOVÁ, J. (1993), 'Soukromé podnikání na startu', *Profit-Ekonomika* (Prague), 36: 5–7.

WINIECKI, J. (1993), *Macroeconomics of Transition in East-Central Europe* (Warsaw: A. Smith Research Centre).

WŐRGŐTTER, A. (ed.) (1994), *The Czech Republic—More than Prague* (Vienna: Institute for Advanced Studies and Bank Austria).

10

The Social and Cultural Embeddedness of Entrepreneurs in Eastern Germany

THOMAS KOCH and MICHAEL THOMAS

INTRODUCTION

Market structures and entrepreneurship in eastern Germany have idiosyncrasies that stem from relatively transparent processes at work in the transformation of a planned society into a market society. In some ways, eastern Germany is a special case of such change. The key problem faced by other former socialist countries in the transformation process—simultaneously having to build a democracy, market structures, entrepreneurship, and even a nation (Offe 1991)—has not confronted the people and institutions in what used to be known as the German Democratic Republic (GDR) (Wiesenthal 1992). With that state's accession to the Federal Republic of Germany (FRG), all western German institutions were adopted in the eastern part of unified Germany. It seemed relatively straightforward to expect eastern Germany to use those new institutions, structures, and instruments and manage all problems by leaving them to Adam Smith's famous 'invisible hand' of the market. With the process being sustained by political and economic arrangements with the FRG, the transformation was regarded as a more or less technical matter to be completed rapidly (Brie and Klein 1993; Offe 1994).

This misconception has created many unintended and unforeseeable obstacles to the adaptation of the eastern German economy, the development of endogenous potential, and, hence, to the emergence of powerful market structures. Economic union with the FRG, which jump-started the eastern German economy in October 1990, was also an external shock for it, destroying endogenous potential (see Hoffman 1993; Matzner *et al.* 1992). In these respects, eastern Germany has been a special model that illustrates the consequences of administering shock therapy and having external actors control and dominate all the attendant processes (Pickel 1993). The adaptation of endogenous potential and the development of endogenous actors has, in some ways, been more difficult in eastern Germany than in other former socialist countries. These circumstances, in turn, have entailed serious problems and conflicts affecting social transformation (see Brie and Klein 1993) in the former GDR despite the fact that the region has enjoyed better economic conditions than other post-socialist countries.

Though these problems and conflicts are not the topic of our chapter, they provide additional incentive to analyse the 'marginal' processes in the development of endogenous potential and actors in eastern Germany. Our argumentation is focused on a very limited aspect of the nature of eastern Germany's new entrepreneurs (people who founded their businesses upon implementation of the market economy in eastern Germany). We try to show that 'the new does not come from the new, or from nothing, but from reshaping existing resources. These resources include organisation forms . . . habituated practices, and social ties, whether formal or informal. Thus, transformation will resemble innovative adaptations that combine seemingly discrepant elements, or bricolage, more than architectural design' (Stark 1992: 301).

We begin by outlining the legacy of entrepreneurship and self-entrepreneurship in the former GDR. Because the process of creating free enterprise in the former GDR has been shaped by the heritage of socialism and the impacts of privatization methods, we then examine methods of privatization and the structure of ownership in eastern Germany since the regime shift of November 1989. Against this background, we consider, in the second section, various aspects of the social and cultural embeddedness of new entrepreneurs in eastern Germany: (1) different group origins (*Herkunftsgruppen*) and their cultural capital; (2) biographical resources, skills, and professional experience; and (3) networks and ties. Finally, we comment on subjective interpretations of the new entrepreneurs, quotations from whom give an impression of their roles and role conflicts.

Our thesis is based on one of Mark Granovetter's key concepts, that economic life is embedded 'in concrete, ongoing systems of social relations' (Granovetter 1985: 483), or, as he later put it, that there is an 'intertwining of economic and noneconomic motives' (Granovetter 1992: 234) in economic action. In this vein, we briefly examine the social relations, or networks, in the formation of entrepreneurship (see also Bögenhold 1989). We then turn more to cultural aspects of embeddedness—the function and influence that capital, especially cultural capital (Bourdieu 1982), has for different social groups in the creation of entrepreneurship in eastern Germany. In the tradition of phenomenological sociology (Schütz 1932; Grathoff 1989), we also consider the consequences that past biographical and life-world experiences have for the strategies and paths that individuals are pursuing in their new social field. These three aspects underscore our sociological approach and the relevance of social and cultural facts as important for the question of 'how to become an entrepreneur' in eastern Germany.

THE LEGACY OF THE PAST:
ENTREPRENEURSHIP IN THE GDR

The various stages, turning-points, and peculiarities of private business and entrepreneurship in the GDR diverged from those of other socialist countries and the Soviet model of socialism (Pickel 1992). Seen as a whole, however, the East German history of the socialist planned economy contained the same seeds of collapse and the same problems obstructing transformation and the emergence of market actors. As Figure 10.1 indicates, private entrepreneurship in the GDR was reduced in several 'waves'. It is, of course, a simplified, very idealized picture of GDR history. It shows none of the divergence that existed and concentrates only on the differences between planned and market economies. Neither economic system is depicted as it actually functioned, only as an ideal type. Former socialist economies are misconceived when thought of as totally state-directed, as based solely on one principle. 'Nowhere have Communist regimes been able fully to eliminate private economic activity, nor have they always and uncompromisingly sought to do so' (Pickel 1992: 3). On the other hand, this simplification and idealization is necessary to underline the main trend and point out the great difficulties of founding endogenous businesses in the process of transformation in eastern Germany.

Aside from the peculiarities that set eastern German private business and entrepreneurship apart from that in other former socialist countries and,

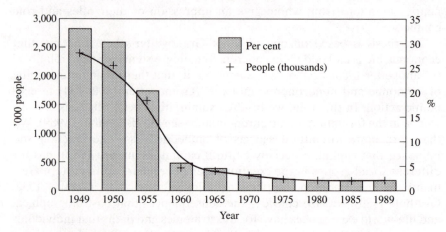

FIG. 10.1. Percentage of entrepreneurs in the East German labour force. Source: Lindig (1993: 7)

more generally, from orthodox Soviet socialism, there was really no opportunity or room for private ownership to develop in the GDR. On the
contrary, the GDR's proportion of entrepreneurs to employers, which, at
30 per cent, was higher than average in post-war Germany until the late
1940s, decreased to 2.2 per cent by 1989 as compared to 11.2 per cent in
West Germany in the same year. With the demise of the GDR, there were
no more than 185,000 entrepreneurs in eastern Germany, most of whom
were engaged in trade, as compared to 2.4 million in 1949.

The fact that the GDR never underwent complete nationalization, never
abolished private entrepreneurship, and even attempted to develop the
private sector from 1986 onward did nothing to modify the general trend
significantly. Socialist development, the centralization and abolition of
small firms, the declining opportunities for autonomous factory management, and the erosion of ways of life, life-worlds, and cultural patterns of
the so-called middle classes were some of the factors impeding modernity in
the GDR.

In this highly complex process of socialist industrial Fordism—centralized planning, nationalization, the dominance of vast structures, and large-
scale manufacturing with wholly dependent enterprises (combines)—the
lack of entrepreneurship as a factor in continuous modernization led the
country into a modernization trap (*Modernisierungsfalle*), with consequences for the small private sector. There were few opportunities for
individuals to accumulate capital or gain experience in managing their own
or autonomous enterprises. Market links and strategies rarely formed.
Moreover, the country's bureaucratically planned society stunted the creativity, competence, initiative, and performance of individuals and social
groups (see Thomas 1992).

Creating indigenous entrepreneurs is, therefore, not the same as founding businesses in established market economies. Moreover, the influence of
the socialist system on the GDR's private sector (trades, crafts), that sector's envelopment in the planned system, and the control of the private
sector by the planned system had similar consequences. The expectation
that this private sector and its entrepreneurs would probably provide the
basis for gradual transformation to a market economy (see Pickel 1992, for
example) appears to have been overly optimistic not only because of the
jump start afforded by the currency union on 1 July 1990. Outmoded
technologies and equipment, insufficient capital, the confining niches of the
production and service sectors, and the lack of market competition in the
GDR also posed serious problems for this sector in the transformation
process. Almost half of the 185,000 'old entrepreneurs' (*alte Selbständige*)—
the business people who had been operating under these conditions of the
socialist economy's private sector—went bankrupt in the first two years.
The construction sector was stabilized by the founding of new firms, not by
the old entrepreneurs. Of course, it was difficult in the GDR to create a

business and become an entrepreneur, but for the few entrepreneurs who did exist there the conditions in the GDR were in some ways a shelter protecting them from competition. In that sense, the introduction of the market economy in the GDR was 'square one' not only for the new entrepreneurs but also for the old, who led their businesses into radically different conditions.

PRIVATIZATION AND OWNERSHIP STRUCTURE IN EASTERN GERMANY

The current process of change is shaped by the heritage of socialism and the impacts of privatization methods (see Heidenreich 1994). The expectation of successful privatization and new foundings based on the development of small business and the involvement of West German entrepreneurship now appears to have been too optimistic. Shock therapy has failed in crucial respects. Furthermore, transformation by means of unification has had both advantages and disadvantages. With regard to the restructuring of firms and property relations, the emphasis has been on the state-conceived privatization programme in East Germany. It is no secret that the Treuhand, the government trust set up to sell off or liquidate what used to be called nationally owned businesses and property of the former GDR, put more than 80 per cent of those holdings into the hands of West German firms or persons of West German origin.

It is impossible to effect a transformation only from the outside. It is necessary to look for endogenous pre-conditions, actors, and patterns of action and activities. But instead of pursuing a more gradual transformation based on what little did exist in terms of eastern German industrial enterprises, regional networks, market connections, and human capital, shock therapy and top-down privatization have largely blocked and terminated these resources. What does this mean for the emergence of indigenous entrepreneurship and its socio-economic role? There are three points we would like to make.

1. The flow of West German and foreign capital into eastern Germany has drawn a special kind of dividing-line between big business and small business. Eastern German players are not big businessmen. They are found mostly on local markets. From north to south, big business is West German or of foreign descent. Big business determines the patterns of competition and sets more or less high barriers to entry into the local markets. It affects the development of small and medium-size structures in eastern Germany. The former power élites have less opportunity in eastern Germany than in other post-communist countries to win new status in the free-market economy (see Mayer 1991: 95; Benácek: 1993).

2. One of the clear objectives of the transformation process in eastern

Germany has been to create a class of indigenous private owners and entrepreneurs. The founding of new businesses has been encouraged, and demand in general has been high (cars, electronics, and furniture). However, the previously cited conditions on the private market in eastern Germany have seriously hampered the effort. In the five years since the fall of socialism in eastern Germany, the small-business sector is based on the founding of firms by the new entrepreneurs (see Fig. 10.2).

3. Empirical studies in market societies have shown that 'unemployment did not promote the founding of establishments . . . On the contrary, a prosperous environment with low unemployment and high wage levels seemed to stimulate start-ups' (Fritsch 1991: 240). For East Germany, we have observed a process of deindustrialization and the dynamics of high unemployment. Of course, private ownership in East Germany has developed, too. Indeed, its pace in 1990 and 1991 has commonly been compared to that experienced during Germany's period of rapid industrial development during the first years of the empire in the latter quarter of the nineteenth century (*die Gründerzeit*). From the outset, however, the development in the early 1990s was unstable because of the negative

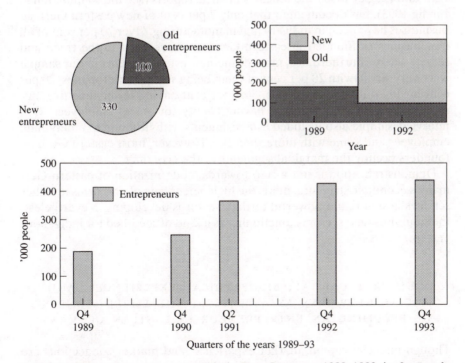

FIG. 10.2. Indigenous entrepreneurship in East Germany, 1989–1993, in thousands of people. Source: German Federal Ministry of Economic Affairs

TABLE 10.1. *New firms in different sectors*

Sector	*Land* Brandenburg	East Berlin
Manufacturing	7.2	6.5
Construction	11.1	18.4
Trade, restaurants	47.8	38.3
Transport	4.0	3.6
Credit, insurance	1.7	1.2
Other services	28.2	32.0

Source: '"Neue Selbständige" in Ostberlin und im Land Brandenburg 1992–1993'. Forschungsbericht und Arbeitsstudie von Gabriele Valerius und Petra Wolf-Valerius, in *BISS Forschungshefte* (Berlin: BISS, 1993), 8: 11.

tendencies in industry—ongoing deindustrialization and the dearth of new firms (see Table 10.1).

Our research, which confirms the findings of other investigations (see Hinz and Ziegler 1995) and official statistical reports (see the compilation in Lindig 1993), has documented that only 7 per cent of new eastern German businesses have been in industry and manufacturing. Over 70 per cent of all new businesses founded in eastern Germany have been in the trade and service sector. Furthermore, most of the new establishments in our sample were very small, with 20 per cent of them being sole proprietorships, 20 per cent having only one employee, 30.8 per cent having fewer than five employees, and only 8.8 per cent having twenty (or more) employees. Our interview sample also included establishments with fifty-one to ninety-nine employees and some with more than 100. However, most eastern German founders occupy the marginal segments of the economy.

Deindustralization is not a step towards modernization of eastern Germany's economic structure, nor is the high percentage of new firms in 'other services' a sign that a powerful tertiary sector is developing. Nevertheless, the small-business sector is functioning as a kind of seed-bed for indigenous entrepreneurship.

CULTURAL CAPITAL, BIOGRAPHICAL EXPERIENCES, AND SOCIAL NETWORKS AS ASPECTS OF THE EMBEDDEDNESS OF BECOMING AN ENTREPRENEUR IN EASTERN GERMANY

Though financial capital, market experience, and market connections are essential for actors in eastern Germany's new economic context, their interaction is also marked by useful, if less specific, social and cultural facets at both the collective and individual level. To analyse how actors go about becoming entrepreneurs, we have tried to examine different social groups and individuals for their constellations of economic, social, and cultural capital (in Bourdieu's sense), the role of social networks, and that of biographical resources. Without delving into the entire issue of the contradictions inherent in the social and cultural heritage of socialist societies in transition, we now offer three examples of the ways in which unspecified social and cultural aspects function in eastern Germany's new economic setting.

Social Groups of Origin and Cultural Capital

The probability that a new firm will be founded is influenced by several personal and collective characteristics of the founder. Personal characteristics include skill level, especially tacit skills and career experience, managerial skills, self-entrepreneurship, and interpersonal skills such as the ability to communicate, co-operate, empathize, and lead; and a sense for opportunities. Collective characteristics encompass patterns of action, biographical resources, and the schemes and scripts of middle-class culture as opposed to working-class culture, and so forth. Because these aspects play a role in the founding of establishments, our research focuses on the social and cultural roots and backgrounds of potential entrepreneurs, that is, on their social and cultural embeddedness.

This approach is based on two assumptions. First, individuals are able to transform their given skills and scripts, their own biographical project. Second, other 'assets' belonging to a person can be used as 'capital' (Bourdieu 1982). Social and cultural capital can help overcome the barriers of economic capital. Bourdieu has drawn attention to the fact that the entry into the market may be stimulated by an individual's cultural capital. There are people who are intimately familiar with the habits, needs, values, dreams or existential fears, and cultural patterns of social groups. The special kind of cultural capital that such people possess must be considered capital stock. Our research on eastern Germany confirms this view and, on this point, is consistent with the findings of studies by Bourdieu in France.

Despite the 'slight' difference between French society and society as it was in the GDR (see Alheit 1994), it is possible to follow Bourdieu in a special manner. Although the rights of private property or ownership were limited in the GDR, the most important point to us seems to be the role of political capital (as a kind of social capital). All in all, two structuring principles of GDR society must be noted in retrospect: political capital and cultural capital. Drawing on Bourdieu's (1982) ideas of 'space' with regard to the state-socialist countries, we found that the new entrepreneurs in eastern Germany represented a variety of the former GDR's social groups of origin (see Table 10.3), but these entrepreneurs were not usually society's underdogs. Indeed, all the social groups from which they came can be found at upper levels of the social 'space'. However, social groups of origin differ in their economic, cultural, and social capital. Each group has special resources, patterns of action, social ties, qualifications, and subjective dispositions. The constellations for launching a business and the manner in which individuals pursued this commitment thus also differed (see Koch *et al.* 1993).

To illustrate the importance of cultural capital, consider a social group of origin with a high level of cultural capital, the intellectuals (former researchers in social sciences, former artists, and people who used to be employed in the cultural sector). As Mannheim (1936) wrote: 'In every society there are social groups whose special task it is to provide an interpretation of the world for that society. We call these the "intelligentsia".' Compared to top-class professionals, members of the intelligentsia in the GDR had middle-level resources. Although they were rather well educated, they were more 'experts in general'. Many of our interviewees had long worked without proper qualification (as theatre actors, assistant stage directors, and radio show hosts). We think that must be interpreted as an indication that these interviewees had acquired a high aptitude and transferable skills. Many founders from this social group of origin were persuaded to cross sectorial boundaries when they started their own businesses. Furthermore, everything they did was used to develop their own individuality as well. One of their most important values was personality, the right to live their own lives. The idea of personality seemed to be one of their most important 'tools'. That is why new entrepreneurs from this social

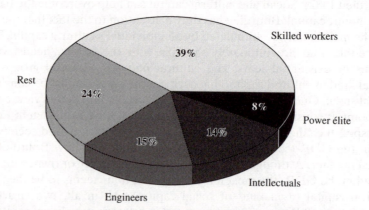

FIG. 10.3. Share of founders by social group of origin in East Berlin and the *Land* of Brandenburg. Source: '"Neue Selbständige" in Ostberlin und im Land Brandenburg 1992–1993'. Forschungsbericht und Arbeitsstudie von Gabriele Valerius und Petra Wolf-Valerius, in *BISS-Forschungshefte* (Berlin: BISS, 1993), 8. 32

group of origin emphasized that 'You don't sell any goods; you sell yourself' and 'I am presenting *my* style and *my* choice of clothes'. Style and choice of attire, furniture, and similar goods enable people to exercise an element of self-presentation and social identity. The intellectuals preferred to establish firms that afforded a chance to demonstrate the meaning of style, adventure, different subcultures, self-experience, and so forth (bookshops, publishing houses, record companies, boutiques, travel agencies, pubs with a special flair, and educational establishments).

There were slight differences between the intellectuals and groups of engineers, natural scientists, and industrial researchers with regard to their ideas of occupation, career experience, importance of formal certificates, and types of social action. Compared to engineers and members of the former power élite, the intellectuals were also masters over their own working hours. In other words, intellectuals had cultivated behaviour patterns similar to self-entrepreneurship.

These examples seem to show that Bourdieu's interpretation of the function that cultural capital has for intellectuals in the founding of a business may be relevant to the special case represented by eastern Germany.

Biographical Resources, Skills, and Professional Experience

One's own biography, including personal experiences, concepts of life, and schemes and scripts, is an important factor to the acting individual. For better or worse, each person is a prisoner of his or her own life-world and biography. The issue is one of bridges and linkages, of chances to transform one's own biographical project and act in a new social situation (see Joas 1992). Quite apart from the abruptness of change in the political and economic system and in all institutions, structures, and role patterns, the individual's subjective activity is, as it was for our sample in particular, crucial to the ways in which those institutions, structures, and roles are received and designed.

Not surprisingly, we found that the proportion of new entrepreneurs among all private sector business people in eastern Germany differs in two ways from that in western Germany. The new entrepreneurs in eastern Germany are older (37.2 per cent are 31 to 40 years old; 30.5 per cent, 41 to 50 years old; and 18.3 per cent, older than 50) and have higher qualifications, making the issue of life history and life experience important for these actors. Within the framework of the social positions that the individuals used to have, that is, their social group of origin within the GDR, we concentrated on each person's former professional biography (*Berufsbiographie*). Reconstructing it would enable us to find relevant patterns of interpretation and action, strategies of action, and social ties. This professional biography is also the key to social identity, the personal 'start-up capital'. Researching it involves the extensive reconstruction of social and personal history. The following examples may show the extent to which this orientation is significant for the matter of how to become an entrepreneur.

Our representative survey provided interesting data on the connection between the social groups from which new eastern German entrepreneurs had come and their entrance into various sectors of the economy (see Fig. 10.4). This link bears on the question of special resources (capital, social ties, skills, and so forth). We found, for instance, that about 80 per cent of the former power élite and intelligentsia in our survey had gone into sectors of trade and service rather than into industry or construction. In fact, the inquiry showed that it was almost impossible for outsiders to enter the latter two sectors. By the same token, members of the former power élite or intelligentsia who did not have special resources or connections often became dependent entrepreneurs in insurance companies and agents. The passage that this group of individuals made into private ownership was thus less specific, less directly related, to their social origin than that of their well-connected peers.

Similarly, 52 per cent of the groups of engineers in our study opted to found their businesses in industry or the building trade. The engineers were normally older and had long professional experience in these lines of work. We also tended to find these engineers in high-tech services, namely, in those sectors and businesses with a high and specialized level of restricted admission. In other words, the engineers had the 'key'—the qualifications, experience, and resources—they needed as their capital for founding businesses. Many engineers had other opportunities as well and selected their businesses carefully. In many cases, they had already contemplated going into business for themselves years earlier. Consulting banks and lawyers, they acted more strategically in the privatization process than other groups

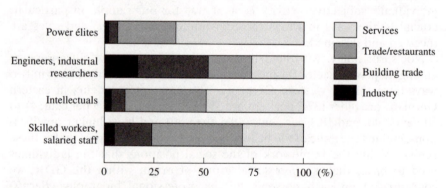

FIG. 10.4. Branch distribution by groups of origin in East Berlin and the *Land* of Brandenburg. Source: '"Neue Selbstandige" in Ostberlin und im Land Brandenburg 1992–1993'. Forschungsbericht und Arbeitsstudie von Gabriele Valerius und Petra Wolf-Valerius, in *BISS-Forschungshefte* (Berlin: BISS, 1993), 8. 37

did. For 500 of the engineers, the opportunity to act on their own ideas was clearly 'very important'; for 450 it was 'very important' to be independent. Characteristically, one of the respondents stated: 'We are not the people who were fired or would have been fired!'

This example shows that people from the GDR can often use their former qualifications and professional experience as capital for their new livelihoods as entrepreneurs. The engineers were convinced that they were well prepared and that they had the social and biographical resources they needed to act in their new social field. Their case, though it is the most obvious and plausible one, holds for other new entrepreneurs as well. Resources and patterns that are somewhat comparable can, for instance, also be found among the groups of skilled workers in our survey. It is too simplistic to assert that the former GDR lags in the modernization of professions, qualifications, skills, and so forth. The same is true of the thesis that lack of modernization in sectorial structure (an underdeveloped tertiary sector) and in the character of traditional working society—as in the FRG in the 1960s (see Geissler 1992; Hradil 1992)—does not relate to the same lack of resources or patterns.

Indeed, the case of the engineers shows the diversity of structures and mentalities in the former GDR, for engineers and skilled workers entering these fields are often highly qualified, professionally knowledgeable, competent, experienced, and flexible. As one engineer said: 'I have no problems as far as technology is concerned.' This statement and the intent to continue working in the same field are indicative. Such sentiments are often heard in developed market societies, especially among engineers. But it may be interesting that it has emerged in the process of systems transformation. The individual's professional knowledge, biographical experiences, and life-world patterns are functioning as a bridge to the new social role.

This example shows that there are elements of the GDR's heritage that have a function in the new social roles being adopted by former eastern German citizens: the unique aspects of their professional biographies, the ways in which they organize their everyday lives, and the reality of having to solve specific and diverse problems. Asked what he thought about the image of the unmotivated eastern German (*Ossi*), one entrepreneur answered: 'It is certainly not an inaccurate cliché, but for us it is not really the main point!' In the processes of transformation and the creation of new entrepreneurs, the social and biographical history of individuals and the social group of origin thus also becomes a central question in a theory of action.

Networks and Social Ties

Our third example of social embeddedness relates to the role of social networks (Granovetter 1985, 1992). The network approach is often used in different ways when it comes to economic transformation, networks between firms, in regions or regional districts, between East and West, and so on. Of special interest for our questions are personal ties, or networks between, say, friends, colleagues, officials, or other market actors engaged in the processes of founding a business.

Of course, the idea of ties can be easily related to eastern Germans and their old system of interdependencies and protectorates (*Seilschaften*, the German term for a rope team of mountain climbers). Members of the *nomenklatura*, the old élites, had opportunities to become entrepreneurs because of their positions, information, and many important connections. As summed up by one young entrepreneur, 'Those who were nothing then will be nothing now.' And vice versa. Some members of the *nomenklatura* do manage to follow this route to entrepreneurship. Given the special conditions in Germany, however, their success is not the norm. For instance, only 7 per cent of the entrepreneurs in our representative survey indicated that they had been a member of the power élite. The 'old-boy' network is thus a special case in the transformation process.

Our survey confirmed the important, but well-known, facts that more than 60 per cent of the new entrepreneurs in eastern Germany received practical support from their wives or husbands when founding their businesses; nearly 50 per cent received such help from friends. More difficult is the question about the extent of assistance from colleagues or acquaintances from the new entrepreneur's former line of work. Such connections constitute crucial networks for information about jobs, business opportunities, market situations, and so forth (Granovetter 1992: 245; Bögenhold 1989). It is not obvious that old connections can remain intact in the transformation from one economic order to another. It is necessary to examine a wide range of relations among former colleagues and the degree of relevance that those relations have. A qualitative network approach may be called for in order to answer the issue of social ties more definitely.

For example, about 600 of our entrepreneurs told us that they had managerial experience and that they found this experience to have been helpful in becoming entrepreneurs. But they were neither necessarily former members of the power élite nor solely managers. The managerial experience to which they referred was a common resource. It was not confined to those individuals who stayed in their former lines of activity or enterprises (such as engineering) but was found among all entrepreneurs in our sample. It was the experience of dealing with people, organizing something, solving problems, thinking and working in a comparatively complex manner. One of our respondents told us: 'Those who used to have the chance to do things differently will continue to do so today.' According to another respondent, 'We had to organize this, to manage; it was a little like a quasi-market situation.' Such former leadership is an important and direct experience and resource in establishing and using ties of trust (*Vertrauensbezie-*

hungen). These kinds of social skills based on professional skills and personal attributes are the foundation for strong ties in the initial steps of setting up businesses. Businesses were founded with friends and colleagues, and there was trust in former staff and the community of people who were 'in the same boat'. Of course, ties, especially ties of trust, are bound to change over time. There will be conflicts in enterprises, and redundancies may be necessary. But such ties are actually a function of the processes involved in building a business, and we can see that the forms of interaction or social order in new enterprises established by the old *Seilschaften* differ from those in enterprises created through ties of trust.

Such bonds between friends and colleagues represent the 'strong ties' involved in the initial phase of founding a business. An important factor governing their dynamics is the length of time they remain intact and how the relevant actors can change or expand them to include the important 'weak ties' (Granovetter) in order to obtain additional information, market contacts, and contracts. Strong ties thus function as a bridge and a special type of social capital for the new entrepreneurs of eastern Germany. The difficult question of widening weak ties has to do primarily with the issue of entry into established networks of western German entrepreneurs, officials, politicians, and so forth. This 'mixture', the peculiar extension into eastern Germany of networks rooted in western Germany, is often reflected in and criticized by eastern German entrepreneurs, most of whom regard these networks as a new wall keeping newcomers out, blocking the establishment of new market connections, and interfering with the flow of information and contracts. Such interaction is, hence, another aspect of the way in which the founding of businesses is embedded in social networks.

THE NEW ENTREPRENEURS: THE HEIRS AND GRAVE-DIGGERS OF EARLIER CODES OF CONDUCT

To conclude this chapter, we turn now to the subjective world and living conditions of the founders (see also Koch and Woderich 1992). Our sample included both social winners and social losers, of whom many are living at subsistence level. All of them are on the road, and their paths into entrepreneurship have been accompanied by changes in status and social identity. How do they deal with the tensions that such changes may entail?

Consider first the self-perception, values, beliefs, and attitudes of entrepreneurs. According to the welfare survey of 1993 (see Landua *et al.* 1993), the overwhelming majority of eastern German founders feel themselves to be members of the middle classes (with 20 per cent feeling themselves to be members of the working class; 10 per cent, the upper class). Our empirical study in East Berlin and the *Land* of Brandenburg suggests that social change is not seen by most founders in terms of upward or downward mobility. Nevertheless, upward mobility is being reflected in the new social status that many of them now have (see Fig. 10.5). Approximately 10 per cent of them regarded their new status as a disruption of their careers. We recorded remarks such as 'I became an entrepreneur out of defiance of the [official] evaluation that led to our enterprise's being closed down.' Too old to find another job in Germany, members of the lost generation often have no choice but to start their own businesses.

We have also detected an increasingly positive retrospective interpretation of the GDR's reality, a relatively high satisfaction with certain conditions of life in the GDR by a majority of eastern Germans and new entrepreneurs (see *Die Zeit* 1993: 17; Valerius 1993). There is no significant difference between the social groups represented in this research. These findings are surprising with regard to the founders—until various aspects are considered. First, the reported attitude resulted from negative and difficult experiences with the market economy and from the special conditions surrounding the process of becoming an entrepreneur in eastern Germany. Eastern German small-business people are facing unfair competition and lack reliable western German partners. The barriers to market entry are high. The difficulties that eastern German small-business people have in making contacts and entering networks must not be underestimated.

Our study of new entrepreneurs has also indicated that these people, in most cases, consider themselves to be East Germans, a feeling that has maintained an East German self-consciousness (which may be a special kind of ethnicity). They share biographical commitments, and business interests are associated with each other. They live with hard competition with western German firms on local markets and the role of local and regional authorities as clients. In Berlin new entrepreneurs prefer ordering

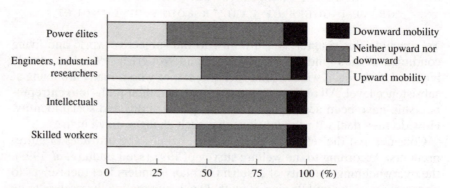

FIG. 10.5. The experience of new status position: upward or downward mobility. Source: '"Neue Selbständige" in Ostberlin und im Land Brandenburg 1992–1993'. Forschungsbericht und Arbeitsstudie von Gabriele Valerius und Petra Wolf-Valerius, in *BISS-Forschungshefte* (Berlin: BISS, 1993), 8.42

from well-known West German firms. The growth of eastern German self-reliance has nourished a growing demand for indigenous goods. 'Made in the East' is, or will be, beautiful. The experience of a distinctive, emerging East German identity is shared by the social 'winners' and social 'losers' of unification, men and woman, old and young, entrepreneurs and workers. (The nexus of interdependencies among eastern Germans and western Germans can be regarded as a 'configuration' encompassing 'The Established and the Outsiders'; see Elias and Scotson 1965.) But in the GDR not all of the population was in the same boat, and the same is true in eastern Germany today. The phrase 'revival of East German self-reliance and we-consciousness' (Koch 1996) therefore also includes a set of distinctions, feelings, and aloofness or unapproachability that marks the differences between social groups of East German origin (see also Koch 1994).

Second, eastern German founders do not feel nostalgic. As pointed out earlier, some of the country's heritage has a function in new social roles—elements in professional biographies, standard ways of organizing everyday life, and different forms of social connections and ties, for example.

Our investigation has indicated that the founders in eastern Berlin and the *Land* Brandenburg prefer comparatively left-wing political parties and orientations. For instance, the Party of Democratic Socialism (PDS), not the right-of-centre Christian Democratic Union (CDU) or the liberal Free Democratic Party (FDP), seems to be the party of eastern German entrepreneurs. Some 20 per cent of the PDS's leaders and 8 per cent of the total party membership in the *Land* Brandenburg are entrepreneurs. The new entrepreneurs enjoy a special kind of solidarity. Retracing the path into entrepreneurship, one encounters the entrepreneur's social pillars (*soziale Stützen*): the friends, family, and former colleagues who help the entrepreneur along the way with money and connections. They stand by the entrepreneur, giving moral support. The phenomenon of social pillars shows how ties and networks that developed under socialism as it was actually practised have been able to generate and mobilize material resources for the new entrepreneurs of eastern Germany.

Another finding of our study was that the new entrepreneurs are both the heirs and the grave-diggers of the collectivism's legacy. Where former work teams set up in business, the manager-owner is seen by the members of the team as *primus inter pares* only. It seems to be a legacy of 'collectivism'. Throughout the history of the GDR, a socialist way of life was propagated in slogans, including 'From me to us'. Perhaps people in the GDR really did move a little 'From me to us'. The internal functioning of the firms can be seen as a mixture of formal relations and informal networks between the manager-owner and the employees. The feeling of being in the same boat prevails. However, the balance of power between workers and the owner-director is changing. The owners are the winners of the power game.

The greatest challenge for all of them seems to be to adopt the role of entrepreneur. One often hears that the new entrepreneurs of eastern Germany try to be better capitalists (Manchestership). Our observations have not confirmed that assertion. Many entrepreneurs do not want to be rich. However, an entrepreneur is defined as an owner of capital who is engaged in the management of an enterprise for the sale of goods or services for profit. Obviously, making a profit in business is not as important a motive for these entrepreneurs as self-fulfilment or self-actualization is. These trends bear witness to the social and cultural embeddedness of small business in eastern Germany.

What are the goals in promoting the private sector? Peter Rutland (1993), who posed this question, responded with a list of general objectives, including 'to reconstitute social norms and cultural values of the pre-communist era' and 'to create a class of new entrepreneurs who will provide a political basis for democracy', a social basis for capitalism. He also noted that many of the goals would conflict with the self-interest, the feeling, of entrepreneurs. We think we agree. The development of entrepreneurial attitudes and behaviour variously include role-taking and role distance as well as the values of independence, innovation, and competition. However, as indicated by our research on the new entrepreneurs in eastern Germany, and by their previously noted political preferences, the players would not accept a quiet reversion to norms and values of the pre-communist era.

All in all, the creation in eastern Germany of a *class* of new entrepreneurs who will provide a social basis for capitalism still has a long way to go. This point, too, is an important reason why we think that capitalism in eastern Germany will have a face of its own for a while.

NOTE

This chapter and the special question of endogenous actors is based on an ongoing research project entitled 'The Making of New Entrepreneurs: Their Social Characteristics, Potential, and Ways' and sponsored by the Volkswagen Foundation. We have drawn on the results of a survey conducted among more than 900 entrepreneurs in East Berlin and the *Land* Brandenburg and a set of about thirty narrative interviews. For more information see Koch *et al.* (1993), Thomas (1991, 1993), and Valerius (1993).

REFERENCES

ALHEIT, P. (1994), 'Strukturelle Hintergründe kollektiver "Verlaufskurven" der deutschen Wiedervereinigung' (Structural Background of Collective 'Trajectories' of German Reunification), *Mitteilungen aus der kulturwissensschaftlichen Forschung*, 17/34: 9–38.

BENÁCEK, V. (1993), 'Toil and Trouble of an Aboriginal Entrepreneur during Transition in the Czech Republic', Paper presented to the Conference on the Social Embeddedness of the Economic Transformation in Central and Eastern Europe, Wissenschaftszentrum Berlin für Sozialforschung, Sept. 1993.

BÖGENHOLD, D. (1989), 'Die Berufspassage in das Unternehmertum. Theoretische und empirische Befunde zum sozialen Prozeß von Firmengründungen' (The Occupational Path to Entrepreneurship), *Zeitschrift für Soziologie*, 18/4: 263–81.

BOURDIEU, P. (1982), *Die feinen Unterschiede. Kritik der gesellschaftlichen Urteilskraft* (The Subtle Differences: Critique of Society's Power of Judgement) (Frankfurt-on-Main: Suhrkamp).

BRIE, M., and KLEIN, D. (eds.) (1993), *Zwischen den Zeiten. Ein Jahrhundert verabschiedet sich* (Hamburg: VSA).

ELIAS, N., and SCOTSON, J. L. (1965), *The Established and the Outsiders* (London: Cass).

FRITSCH, M. (1991), 'Die Übernahme neuer Techniken durch Industriebetriebe' (The Adoption of new Technology through Industry), *Ifo-Studien*, 37: 1–18.

GEISSLER, R. (1992), 'Die ostdeutsche Sozialstruktur unter Modernisierungsdruck', in *Aus Politik und Zeitgeschichte*, B29–30: 15–28.

GRANOVETTER, M. (1985), 'Economic Action and Social Structure: The Problem of Embeddedness', *American Journal of Sociology*, 91/3: 481–510.

——(1992), 'The Sociological and Economic Approaches to Labor Market Analysis: A Social Structural View', in M. Granovetter and R. Swedberg (eds.), *The Sociology of Economic Life* (Boulder, Colo.: Westview), 233–63.

GRATHOFF, R. (1989), *Milieu und Lebenswelt. Einführung in die phänomenologische Soziologie und sozialphänomenologische Forschung* (Milieu and Life-World: Introduction to Phenomenological Sociological and Socio-phenomenological Research) (Frankfurt-on-Main: Suhrkamp).

HEIDENREICH, M. (1994), 'Die mitteleuropäische Großindustrie im Transformationsprozeß' (Central European Big Industry in the Process of Transformation), *Zeitschrift für Soziologie*, 23/1: 3–21.

HINZ, T., and ZEIGLER, R. (1995), 'Businesses Founded in East Germany: Economic Activity and Capital Investment', in H. Brezinski and M. Fritsch (eds.), *The Economic Impact of Post-socialist Countries: Bottom-up Transformation in Eastern Europe* (Cheltenham: Elgar), 233–52.

HOFFMANN, L. (1993), *Warten auf den Aufschwung. Eine ostdeutsche Bilanz* (Waiting for the Upturn: Taking Stock in East Germany) (Regensburg: Transfer Verlag).

HRADIL, S. (1992), 'Die "objektive" und die "subjektive" Modernisierung. Der Wandel der westdeutschen Sozialstruktur und die Wiedervereinigung', in *Aus Politik und Zeitgeschichte*, B29–30: 3–14.

JOAS, H. (1992), *Die Kreativität des Handelns* (The Creativity of Action) (Frankfurt-on-Main: Suhrkamp).

KOCH, T. (1994), ' "Die DDR ist passé, aber die Zeiten des naiven Beitritts auch". Von der Renaissance ostdeutschen Wir- und Selbstbewußtseins nach der Vereinigung' ('The GDR is in the Past, but so are the Times of Naïve Accession':

Of the Renaissance of East German We-Consciousness and Self-Awareness after the Unification), *BISS-Public*, 13: 71–8.

KOCH, T. (1996), 'The Renaissance of East German Group Awareness since Unification', in M. Gerber and R. Woods (eds.), *Changing Identities in East Germany: Selected Papers from the 19th and 20th New Hampshire Symposia* (Lanham, Md.: University Press of America), 189–210.

——and WODERICH, R. (1992), 'Freier Flug oder Fall in die Marktwirtschaft? Existenzgründer in Ostdeutschland', *BISS-Forschungshefte* (Berlin: BISS), 1.

——THOMAS, M., and WODERICH, R. (1993), 'Akteurgenese und Handlungslogiken—das Beispiel der neuen Selbständigen in Ostdeutschland' (Origins of Actors and Logics of Action: The Example of the 'New Entrepreneurs' in Eastern Germany), *Berliner Journal für Soziologie*, 3/3: 275–91.

LANDUA, D., HABICH, R., NOLL, H.-H., ZAPF, W., and SPELLERBERG, A. (1993), . . . *im Westen noch beständig, im Osten etwas freundlicher* (Still Steady on the Western Front, a bit Kinder in the East) (Berlin: Wissenschaftszentrum Berlin für Sozialforschung).

LINDIG, D. (1993), 'Datenreport: Selbständige und Gründungsgeschehen in Ostdeutschland unter besonderer Berücksichtigung der Region Berlin-Brandenburg. Eine Sekundäranalyse' (A Secondary Analysis of Data on Entrepreneurs and Business Foundings in East Germany, with a Focus on the Region of Berlin–Brandenburg), *BISS-Forschungshefte*, 7.

MANNHEIM, K. (1936), *Ideology and Utopia* (London: Routledge & Kegan Paul).

MATZNER, E., KREGEL, J., and GRABHER, G. (1992), *Der Marktschock* (Market Shock) (Berlin: edition sigma).

MAYER, K. U. (1991), 'Soziale Ungleichheit und Lebensverläufe. Notizen zur Inkorporation der DDR in die Bundesrepublik und ihre Folgen' (Social Inequality and Life Courses: Notes on the Incorporation of the GDR into the Federal Republic of Germany and its Impacts), in B. Giesen and C. Leggewie (eds.), *Experiment Vereinigung. Ein sozialer Großversuch* (Berlin: Rotbuch), 87–99.

OFFE, C. (1991), 'Das Dilemma der Gleichzeitigkeit. Demokratisierung und Marktwirtschaft in Osteuropa' (The Dilemma of Simultaneity: Democratization and the Market Economy in Eastern Europe), *Merkur*, 45: 279–92.

——(1994), *Der Tunnel am Ende des Lichts* (The Tunnel at the End of the Light) (Frankfurt-on-Main: Campus).

PICKEL, A. (1992), *Radical Transition: The Survival and Revival of Entrepreneurship in the GDR* (Boulder, Colo.: Westview).

——(1993), 'Die Bedeutung Ostdeutschlands für die vergleichende Transformationsforschung' (Eastern Germany's Significance for Comparative Research on Transformation), *BISS-Public*, 12: 33–8.

RUTLAND, P. (1993), 'The Antinomies of Private Enterprise in the Post-socialist Economy', Abstract for the Conference on the Social Embeddedness of the Economic Transformation in Central and Eastern Europe, Wissenschaftszentrum Berlin für Sozialforschung, Sept. 1993.

SCHÜTZ, A. (1932), *Der sinnhafte Aufbau der sozialen Welt* (Vienna: Julius Springer).

STARK, D. (1992), 'The Great Transformation? Social Change in Eastern Europe', *Contemporary Sociology*, 21/3: 299–304.

THOMAS, M. (1991), 'Neue Selbständige im Transformationsprozeß. Herkunftswege, soziale Charakteristik und Potentiale' (New Entrepreneurs in the Transformation Process: Backgrounds, Social Characteristics, and Potential), Project application to the Volkswagen Foundation.

——(ed.) (1992), *Abbruch und Aufbruch. Sozialwissenschaften im Transformationsprozeß* (Changing Course: Social Sciences in the Process of Transformation) (Berlin: Akademie Verlag).

——(1993), 'Private Selbständigkeit in Ostdeutschland. Erste Schritte in einem neuen Forschungsfeld' (Private Entrepreneurship in Eastern Germany: Initial Steps in a New Research Field), *Soziale Welt*, 44/2: 223–42.

VALERIUS, G. (1993), ' "Neue Selbständige" in Ostberlin und im Land Brandenburg, 1992' ('New Entrepreneurs' in East Berlin and the *Land* Brandenburg, 1992), *BISS-Forschungshefte*, 8: 4–60.

WIESENTHAL, H. (1992), 'Sturz in die Moderne. Der Sonderstatus der DDR in den Transformationsprozessen in Osteuropa' (Headlong into Modern Times: The Special Status of the GDR amid the Transformation Processes in Eastern Europe), in Brie and Klein (1993: 162–88).

Die Zeit (1993), 'Es wächst zusammen' (It's Growing Together), 40 (1 Oct.), 17–20.

III

POLICY NETWORKS:

Restructuring Institutions

11

The Antinomies of Privatization in Eastern Europe

PETER RUTLAND

INTRODUCTION

The usual approach to the question of privatization in Eastern Europe is to plunge into an analysis of successes and failures, and the reasons for these differing outcomes in the various countries. This search for the elusive pre-conditions for successful transition is reminiscent of the 1960s debate over the pre-conditions for economic take-off in the optimistically titled 'developing countries' (Rostow 1960).[1] Both share the teleological assumption that there is a future state of economic well-being which these countries can and must attain. The job of the analyst is to explain how to get there, and to explain why some countries fall by the wayside.

This chapter tries to put this literature into a broader context, by asking why the rhetoric of privatization came to dominate the transition debate, and by trying to unpack the different meanings contained within the term.

WHY THE RHETORIC OF PRIVATIZATION?

Within months of the election of a Solidarity government in Poland in June 1989, discussion of economic policy in Eastern Europe very quickly fell into a standard framework: the teleological rhetoric of the 'transition to the market'. A consensus rapidly emerged among Western economists that the solution for Eastern Europe lay in the policy troika of liberalization, stabilization, and privatization. There was room for disagreement over the pace and sequencing of these policies, but dissenting voices were treated as economic ignoramuses or advocates of communist restoration, and largely excluded from the debate.

There are few historical precedents where a particular set of economic concepts was so rapidly able to establish hegemony over political discourse. This chapter offers some preliminary hypotheses about why this discourse of market transition arose, and how it relates to the actual political and economic processes under way in the region.

There seems to be a radical disjuncture between the language of transition and the actuality of disorientation and collapse. The breakdown of the Comecon trade and payments system and the abolition of the political controls which had steered the region's command economies caused a slump in economic activity which exceeded that of the Great Depression of the 1930s. Yet these developments were interpreted as part of a positive and welcome process—the building of a market economy. Terms like 'depression' and 'collapse' rarely appear in commentaries on the region.[2]

It would be relatively easy to measure success in terms of liberalization and stabilization by looking for evidence of the abolition of restrictions on business activity, the rate of inflation, and the level of the budget deficit. However, how was the overall rate of progress towards the market economy to be measured? The favoured indicator appeared to be 'privatization'—the transfer of productive assets from state to private hands. Other indicators of market transition would include the share of employment and output in new privately owned start-ups, the rate of inflow of foreign investment, and the rate of growth of exports to market economies. However, none of these variables could be summarized in such a crisp and concise term as 'privatization'.

Actual progress in privatization in countries like Poland and Hungary has been much more modest than the rhetoric of transition would suggest. The trajectory of the term 'privatization' in Eastern Europe is reminiscent of Murray Edelman's (1971) book on US public policy subtitled 'Words that Succeed and Policies that Fail'. The term has dominated debates about the region's performance, and debates among specialists about the course of economic policy. And yet actual progress in privatization has been remarkably modest in most of these countries, and its impact dubious in those which have actually implemented such measures.

This gap between policy and reality cannot be reduced to the familiar dichotomy between normative and positive modes of enquiry. The economists commenting on the post-socialist transition seem to inhabit an epistemological no man's land, simultaneously prescriptive and descriptive. On the one hand, they offer normative advice ('This is the best policy'). At the same time, they are at pains to stress the empirical validity of their prognostications; to insist that 'the policies are working'. They are unusually keen to establish their standing as governmental advisers, and anxious to show that their advice is being followed. Yet their approach is hardly empiricist, since it is immune to falsifiability. If inflation does not slow down, if GDP continues to fall, or if no privatizations take place, then it simply means that the government is not following their advice.

The economists picking winners in the transition process have been aided and abetted by the international media. Major publications such as the *New York Times*, *Wall Street Journal*, *Financial Times*, and *The Economist* have promulgated an unremitting propaganda of success—at least on their editorial pages, and often in their news-reporting. In most cases, their commitment to privatization and liberalization probably has more to do with the domestic policy debates in their own countries than the situation on the ground in East Europe. (That is, advocates of, say, further privatization of public utilities in Britain may believe their case will be strengthened if there is a feeling that privatization is sweeping the globe.)

The Role of International Financial Institutions

A crucial role has also been played by the international financial institutions (IFIs), who have provided much of the funding for the 'Marriott brigade' of Western advisers. The international community has given a high level of rhetorical commitment to the development of a private sector in the post-socialist countries. This political commitment has provided a veneer of ideological unity to Western strategy towards Eastern Europe, which has not been matched in their concrete economic and political policies. There are at least two distinct problems in the Western approach: errors based on a misunderstanding of the situation in the region, and errors stemming from the deliberate promotion of Western interests irrespective of the region's needs.

The IFIs had a strong incentive to stake bureaucratic claim to the post-socialist territories. Organizations like the OECD and IMF had been created to manage the institutions of the post-war international economic system (the Marshall Plan, Bretton Woods, etc.). After three decades, however, liberalization and global integration had undermined their *raison d'être*. In the 1970s they tried to find a new mission by tackling the problem of underdevelopment in the Third World, with fairly miserable results. The collapse of the socialist economic system gave them a new role. According to some reports 30 to 40 per cent of IMF and World Bank officials are now working on the transition economies. There was little in the way of preliminary research to discover what was happening in these economies: most studies were tied to policy formulation. Research contracts to study the collapsing socialist economies were not awarded through the usual academic procedures (competing proposals subject to peer review) but on the basis of a rather secretive process in which personal contacts and ideological affinity loomed large.

There were distinct differences between the approaches of the various IFIs, reflecting their past missions and the intellectual background of their staff.[3] The IMF focused on budgetary stringency and currency convertibility as the keys to success. The World Bank was more interested in restructuring state enterprises, on the assumption that the public sector would continue to dominate in these economies for the foreseeable future. The OECD tried to cultivate a market niche for themselves in regional policy and labour retraining, while the European Union PHARE programmes made small-business development a priority. The potential contradictions between these divergent approaches were submerged under the rhetoric of 'transition', which was assumed to be a unified process within which all of these component parts would find a place.

There were also country-by-country differences. Western operators typically provided the services in which they had expertise. Thus, for example, the Belgians offered advice on how to restructure the coal and steel industry; the British on how to retrain the long-term employed; the Americans on how to draw up business plans and solicit loans from banks. Some of this advice was useful and made a substantial contribution to the development of the indigenous private sector. But much of it was superfluous or irrelevant. Whether or not the international assistance matched the immediate needs of the country in question only became apparent months later—by which time the grants which the advisers received had drawn to an end. For example, few of these countries had a problem of long-term unemployment, and few had the need for the sort of basic skills training which is seen as crucial in, say, Britain's labour market. Yet these were the programmes which the British Know How Fund concentrated on in the Czech Republic.

THE INTELLECTUAL BACKGROUND

The collapse of the socialist bloc in Eastern Europe came at an interesting juncture in Western economic thinking—at least, in the thinking which dominated policy-making élites in the West.

At the international level, there was a new confidence in the benefits of global integration. The European Community was moving beyond the promotion of trade, in the direction of 'deeper integration' (the harmonization of domestic economic policies and the free flow of capital and labour). Those countries which tried to insulate themselves from world market forces in the 1960s and 1970s by pursuing strategies of import substitution were trapped by stagnant growth and mounting international debts. The international financial institutions tried to insist on budgetary stringency and the removal of trade barriers as a pre-condition for debt-restructuring. Such 'conditionality' was reinforced by the accelerating pace of international capital flows, which made it increasingly difficult for national governments to pursue independent economic policies. The 'winners' of the international economic system seemed to be those countries, such as the South-east Asian 'tigers', which had made export promotion the central plank of their development strategy (even though initially this had not usually been combined with liberalization of import barriers).

At the domestic level, the post-war economic boom in the developed economies had sputtered out. Fiscal crisis, together with persisting problems of poverty and unemployment, had called into question the viability of the welfare state and the social market economy. By the late 1980s 'privatization' had become the buzz-word of public policy makers. In Britain, this was epitomized by Margaret Thatcher selling off state assets to the general public (from council housing to British Gas and British Telecom). In the United States, it involved contracting out municipal services.

This renewed faith in the market was not, however, unchallenged in the intellectual climate of the Anglo-Saxon world. Many economists doubted whether the market could bring prosperity and stability to the developing world. Within the developed world itself, there continued to be strong advocates of a more active role for government—from the Clinton team in the United States to the exponents of the social market in Germany. The collapse of the centrally planned economies gave a tremendous boost to the pro-market camp in this debate—although the subsequent tribulations of the transition economies may shift the centre of gravity back towards the institutionalists.

Western economic advice towards the socialist bloc can be divided into two phases. The first wave of advisers were those who pre-dated the collapse of the one-party regimes, working in Poland and Hungary since the early 1970s and in the Soviet Union between 1988 and 1991. In this phase, besides liberalization of foreign trade, the key issue was seen to be the abolition of centrally fixed prices, which would clear the way to increased autonomy for factory managers. Apart from modest encouragement for new private businesses, questions of changes in ownership of major state enterprises were not on the agenda—either of policy-makers or of their economic advisers (domestic and Western). Price liberalization was achieved in Hungary, but was blocked in Poland and Russia due to social protest (or manipulation of the threat of unrest by anti-reform politicians). A second theme was promoting trade with the West. Again, this was partly successful in Hungary, but yielded few benefits in Poland and never got off the ground in the USSR.

The lessons drawn from this first phase were that price liberalization and trade promotion were basically sound policies, but had to be pursued more resolutely and had to be accompanied by stricter stabilization measures (to prevent inflation) and by privatization (to create profit-oriented firms). The collapse of the socialist regimes in 1989 and 1991 lifted the political veto on radical reform. Thus the second wave of advisers who flooded into the region after the collapse of communist power in 1989–91 advocated the simultaneous launching of liberalization, stabilization, and privatization. These three policies became the Holy Trinity in the theology of transition.

The Orthodox Transition Model

There was broad agreement among Western economists on what needed to be done. The major arguments were over the speed and sequencing of the reforms: should they be fast or gradual, should they be simultaneous or in stages (McKinnon 1991; Murrell 1993)? A consensus soon emerged that simultaneity was preferable to sequencing, given the interconnectedness of the policy measures. But economists remained divided over whether speedy implementation of the transition package was really feasible, and whether the costs of doing so (in the form of an accelerated slump in output) exceeded the benefits.

The initial wave of successes (Poland and Hungary) faded from attention as their achievements eroded—and as consultancy contracts shifted further east. Enthusiasm for the next wave of successes (Russia and Kyrgyzstan) proved to have an even shorter half-life. The most enduring successes have been Czechoslovakia, Slovenia, and the Baltic republics, particularly Estonia. In all countries, liberalization proved quite easy to achieve. Stabilization proved harder to achieve, but most countries eventually came round to making a credible effort. Privatization has proved very difficult, with only the Czech and Slovak Republics and Russia making any real progress on this front on a large scale (Rutland 1992–3).

In restrospect this hierarchy of success is quite easy to explain. Liberalization simply meant doing less of something—regulating the economy—which they did not intrinsically want to do. Stabilization involved spending less money—always a painful decision. But unlike the other two policies, privatization required positive action: the break-up of companies, the seeking of new owners.

PRIVATIZATION: FOR WHAT, AND FOR WHOM?

Privatization, then, was assumed to be a Good Thing, both in the West and among the policy élites of Eastern Europe. However, the goals which are supposed to be advanced by privatization are varied, ill defined, and often tend to be contradictory. It is instructive to draw up a list of the range of objectives laid down for privatization by various leaders at various times:

- to restructure industry and promote more efficient production;
- to speed up the shedding of inefficient labour and eliminate hidden unemployment;
- to create competitive markets;
- to provide an improved level of goods and services for consumers;
- to soak up unemployed workers released from inefficient state-owned industry;
- to generate profits and investment;
- to create a class of new entrepreneurs who will provide a political basis for democracy;
- to give ordinary citizens a feeling that they have a stake in the transition process;

- to correct historical injustices by restituting property to expropriated owners;
- to facilitate the inflow of foreign business and investment;
- to hinder the inflow of foreign business;
- to reduce state subsidies to industry; and
- to generate revenues for local and national governments.

Obviously, no single policy package can hope to realize all of these goals. Trade-offs have to be made, or uncomfortable and possibly unstable compromises reached. By way of illustration let us take two sets of choices, using the Czech Republic as an example.

The Czechoslovak government opted for a two-track strategy. Key industrial assets in urgent need of new technology and access to international markets would be sold to foreign buyers. However, it would be impossible to find sound foreign buyers for the bulk of Czech industry, and anyway it was important to build up a social basis for the new democracy by creating a class of indigenous entrepreneurs and by giving ordinary citizens a stake in the privatization process. This was to be achieved through a range of programmes available exclusively to Czech citizens: restitution of property nationalized after 1948, the auctioning of leases on small shops, and the celebrated voucher privatization programme (Ceska 1994; Marcinin 1994).

Foreign or Domestic Ownership?

The Czechs wanted both to build up a native capitalist class and to open the country to foreign investors and expertise. How are these conflicting goals to be reconciled? Foreign investors are unlikely to be willing to lend money without some equity stake. This means that decisions involved in rebuilding key sectors of the country's economy will be made with the interests of transnational firms in mind—and the profits thereby generated will accrue to them. There was a fear that some multinational investors would indulge in 'spoiling' operations—buying a Czech firm merely to prevent a foreign competitor from taking over the plant. In order to deter such buyers, the Czech government tried to write guarantees on future investments and hiring levels into the purchase contracts. There was also talk of the government retaining a 'golden share' in privatized firms, giving them veto power over key decisions. Foreign buyers proved to be very wary of such vague arrangements.

Moreover, foreign firms are likely to target those enterprises which offer the best investment prospects. Such 'cherry-picking' will leave Czech entrepreneurs and investors with the worst of the crop. The same logic is at work when foreign banks are allowed to start making loans to domestic firms. None of the newly independent indigenous banks can compete with multinational banks in terms of reputation, experience, range of services, and, above all, interest rate. Foreign banks can select the strongest candidates among loan applicants (particularly among large firms)—leaving Czech banks with a disproportionately small number of sound clients among their risk pool. (The same criticism can be made of the small-loans programme of the US Enterprise Funds set up in each country.)

Initially, the Czechs anxiously sought foreign investors with ready cash and the willingness to bring much-needed technology to modernize a given sector. In 1990–1 the new government was keen to demonstrate that Czechoslovakia was 'returning to Europe' to ward off the threat of some sort of socialist restoration. Thus the government of Prime Minister Petr Pithart pulled out all the stops in 1991 to close the purchase of Skoda Mlada Boleslav by Volkswagen and of Tabak Kutna Hora by Philip Morris.[4] Both these firms were monopoly producers in the Czech market, and the government provided guarantees regarding future levels of import tariffs to ensure that they would maintain their monopoly position even after privatization. Belgian and German companies were also allowed to buy up most of the glass and cement industries. However, when it came to smaller, low-tech industries where Czech national pride was involved ('the family silver', in the words of Privatization Minister Tomas Jezek), the government strove to keep out foreign buyers. This applied in particular to breweries and porcelain, although the government was also forced to recognize that these sectors urgently needed access to foreign technology and marketing networks.

However, after 1991 the government started to apply the national-pride argument to some of the core industrial sectors whose state-appointed managers were struggling to avoid foreign ownership. The Skoda Plzen engineering giant spurned such eminent suitors as Siemens and Westinghouse, and in November 1992 the government orchestrated a buy-out by a consortium of Czech banks and a company owned by Plzen's former managing director. Similarly, in May 1994 the government rejected a $US550 million bid for the two Czech oil refineries from an international consortium led by Agip and Conoco, and opted instead for the so-called 'Czech path', i.e. selling the refineries to a holding company owned by other Czech firms (Marsh 1994). The government cited strategic concerns, but it is clear that control of the profits from oil-refining is the real issue. In the face of opposition from free-market advocates within the ruling coalition, the government reopened discussion of oil industry privatization in July.

The Czech government's shift away from foreign participation can partly be attributed to some negative experiences with foreign investors. In 1992 Dow withdrew from a provisionally agreed $100 million deal to purchase the Litvinov chemical plant. Then in late 1993 Volkwagen abruptly and unilaterally decided to cut their promised investment in Mlada Boleslav by more than half. Czechs were surprised to discover that the deal signed by Volkwagen did not include any legally binding commitments to provide the promised investments. Total direct foreign investment in the Czech Republic amounted to a disappointing $2.5 billion by June 1994, compared to $6 billion in Hungary (*Business News* (CTK), 10 Aug. 1994; *Central European*, June 1994, 5).

Also, paradoxically, the move away from foreign investors is partly a result of the very success of their liberalization policies. The Czech crown held its value against the dollar after price liberalization in January 1991, while inflation fell to less than 10 per cent in 1994, while the government ran a budget surplus. As a result, the international investment agencies raised the rating of Czech bonds to investment grade (BAA). The Czech government found itself awash with cash, and realized that they might be able to raise investment capital on international markets without relinquishing equity control to foreigners (Robinson 1994). In 1994 the Prague Council and the electricity monopoly CEZ successfully floated international bonds, and there was a surge of international portfolio investment in the infant Czech stock market.[5] Thus the Czech success in liberalization and stabilization seems to have militated against further progress in privatization, in so far as this is taken to mean the influx of new foreign owners with the technology, expertise, and incentives to restructure Czech industry.

An additional complication is the fact that among the most active foreign partners seeking involvement have been state-owned corporations (such as Deutsche Telekom and Renault). At times the rubric of privatization seemed to be serving as a cover for the international expansion of Western state-owned corporations. These companies have close ties to international lending agencies, particularly the European Bank for Reconstruction and Development. One suspects that foreign state-owned companies may be no more efficient than domestic state-owned companies—as the Czechs discovered when Air France, with EBRD participation, bought 19 per cent of Czechoslovak Airlines in 1992. In 1994 the Czech government bought back the shares in the face of mounting losses at CSA.

Efficiency versus Social Equity

The choice between foreign and domestic buyers for state property is relatively clear and direct. The tension between efficiency and social equity is less obvious, but no less important.

The central purpose of privatization is to improve economic efficiency. One of the by-products of improving efficiency—and an indicator that productivity is actually improving—is the shake-out of excess labour.[6] However, unemployment will erode the government's popularity—however much they explain that it is a sign of economic restructuring. One way of keeping unemployment low is to hold down real wages—the cheaper the worker, the more will be hired. Despite their *laissez-faire* rhetoric, the Czech government has been able to hold down the real wage through a strict excess wage tax.[7] This tax was applied not only to state-owned firms, but also to privatized enterprises. The wage tax is probably the main reason why unemployment in the Czech Republic has been kept at an astonishingly low 3.2 per cent (as at July 1994) (*Business News* (CTK), 8 Aug. 1994).

A strict wage control policy may be useful if one is threatened by inflation, but it is inefficient from the economic point of view. It discourages investment in physical capital and in skill acquisition, and distorts the operation of the labour market (making it more difficult for efficient producers to expand their work-force).

The maintenance of wage controls in the Czech Republic is connected to the second major reason for the low rate of unemployment—the explosion of self-employment. The number of registered self-employed rose from 20,000 in 1989 to 640,000 in 1993 (*Business News* (CTK), 3 Aug. 1994).[8] These are mostly sole practitioners, without hired labour. There are an additional 150,000 firms with less than twenty-five workers, with a total of 1.2 million working in the self-employed sector and in private companies with less than twenty-four employees (*Business News* (CTK), 20 June 1994). These are very impressive figures in a country with 10 million inhabitants and a labour force of 6.5 million. The government has encouraged this phenomenal explosion of entrepreneurship through their programmes for property restitution and the auctioning of small shops (on a five-year lease). They have also instituted active labour market policies, which involve subsidies for small entrepreneurs who employ school-leavers.

This expansion of private entrepreneurship has obviously helped to keep a growing number of workers out of the ranks of the unemployed. Whether it is economically efficient to redeploy labour into this host of small businesses is an open question.

On the one hand, it can be argued that the service sector was grossly under-represented in the socialist economy in comparison with Western economies. The explosion of private cafés, computer consultancies, construction firms, and appliance repairers is a healthy corrective. All consumers benefit from the ready availability of services which were hitherto lacking (although price rises may keep services beyond the reach of the poor).

On the other hand, many of the new private entrepreneurs lack experience and capital, and their numbers soon saturated local markets. Most of them will fail, perhaps as many as 80 per cent. (This is roughly the proportion of new business start-ups which fail within five years in established market economies.) Many of them are only able to stay afloat by avoiding taxes—which is unfair to more efficient businesses, and pushes up the general taxation level for legitimate payers. Many of them have drawn their skills and expertise from the state sector, and continue to maintain close business ties with state-owned enterprises (Webster 1992; Swanson and Webster 1993). As the state sector continues to contract, the new private firms will have to seek new customers.

Much of the new private sector is relatively impervious to foreign competition—particularly as the small privatization programme was restricted to Czech residents. In the first three years after 1990 the government only allowed a handful of foreign retailers to acquire property and enter the market (Ikea, McDonalds, K. Mart). As foreign-owned retail chains steadily infiltrate the Czech market, they will increase the competitive pressure on local entrepreneurs. McDonalds has already taken a commanding position in the fast-food business in Prague.

Thus one sees a very complex interaction of competing concerns pertaining to economic efficiency and social engineering. There is no evidence that the government sat down at any point and drew up a coherent and explicit blueprint for steering the transition process. Rather, different parts of the governmental bureaucracy follow their own logic, and as a result pull in different directions. The Finance Ministry will push for tighter licensing and reporting requirements, while the Labour Ministry will be more interested in increasing spending on job subsidization programmes. Municipal authorities and national officials come under conficting pressures from local entrepreneurs and foreign companies—both invoking the rhetoric of privatization.

If there exists an overarching force tying together these various pressures, it will be found in the sphere of politics. The next section examines the political assumptions underlying the debates about the adoption of the reform package. Unfortunately, the prevailing hypotheses about the politics of privatization fail to provide a framework to explain or reconcile its social and economic antinomies.

MODELLING THE POLITICS OF PRIVATIZATION

The main threat to the reform package was seen to be potential opposition from social groups who stood to lose the economic privileges they had enjoyed under socialism—mainly workers, managers, and bureaucrats in heavy industry. These strategically placed groups still had the potential capacity to disrupt economic life, to block the implementation of the reforms, or perhaps to mount organized political opposition to the programme. The second source of political threat was the newly enfranchised general population, who would be asked to sustain considerable disruption to their way of life and a sharp cut in their living standard for at least several years. If this potential opposition could be overcome, it was assumed that the population would be able to see the long-term benefits of marketization and would not vote the reformers out of office.

There were four main schools of thought on how to deal with these political challenges to the reform process. All emerged in a rather *ad hoc* fashion, and have rarely been systematically explained.

1. *'Pay-off'*. The argument here is that key strategic groups must be compensated for the losses they incur, and persuaded that they too will have a share in the benefits of marketization. This means giving workers shares in the privatized firms, giving managers a role in the design of privatization projects, and so forth. The difficulty with this approach is that so much may be given away in the form of concessions to get the programme accepted that there is very little of the programme left when (if) it is actually implemented. The most glaring example is the Russian privatization programme, where three-quarters of firms opted for the variant allowing the firm's workers to buy 51 per cent of the shares (Rutland 1994).

2. *'Window of opportunity'*. Poland's first post-communist Finance Minister, Leszek Balcerowicz, argued that it was neither prudent nor necessary to wait for the construction of a political coalition for reform. Given the pattern of social interests and attitudes inherited from the socialist era, it was unrealistic to expect the new, inexperienced political leadership to build a political coalition for reform. Instead, the reform government should seize the opportunity created by the collapse of the communist political order to rush through as many irreversible reforms as possible, before the conservative forces out there in society regrouped. This kamikaze mentality was also espoused by the Gaidar leadership in Russia in the first months of 1992. This approach carries quite obvious dangers. What are the chances that such hastily introduced policies will work? What is to stop subsequent governments reversing the process?

3. *Populism*. While the 'window of opportunity' school is rather dismissive of the benefits of democracy, the third approach seeks to use the opportunity provided by democratization to forge a new political coalition for change. Unlike the 'pay-off' philosophy, which concentrates the benefits on strategic groups inherited from the old regime, the populist approach tries to enlist the broad ranks of the population in support of the reform agenda. The outstanding example is, of course, the voucher privatization pioneered in Czechoslovakia and emulated, somewhat less successfully, in Russia. Lithuania and Poland have also tried to introduce voucher schemes, but have run into implementation problems. A still more widespread populist measure is to preserve subsidies for housing, utilities, and transport so as to mitigate the impact of price liberalization on these basic commodities where the poor cannot easily cut consumption. By distributing vouchers to the entire adult population the Czechoslovak government gave them a stake in the continuation of privatization and helped ensure the victory of Vaclav Klaus's party in the June 1992 elections. (The elections took place just one month after bidding began for shares in state enterprises.) The cash value of the vouchers in the Czech Republic turned out to be around $300–500 (a sum roughly equivalent to two months' salary). The Russian vouchers are only worth some $30, because fewer valuable assets were put into

the programme, and because, as described above, most firms opted for worker buy-outs. The populist approach carries certain dangers. Voucher privatization will tend to delay the transfer of assets into the hands of new outside investors (domestic or foreign), who will carry out the necessary restructuring. By distributing assets at no cost it does nothing to raise new capital or generate additional budget revenue. (Populist subsidies for housing and so forth obviously have an even more direct impact on government finances.) It was for these reasons that World Bank experts opposed the introduction of voucher privatization in both Czechoslovakia and Russia. A further drawback of populism is that it is gambling with the political moods of a volatile and largely unknown electorate. In both Russia and Czechoslovakia there was a surge of enthusiasm when the privatization vouchers were issued and lavish advertising campaigns raised citizens' hopes for a killing in the privatization lottery. There was inevitably a backswell of disillusion as the riches failed to materialize (even in Czechoslovakia, where the vouchers did prove to be valuable assets). In each country there were corruption scandals and a widespread sense that others had unfairly benefited from the programme. The populist strategy can easily backfire, with political opportunists moving in to exploit the popular discontent.

4. *The social safety net.* Early on in the process, the international financial institutions recognized that the social costs of market transition could be severe. They therefore advocated the erection of a social safety net to protect the 'losers' in market reform. This approach, typical for economists, regards politics as a constraint which, once acknowledged, frees policy-makers to maximize the key variable—market reform.

These societies already had a system of pensions in place, and unemployment legislation was swiftly introduced. However, the existing social security systems were geared to work experience rather than some assessment of actual need (penalizing women who had been out of the labour force, for example). The main problem, however, was the lack of money to prevent the erosion in the real value of these benefits, which in most cases were quite generous relative to the prevailing wage. It was easier to continue subsidizing existing firms than to close them down and throw all their workers on to the labour market.

The heavy emphasis placed by Western advisers on building up the social safety net became increasingly unrealistic as these governments (with the exception of the Czechs) struggled to control mounting budget deficits. In no country have social security measures been able to prevent the poor from bearing a disproportionate burden of the costs of transition. The international experts' persistence in this line of approach was a product of wishful thinking. It was also a reflection of their own personal expertise, and of the fact that safety nets had come to be a priority in development assistance to the Third World (where social security was much less developed than in Eastern Europe).

In reality, of course, the disadvantaged groups who would be assisted by a social safety net did not pose any serious threat to the reform process. The poor and dispossessed, including women, children, and the elderly, by definition lack the resources necessary to become effective political actors. The family, as ever, has been called into service as a social shock-absorber for the costs of transition. The fact that women had been asked to bear a disproportionate share of these costs makes the almost total absence of gender issues in the mainstream economic transition literature even more galling.

THE PARADOXES OF PRIVATIZATION

None of these hypotheses about the politics of privatization provide a satisfactory account of the overall dynamics of the process. These approaches share the view that privatization is the goal and the analyst must explain the politics of how to get there—by building coalitions, by neutralizing opposition, etc. This chapter will sketch out an alternative, non-teleological explanation of the dynamics of privatization. The East European countries have made a systemic break with the socialist past, but they are not in the process of constructing a capitalist future in the same way that one might set about constructing a house (e.g. Poznanski 1992; Csaba 1994). Societies do not consist of a set of discrete institutions connected according to some sort of blueprint (a fallacy which David Stark discusses in terms of 'designer capitalism') (Offe 1991; Stark 1994). Rather, they evolve over time ('path dependency'), and consist of a complex of social practices whose character and interrelationship varies from case to case.

With reference to the privatization of formerly socialist economies, one can identify some patterns of interaction which are common across these diverse societies. These regularities are cyclical rather than teleological, and are best understood as a response to contradictory and ambiguous pressures, rather than the erection of components of a predetermined capitalist future.

Building Capitalism—With a Human Face

The central antinomy of the politics of transition is the tension between the overarching theme of international integration and growing domestic dissatisfaction with the impact of reforms. The desire to be accepted as a legitimate partner by the alphabet soup of Western institutions (IMF, GATT, EU, NATO) is so widely acknowledged that the small band of nationalist extremists who reject this aspiration stand little chance of acquiring power.

While accepting in principle the advantages of the shift to democracy, most of the citizens of Eastern Europe quickly became disillusioned with the performance of their newly elected democratic governments. Thus in the second wave of elections, one has seen a succession of reformed ex-communist parties return to power—in Lithuania, Poland, and Slovenia.

Ironically, these social-democratic parties seem to be as firmly committed to continuing the policies of market transition as their liberal rivals, at least as far as liberalization and stabilization are concerned. Their stated goal is to combine these policies (and privatization) with more concern for social equality. It remains to be seen whether the circle can be squared, but one can expect politics to oscillate between these contrary tendencies for the next several years.

The New Politics of Privatization

The economic changes under way have created new patterns of political lobbying, but most interest group activity tends to reflect the features of the pre-1989 society. Some social groups have been more silent than expected, while others have been more vociferous.

Industrial workers have on the whole been strangely passive, given their numbers, level of organization, and often important role in the overthrow of the old system. Even in Poland, where workers were well organized and highly mobilized, they proved unable to mount an effective challenge to the invading market orthodoxy (Ost 1994). Surprisingly, farmers in almost all countries have turned out to be one of the social groups best able to seize the opportunities created by the arrival of 'market democracy'.[9] The reason seems to be that they are a single-issue group whose interests are clear and simple: subsidies for domestic food producers and protection against foreign imports. The interests of industrial lobbying groups are more diverse, and more likely to be in conflict between themselves. They are also able to appeal to nationalism, since village life is universally associated with the pre-communist past.

The new economic actors which marketization was to create have been relatively slow to make their début on the political stage. New private businessmen are now responsible for generating 30 to 40 per cent of GDP in most of these countries, but they have not been successful in creating formal organizations to articulate their interests. They have also shown relatively little interest in participating in political parties. There have been only a handful of cases where businessmen have played a visible role in political life (such as the entry of *émigré* businessman Stanislav Tyminski into the Polish presidential election).

Why has private capital apparently been so slow to organize itself? Partly this reflects the widespread contempt for politics inherited from the old socialist order, plus, therefore, a lack of experience in the possibility (and necessity) for participation in a democratic polity. However, one must also bear in mind the continued importance of the informal economy.

The Rise of the Informal Economy

Far from diminishing with the arrival of the market, the black economy in Eastern Europe has probably increased in scope and scale. Much of the activity of the new and expanding private sector is unreported and untaxed. Liberalization increased the opportunities for the informal economy, while government efforts to stabilize the budget through increasing taxes only drive more activity into the informal sector.

Entrepreneurs who rely on unrecorded activity for much of their profits will see little reason to band together to lobby for legislative changes—since they do not obey the laws anyway. They will also worry that overt political involvement might expose themselves to public scrutiny. Thus they will probably confine themselves to covert political activity (bribery, offering consultancies to politicians and government officials, and so forth). They will see political involvement as involving lobbying for particular favours, rather than collective action to improve business conditions for private enterprise.

The Creation of New Political Lobbies

The proponents of rapid market reform argue that privatization will bring about the depoliticization of decision-making, since it involves the introduction of the politically neutral logic of the market. Privatization means that the government's role will be limited to setting up the rules of the game within which efficient entrepreneurs will flourish.

One only has to spell out this line of thinking to reveal its untenability. The privatization process has been unavoidably political, involving as it does the reallocation of property rights on an unprecedented scale. Far from depoliticizing economic decision-making, privatization necessitates the exercise of political discretion and creates massive opportunities for political manœuvring. It creates new groups with claims on the state (would-be property restitutents, voucher-holders, investment funds, etc.) while doing little to deal with the opposition to restructuring from 'old' groups (such as workers in heavy industry). There is no reason to suppose that newly privatized firms will be any less adept at lobbying for special favours from the government than were their state-owned predecessors. Even if a reformist government is willing to bear the social costs of closing down loss-making state-owned enterprises, they may be less willing to allow newly privatized firms to go bankrupt because it would call into question the validity of the market transition programme.

CONCLUSION

The central theme to emerge from these observations is that of complexity and contradiction. The transition process does not involve the unfolding of the innate logic of a market economy—a process that may go well or badly depending on the ability of leaders to overcome the political barriers to reform. Rather, privatization sets in train a complex pattern of relations in which domestic and international actors pursue their various interests.

Thus the course of transition is not predetermined by a given economic logic, but is very open to political and social processes. Each society is making the transition from Soviet-type socialism in its own way, and will take a different path to a different end-point. Despite the favoured rhetorical cry of the shock therapists, 'There is no alternative!', the events of the past four years show that in fact each country has crafted its own transition package. To be sure, the results have usually been inferior to the hypothetical results which were to be obtained from a pure, surgical application of shock therapy. But one should beware of 'comparing muddle with model'.

Perhaps one of the more worrying implications of the orthodox economic literature on transition is the widespread assumption that politics is a problem, something that interferes with the logic of the market that is best ignored, or at least grudgingly recognized as a constraint on the introduction of the market. On the contrary, politics must be placed at centre-stage, and recognized as the key factor affecting not only the adoption but also the design of this or that element in the transition package. The advent of reform communist governments in several East European countries (all of whom remain verbally committed to market reform) will presumably force economic advisers to be even more cognizant of the political context within which market transition is taking place.

NOTES

1. For a sample of the new literature, see Islam and Mandelbaum (1993).
2. One of the most trenchant advocates of the view that depression is the dominant characteristic of the transition is G. Kolodko, since Apr. 1994 Finance Minister of Poland. See Kolodko (1993).
3. On this, see Rutland and Dobes (1992). This report was based on interviews with officials in ten international agencies and twenty regional business centres.
4. In every country, incidentally, from Lithuania to Kazakhstan, it seems as if the tobacco companies have been the first off the plane. And the second off the plane are the detergent giants—Unilever and Proctor & Gamble.
5. Portfolio investment amounted to $350 million—12 per cent of the total (Kayal 1994).

6. It is conceivable, but unlikely, that all freed labour could be re-employed by their current employer, and thus not show up on the labour market at all.
7. The real wage dropped 5.5 per cent in 1990 and 26.3 per cent in 1991, but grew by 10.3 per cent in 1992 and 5.2 per cent in 1993. It remains about 15 per cent below its 1989 level (EC Commission 1993).
8. In contrast in Poland in 1989 there were already 4.4 m. self-employed, and in Hungary 412,000 (EC Commission 1993).
9. Ironically, some EU officials have been encouraging the East Europeans to introduce a system of agricultural price supports along the lines of the Common Agricultural Policy, so as to facilitate their entry into the EU.

REFERENCES

CESKA, R. (1994), 'Results of Privatization through 1993', *Privatization Newsletter* (Mar.–Apr.), 21–2.

CSABA, L. (1994), *The Capitalist Revolution in Eastern Europe* (London: Elgar).

EC COMMISSION (1993), *Central and Eastern Europe Employment Observatory*, no. 5 (Brussels).

EDELMAN, M. (1971), *Political Language: Words that Succeed and Policies that Fail* (New York: Academic Press).

ISLAM, S., and MANDELBAUM, M. (eds.) (1993), *Making Markets* (New York: Council on Foreign Relations).

KAYAL, M. (1994), 'Regional Rivals Take over Lead in Investments', *Prague Post*, 24 June, 8.

KOLODKO, G. (1993), 'From Recession to Growth in Post-communist Economies', *Communist and Post-communist Studies*, 26: 123–43.

McKINNON, R. (ed.) (1991), *The Order of Economic Liberalization* (Baltimore: Johns Hopkins University Press).

MARCININ, A. (1994), 'Voucher Privatization and Ownership Structure', *Privatization Newsletter* (June), 4–8.

MARSH, A. (1994), 'Klaus Wants Oil Refineries to Go the Czech Way', *Prague Post*, 25 May, 5.

MURRELL, P. (1993), 'What is Shock Therapy?', *Post-Soviet Affairs*, 9/2: 111–40.

OFFE, C. (1991), 'Capitalism by Democratic Design?', *Social Research*, 58/4: 865–92.

OST, D. (1994), 'Class and Democracy: Organizing Antagonisms in Post-communist Europe', Paper presented to the International Political Science Association, Berlin, 21–5 Aug. 1994.

POZNANSKI, K. (ed.) (1992), *Constructing Capitalism* (Boulder, Colo.: Westview).

ROBINSON, A. (1994), 'Too much of a Good Thing', *Financial Times*, 29 July.

ROSTOW, W. W. (1960), *The Stages of Economic Growth* (Cambridge: Cambridge University Press).

RUTLAND, P. (1992–3), 'Thatcherism, Czech Style: Organized Labor and the Transition to Capitalism in the Czech Republic', *Telos*, 94: 103–29.

——(1994), 'Privatization in Russia: One Step forward, Two Steps Back?', *Europe/Asia Studies*, 46/8: 1109–32.

——and DOBES, A. (1992), *Shaping the Future: International Assistance for Small Business Development in Czechoslovakia*, OECD Research Report (Paris: OECD).

STARK, D. (1994), 'Recombinant Property in Eastern Europe', Program on Central and Eastern Europe Working papers no. 33 (Cambridge, Mass.: Harvard University, Center for European Studies).

SWANSON, D., and WEBSTER, L. (1993), 'Private Sector Manufacturing in the Czech and Slovak Federal Republic', Working paper no. 68 (Washington: World Bank, Industry and Energy Dept.).

WEBSTER, L. (1992), 'Private Sector Manufacturing in Poland', Working paper no. 66 (Washington: World Bank, Industry and Energy Dept.).

12

Privatization by Means of State Bureaucracy? The Treuhand Phenomenon in Eastern Germany

WOLFGANG SEIBEL

INTRODUCTION

Privatization is, by definition, a state affair. Despite good intentions, the state is still confronted with the same problems as a state-planned economy. The state has to make decisions without sufficient information and without sufficient capacity for control. The state must decide when to privatize which enterprise, to whom to sell it, and at what price. Each of these decisions has consequences for the allocation of commodities and capital, for labour migration, and for the future of firms and production sites. Quite rightly, the public holds the democratic state liable for the effects of these decisions, yet the state can neither exactly predict these effects nor effectively influence them. Thus, privatization in a democracy represents a classic dilemma from the very beginning.

When it comes to privatizing an entire economy, these problems multiply. Affected are not only individual firms and production sites, but entire industries and regions. Not only does a certain sales price bring a little more or a little less money into the state coffers, but the entire federal budget is altered according to whether privatization of the state's industrial assets tends to bring more or less profit. It is not just the employees of a single company who are affected, but entire areas and, by virtue of the impacts on the federal budget, the entire nation.

The state's dilemma of having to do things it cannot completely control and for whose effects it is nevertheless held liable is made more tangible by every attempt to cope with it. The more the state broadens its database and strengthens its capacity for control, the less it does what it actually should do: to withdraw from the economy instead of intervening in it, to dismantle its own control apparatus instead of expanding it.

In addition, 'the' state is neither a monolithic nor a rational actor. It is free neither in its ability to act nor in its choice of institutions. The public's preformed habits and expectations and the predetermined structure of institutions specify the pathways to decision-making from which policy-makers themselves could not necessarily stray even if they had a clear goal and a well-defined plan of action. Often, however, policy-makers do not have these clear goals and well-defined plans of action; often they recognize problems too late, if at all. When a problem is recognized and acknowledged as important, policy-makers are often pressed to accept compromises and problem-solving strategies of questionable effectiveness, and it may even be uncertain whether these compromises and strategies can be practically implemented or realized at all.

In this chapter I attempt to explain that the real process of privatization is composed of a chain of constraints and dilemmas and that the institutional design of privatization plays a central role in coping with these constraints and dilemmas. Although I refer to the economic fundamentals of privatization, it is only by way of partial analysis. The chapter focuses on the creation and adoption of the institutional design of privatization, the linchpin of which was the East German Treuhandanstalt, the government holding company set up to sell off or close down the state-owned businesses and property of the former German Democratic Republic (GDR). In particular, I attempt to describe and explain the institutional dynamics of the privatization process in the former GDR as it is reflected in the organizational development of the Treuhandanstalt. The logic of these dynamics was threefold. It was shaped by (1) the need to build up and control an organization of around 4,000 employees in less than twelve months; (2) the need to control the social and political costs of privatization, particularly those incurred by massive unemployment; and (3) the need to cope with the economic risks surrounding the extreme rapidity of privatization, whose pace characterizes the policy of economic transformation in East Germany.

THE TREUHANDANSTALT AS LEGAL HEIR TO THE GDR'S ECONOMIC ADMINISTRATION

In micro-economic terms, the German *institutional choice* for privatizing the East German economy was to have a single authority as the privatization agency, the Treuhandanstalt, which was in existence from 1990 to 1994. With its headquarters in Berlin, the Treuhandanstalt was a bureaucracy with 4,000 employees whose job was to return the former GDR's state-owned businesses to their former owners; to place them under the jurisdiction of other public authorities, especially local authorities (such as local traffic, water supply, and waste management); to sell firms to private entrepreneurs; or to liquidate them. On 1 July 1990 the Treuhandanstalt possessed 12,132 firms with about 4 million employees. By 31 December 1994, 97 per cent of the portfolio had been sold to private owners or had been reprivatized, transferred to the municipalities, or liquidated (Treuhandanstalt 1994).

The 'institutional choice' of a central privatization authority had not been a conscious weighing of advantages and disadvantages but rather an implicit avoidance of alternative costs. A change in the institutional status quo certainly would have been costly, and the advantage to the institutional alternative was uncertain. The Treuhandanstalt, founded in March 1990, barely three weeks before the first free elections in East Germany, was a creation of the GDR's communist-led government. At that time, the authority's task was to legally convert the state-run companies according to the prototype of West German corporate law. As before, however, the state was to be the sole owner of these firms. Thus, the Treuhandanstalt was something like a branch for the legal affairs of the GDR economic administration. Because of this arrangement, the organizational design of the Treuhand reflected the governance structure of the state-owned economy, with headquarters in East Berlin for the large industrial conglomerates (*Kombinate*) and branches being run decentrally in the fourteen districts of the GDR for the *Volkseigene Betriebe* (literally: enterprises owned by the people).

On 17 June 1990 the Treuhandanstalt's legal basis was revised, making the selling of state-owned enterprises its principal task. As is known today (see Fischer and Schröter 1996; Seibel 1993), the influence of West German policy-makers, too, was certainly felt in the drafting of this law, although it was not a decisive factor. In general, the institutional side of reunification received little attention. The problem of institution-building seemed to have been solved through a simple, yet promising, model—the wholesale transfer of West German political, legal, and economic institutions to what had been the GDR. The Treuhandanstalt, however, is a remarkable exception to that rule because there was no West German institutional equivalent to it. Thus, it became the only significant institution of the GDR to survive Germany's reunification.

In October 1990 the Treuhandanstalt was, and remained, a foreign institutional body that did not fit into the polity of what had been until 1989 the Federal Republic of Germany. The principal institutions of German public administration are the *Länder* (the federal states) and the municipalities. The Treuhandanstalt as the direct successor of the economic administration of the GDR was a centralized state agency. When it came to building a market economy, the perpetuation of this particular institution could therefore hardly be an appropriate message. Accordingly, political and constitutional considerations would have urged its dissolution and its subsequent decentralization into institutions of the East German *Länder* on 3 October 1990, the date of the GDR's accession to the FRG.

This option was not realistic for two reasons. First, one would have assumed in the summer of 1990 that the Treuhandanstalt, as a federal institution (*Bundesanstalt*), was a provisional entity as imperative for the efficient organization of privatization as for the short-term necessity of refinancing the federal government. At that time, the illusion in Bonn was that reunification would in some way finance itself.[1] It was not assumed that the reorganization of the state and economic order in East Germany would require continuing redistribution of resources from West to East (see Seibel 1992). During the campaigns for the first all-German elections that had been scheduled for December 1990, the West German federal government categorically refused to raise taxes to finance the burdens of reunification. From this perspective it seemed reasonable to rely on the sale of the Treuhand's property for refinancing the accumulating short- and medium-term public debt. The state treaty for the unification of West and East Germany (*Einigungsvertrag* of 31 August 1990) then stipulated that the Treuhandanstalt remain a federal holding of the GDR's formerly state-owned enterprises and be assigned to the Ministry of Finance.

The second reason for maintaining the Treuhandanstalt as a central authority for the state government was that the former GDR did not yet have a decentralized administrative substructure. In the summer of 1990 *Länder* were drawn on GDR territory on the basis of the West German model. At that time, however, the East German *Länder* existed merely as territorial borders. The official organization of the East German *Länder* coincided with the first elections for the state legislatures on 14 October 1990, some ten days after the Day of German Unification on 3 October. It was also foreseeable that the construction of a viable administration at the *Land* level would take much longer than the desirable life-span of the Treuhandanstalt in the summer of 1990. Thus, practical necessities alone spoke for the temporary continuation of the Treuhandanstalt as a central privatization agency.

As it turned out, however, the institutional side of privatization developed its own dynamics, over which policy-makers had but limited control. Only with ideological formulas and the respective political rhetoric could the truth be veiled—that the Treuhandanstalt, down to its internal structures, was a continuation of the GDR's economic administration and, hence, the exact opposite of what it actually should have been. This was not due to any single monumentally wrong decision but was more the almost unavoidable consequence of piecemeal decisions, each of which appeared to be plausible and appropriate. This pattern can be seen in the many hectic changes to which the Treuhand's organizational structure was subject in the summer and fall of 1990 (Seibel 1993). At times, Treuhand law was crassly broken by these measures for reorganization, but in the agony of the GDR, parliament and the public took little notice.

By this law, the creation of five multi-industry stock corporations was provided for at below Treuhand headquarters level. The fourteen branches of the Treuhandanstalt, which still existed as a legacy of the GDR economic administration, were to be dissolved, while the federal government was to remain the sole owner of the stock companies. The founding of the stock companies was, nevertheless, to symbolize the capitalist new beginning and serve as an attractive institution for the managers who had to be recruited from the western part of Germany for the boards of directors and the executive committees.

This stock corporation model failed, however. To be precise, it was stopped abruptly by the president of the Treuhandanstalt in August 1990 out of concern that the gigantic stock companies would develop into power centres that would hinder privatization more than help it. Thus, the East German economy, as during the times of the GDR, remained under the direction of a single authority.

But the Treuhandanstalt did strive to decentralize its own structures. The fourteen branches were not dissolved as originally planned, but rather strengthened and renamed the *Niederlassungen*. A division of labour according to company size took place between the head office in Berlin and the district offices. The district offices managed all firms with fewer than 1,500 workers; the head office, all firms with 1,500 workers or more.

The head office in Berlin was itself reorganized as well. For ideological reasons, it was desirable to avoid a structure divided according to industries because that approach would have corresponded exactly to the organization of the GDR economic administration. Instead, headquarters were restructured along functional lines. The principal tasks as outlined by Treuhand law were emphasized through two large key departments for privatization (*Privatisierung*) and reconstruction (*Sanierung*). Each of these departments would have had more than 2,000 firms to manage. In the fall of 1990 this model proved unviable because the sheer number of companies would have been too great for those key departments to manage. In particular, it turned out that effective privatization and reconstruction of firms depended on organizational knowledge being structured much like the economy itself—according to sectors. There was nothing else to do but give the Treuhandanstalt's headquarters a new divisional structure according to industrial sectors. That done, however, the structure of the Treuhand's head office was almost a blueprint of the former GDR's branch ministries. The culmination of this reorganization was the Treuhandanstalt's transfer to the GDR's former House of Ministries in May 1991, the very building in which the GDR's branch ministries had had their seat.

Thus, to the degree that the Treuhandanstalt did consolidate (around the beginning of 1991), it edged more and more closely towards perpetuating the GDR's economic administration. In terms of the industrial structure of the Treuhand headquarters and the strengthening of old district offices, the institutions of privatization were now practically the same as the institutions of the GDR's state-planned economy.

The logic of institutional dynamics had hitherto been rooted in the decision not to dissolve the Treuhandanstalt upon German reunification and to make it the country's central privatization agency instead. However, 1 July 1990 was a strategic turning-point. On that day, West German currency became the legal tender in the GDR. From then on, there unfolded another developmental logic that eclipsed the institutional dynamics of the Treuhandanstalt: the rapid decline of the East German economy, which was thrown on to the open world market overnight. From then on, two processes ran parallel: the formation of an efficient privatization agency and the erosion of its assets. This dual developmental logic forced the continuous process of institutional learning that is outlined in the remainder of this chapter.

INSTITUTIONAL LEARNING AS A PROCESS OF DISILLUSIONMENT: THE DEVELOPMENT OF THE TREUHANDANSTALT'S STRATEGIC BASELINE

While the blueprint of the Treuhandanstalt's organizational structure was being drafted in the fall of 1990, there was still much obscurity about how to put the agency's goals into operation. The fall of 1990 was shaped by the election campaign for the first all-German parliament since 1933, not a setting in which general public attention was attracted by such difficult questions as the putting privatization into operation strategy. Not even the strategic actors in the Treuhandanstalt—the president and his council—had access to much information. No one knew exactly how many firms the Treuhandanstalt possessed, let alone what condition they were in. It was a demand-driven market in which small and medium-size businesses were in particular demand. Stable demand enabled the privatization of the retail and gastronomic trades to progress more quickly than other sectors.

Determining the selling criteria was among the decisions that had to be made. It had to be established whether the buyer was actually interested in the business itself and in its economic future (rather than, for example, the attached real estate or the take-over of a potential competitor). Thus, the selling criteria laid down in summer 1990 encompassed (1) the potential investor's concept for product development, marketing, and finance; (2) the amount of the planned investments; (3) the number of future jobs; and (4) the purchase price. With this list to hand, the Treuhandanstalt subjected the purchase offers to the judgement of a particular board, the *Leitungsausschuß*, which was composed of four top-level West German managers assisted by a staff of some eighty analysts.

By fall 1990 most Treuhand firms had proven to be uncompetitive in their current state and could therefore not be sold profitably. The firms in all significant industries lacked modern technology, managerial know-how, and, hence, competitive products. Foreign customers, 70 per cent of whom were located in Comecon countries and up to 40 per cent in the Soviet Union alone, now had to pay for their East German imports in hard currency. This led to dramatic slumps in sales and to deferments in payment even before the dissolution of the Soviet Union in 1991. Given these realities, the Treuhandanstalt came to a fork in the road. The question was whether the firms were to be first reconstructed and then sold at the highest possible price or whether they were to be sold at a low price and then reconstructed by a private owner.

Time for a considered decision quickly ran out. Within the decisive six months between fall 1990 and spring 1991, the Treuhandanstalt's options were dramatically reduced. In the first quarter of 1991 industrial output in East Germany fell to 30 per cent of the level it had had in the fourth quarter of 1989 (DIW and IWK 1993). Two million of the 9.7 million employed in the fourth quarter of 1989, or more than 20 per cent, had lost their jobs or migrated to West Germany. All of this was the unavoidable consequence of the abrupt currency union between East and West Germany in the summer of 1990. Moreover, illusive hopes had been raised by the West German government when it propagated the idea in the election year of 1990 that a *Wirtschaftswunder* (economic miracle) in East Germany would occur via a market economy just as in West Germany during the 1950s. The discrepancy between the East German hopes for the Deutschmark and its real effects was both politically and economically risky.

This mix of misperception and illusion had two essential consequences. First, the amount of time that would be required to make the transformation from a planned economy to a competitive market economy went unappreciated, as did the concomitant social costs in the form of massive unemployment. Second, the promises for rapid economic growth and a high standard of living for the entire East German population produced a political climate that the unions were able to use to push through high wages that had no basis in labour productivity. This also resulted in a situation in which the major share of the state transfer payments from West to East Germany primarily went to finance unemployment funds, retirement plans, and the like rather than the critically needed investments in public infrastructure.

Inevitably, the Treuhandanstalt became an institutional hinge of the economic, social, and political consequences arising from the discrepancy between ideology and reality. Until early 1991 the Treuhandanstalt had survived in a protected political niche. In February 1991, however, came the first massive strikes in East Germany against what was realistically perceived as a disastrous economic breakdown. Workers occupied dozens of firms. In Schwerin, the capital of Mecklenburg–Western Pomerania, workers even occupied the state legislature. The prime ministers of the East German *Länder* strongly criticized Treuhandanstalt's privatization policy, demanding that it be dismantled into regional agencies and that the latter be transferred to the respective *Länder*. Trade unions and the East German

Länder called for a 'change in the course' of the Treuhandanstalt toward state-controlled 'reconstruction' of the economy instead of accelerated privatization.

This overt political pressure forced the Treuhandanstalt to decide upon its strategy at last. Inevitably, its perspective was diametrically opposed to the perspective of those directly affected by its policy. Conversely, the massive production set-back, which caused the East German *Länder* and the trade unions to seek the state-controlled reconstruction of firms, sent a clear signal for the Treuhand to dismiss this strategic option once and for all.

From the Treuhandanstalt's viewpoint, comprehensive state-controlled reconstruction of the East German economy would have required such an enormous sum of money that it could only have been financed through an uncontrollable federal debt. In turn, this reality raised the fundamental question of whether the state (i.e. the Treuhandanstalt) would be able to allocate its resources appropriately. Accordingly, there was no other choice but to privatize the Treuhandanstalt's assets as quickly as possible and to limit the unintended economic and socio-political effects as far as possible.

With that option set, however, there was no doubt that new dilemmas would arise from it. Maximizing the speed of privatization would not only increase unemployment and its attendant social and political tensions but would also severely depress the prices of the Treuhand firms (Sinn and Sinn 1992). Falling prices, however, have meant lower proceeds for the state and thus fewer resources for what remained in terms of state-controlled economic reconstruction.

Institutional Learning as Organizational Differentiation: Control over Social and Political Costs, Control over Timing

It is important to acknowledge that the Treuhandanstalt was not simply an executor of a rapid privatization scheme. If it had been, it could have been dispensed with: a sales catalogue from the federal government would have been sufficient. In reality, however, the Treuhandanstalt had basically abandoned control over the pace of privatization but, for the sake of political legitimacy, it could not abandon control over the social and political consequences of privatization.

Therefore, the Treuhandanstalt had to make compromises aimed at minimizing the social and political costs of its policy without changing the substance of that policy too much. Besides that, control over the pace of privatization had to be partially regained without the Treuhandanstalt becoming burdened with the tasks of state-controlled economic reconstruction. These compromises were reified as an institutional differentiation of the Treuhandanstalt. Differentiation allowed the Treuhandanstalt to improve control over social and political costs and institutions and over the

time schedule of privatization as a critical factor of the economic transformation process in East Germany. Needless to say, these functions cannot be
neatly separated; every institution has its overlapping functions. Nevertheless, the institutional dynamics of the Treuhandanstalt seem to have
followed this particular logic for the most part.

Control over Social and Political Costs

By virtue of its character as an independent state agency alone, the
Treuhandanstalt had already fulfilled an important role in mitigating political conflicts and, accordingly, lessening political risks of legitimacy. A loose
coupling established between the privatization agency and the federal government was significantly more advantageous for both the federal government and the Treuhand than a tight coupling of the state-run firms with the
government in Bonn. The effect was indeed that the Treuhand, not the
federal government, was able to be made the scapegoat for the social
consequences of privatization—the closures of non-competitive firms and
the loss of millions of jobs. But an essential risk was also minimized for
the agency itself. In a way, there was an implicit contract between the
Treuhandanstalt and the federal government. The Treuhand lowered the
government's political costs (loss of legitimacy), and the government
granted the agency relative independence.

Furthermore, the crisis in the spring of 1991 led to considerable improvements in co-ordination between the Treuhandanstalt, the East German
Länder, and the trade unions, a change that increased the
Treuhandanstalt's political entrenchment. On 14 March 1991 principles for
co-operation between the federal government, the new *Länder*, and the
Treuhandanstalt (*Grundsätze zur Zusammenarbeit von Bund, neuen
Ländern und Treuhandanstalt*) were issued. They envisaged regular meet-
ings between representatives of the Treuhandanstalt and the ministers of
the East German *Land* governments. In the fall of 1991 the introduction of
an 'early-warning system' followed, through which the governments of the
Länder were to be informed about the imminent closures of Treuhand
businesses in their respective territories. A joint statement by the trade
unions and the Treuhandanstalt on 13 April 1991 and, lastly, an agreement
setting up Societies for Job Creation, Employment, and Structural Development (*ABS-Gesellschaften*) on 17 July 1991 resulted from these improvements in political co-ordination.

These measures had their share of success. Basically, the East German
Länder and the trade unions started to accept the Treuhandanstalt as it was.
The structural effect of these measures was that the Treuhandanstalt began
to adapt to the fundamental elements of the West German political system:
federalism and corporatism. Although consolidation into a more or less
efficient federal agency bequeathed to the Treuhand a core organization

resembling the economic administration of the bygone GDR, the improvement in the Treuhandanstalt's political embeddedness followed the traditional West German model. It is not surprising that organizational management of social and political uncertainties followed the West German pattern. Less obvious, however, is that coping with the time-consuming character of economic reconstruction was a main factor shaping the organizational differentiation of the Treuhandanstalt.

Control over Timing

The weak point of a privatization policy oriented to rigorous acceleration in sales is the loss of control over the timing of economic reconstruction. Control over timing is a characteristic of every hierarchy as opposed to markets. In principle, this truth also applies to the characteristics and possibilities of an authority such as the Treuhandanstalt. When circumstances are not too complex, a competitive advantage enjoyed by hierarchies is that they co-ordinate things more quickly. For this reason, for instance, fire protection and surgical operations tend to be entrusted to strongly hierarchical organizations.

However, the actual advantage of the hierarchy is not speed itself but rather the possibility of expediting or decelerating processes in a controlled fashion. Only hierarchies and the authority and discipline associated with them can prevent processes from running too quickly or too slowly. Firms need time to develop new products, and they can only do so by allocating staff to this purpose by hierarchical directive long before the market signals that the old products are no longer being sold. The most common examples are interventions to speed up or slow down economic development through the hierarchical order of the state. Since its emergence, the modern state has thus ensured that raw materials such as wood and coal are not stripped away too quickly and that over-exploitation is avoided. This function led to the emergence of entire administrative industries such as those regulating forestry and mining.

Control over timing and the formation of institutions appropriate for it have presumably been a key difficulty in every process of economic transformation. However, the demise of the planned economy in Central and Eastern Europe has an additional dimension, the 'dilemma of simultaneity' (Offe 1991). Too much disintegrates at once, with new structures emerging too slowly. Basically there is good reason to assume that the state, whatever its institutional form, must tend to decelerate the decay of the old and accelerate the creation of the new.

The Treuhandanstalt indeed tried to regain a degree of control over the rate of decline of the old economic structures and the creation of new ones. This effort focused primarily on the privatization of land, the regeneration of an entrepreneurial and managerial class, and the reconstruction of local

and regional industrial networks. In all three cases, the circumstances stemming from the legacies of the East German economy all but precluded appropriate allocation without government intervention. The
Treuhandanstalt partly volunteered and was partly compelled to react to
these flaws by modifying the pace of the privatization process. In doing so,
it again diversified its organizational structure.

The Privatization of Land

In the former GDR land was completely state-owned. In the capitalist
world, land is both a means of production and a collateral for borrowed
capital. A special feature about land as an economic commodity is that it
lacks technological components (and therefore cannot become 'obsolete')
and that it is not infinitely reproduceable. Apart from the risk of contamination by noxious substances, the state-owned land in the former GDR is
certainly a secure investment.

By the end of 1994 the Treuhandanstalt owned approximately 35 per cent
of all East German soil and was therefore almost a monopoly supplier of
land. The other areas continue to belong to the federal government, the
Länder, the municipalities, and the firms, which usually use the land and do
not want to sell it. Private ownership of land is still relatively limited,
primarily because of the complicated process of clarifying ownership prior
to the several waves of land expropriation under the communist regime.

As the monopoly supplier of land, the Treuhandanstalt had two tasks to
complete. First, it had to prevent land speculation. Second, it had to control
the timing of depreciation by selling surplus land. Both conditions were met
in that the sale of land was organizationally separated from the
Treuhandanstalt's other business of selling. For this reason, all land associated with a firm but not necessary for the firm's operation had to be
dealt with separately. This approach was designed to prevent investors
from buying a firm simply for its land. A special agency, the
Liegenschaftsgesellschaft der Treuhandanstalt (TLG, or Agency for
Landed Properties), was founded for the sale of land that was not necessary
for business operation.

A loss of control over the timing of land sales and a resulting depreciation
due to over-supply would not only mean lower revenues for the
Treuhandanstalt. Because land as an investment commodity lacked technological risk, such loss of control also meant that it could not be regionally
limited. Both in the East and West, the result would be a depreciation of
collateral for private and institutional debtors and a destabilization of the
capital market.

As far as the particular commodity of land is concerned, the Treuhand
acted in exactly the opposite way from how it did in the sale of its firms. The
loss of control over timing could have had catastrophic economic ramifica-

tions. However, it is not certain that this prospect alone would have triggered the depicted institutional learning effect. By their very nature, economic ramifications would show up on the West German market, and they are relatively easy to comprehend. Thus, strong West German interests and the simplicity of information were two advantages that favoured the institutionalization of a particular mechanism for delaying the sale of land, thereby securing an elementary economic factor: land itself and capital procurement.

The Formation of an Entrepreneurial Class

By expropriating the last private entrepreneurs and forming *Kombinate* in the 1970s, the communist regime of the GDR had destroyed the final remnants of traditional German industrial governance. The rest of what had remained in terms of small and medium-size businesses, an industrial middle class, and regionally focused suppliers and customers was eliminated. Output was organized largely on the basis of industrial mass production and a nationwide sales area of supply and delivery. The centrally directed conglomerates were supposed to match factory production with the proper suppliers and customers throughout the GDR. The relations between a given industry's dominant firms and their suppliers were no longer regionally agglomerated, and they no longer relied on a division of labour between independent small and medium-size firms. Thus, the destruction of small business and the destruction of regionally focused supplier–customer relations were complementary. At the same time, this meant a high degree of vertical integration within the *Kombinate* that was repeated at the level of individual firms because those firms always tried to make themselves independent of notoriously unreliable suppliers. Because of this structure, the conglomerates as such were not sellable; they had to be dismantled. That dismantling brought the destruction of an organizational principle, but no new one to replace it.

Creating a new industrial structure through the market is a time-consuming process. This process has both an organizational and a sociological component. The organizational component is the emergence of a stable network of labour among dominant firms, suppliers, and customers in a given region. The sociological component can be seen in the development of an indigenous class of entrepreneurs and managers. From 1991 on, the Treuhandanstalt promoted the sale of small and medium-size firms with concessions in their purchase price and special assistance in capital procurement. The declared goal was to strengthen the entrepreneurial middle class. Assistance with management buy-outs (MBOs) was a particular way of promoting this effort. MBOs, the majority of which involved small and medium-size businesses, accounted for 20 per cent of all business privatization in 1993 (Treuhandanstalt-Zentrales Controlling 1993).

Experts are sceptical about the economic prospects of the MBOs, however. According to Dreher and Michler (1992), the essential motive behind an MBO is to save the business and/or part of a business and its jobs. Thus, when MBOs occur, the reasons are almost always defensive, not active, entrepreneurial ones. The managers lack the necessary know-how, particularly in the areas of finance, marketing, and sales promotion. Moreover, there is very little owner's equity because most available financial resources have already been used to acquire the business in the first place. The low chance of procuring capital, in turn, hinders research and development for new products and the building of a production system. In this situation, many new ownership teams have tended to reactivate at least the relations between subcontractors and customers that once existed under the conglomerate, thus reconstructing the dismantled conglomerate structure 'from the bottom up'. But this outcome is precisely what hinders product innovation, the improvement of new markets, and the development of the new firm's ability to stand on its own two feet. Because everyone in these old structures is in the same situation, business failures are perennial, destabilizing relations between subcontractor and distributor. Because of this instability, however, many new ownership teams must rely on manufacturing depth in terms of pre-products and services. This need, in turn, raises the costs of production, lowers profit margins or increases losses, and restricts entrepreneurial leeway—perfect ingredients for a vicious circle.

From all of this, one can conclude that the sociological consequences of eliminating a self-reliant entrepreneurial class in the GDR can hardly be dealt with through government promotionals. In any case, the MBO so favoured by the Treuhandanstalt is little more than a symbolic measure. Sociological processes such as those involved in developing an entrepreneurial class are far beyond government control anyway. All in all, one is left only with the irreversible consequences of the Treuhandanstalt's policy of dismantling the conglomerates.

The vicious circle exemplified by the MBOs is the central risk of privatization: the constant threat of deindustrialization. If it is not possible to mobilize enough capital and management know-how for the obviously long haul of East Germany's economic reconstruction, then there might eventually be a chain reaction of business failures and of labour migration due to adverse synergetic effects. These dynamics show how central the time issue is and how crucial it is to ask whether appropriate institutional forms of control can be found for slowing the demise of the old structures and for accelerating the creation of new structures (Albach 1992).

The Formation of Industrial Networks

The Treuhandanstalt certainly did not ignore the risk of deindustrialization. On the contrary, of necessity it realized it earlier than all other policy-makers. As early as in the summer of 1991 a study authorized by the Treuhandanstalt and conducted by the consultant firms McKinsey and Goldman & Sachs described the risk of deindustrialization, using the East German chemical industry as an example. In a public speech in November 1991, the president of the Treuhandanstalt, Birgit Breuel, demanded that 'the core industrial regions [be] maintained' in East Germany (*Handelsblatt*, 2–3 Nov. 1991: 17).

Two things are remarkable about this initiative. The first is that the Treuhandanstalt commented at all about such an affair, which, according to the official distribution of duties and to general policy, should be the jurisdiction of political decision-makers, and not that of the Treuhandanstalt. Second, the phrase 'maintenance of core industrial regions' could make it seem that the Treuhandanstalt concerned itself with the preservation of existing industrial structures instead of with their rapid adaptation to the demands of the market. This public stance can only be explained by recalling the particular position the Treuhandanstalt occupied between market and government, between the logic of the allocation of goods and the logic of maximizing votes and political support. Furthermore, it is remarkable that the Treuhandanstalt did not just defensively oppose the political pressure exercised by the German *Länder* and the trade unions. It also converted such pressure into operational concepts of modifying the privatization strategy and institutional innovation. It should be borne in mind that in 1991 the Treuhandanstalt was still a large jump ahead of the rest of the state and societal actors in East Germany in terms of information, professionalism, and administrative consolidation.

In the summer of 1991 the Treuhandanstalt had thus tacitly acknowledged that the risk of deindustrialization was real and not simply an ideological formula thought up by the East German *Länder* and the West German political Left. At the same time, the Treuhandanstalt realized that what mattered was the prevention of political coalitions that might rally spontaneous interest in conserving old and non-competitive firms and industrial structures. The Treuhandanstalt had to make an acceptable offer on the political market without fostering non-competitive structures on the market for firms. The political offer had to be packaged in a clever, rhetorical fashion, but it had to be more than just plain rhetoric. Naturally, the dilemma still existed that the Treuhand had an interest in both safeguarding its autonomy and mobilizing policy-makers for the task of promoting economic structural development. The Treuhand could not promote structural development on its own and had not actually been authorized even to reflect on the issue.

'Maintaining the industrial core regions' was such a rhetorical offer, but it was formulated vaguely enough so as to not to bind the Treuhandanstalt to an exact model. Between the fall of 1991 and the spring of 1992 two institutional forms for improving control over the economic structural development of the former GDR emerged: the *Management Kommanditgesellschaften* (MKGs) and the Saxon ATLAS model. The MKGs were the initiative of the Treuhandanstalt, the ATLAS model, the initiative of the *Land* government of Saxony.

The MKGs were holdings owned exclusively by the Treuhandanstalt. The portfolio of these holdings consisted of firms that the Treuhandanstalt assessed as having a chance to become competitive but that could not be sold at that time. Every holding has continued to be directed by a well-paid, experienced West German manager receiving an additional premium depending on the success of the privatization. The portfolio's composition of the first two holdings founded in the spring of 1992 was not focused on particular industries or regions but rather on the restoration and ensuing sale of single firms. The Treuhandanstalt guaranteed sufficient capital resources for the firms of the holding. The firms could be sold at any time.

The model of the MKGs signified the attempt at reconstruction in an entrepreneurial style and was a remarkable exception to the Treuhandanstalt's policy, according to which the reconstruction of firms *before* their sale was not the agency's business. The exceptional character of this institutional solution was mirrored by the fact that in 1992 just 10 per cent of the Treuhand's firms were earmarked for the privileged status of MKG firms. The policy was clearly designed to promote the competitiveness of each individual firm. The focus on the individual firm and on the strong personality of the holding boss was both the strength and the weakness of this model. The strength lay in the fact that the goal was the creation of a competitive business and not the conservation of certain industries or production sites. By the same token, the weakness lay in the fact that the companies' existing relations with suppliers and customers were not considered. Synergistic effects were consciously not aimed at, for the concern was that 'synergies' would only mean reactivation of previous supplier–customer relations from the days of the *Kombinate*. This approach, however, tended to ignore the risk that even capably managed firms may remain uncompetitive as long as, for instance, the absence of capable suppliers and business-related services forces them to maintain a costly vertical integration of production and services.

The ATLAS model, which the Treuhandanstalt had accepted only under political pressure, signified the attempt to make firms competitive in a *corporatist* style. ATLAS stands for *Ausgewählte Treuhandbetriebe, von der Landesregierung angemeldet zur Sanierung* (selected Treuhand businesses registered by the *Land* government for reconstruction). From the very beginning the East German *Länder* have pressed for improved opportunities to have a voice, in particular, in the Treuhandanstalt's decisions about reconstruction and closure procedures. In April 1992 the *Land* of Saxony reached an agreement with the Treuhand according to which the *Land* government was to name those Treuhand enterprises that were especially important for a particular region. These enterprises were then closely supervised by the Treuhand if the *Land* government simultaneously subsidized those firms with federal funds it had received for the promotion of the regional economic structure. A non-profit organization with two managing directors acted as a co-ordinating mechanism; one director was nominated by the trade unions, the other, by the employers' associations. In addition, there were two advisory councils, one representing both trade unions and employers, the other representing state legislators. The Treuhandanstalt had the final say on the future of the ATLAS firms, but it has been admitted that institutional lobbying by the state legislators and the particularly intensive examination of the ATLAS firms offered a second chance. ATLAS was recommended by the federal government in December of 1992 as a model for all East German federal States (*Neue Bundesländer*) for saving the 'industrial core regions' in East Germany.

If one compares the MKGs with the ATLAS programme, the Treuhandanstalt's dilemma is salient. The MKGs focused on individual businesses. The individual firms, networks of core production, suppliers, and services were not considered or organized. Possible synergies were not used. By contrast, ATLAS had a regional, industry-related focus, but the interests of existing production sites and existing jobs were dominant, thereby limiting the innovation of products and industrial organization.

The core of this dilemma is that the government as the owner of firms, according to the Hayek theorem, can never match the market's capacity of processing information, nor can it create social classes such as middle-class entrepreneurs and managers. Nor can the government design and foster new structures of industrial organization. The technological trends for development and the chances on the market for an industry or line of production can only be recognized and used by those who have the required knowledge, experience, and vested interest in the survival of a business. This applies to the entrepreneur as well as to the managers. The existence of entrepreneurs and managers, however, is a sociological phenomenon found in the creation of an economic élite that requires many conditions and decades to form. The same applies to the formation of production patterns based on a regionally or locally concentrated division of labour and of networks for core production, suppliers, and services that build on such patterns. Normally, these structures are formed step by step as a historical result in unco-ordinated fashion in a relatively long evolutionary process with tight interdependencies.

THE LOGIC AND MORPHOLOGY OF INSTITUTIONAL DYNAMICS: PATH-DEPENDENCY, IMITATION, INNOVATION, AND THE LIMITS OF STATE-CONTROLLED PRIVATIZATION

The scope for the German federal government to shape the institutional side of privatization of the East German economy rapidly shrank during

1990. Institutional aspects did not play a crucial role in the important strategic decisions on the future of East Germany's economic development. The central privatization agency in East Germany, the Treuhandanstalt, was set up under the final Communist government in March 1990. Neither the first and last democratically elected GDR government nor the government of unified Germany questioned the existence of the Treuhandanstalt.

Further political and economic decisions and developments continued to narrow the room for manœuvre in economic policy for East Germany in 1990. The most important of these factors were (1) the establishment of monetary union between the two German states on 1 July 1990; (2) the expectation, systematically raised especially by the governing parties in the election year 1990, that East Germany would enjoy rapid economic growth through monetary union and through reunification on 3 October 1990; and (3) East German industry's loss of markets in Central and Eastern Europe, caused by both the conversion to hard currency and political turbulence in that part of the Continent. All these decisions and processes lay beyond the control of the Treuhandanstalt.

From the very beginning, the Treuhandanstalt's scope for institutional self-initiative was thus limited to tactical adaptation. None the less, this institutional flexibility and its success or failure were of utmost importance for the strategic ability of the German federal government's privatization policy. In the summer of 1990 the federal government had already lost the initiative for controlling the economic process of transformation in East Germany. It was already foreseeable at that time that East Germany's shock-like entry into the world market upon monetary union on 1 July 1990, together with the political promises of a rapid rise in the standard of living, which was achievable only through higher wages, would inevitably lead the East German economy to its own collapse. This was tantamount to an abrupt devaluation of Treuhand assets. In consequence, the government of reunited Germany could neither obtain the profits that it hoped to reap from the sale of Treuhandanstalt assets nor come up with the enormous sums that would have been necessary to reconstruct state-owned firms prior to their sale.

In this way privatization changed from a pragmatic means of achieving a stable, economic transformation of the East German economy into a crude end in itself. This change made it necessary to give the swiftness of privatization absolute priority. The relative success of the Treuhandanstalt is that it institutionally stabilized this one-sided goal, which was compelled by external circumstances and ideologically justified by the federal government after the fact. The Treuhandanstalt achieved not only the political objective of rapidly privatizing the East German economy but also reduced this policy's political costs to the federal government without itself collapsing under the political pressure resulting from it. This achievement was made possible by the Treuhandanstalt's institutional status as an independent federal agency and its step-by-step differentiation in a rigid centre with a flexible periphery, a process that gradually developed after crisis-like phases. In this way, the Treuhandanstalt balanced out not only the political dilemmas of the drastically accelerated privatization process but also the tension between the short-term task of privatization and the long-term process of economic structural transformation.

The institutional side of privatizing the East German economy was subjected to a threefold logic of development: that of administrative efficiency, social and political cost reduction, and compromise between incompatible goals of privatization. These three overlapping logics of development produced a certain institutional morphology related, in turn, to three different patterns of development: path dependency, imitation, and institutional innovation.

In the second half of 1990 the logic of administrative efficiency made it necessary to realign, step by step, the Treuhandanstalt's organizational structure with the structures of the GDR economic administration, which, ironically, the Treuhandanstalt should have overcome. The pattern of path dependency dominated in this respect. Although it had been planned otherwise, the Treuhandanstalt had to give up the model of overarching stock corporations for managing state industrial assets and abandon the functional organizational structure of the Treuhand's head office. Towards the end of 1990 the Treuhandanstalt had become a central administrative authority with regional subunits.

The Treuhand's head office, in turn, was organized by sector, just as the GDR's branch ministries of trade and commerce had been. This organizational structure had not been desired; external circumstances had forced it. It had become apparent that a functional structure of organization would raise major problems of co-ordination and that the necessary expertise in privatization and in the reconstruction of the Treuhand's firms could only be mobilized with a divisional structure organized according to sectors.

The logic behind the necessary reduction of social and political costs led to the peripheral differentiation of the Treuhand organization according to the model of West German federalism and neo-corporatism. The pattern of institutional imitation dominated in this regard. The co-optation of the East German prime ministers and trade unions in the administrative council of the Treuhandanstalt, the establishment of 'Treuhand cabinets' and of East German *Land* governments, and the conclusion of several general agreements on pension funds for laid-off workers and on subsidized employment agencies decidedly improved the political entrenchment of the Treuhandanstalt. Only in this way could it mitigate the political pressure generated by the massive unemployment that accompanied privatization.

The logic of compromise between the incompatible economic goals of privatization led to the Treuhand's own institutional innovations where there were no historical models to follow. The rapid privatization of industrial assets and the slow privatization of landholdings could be reconciled only by transferring the privatization of landholdings to formally private agencies controlled entirely by the Treuhandanstalt (the TLG and the Bodenverwertungs- und verwaltungsgesellschaft, or BVVG). The same applies to the MKGs—the type of holding whose subsidiaries were considered capable of being reconstructed, but not of being sold on an *ad hoc* basis. Here, too, the process was purposely decelerated for certain firms, something that could only happen by means of organizational subdivision.

How will the institutional morphology of the relation between the government and the economy ultimately look in East Germany? One can only speculate at present, but several tendencies can be discerned. It is not probable that the Treuhandanstalt, which from the very beginning was bound to an alien element in the German constitutional and economic order and which continues to exist under the enigmatic label Bundesanstalt für Vereinigungsbedingte Sonderaufgaben (Federal Agency for Special Tasks Arising from Unification, or BVS), will be completely absorbed by this (West German) constitutional and economic order. It is possible rather that the relation between the state and the economy in East Germany will be characterized in the long run by a higher degree of centralism and government intervention. How is this prognosis arrived at?

First, the logic of administrative efficiency did not end with the dissolution of the present Treuhandanstalt on 31 December 1994. Important tasks of the Treuhandanstalt, such as managing contracts of purchase and clarifying the ownership of firms in the hands of the Treuhand, have been left up to the federal government, not transferred to the East German *Länder*. This solution may be efficient, but it is unconstitutional. According to the constitution of the FRG (the Basic Law), the East German *Länder*, not the federal government, are responsible for regional industrial policy.

The logic behind the necessary reduction of social and political costs leads to imitation of West German industrial patterns that have little or no societal and political basis in East Germany. Half a decade after reunification in 1990, the East German *Länder* are not equal partners in the system of German federalism. The East German prime ministers can only exercise as much influence on the federal government as they can afford in view of their heavy dependence on direct financial assistance from the federal level.

The logic of compromise between the incompatible goals of privatization policy has led to institutional innovations that favour the centralism of federal authority and call into question the strengthening of the authority of the East German *Länder*. Similarly, the agencies for the privatization of land and the reconstruction of potentially competitive firms that had become autonomous organizations cannot be taken over by the East German *Länder*. Such an arrangement would exceed both their financial and their managerial capacities. The process by which these organizational units become legally independent eventually perpetuates the existence in East Germany of powerful quasi-non-governmental organizations (quangos), which lie beyond the influence of the East German *Länder* and direct democratic control.

All in all, it is probable that the centralist and statist elements of institutional arrangements will persist at the intersection between government and market in East Germany rather than decentralizing and market-driven elements. Even though the Treuhandanstalt was officially dissolved at the end of 1994, the Treuhand phenomenon has continued to shape the relation between the government and the economy in East Germany and beyond. After fifty-six years of dictatorship and central economic administration, East Germany still lacks the necessary means for sustainable institutional development along the lines of the West German model. These conditions can be neither created nor replaced by institutional imitations and innovations. The emergence of a professional entrepreneurial class, the formation of industrial networks with a division of labour between big industry and small and medium-size firms, the self-organization of business and employees, and the creation of strong *Länder* that do not depend financially on the federal government are all prerequisites that grow only within medium- and long-term historical processes. These processes not only lie outside state control but also continually invite government intervention. Despite good intentions and favourable circumstances, it remains to be seen whether government-controlled privatization is an unsolvable dilemma in Germany.

NOTES

This chapter is based on empirical research in and around the Treuhandanstalt, East Germany's privatization agency, since Nov. 1992. It draws on documents which were kindly provided by the Treuhandanstalt and collected by a major interdisciplinary research project that was co-ordinated by Professor Wolfram Fischer of the Free University of Berlin, and to which I contributed an analysis of the organizational development of the Treuhandanstalt (see Seibel 1996). Furthermore, I was able to conduct some thirty interviews with Treuhand executives (Feb.–May 1993) as well as a questionnaire-based survey on job attitudes and other staff-related variables in Mar. 1993. I am indebted to Stephan Kapferer and Jutta Wietog for technical assistance and to Roland Czada, Gerhard Lehmbruch, and Hartmut Maassen for helpful comments on earlier German drafts of this chapter.
1. See Milbradt (1993). Milbradt is Saxony's Minister of Finance.

REFERENCES

ALBACH, H. (1992), 'Kein Geld, keine Zeit—und kein Geld für den Kauf von Zeit' (No Money, no Time—and no Money to Buy Time), Paper presented at the Wissenschaftzentrum Berlin für Sozialforschung, 30 June 1992.

DIW (Deutsches Institut für Wirtschaftsforschung) and IWK (Institut für Weltwirtschaft Kiel) (1993), *Gesamtwirtschaftliche und unternehmerische Anpassungsprozesse in Ostdeutschland* (Macro-economic and Micro-economic Processes of Adaptation in Eastern Germany), Report no. 8 (Berlin: DIW).

DREHER, C., and MICHLER, T. (1992), *Die Entwicklung und Chancen der mittels MBO/MBI enstandenen mittelständischen Industrieunternehmen in Ostdeutschland* (The Development and Opportunities of Small Business Born of MBO–MBI in Eastern Germany) (Karlsruhe: Fraunhofer-Institut für Systemtechnik und Innovationsforschung).

FISCHER, W., and SCHRÖTER, H. (1996), 'The Origins of the Treuhandanstalt', in W. Fischer, H. Hax, and H. Schneider (eds.), *Treuhandanstalt: The Impossible Challenge* (Berlin: Akademie Verlag), 15–39.

MILBRADT, G. (1993), 'Die Finanzausstattung der neuen Bundesländer' (The Financial Resources of the New Federal Länder), in W. Seibel, A. Benz, and H. Mäding (eds.), *Verwaltungsreform und Verwaltungspolitik im Prozeß der deutschen Einigung* (Baden-Baden: Nomos), 272–87.

OFFE, C. (1991), 'Das Dilemma der Gleichzeitigkeit' (The Dilemma of Simultaneity), *Merkur*, 45: 272–92.

SEIBEL, W. (1992), 'Necessary Illusions: The Transformation of Governance Structure in the New Germany', *Toqueville Review*, 13: 178–97.

——(1996), 'The Organizational Development of the Treuhandanstalt', in W. Fischer, H. Hax, and H. Schneider (eds.), *Treuhandanstalt: The Impossible Challange* (Berlin: Akademie Verlag), 112–47.

SINN, G., and SINN, H.-W. (1992), '*Kaltstart*' Volkswirtschaftliche Aspekte der deutschen Vereinigung, 2nd edn. (Tübingen: Mohr).

TREUHANDANSTALT (1994), *Treuhandanstalt-Information*, no. 21 (Dec.).

TREUHANDANSTALT-ZENTRALES CONTROLLING (Treuhandanstalt Central Controlling) (1993), *Monatsinformationen der THA*, 31 Oct.

13

Mediating Institutions in the Transition from State Socialism: *The Case of Local Government*

CHRIS PICKVANCE

INTRODUCTION

It is often observed that the way in which questions are phrased controls the answers which are given to them. Hence it is useful to start with a few comments on the terms in the title of this chapter.

The concept of transition from state socialism (1) identifies a starting-point for a process and (2) names that process as a transition. This gives rise to two dangers. The first is that state socialism is treated as a homogeneous entity which functioned in the same way in each country. The concept of state socialism is undoubtedly useful in referring to the family resemblances between the socio-economic systems of Eastern Europe and the former Soviet Union. However, there is a danger that ideal concept and reality are confused and that the differences between state-socialist societies are ig-nored, e.g. differences in degree of tolerance of private land, private hous-ing, private business, and of political opposition (Kornai 1992). Such differences are obviously important in understanding the process of transition.[1]

Secondly, the concept of transition process is open to objection. By definition, a transition process can only continue for a determinate period, until an end-state is reached, after which the transition finished. The danger here is twofold. First is the teleological assumption that the end-state is known in advance (e.g. liberal democracy or welfare capitalism). The choice of end-state may reflect the aims of those involved in transferring institutions, as well as the hopes of groups in society, but sociologically the assumption of a known end-state is untenable. For example, capitalism can operate at varying levels of economic development, and in a variety of political contexts, authoritarian as well as democratic, any of which might be the end-state in former state-socialist societies. The second danger is that the concept of transition process may make one think in terms of contrasts between transition period and end-state such as confusion and order or rapid change and stability which belong more to the metaphor of transition than to the reality 'out there'. This may divert attention from similarities and order in transition processes and on the other hand exaggerate the stability and lack of conflict in the end-state societies.[2] The term 'transition' will be used in this chapter in implicit quotation marks: no assumption is made about the duration, pace, extent of change, or end-state of the process.

The other term in the title of this chapter is 'mediating institutions'. The assumption here is that some institutions are crucial in instigating change, and others respond to it. For example, the household or family is often seen as a coping institution which responds to change introduced at 'higher' levels in society. However, the question could well be asked whether under the Hungarian variant of state socialism, the second economy did not represent a household-driven social form which expanded to a degree unpredicted by the party-state and eventually provided an economic element in its downfall (Sík 1992). I would draw the conclusion that whether an institution is mediating or instigating can vary over time, and that the two functions can even coexist in a single institution.

There is also an ambiguity in the idea of mediating. For some writers, mediating means 'passively' transmitting, e.g. when we see a mediating institution as passing on initiatives external to itself without altering them. For other writers, mediating can mean 'actively' shaping, e.g. when we see a mediating institution as imposing its own stamp on some externally initiated process and giving it a change of direction or speed. Local government is a good example of such ambiguity since it can be seen as simply implementing central government policy, or as providing scope for local political forces to modify the implementation of central policies such as housing privatization, or to initiate local policies.

The chapter is divided into three parts. Firstly, it is shown that under state socialism local government was subordinate to central government and state enterprises, had relatively few functions, and access to the benefits of local government activities was controlled by a party-based élite network. Secondly, it is argued that after state socialism local government becomes in many respects a more active mediating institution and control over its functions becomes a highly contested issue in local politics. For example, local government is a significant source of demand and a significant owner in urban real estate and hence shapes the development of the private sector of the economy. The central questions are how far it gains autonomy from former economic and political centres of power, and how far it is subordinate to new sources of economic and political power. Finally, the extent to which the network capital built up under state socialism is still a valuable resource is discussed.

LOCAL GOVERNMENT UNDER STATE SOCIALISM

Under state socialism, local governments were formally elected bodies responsible for service provision in local areas. They were financed by a mixture of central grants and taxes on local state enterprises. They followed allocation principles set up by the superior regional and central government departments. They had a very low degree of decision-making autonomy and had no fiscal autonomy (they could not levy their own taxes) (see Jacobs 1983; Ross 1987; Elander and Gustafson 1993; Lengyel 1993).

In reality this picture was partly correct and partly misleading. The real centres of power in state socialism were the party hierarchy and state enterprises. Although state enterprises were formally 'simply' economic units receiving centrally decided investment allocations, the fact that they were the source of all employment and *were* the economy gave them huge political significance and hence real leverage over resource allocation—this is manifested in what Kornai baptized the 'soft budget constraint'.

The implications for local government were of great importance. *De facto*, local government was controlled by the party hierarchy and heads of local enterprises, and the composition of 'local executives' reflected this. Elections were contested by candidates who had been vetted by the party, and meetings of the local council were infrequent and simply rubber-stamped the decisions of the local executives who had real power. The local executive needed a certain degree of autonomy in order to reconcile differences in interest between different levels of the party apparatus and local state enterprises. In cases such as Hungary where by the 1970s managers of state enterprises had been allowed more autonomy, the degree of autonomy of local government was somewhat greater. In essence, local government should be seen as part of the party–administrative–industrial nexus which had to cope with the failures of co-ordination and performance of state socialism in practice (Hough 1969; Andrle 1976).

Economically, too, local government had little autonomy under state socialism. Firstly, since state enterprises were the economy they were privileged in the ministerial allocation of state funding compared to local government: as a result there developed an 'occupational welfare state' in which state enterprises provided housing, health, recreational, vacation, and other facilities for their employees (Shomina 1992). In other words many of the functions of local government in welfare capitalist societies were performed by state enterprises. Another effect of the niggardly funding of local government was that it often had to turn to state enterprises for the execution of local public works projects, e.g. the construction of roads or buildings.

Secondly, since state enterprises were the only *local* source of funding for local government, local government could not deviate too far from the priorities of state enterprises in case this supply of funds was cut off. Local governments had no autonomy to levy additional local taxes.

In terms of resource allocation, a major local government function was the allocation of housing. The Hungarian case has been extensively re-searched and can be taken as a model for the examination of the question 'Who benefits?' in resource allocation. The results can be summarized as follows:[3]

1. Up to the 1960s state flats were considered the most attractive form of urban housing and the best-quality and best-located flats were allocated to the most prestigious occupational groups. Some state flats were employer-allocated but even when they were allocated by councils, employers were always consulted in the allocation decision. Tenants of state flats had many of the rights of owners, and in particular could sell their tenancy. This allowed exchanges between tenants, who could thereby trade a good location for cash if they chose.

2. From the 1970s state support was introduced for the private housing sector in the form of subsidized loans which led to the creation of private flats which were ranked above the best state flats in desirability.

3. As a result, there was an outflow of the highest-income tenants (in the best state flats) into private flats. Given the quasi-market in state flat tenancies, those involved could sell their tenancy, thereby 'cashing in' the advantages of their initial favourable housing allocation. The subsidies for private house purchase allowed them to gain further advantages.

4. Subsequently, state flat allocation was altered in order to give higher priority to 'social need'.

Overall then, state housing institutions have favoured the higher-status occupational groups,[4] and local government worked with employers in deciding on flat allocation (for more on the relation between employers' interests and housing, see Pickvance 1988).

To summarize the argument so far, local government under state social-ism was largely controlled by the party hierarchy and local state enterprises and employers such as administrations. It had a limited mediating role (limited to what was necessary to try and overcome some of the defects of state-socialist economic performance) and to a large extent its allocation of resources reflected the priorities of an élite.

LOCAL GOVERNMENT IN THE TRANSITION FROM STATE SOCIALISM: A NEW OPPORTUNITY STRUCTURE

We approach this subject in two stages. In this section we look at how far local government has changed and in the next section we speculate about how individual actors have responded to the new opportunities it offers.

It is beyond the scope of this chapter to consider how local government has changed throughout Eastern Europe and the former Soviet Union. We shall refer only to the cases of Hungary and Russia.[5] We consider in turn local democracy, local government structure, and the resources (financial and otherwise) of local government.

Local Democracy

In Hungary, local elections were held in autumn 1990 after the general elections in March. These were freely contested by political parties, most of which were anti-communist. In rural areas some supporters of the previous regime were elected but in the cities those elected were mainly opposed to the former regime. In Budapest, the Free Democrats won power at the city level and in almost all of the district councils, but this did not guarantee harmonious relations between them.

No research has been done to my knowledge on the subsequent relations within majority party groups, or between politicians and permanent officials. The questions of interest are: how far a 'clean break' with the past can be made in policy terms; how far the existing staff can exercise continuing power over the newly elected politicians and if so what resources they deploy (social networks, information, etc.); and how far politicians have real power or how far external interests such as large enterprises still exercise power (as in capitalist societies). Our own study has revealed some evidence that grass-roots groups find the new structures as unresponsive as the old.

In Moscow, local elections were held in March 1990 after the general elections of March 1989. The period 1988–90 saw a mushrooming of discussion clubs and other groupings who were suspicious of the term 'party' (Brovkin 1990; Fish 1991; Pickvance 1995). The local elections were contested by some temporary groupings but loyalties were centred on individuals rather than programmes and the term 'political party' exaggerates the stability and coherence of the groupings that formed. The studies of local government since then have all emphasized the experience and high hopes of the newly elected representatives and the conflicts (1) over the competence of each level of local government and (2) between mayor and senior officials and rank-and-file representatives over their respective powers. The simultaneous dissolution of the USSR, the lack of a new Russian constitution to replace the Soviet constitution, and economic dislocation all contributed to the chaotic situation in local government and help to make sense of the reassertion of central authority over local government from late 1990 (Alexejev *et al.* 1991; Campbell 1992; Boyce 1993; Hanson 1993).

In Hungary the democratic election of local governments occurred in a context where economic reform had been taking place for over a decade— though it would be wrong to claim the insecure partial measures as first steps which would necessarily eventuate in a new economic system. In Russia, on the other hand, there had been minimal change from the centrally planned economic model.

Thus the fact that anti-communist majorities were often brought to power by the first local elections cannot be expected to have the same effects. Some evidence about changes in the practices of local government is presented below.

Local Government Structure

A second question concerns the structure of local government.

In Hungary there has been a reform of the local government system. Central control was seen as part of the old regime and its tendency to reinforce social inequality (see Rév's statement that 'redistribution by central authority creates inequality'; Rév in Ladanyi 1992). In its place, in Budapest, a new structure was introduced replacing Budapest city council by a city council and twenty-two district councils which had the main powers. Whatever the intentions of the reformers the result has been to decentralize too many competences to the district level and create a weak centre. By 1993 Budapest city council was funding three research groups to produce alternative models of local government for the future (e.g. in case the conservative-nationalist government led by the Hungarian Democratic Federation lost the general election in 1994, which it did, bringing into power a socialist–Free Democrat coalition).

In Moscow initially there was no change of local government structure. The March 1990 elections took place within the old system of a city council and thirty-three district councils. Ironically, this structure, which had been the mechanism of central power until 1990, proved capable of facilitating challenges to the power of Moscow city council once new councillors (many of them under 'reform' or 'democratic' labels) were elected. Serious conflicts broke out, including attempts by district councils to usurp functions of the city council.

In autumn 1991 the city council responded drastically to this challenge by abolishing the thirty-three district councils and regrouping their administrations under ten prefectures each reporting directly to the mayor of Moscow. The aims of this reform were:

- to remove rival power centres which had challenged the powers of the city council;
- to weaken the political forces influential at the district level;
- to gain control of urban real estate held by district councils—whose importance we shall return to below; and
- to strengthen the position of the mayor of Moscow against the elected representatives on the city council.

In October 1993 Moscow city council was itself abolished, by presidential decree.

Local Government Finance

A third question concerns the financial resources available to local governments. Under state socialism, personal incomes were not taxed and local state enterprises were the only local source of local taxes. A major legacy of this is the reluctance of local governments to levy taxes on the population.

In Hungary local governments receive a share of personal income tax paid to central government as well as a block grant (Peteri and Szabo 1991). They have also been given powers to levy taxes on private persons (on private buildings, dachas, agricultural and urban land, communal buildings, and tourists) and on companies (on their premises, vacant land, payroll, and profits). However, they have been very reluctant to impose these taxes—by 1990 they only represented 1 per cent of local government current income (Lengyel 1993). Instead, their main new income source has been through the sale of council flats which by June 1993 had reached 35 per cent of the stock in Budapest (Hegedus and Tosics 1993; Pickvance 1994*b*).[6]

In Moscow, there is a similar reluctance to levy new local taxes. A 0.1 per cent property tax has been legislated but by 1993 had not been implemented. This is a key issue for owners of flats. The housing privatization programme in Moscow started very slowly in 1990 but by August 1993 had reached 35 per cent. Since it is 'free privatization' involving a transfer of ownership without payment, it provides no income to the city government beyond a transfer charge of 2,000 roubles ($US2) per flat. But the large percentage of owners now constitutes a further obstacle to the levying of a property tax. On the other hand, once urban real estate is resold, it is subject to a 50 per cent capital gains tax (announced in April 1993).

The other likely sources of new local government income in Hungary and Russia are increased rents and increased charges by state property maintenance organizations.[7] In Hungary, the latter are financially interdependent with local governments; in Moscow, it is planned to replace existing property maintenance organizations with private ones.

Local governments have other assets and although there is little systematic evidence it is likely that these are a key source of new income in the present transition period. Local governments are owners of commercial premises such as shops and offices. These are a more significant income source than flats, and their sale is a tempting way to generate a quick income. In Moscow, the renting of commercial space allows local governments to generate foreign-exchange incomes from foreign companies. Control of such space was one issue in the Moscow local government conflict

(Boyce 1993) as well as for the protest groups known as 'housing partnerships' (Pickvance 1994*b*). There is also anecdotal evidence of local governments placing empty flats for sale for hard currency rather than allocating them through the waiting-list (*Guardian*, 5 May 1993). One estimate is that 10 per cent of new housing built in 1992 in Moscow was sold off (Berezin and Kaganova 1993).

The sale of shops is another option. In St Petersburg, 'about two thirds of shops and services have been privatized' (Berezin and Kaganova 1993: 6). In Budapest, a law passed in summer 1993 gives tenants of shops a right to buy them. Depending on the level of discount set, this could yield a considerable one-off income for local government but would deprive it of future revenue flows. According to Hegedus and Tosics (1993) income from commercial space pays for about one-third of all housing maintenance and repair expenditure by state housing maintenance organizations. Loss of this income would sharply increase costs for those (poorer) households who continue to live in state flats.

However, a query must be raised about whether, at least in Russia, local government, as distinct from individual local government officials, always benefits from municipal real-estate transactions. According to Kaganova (1993), the local government executive in St Petersburg has a policy of privately negotiated transactions, with no competitive bidding and no public access to information about the transaction. 'Five committee approvals . . . and about thirty-five permissive signatures are required, along with an indeterminate number of coordinating approvals [allowing] an open channel for private profit through corruption' (Kaganova 1993: 46). Kaganova also cites a joint venture in Moscow involving $4.5 million worth of land in which 'profits will be remitted to a special hard currency (not rouble) joint venture account, but only the Executive Branch can withdraw funds. This removes it from control by the City Council and prevents its inclusion in the city budget' (1993: 46).

In brief, though some diversion of funds has occurred, the proceeds of housing privatization (where it is not free) and of the sale or renting of commercial property have allowed local governments in former state-socialist countries to increase their incomes without levying new taxes. (Since average real incomes have been declining and new central taxes imposed, new local taxes would have been very unpopular and possibly ineffective.) However, the sale of assets is a short-term solution and future conflict over income sources is inevitable. It is not clear whether local taxes on enterprises have declined in importance, but this seems highly likely due to the economic difficulties faced by enterprises, and to the tactic of withholding taxes in enterprise–local government conflicts, e.g. over pollution penalties or the transfer to local governments of profit-draining enterprise-provided utilities and facilities.

Local Government Resources

We have already referred to land, housing, and commercial property as local government assets. We now need to consider local government resources more systematically.

These can be listed as follows:

1. economic power:
   - power to tax,
   - power to purchase goods and services,
   - power to undertake capital investment projects, and
   - power to provide subsidies, grants, and tax reliefs to local firms;
2. power to provide services, e.g. state flats, schools, refuse collection;
3. power as an employer;
4. regulatory power (to license economic activities, to allocate land for different purposes), and
5. power as owners of assets, e.g. housing, land, and commercial and industrial property.

This list immediately makes clear why local government has the potential to be an active 'mediating institution'. In its own right it is an economic actor and a political actor of major importance which does far more than passively reflecting changes from above. As a political actor it has to calculate whether to introduce nationally legislated taxes in the light of their local political impact. As an economic actor it influences the pace of marketization. Its licensing and regulatory decisions affect the development of the private economic sector. Its purchasing decisions affect the market shares of new and existing enterprises. Its provision of grants and subsidies can be used to differentially influence the prospects of different firms. Its power to provide services can be used to favour certain social categories or certain neighbourhoods. Its decisions on where to invest on housing maintenance can affect the relative desirability of different neighbourhoods. Capital investment projects like roads and means of transport have major impacts on land and property values and on investment opportunities for private sector actors. As an employer at a time of rising unemployment, local government offers security. All of these activities offer scope for illegal payments or relationships.

Finally, the question must be raised as to how far local governments are seeking to sell or preserve their assets. This question has already been touched on in relation to real estate. The argument can now be extended to those industrial assets in which Russian local governments have a stake. The ownership of such assets usually confers the right to sell, and when the privatization process is decentralized as in Russia, local governments stand to benefit from privatization. However, as Shleifer and Boycko point out, they may choose not to sell since benefits accrue to them from being managers of industrial enterprises: this allows them 'to assure the supply of goods to their areas, as well as power and bribes for themselves' (1993: 49–50). These authors go on to argue that local government is the 'greatest danger to privatization' in Russia (1993: 74).

So far we have indicated that the resources possessed by local government allow it to be far more than a passive mediating institution. Its role in the transition depends on how it allocates these resources, and this depends on the centres of economic and political power in the external context, and on how 'internal' actors exploit their opportunities.

Existing theories of local government in capitalist societies range from those which see it as a weak force responding to powerful external economic actors, and those which see it as a strong force able to intervene considerably in economic growth. In recent years, the global recession and the rise of neo-liberal ideologies have translated into local fiscal crises and a concern with local economic growth. As a result, local governments have sought to co-operate with economic actors rather than obstruct them (Pickvance and Preteceille 1991).

How far will local governments in former state-socialist societies move towards this model? What leverage do external state institutions or private enterprises have over local government? Does local government encourage the creation of private firms controlled by its own staff? Does it favour new private suppliers over old state suppliers? Does competitive tendering exist? How does it use its planning and subsidizing powers? Does a 'machine politics' develop in which votes are given in exchange for promises of jobs?

All of these questions apply to local government in former state-socialist societies. But so do a further set of questions relating to the coherence of local government institutions. How far does local government act in a co-ordinated way? Do its different departments pull in the same direction or do individual staff members and individual politicians each pursue their own economic strategies? Does local government have any global capacity to pursue policy, or do its different departments simply engage in deals with any willing business partner? If its lack of tax income makes it more dependent on asset sales which have a one-off character, does this encourage person-to-person relations which facilitate corruption? Certainly the vague and contested legal framework in Russia (in contrast to Hungary) means that there is considerable scope for creativity in presenting transactions as legal.

These are all questions which need to be answered before we can establish how active a mediating institution local government is and in whose interests it is acting. Overall, there is evidence that local government in former state-socialist societies is at the hub of what Lorrain (1982) calls the 'local public sector' and is exercising increasing economic and political power. For example, according to Shleifer and Boycko, in Russia local governments have legitimacy as elected bodies and have been given control over electricity, water and other utilities which they can translate into influence over firms: as a result, they 'have found tremendous room to govern their localities' (1993: 48).

LOCAL GOVERNMENT, SOCIAL NETWORKS, AND TRANSITION

We now move from the level of structures to the level of actors and their relationships.

Social networks are a form of what Bourdieu calls 'social capital' which stands alongside economic capital and cultural capital in his terminology. Sík (forthcoming) uses the term 'network capital' to emphasize the value of social connections. The question of the role of such capital in the transition from state socialism has been raised both by authors such as Sík, who has written at length about its scale, and Grabher (Chapter 4, this volume) who has asked whether 'old' networks inhibit marketization.

The key question is whether network capital created under state socialism retains its value today, and if so, whether it helps or hinders processes in the transition period. In this section, we will discuss this question with reference to some of the processes affecting local government discussed earlier.

To start with, some general comments need to be made. Without taking the network capital metaphor too literally, it is nevertheless true that social networks (1) can depreciate in value as well as maintain their value, (2) require activity to sustain them—otherwise they will fall into disuse, and (3) can increase or decrease in value because of changes in the context in which they exist. Network capital may also be partly substitutable for the other types of capital. Finally, new social networks can be created which can compete with or even displace existing networks.

Writers on network capital tend to start from the existence of a stock of such capital and ask how it is deployed (Czako and Sík 1993). For example, Sík makes the bold claim that 'since post-communism follows communism and since in communism network capital was very widespread, it follows that network capital cannot be less widespread in post-communism, except if it was destroyed or became useless' (forthcoming: 57). He denies that the latter exceptional conditions are likely, due to the 'ample room to use network capital both as coping and as grabbing means' and because of the peaceful transition in Hungary: 'both its cultural basis and the network itself is characterised by huge inertia' (forthcoming: 57). Sík's concept of network capital seems to imply an infinite convertibility for new purposes and a neglect of the creation of new networks.

In this section, by contrast, I wish to draw attention to some of the conditions which 'devalue' existing network capital and provide opportunities for the development of new social networks, or obstruct the deployment of social networks, new or old.

The first process which could devalue existing networks is the changes in occupational and other roles which accompany transition. The networks by which industrial managers tried to cope with the obstacles to production and which involved party officials as well as other managers (which Sík, forthcoming, calls 'managers' reciprocal transactions') are likely to decline as party structures collapse[8] and market processes take the place of network linkages.[9] Likewise occupational changes among network members are as likely to devalue network capital as to maintain it, and will create the basis for new networks.

A second process weakening the value of old networks is a reduction in the level of trust and the development of one-off deal-making. The term 'social network' is used here to refer to relations involving reciprocity between partners of similar social status. (This excludes relations involving power and dependence which are part of the wider definition used by Czako and Sík 1993.) Network relations are enduring and can be contrasted with one-off transactions which are instantaneous and where there is no necessary equality of status between partners.

The relevance of trust in social networks is that reciprocation is not immediate and creates 'indebtedness' over time. If *ego* helps *alter* today, *ego* expects *alter* to reciprocate in the future. In the meantime *alter* is indebted to *ego*. *Ego*'s willingness to wait for a return depends on his or her willingness to trust that *alter* will honour the obligation. (One expects a proportionality to exist between level of indebtedness and level of trust. However, there may be cultural differences in this ratio.) In a period of transition, and especially when the transition is rapid, trust[10] is threatened as people change occupational and other roles and as new modes of behaviour become dominant. Network links which require high levels of trust may be sacrificed in favour of one-off transactions which require low levels of trust as short-term orientations increase in importance as a response to the uncertain and turbulent environment.

In the case of local government officials, the relative attraction of relying on network links and one-off deals will depend on the task in question and on prevailing levels of trust. Some tasks will be intrinsically more likely to be the subject of one-off deals than network relations, e.g. when they increase the ratio of indebtedness to trust beyond a 'normal' level; or when the official is obliged to obtain an immediate cash settlement. For example, information (e.g. about the location of development land) may be more likely to flow through networks (especially when there is no requirement for open tender), whereas property is more likely to be the subject of one-off deals since the ability to purchase is not a general one. The concentration of ability to purchase among a restricted set of individuals could mean that local government officials charged with selling real estate encounter the same people again and again. But this would be more a case of deal-making with a limited set of partners than the establishment of a network.

However, I would not argue that network relations cease to be important.

In a transition period, roles are by definition likely to be less stable and less predictable than at other times. To perform a job considerable discretion may be given to or taken by an official since the context is more turbulent, and rigid role definitions would be impossible to specify or apply. The looser the definition of roles, the more discretion the official has. One consequence of this is that the use of network contacts may be perfectly compatible with executing an official role. For example, in the situation described earlier for St Petersburg, where local government property transactions are privately negotiated and not subject to competitive tender or to public knowledge, there would be no obstacle to officials relying on network contacts. The boundary between legal and illegal action is also hard to establish when the laws are vague or conflicting and role definitions imprecise.

However, the concept of corruption is not lost altogether as is apparent from the following report on Leningrad (as it then was) in 1990: 'in the district Soviets (councils), there was a noticeable strengthening of ties between various forms of enterprises (cooperatives, small businesses, etc.) and the deputies (councillors) who became the legal sponsors and partners of the former. This tended to lead to corruption at the district level. In contrast, the Soviet (city council) limited the business activities of its deputies and the Executive Committee apparatus' (Alexejev *et al.* 1991: 15). It is perhaps straining credibility to believe that politicians at city level are more resistant to overtures from entrepreneurs than those at district level, but this quotation gives perhaps a new meaning to the phrase 'local corporatism' (Stoker 1991), which has been coined to refer to the more formalized business–local government co-operation and interdependence found in the West (Squires 1991).

Whether it is useful to conceptualize these business relations as network links depends on the type of task and level of trust. The more the task is recurrent or lends itself to reciprocity and the greater the level of trust, the more likely network links are to be involved. These links could of course be 'old' or 'new'.

A final consideration concerns the maintenance of network capital. An existing stock of network capital will only survive if it is maintained. This means that the links must be used, otherwise they will cease to be operative. The frequency with which they need to be used is a variable. If we conceive this maintenance work as involving time and energy, then it is clear that it has an opportunity cost. The more effort is devoted to the maintenance of an old network, the less is available for the development of a new network, and vice versa. If, as has been argued, transitions are characterized by changes in roles, changes in contexts (and hence the 'demand' for network use), and changes in levels of trust, it is clear that there are reasons to expect a decline in certain types of network, and an increase in others, as well as an increase in non-network relations such as deal-making outside reciprocal ties.

In sum it can be argued that the transition creates new opportunity structures for the use of social networks, but that these will vary between societies just as the character and speed of transitions vary. However, contrary to some other authors, one cannot assume that network capital inherited from state socialism is capable of surviving and/or meeting the new demands placed on it. Especially in fields such as local government where the pace of change has been great, one would expect old networks to lose their efficacy, new networks to develop, and relations involving low trust to compete with both old and new network capital.

CONCLUSION

To sum up, we have argued that local government is a key mediating institution in the transition from state socialism because it controls resources which can play an important part in the development of marketization.

To judge how far local government is an active or a passive mediating institution can only be the result of empirical research on local government policies. It would be necessary to examine how far these policies reflect autonomous internal interests rather than the interests of external bodies such as central government and local firms.

At this stage, although quite a lot is known about certain policies (e.g. housing privatization in Hungary), there are numerous other cases where only fragmentary or anecdotal information exists. These include local government purchasing, licensing, subsidizing, and planning activities. Since these are all activities which lie at the interface of the relation between state and market institutions and have a potentially strong bearing on processes of privatization and marketization in the economic sphere, the lack of research is very striking.

A theme of this chapter is that in both countries considered, the development of land and property markets and the policy of privatization of council property has allowed councils to gain significant income from property sales and leases, thereby avoiding the need to implement new taxes with the probability of alienating voters. Since markets in this field were often poorly developed,[11] local authority action has been critical in developing land and property markets.

The economic roles of local governments bring them into contact with a wide variety of types of enterprise. But what is unknown is how far these enterprises differ from those in the past. Likewise, it remains unknown how far the strong leverage of state enterprises over local government in the past has completely disappeared, or how successful enterprises have been in bargaining with local government over their tax payments. At least the influence of large firms will be much more concealed than in the past when leading managers were members of local executives. Clearly the answers to these questions will differ between countries.

Finally, this chapter has raised some questions about the relevance of network capital inherited from the past: my question has been how far the tasks typical of a 'transition' period—and particularly those falling on local government—have been ones where old network capital could be drawn on and how far not. In the former case, the effect is to reproduce old networks, whereas in the latter it is either to create new ones or to encourage one-off deals rather than networks. It has been argued that three aspects of the transition from state socialism have affected the role of local government officials' reliance on their previous social networks in the real-estate field. Imprecise role definitions have facilitated the use of social networks (and the spread of corruption) and certain tasks (the diffusion of information) have lent themselves to reliance on social networks. However, the decline in levels of interpersonal trust characteristic of transition periods works in the reverse direction, favouring one-off deals, as do tasks which would place too much strain on interpersonal relations. Thus, it is not possible to conclude that 'old' networks become more important or less important in transitional periods. There are factors working in both directions.

The aim of this chapter has been agenda-setting. The question of whether local government takes an active or passive mediating role in the transformations currently taking place in Eastern Europe and the former Soviet Union can only be answered on the basis of much more research. There is a great danger that with political scientists focusing on local government as an arena of democratic change, and economists focusing on changes in the local (and national) economy, the interaction between the two fields will remain unstudied. The present wave of privatization of municipal assets cannot be enduring, but the other economic activities of local government make its mediating role a continuing focus for research.

NOTES

1. Stark (1992) has usefully distinguished different modes of 'extrication' from state socialism—reunification (EG), capitulation (CZ), compromise (P), and electoral competition (H). It remains to be shown how far they can be systematically linked to differences between state-socialist societies, and whether they will have lasting effects on subsequent developments.

2. This topic is discussed further in Pickvance (1994*a*).
3. They refer to urban housing. In rural areas, state housing was virtually absent and private (often self-built) housing was predominant. The following paragraphs are based on Szelényi (1983), and Hegedus and Tosics (1983).
4. The debate about the above sequence is between those such as Szelényi (1978) who argue that under state socialism, state institutions such as local government necessarily act in an inequitable way, redistributing resources towards the privileged, and those such as Ferge (1979) who deny this. In particular, debate centres on the final stage described above. Both sides acknowledge that the outflow of households from the top of the state flat sector made it easier for local government to alter their allocation policy in favour of those most in need. They also acknowledge that the subsidization of private housing favoured those who could afford it. The point of debate concerns the relative importance of these two pieces of evidence. Szelényi (1987) focuses on the continuing favour shown by the state towards the better-off and Tosics (1988) focuses on the change in state flat allocation policy. Szelényi considers his thesis is intact and that it is simply the form in which the state helps the better-off which has changed; Tosics argues that the change in flat allocation policy shows the state can favour lower-income groups.
5. This chapter draws on the project 'Environmental and Housing Movements in Hungary, Estonia and Russia' being financed by the Economic and Social Research Council and carried out at the University of Kent at Canterbury from 1991 to 1994. I would like to thank my colleagues Nick Manning, Katy Pickvance, and Sveta Klimova for their general support and stimulation and for translations from Russian and Hungarian documents. The project involves interviews with housing and environmental activists and officials and public opinion surveys.
6. The terms of the sale offer very large discounts on the 'market' price of the flat and a further discount for payment in cash in full. This privatization process can be seen as one by which the best-off members of the stratum in the state flat sector who had not moved to the private sector are able to secure their position. Tenants with very low incomes, or in houses of poor quality, are unlikely to buy their flats; see Pickvance (1994*b*).
7. In both countries rents have been frozen in money terms at a time when inflation was rising (20–35 per cent p.a. in Hungary; up to 1,350 per cent in Russia). The effect has been to moderate slightly the decline in real household incomes, but to reduce local government incomes. (In summer 1993 housing rents in Hungary were frozen for a further year by national legislation until after the 1994 general elections.)
8. The problem of establishing how far this has happened is well brought out by Teague's (1994) example of how some Russian party officials became local election candidates (and won council seats) when the party's authority started to weaken, and then when local councils lost their influence, took administrative positions in local governments. Whether such trajectories enabled party officials to maintain their power or whether (as is more likely) they show the difficulties of doing so remains unknown. This example is open to the general methodological problems of 'where are they now' studies of one-time communists: (1) Communist Party power lies in structural relations rather than the situation of

individuals, (2) such studies reveal nothing about their present orientations, and (3) in countries like Hungary, party affiliation may have been secondary to technical competence.

9. There is a danger here of treating market linkages as independent of personal linkages which has been rightly attacked by writers on the 'social embeddedness of economic action'—see Swedberg and Granovetter (1992)—but there is undoubtedly a difference of degree in the importance of network relations when market processes replace administrative processes supported by managerial networks.

10. Trust in institutions may also be weakened. In both Hungary and Russia, there is suspicion and cynicism towards governments. But in Hungary people are willing to save in government financial institutions whereas in Russia the 1,350 per cent inflation rate of 1992 wiped out savings and destroyed trust in financial institutions.

11. The fact of private property ownership was not always accompanied by the right to sell private property—hence, private housing could exist without a private housing market in certain countries.

REFERENCES

ALEXEJEV, A., GELMAN, V., KORNEV, N., KOSTJUSHEV, V., and ETKIND, A. (1991), 'The Social Movements and the Development of New Power in Leningrad, 1986–1991', MS, Institute of Sociology, Leningrad.

ANDRLE, V. (1976), *Managerial Power in the Soviet Union* (Farnborough: Saxon House).

BEREZIN, M., and KAGANOVA, O. (1993), 'Real Property Market as Capitalization Factor of Russian Cities', Paper presented to the Conference of the European Network for Housing Research, Budapest, Sept. 1993.

BOYCE, J. H. (1993), 'Local Government Reform and the New Moscow City Soviet', *Journal of Communist Studies*, 9: 245–71.

BROVKIN, V. (1990), 'Revolution from Below: Informal Political Associations in Russia, 1988–1989', *Soviet Studies*, 42: 233–57.

CAMPBELL, A. (1992), 'The Restructuring of Local Government in Russia', *Public Money and Management*, 12/4: 19–24.

CZAKO, A., and SÍK, E. (1993), 'On the Role of Network Capital in Economic Transactions in Post-communist Hungary', Paper for the Conference on Legacies, Linkages and Localities: The Social Embeddedness of the Economic Transformations in Central and Eastern Europe, Social Science Research Centre, Berlin, Sept. 1993.

ELANDER, I., and GUSTAFSSON, M. (1993), 'The Re-emergence of Local Self-Government in Central Europe: Some Notes on the First Experience', *European Journal of Political Research*, 23: 295–322.

FERGE, Z. (1979), *A Society in the Making: Hungarian Social and Societal Policy, 1945–1975* (Harmondsworth: Penguin).

Fish, S. (1991), 'The Emergence of Independent Associations and the Transformation of Russian Political Society', *Journal of Communist Studies*, 7: 299–334.

Hanson, P. (1993), 'Local Power and Market Reform in Russia', *Communist Economies and Economic Transformation*, 5: 45–60.

Hegedus, J., and Tosics, I. (1983), 'Housing Classes and Housing Policy: Some Changes in the Budapest Housing Market', *International Journal of Urban and Regional Research*, 7: 467–93.

——— (1993), 'Changing Public Housing Policy in a Central European Metropolis: The Case of Budapest', Paper presented to the Conference of the European Network for Housing Research, Budapest, Sept. 1993.

Hough, J. (1969), *The Soviet Prefects* (Cambridge, Mass.: Harvard University Press).

Jacobs, E. M. (ed.) (1983), *Soviet Local Politics and Government* (London: George Allen & Unwin).

Kaganova, O. Z. (1993), 'Creating an Urban Real Estate Market in Russia', *Real Estate Issues*, 18/1: 45–8.

Kornai, J. (1992), *The Socialist System* (Oxford: Clarendon Press).

Ladanyi, J., *et al.* (1992), 'Local Government Reorganization and Housing Policy in Budapest: A Roundtable Discussion', *International Journal of Urban and Regional Research*, 16: 477–88.

Lengyel, I. (1993), 'Development of Local Government Finance in Hungary', in R. J. Bennett (ed.), *Local Government in the New Europe* (London: Belhaven), 225–45.

Lorrain, D. (1982), 'Le Secteur public local: Entre nationalisation et decentralisation', *Annales de la Recherche Urbaine*, 13: 53–104.

Peteri, G., and Szabo, G. (1991), 'Local Government in Hungary: Transition Renewal and Prospects', in I. Elander and M. Gustafsson (eds.), *The Re-emergence of Local Self-Government in Central Europe: The First Experience* (Orebro: University of Orebro, Centre for Housing and Urban Research).

Pickvance, C. G. (1988), 'Employers, Labour Markets and Redistribution under State Socialism: An Interpretation of Housing Policy in Hungary, 1960–1983', *Sociology*, 22: 193–214.

——— (1994a), 'System, Transition, Legacy and Bricolage: Thinking about Change in Eastern Europe', Paper presented to the 13th World Congress of Sociology, Bielefeld, July 1994.

——— (1994b), 'Housing Privatization and Housing Protest in the Transition from State Socialism: A Comparative Study of Budapest and Moscow', *International Journal of Urban and Regional Research*, 18: 433–50.

——— 1995, 'Social Movements in the Transition from State Socialism: Convergence or Divergence', in L. Maheu (ed.), *Social Movements and Social Classes: The Future of Collective Action* (Newbury Park: Sage), 123–50.

——— and Preteceille, E. (eds.) (1991), *State Restructuring and Local Power: A Comparative Perspective* (London: Pinter).

Ross, C. (1987), *Local Government in the Soviet Union* (London: Croom Helm).

Shleifer, A., and Boycko, M. (1993), 'The Politics of Russian Privatization', in O. Blanchard (ed.), *Post-communist Reform* (Cambridge, Mass.: MIT Press), 37–80.

Shomina, E. S. (1992), 'Enterprises and the Urban Environment in the USSR', *International Journal of Urban and Regional Research*, 16: 222–33.

Sík, E. (1992), 'From Second Economy to Informal Economy', *Journal of Public Policy*, 12: 153–75.

——(forthcoming), 'Network Capital in Capitalist, Communist and Post-communist Societies', in B. Wellman (ed.), *Networking in the Global Village* (Boulder, Colo.: Westview).

Squires, G. D. (1991), 'Partnership and the Pursuit of the Private City', in M. Gottdiener and C. G. Pickvance (eds.), *Urban Life in Transition* (Newbury Park: Sage), 196–221.

Stark, D. (1992), 'Path Dependence and Privatization Strategies in East Central Europe', *East European Politics and Societies*, 6: 17–51.

Stoker, G. (1991), *The Politics of Local Government* (London: Macmillan).

Swedberg, R., and Granovetter, M. (1992), Introduction, in M. Granovetter and R. Swedberg (eds.), *The Sociology of Economic Life* (Boulder, Colo.: Westview Press), 1–26.

Szelényi, I. (1978), 'Social Inequalities in State Socialist Redistributive Economies', *International Journal of Comparative Sociology*, 1: 63–87.

——(1987), 'Housing Inequalities and Occupational Segregation in State Socialist Cities', *International Journal of Urban and Regional Research*, 11: 1–8.

——(1983), *Urban Inequalities under State Socialism* (Oxford: Oxford University Press).

Teague, E. (1994), 'Russia's Local Elections Begin', *RFE/RL Research Report*, 3/7: 1–4.

Tosics, I. (1988), 'Inequalities in East European Cities: Can Redistribution ever be Equalizing, and if so, why should we Avoid It? A Reply to Ivan Szelényi', *International Journal of Urban and Regional Research*, 12: 133–6.

14

Between Institutional Transfer and Legacies: *Local Administrative Transformation in Eastern Germany*

HELLMUT WOLLMANN

INTRODUCTION

In dealing with the transformation of local authorities in East Germany since the collapse of the communist regime, this chapter dwells on two distinct, yet interrelated, sets of questions. I begin by addressing the process of institution-building in terms of the formation of formal organizations. Technically speaking, the formation of formal institutions is treated in the following pages as a dependent variable, and factors that explain the process are sought. This chapter starts with the obvious—that the transformation process in East Germany has been shaped to a significant degree by the 'old' Federal Republic of Germany (FRG) as an 'external change agent'. From that point of departure, I focus on 'exogenous' factors (see Lehmbruch 1994 for a similar distinction; see also Wollmann 1994, 1995, 1996), that is, ingrained features of the FRG's legal, organizational, and personnel structure that impinge upon the transformation process in East Germany. Such exogenous factors include the constitutional and legal norms extended from West to East Germany, the organizational blueprints and models transferred from West to East, and West German officials 'going East' with their 'baggage'[1] to occupy, as a rule, leading positions in East Germany's new administrative structures.

At the same time, I try to identify endogenous factors rooted in and derived from East Germany as 'legacies' of organizational patterns, mind-sets and value-bound 'frames' of reference (see Wollmann 1991, for an early reference to the analytical and practical relevance of legacies in East Germany's transformation). A review of the transformation process suggests that two kinds of legacy may now have to be distinguished: (1) organizational and cognitive legacies of the kind shaped during the GDR's existence and carried over to post-communist development, and (2) endogenous givens specifically generated by the organizational and cognitive offshoots and dynamics engendered in the heady days of East Germany's 'peaceful revolution' from the collapse of the communist regime in October 1989 until the GDR's accession to the FRG on 3 October 1990. Granted, the former GDR differs greatly from the other post-communist countries in Central and Eastern Europe by virtue of the weight and salience of exogenous factors impinging upon its transformation process. But the similarities between the former GDR and these other countries may be substantial as far as the salience of endogenous elements is concerned.

In the second part of this chapter, I ask whether and how formal institutions, once transferred from West to East or established in the East, are applied or run by East German actors. In that respect, a wider understanding of institutionalization is employed to distinguish between the formal structures of institutions (the systems level) and the action orientations and behavioural patterns of individuals (the actor level) (see Mayntz 1994). At the systems level, it is therefore assumed that institutions consist of formal structures as well as operational role prescriptions meant to guide and direct the individual actors as members of the organization. At the actor level, it is the individual who, through subjective cognitive orientation and skills, affects the operation of the formal organization by 'bringing it to life' and 'making it run' (Göhler 1994). By virtue of this wider conceptualization of the process by which institutions are formed, the cognitive orientations and qualifications of the members of an organization (as well as such intra-organizational socio-cultural givens as 'organizational culture') can be recognized as the 'cultural' and 'subjective' dimensions of the institutional process that are functionally complementary to its 'organizational' and 'objective' dimensions. One can therefore plausibly hypothesize that the neater the match between the organizational structures and the cultural texture of a formal institution, the more smoothly that institution operates. Conversely, the wider the mismatch between the organizational and cultural fabrics, the less smoothly the formal institution runs.

From this point of view, the process of institutionalization in East Germany is both analytically and politically intriguing because the transfer and building of formal institutional structures occurred with exceptional speed at the systems level, whereas there is every reason to surmise that the emergence of individual mind-sets and socio-cultural contexts to match the formal organizations has been much slower. People and socio-cultural contexts are more resistant to change and are apt to persist as a legacy of the past. If this is true, two engaging questions can be raised. First, how do formal institutions fare when operating in a socio-cultural context that is still somewhat alien to them? Second, in what ways, if any, do these endogenous cognitive frames of reference and socio-cultural contexts come to be institutionalized within, and even despite, new formal organizational structures?

THE FORMATION OF ORGANIZATIONAL STRUCTURES OF EAST GERMAN LOCAL AUTHORITIES

Institutional Formation Driven Primarily by External (Exogenous) Factors?

The institutional transformation in East Germany initially appears to offer a case of 'institutional transfer' (Lehmbruch 1994) in which the West German model has been largely extended to, if not imposed upon, East Germany. By virtue of the GDR's accession (*Beitritt*) to the FRG—the arrangement by which German unification became effective on 3 October 1990 (Derlien 1993*b*: 320–1)—the constitutional and legal order of the old FRG, along with the attendant organizational models, was expanded to include East Germany. At the same time, most of the GDR's constitutional and legal order was abolished, including the central government structures, most of the regional administrative apparatus, and the country's existence as a separate sovereign state. With this type of institutional transfer, which Rose *et al.* (1993) have called the extension or transplantation of a 'ready-made state', the transformation in East Germany is set conspicuously apart from that in the other post-communist countries in Central and Eastern Europe.

Second, the formation of new institutions (ministries and agencies) at the *Land* level and the basic remoulding of existing local institutions were accompanied by a massive transfer and influx of administrative personnel from West Germany to East Germany in what was called administrative aid (*Verwaltungshilfe*), a term tellingly analogous to development aid provided to development countries. East German county and municipal authorities have been receiving administrative aid through sundry channels (Scheytt 1992: 38):

1. Partnerships (*Städtepartnerschaften*) between East German and West German counties and municipalities began forming even before the GDR's final demise. They mushroomed after the collapse of the communist regime.[2] Particularly in the early stage, these sister-city relations facilitated material assistance, practical advice, and the transfer of know-how, often on a daily basis, whether by phone, short-term consultancy and coaching of an East German counterpart by West German municipal personnel, or internship of East German personnel with a West German local authority.

2. Special funding programmes were set up by the federal government and by the West German *Länder* to encourage West German personnel to move to East Germany for extended periods to assume positions in local authorities (Bundesvereinigung der kommunalen Spitzenverbände 1994). About 4,000 West German municipal experts and employees presently work with East German local authorities (Keller and Henneberger 1993: 183). Both the percentage and absolute number of West Germans engaged

in municipal service are considerably smaller than those in administration at the *Land* level, but they constitute a significant personnel transfer none the less.[3]

The existence of two such powerful levers—institutional transfer and personnel transfer—seem to suggest that institutionalization in East Germany is driven to a large extent by external or exogenous factors. Small wonder that some authors have called this process of institutional formation a 'photocopy' or 'blueprint' approach (*Blaupausenansatz*) (Reichard and Röber 1992).

Institutional Formation Shaped by Internal (Endogenous) Factors?

If the institutional formation in East Germany is studied in more depth, however, a more discriminating picture emerges (for more detail, see Wollmann, forthcoming). To begin with, the very concept that West Germany's ready-made state was extended to include East Germany needs reconsideration. Granted, a broad set of key institutional arrangements was transplanted to East Germany, particularly the Basic Law (*Grundgesetz*)—the federal constitution, with its distribution of power between the federal government and the states (*Länder*) and the 'institutional guarantee' of local self-administration (*kommunale Selbstverwaltung*). In addition, the enormous body of West Germany legislation that was extended wholesale to East Germany was part and parcel of West Germany's ready-made state. But within the 'corridor' marked out by these general basic constitutional and legal stipulations, the organizational differentiation and variability of the FRG's political and administrative system is remarkably great both vertically and horizontally. This is as true of the *Länder* administration as it is of the county and municipal authorities (see also Goetz 1993). They have a broad repertoire of organizational solutions and options. Far from being an institutional monolith, West Germany's ready-made state appears as a conglomerate rich in organizational alternatives for East German actors to choose from, adapt to, or convert.

The local political and administrative arena came to play an ever greater role in producing such institutional variations and bringing endogenous factors to bear. On 6 May 1990 the first democratic elections for new local councils ushered in sweeping change. Nearly all senior county and local administrative officials were replaced. Most of the new administrative leaders (mayors, deputy mayors or division heads, and section heads) were newcomers to public administration. Belonging to the technical and economic intelligentsia, they had been employed in clerical and management positions in state enterprises before seeking or accepting political and administrative careers in 1990.[4] The same may be said of the 'old hands', that is, the victorious candidates who had been working in the government administration before 1989, mostly as subordinates. As for local administration, it has already been mentioned that West German administrative aides (*Verwaltungshelfer*) have played a comparatively small role.[5] Keeping in mind these two hypotheses about the salience of exogenous and endogenous factors, let us now examine and discuss the process of institutional formation.

STAGES OF INSTITUTIONAL FORMATION AND TRANSFORMATION

In order to grasp the scope of the organizational turnover to which local administrative institutions have been exposed, one must remember certain basic features of the organizational structure that characterized the GDR's administrative apparatus in the counties (*Landkreise*) and incorporated municipalities (*kreisfreie Städte*). Although the districts (*Bezirke*) constituted the regional administrative backbone of the East German regime, the counties and incorporated municipalities were the lowest administrative layer of centralist rule. The many county-subordinated municipalities and localities, half of which had fewer than 500 inhabitants, had little administrative role to play.

Tailored in principle on the former Soviet Union's organizational scheme of centralist party and state rule that had been introduced in the GDR in 1952, county and incorporated municipal administration was headed by an administrative directorate (the *Rat des Kreises* in counties and the *Rat der Stadt* in incorporated municipalities). This body passed formally as the executive committee of the elected local council. In keeping with the centralist grip on local administration, administrative functions and responsibilities were enumerated and prescribed in a uniform, nation-wide scheme that, in the late 1980s, comprised nineteen administrative divisions (*Fachabteilungen*), each directed by one member of the *Rat des Kreises* and one member of the *Rat der Stadt* (on county administration, see Schubel and Schwanengel 1991: 251). Even comparatively small incorporated municipalities that lacked serious administrative tasks had a considerable number of city councilors (*Stadträte*) and corresponding administrative divisions also with councillors. One incorporated municipality of about 30,000 inhabitants, for example, had fourteen administrative councillors. This system resulted in over-staffing and a disproportionately high number of senior administrative positions to rank-and-file personnel (Rapsch and Simanski 1991: 196).

Between late 1989 and 6 May 1990 civic groups and reformist party groupings seized local political power in many places and exercised it through 'round-table' negotiations and agreements (for details see Berg, Nagelschmidt and Wollmann 1996, ch. 2). The members of the *Rat des Kreises* and the *Rat der Stadt* were increasingly pushed out of office, and the

Soviet-type organizational structure began to be dismantled. The way was thus open to organizational changes oriented to forms of local administration common in West Germany (see Schubel and Schwanengel 1991: 251 for an account of a county administration). The municipal elections of 6 May 1990 and the enactment of the new municipal charter of 9 May 1990, which established the basis for reintroducing local self-administration, legally and politically paved the way for recasting the organizational structures of county and municipal administration.

Given the all but paradigmatic rupture (Wollmann 1991) of the political and constitutional framework and of the responsibilities of the local authorities, East German counties and municipalities turned first primarily to their West German partner authorities for organizational advice and assistance. Another important source of guidance was the Kommunale Gemeinschaftsstelle für Verwaltungvereinfachung (KGSt), a prestigious, municipally funded consulting agency that had established itself in West Germany as an authoritative voice on matters of county and municipal organization. Empirical data show, however, that the institutional transformation of local administrative structures in East Germany was not a mere photocopy or blueprint approach to institutional transfer. Although the organizational schemes communicated to East German actors by the KGSt and other sources did provide important conceptual guidance, many local authorities pursued an incrementalist, step-by-step, and trial-and-error type of organizational change rather than an organizational master plan or recipe-type scheme from West Germany.

In fact, local authorities changed the number and functional definition of their administrative divisions (*Dezernate*) and the number and organizational assignment of their administrative sections (*Ämter*). This action indicated an ongoing organizational learning process in which often divergent organizational advice from West Germany converged with accumulating local experience in the effort to tailor an organizational structure based on endogenous needs. In response to the political power play endemic to local democratic systems, the crucial decisions on organizational issues were shaped by local political parties and groupings pressing for their share in the distribution of important administrative positions.

The decision on the number of administrative divisions provides an intriguing example illustrating how different endogenous factors mix in a peculiar way. No doubt, there were political and personal interests in favour of raising the number of such positions. At the same time, the GDR's legacy of having almost twenty senior administrative positions in the *Rat der Stadt* was probably still in the actors' minds (Rapsch and Simanski 1991: 196). This syndrome proved to be a significant endogenous factor in shaping the organizational framework of East German local authorities and their subsequent resistance to reducing the number of these positions.

With regard to internal reorganization, East German local authorities had a peculiar mixture of radical change and conspicuous continuity. Whereas the administrative structure of East Germany's central government and districts was dismantled, the organizational structure and personnel at the county and municipal administrative level survived, except the ousted administrative élite. Unlike the new *Länder*, in which the ministries and agencies had to be established from scratch, the local authorities had to deal with existing organizations and personnel in revamping their administrative structures. When it came to equipping and staffing the newly designed and tailored administrative divisions and sections, the local authorities were understandably prone to draw as much as possible on existing administrative contexts and personnel and simply transfer them wholesale to the new administrative units. This approach was particularly apparent in fields where the units of the former and the new municipal system bore at least some obvious degree of functional similarity, such as in finance, planning, and construction. By contrast, the many municipalities that were subordinated to a county had had few administrative functions or related personnel and were therefore confronted with the task of building local administration from the ground up.

By and large, East German counties and municipalities succeeded in putting viable organizational structures into place. Beset by unprecedented problems, they managed in a couple of years to forge local agencies that had taken West German local authorities much longer to create (on local institutions for combating unemployment, for instance, see Wegener *et al.*, forthcoming).

By contrast, East German local authorities have been cautious and hesitant about embracing municipal administrative reform currently debated and touted as New Public Management. In West German *Länder*, about seventy municipal authorities and a number of county authorities have embarked upon reform concepts related to ideas of New Public Management (Reichard 1994: 67).

MATCH OR DIVERGENCE BETWEEN THE INSTITUTIONS AND THE PERTINENT MIND-SETS AND SKILLS OF THE ACTORS?

As stated out the outset, this chapter presents an understanding of institutional transfer and structures that goes beyond formal organizations themselves to encompass the related roles prescribed for organizational members as well as an organization's standard operational procedures and internal routines. For the sake of the argument, let institutional transfer and formation also include the set of legal norms that organizations are basically expected to apply. With this perspective let us now explore the degree to which the actors in East German local authorities have already adapted their mind-sets (the individual level) to the role and skill requirements of the new institutional structures (the systems level). Conversely, to what degree are their mind-sets still shaped by orientations moulded in the GDR's past (i.e. legacies)? I begin by elaborating crucial role prescriptions related to the institutions that have been recently transferred or formed. I then identify related cognitive frames and skills moulded in the GDR's past. Drawing on still sketchy and sparse evidence, I conclude this section by proposing statements on the match or divergence between the new institutions and the actors' mind-sets and skills.

INSTITUTIONAL TRANSFER, INSTITUTIONAL FORMATION, AND ROLE REQUIREMENTS

Institutional transfer, institutional formation, and role requirements entail two dimensions of particular interest. One is the rule of law (*Rechtsstaat*) embodied in myriad legal statutes that have been extended to East Germany, most of which are to be applied by the local authorities. The other is the rules and routines regulating the operation of public bureaucracies.

The FRG's rule of law and the GDR's socialist legal order (*sozialistische Gesetzlichkeit*). With nearly five decades of legislation by West Germany's parliament and comprehensive judicial review, public administration is instructed in its activity by an ever denser body of law and an elaborate court system to oversee it. For some time over-regulation and the over-density of judicial review have come under critical fire. The traditional primacy of legal regulations in guiding administrative actions is reflected in the fact that most senior civil servants (*höherer Dienst*) are lawyers and that the study of law has been important in the training of members of the upper intermediate service (*gehobener Dienst*), the backbone of public administration. Though formally correct application of legal rules and the ability to hold up under subsequent judicial review is a crucial element of administrative activities, administrators have been eager to identify and explore the legal latitude for informal action (*informales Handeln*) (Bohne 1981) outside the law (*praeter legem*), not against it (*contra legem*). The search for such informal margins, based on expert knowledge of formal law and of the limits that the judiciary has placed upon such informalities, is regarded among administrators as the high art of administration.

In the GDR the regulatory function of law was of a completely different nature (König 1993). As part of the socialist legal order, enactments by parliament had an ancillary status. The class rule of the proletariat exerted by the Communist Party had primacy. Subject to revocation, nullification, and amendment by party decree or ordinance at any time, the regulations of public administration were not a matter for judicial review. The result, by and large, was what has been called legal nihilism (*Rechtsnihilismus*) (Will 1990: 30).

The FRG's variant of 'classical European administration' and the GDR's communist 'cadre administration'. By and large, the FRG's variant of what has been termed classical European administration (König 1993) still corresponds basically to Max Weber's model of bureaucracy. Its hallmarks are the distribution of functions and responsibilities (*Zuständigkeiten*) within the organization; the assignment thereof to specific administrative units; top-down hierarchical control; the practice by which administrative acts, decisions, and rules are formulated and recorded in writing (*Aktenmäßigkeit*) (Weber 1922/1978: 219); and, with regard to personnel, administrative professionalism rooted in related preparatory training, life-long job security in the civil service system (*Berufsbeamtentum*), and the imperative of impartiality.

Modelled on the system practised in the Soviet Union, the cadre administration (*Kaderverwaltung*) that the GDR installed when it was founded in 1949 was diametrically opposed to the classical European model in almost every way (Wollmann and Jaedicke 1993: 110). Written schemes about the distribution of responsibilities and standard operating procedures hardly existed. Orderly administrative files were scarcely kept—in paradoxical contrast to the state security service (*Stasi*), with its mania for compiling Kafkaesque files. It is true that county and municipal administration circumscribed functions and assigned specific responsibilities to individual administrative units, but such delineation of decision-making authority was always placed in question, if not nullified, by pervasive, higher-order centralist control by the party and state. Bottom-line administrators therefore shied away from making decisions on their own, preferring to wait for instructions from above.

Among senior officials in particular, cadre administration was based on the principle that political and ideological loyalty to the ruling party was more important than professional competence. The recruitment for and appointment to top administrative positions was handled through a system of patronage (*Nomenklatura*), the party's crucial personnel pool for staffing all senior positions at the party's discretion. Cadre administration was thus a breeding-ground for what was called politicized incompetence, not administrative professionalism (Derlien 1993*a*).

In striking contrast to the political world essentially forged by the party's centralist top-down rule, a 'second world' permeated the reality of administrative, economic, and everyday life of East German citizens (Wollmann 1991: 249–50). It was one in which the individual actors developed their own strategies and skills for coping with the many constant supply bottle-necks of the GDR's deficit-ridden, centrally directed political and economic system. This 'competence for dealing with chaos' (Marz 1992; Klinger 1994*a*: 72–3) and an ability for *ad hoc* improvising can be seen as the individual's bottom-up strategy to beat the system. In addition, a kind of self-protective group mechanism is recognizable in important interactive, communicative, and emotional functions that the rank-and-file employees attributed to the collective group (*Kollektiv*) at the workplace. In at least one way, the collective group can be interpreted as a social bottom-up mechanism in the second world that was set against the top-down centralist system.

New Institutions, their Role Prescriptions, and the Mind-Sets and Skills of the Actors: A Match?

To which degree have East German actors already adapted their mind-sets and skills to the new institutions? To which degree are those frames of reference and skills still shaped by legacies of the past? Despite the broad range of research findings now available, the empirical evidence for answers to these questions is still impressionistic and anecdotal rather than systematic.

The advent of the rule of law. As noted above, a huge body of law had been built up in the FRG over four decades of legislative production, if not over-production. Extending and transferring it virtually overnight to East Germany clearly posed an unprecedented challenge to local authorities and their actors. After all, when West Germany's complex legal system arrived at midnight on 3 October 1990, the only remaining administrative structure was that at the local level. It was in any case the most important agency for applying norms under the new administrative model.

According to Wollmann and Berg (1994: 262), the vast majority of senior local administrative personnel have been remarkably swift in becoming familiar with the new body of law. The speed of this learning process bears out other findings that the ability of East Germans to 'learn fast' generally equals, if not exceeds, that of West Germans (Becker 1992; Stratemann 1992). However, there are indications that East German actors still have a different understanding of the basic function of legal regulation. First, the very rationale behind the rule of law—'equality before the law' (Weber 1922/1978: 980)—appears to be questioned on the grounds that under specific circumstances it can result in decisions that some individuals may call politically, socially, or otherwise very unjust by the standards of their strong personal convictions and beliefs. This argument holds particularly for the politically, economically, and morally complicated process of unification, in which a communist East Germany undertook a transition to a democratic system and in which the eastern and western parts of the country were to grope their way back together.[6]

Second, East German administrators relate to the legal order differently from their West German counterparts, perhaps in part because of past experience with legal nihilism and rule evasion. West German administrators have been brought up in the FRG's tradition of due process, which is based on the notion that laws are binding in principle and subject to judicial review. These officials tend to see the legal norms as the framework that *enables* administrative activities. With thorough knowledge of the rules, they then seek informal flexibility and discretion within the legal setting. By contrast, the East German actor is inclined to regard legal regulations as a set of prescriptions limiting, and even *preventing*, action and tends to seek informal flexibility outside and against the legal setting. Applying the law at the local level, the individual actor identifying with the citizen who seeks counsel and action (say, in matters of social assistance) may be tempted to go beyond the pertinent legal rules and standard operational procedures in order to find a just solution for the individual case. It may be that the inclination to seek an individually just solution by exercising informal discretion, possibly even outside and against the law, is promoted by what used to be the voluntary practice of improvising from case to case and trying to beat the system.

The advent of the West German variant of classical European administration. Although local East German authorities have been quick and effective in revamping their formal organizational structures since late 1989, particularly after May 1990, they have been considerably slower at introducing internal written organizational charts, laying down standard operating procedures, and internally regulating the maintenance of administrative files (Bundesvereinigung der kommunalen Spitzenverbände 1994: 39). These organizational deficiencies reflect a persistent neglect of formal Weberian elements that are basic to the effective functioning of modern bureaucracy. They appear to be shared by the two main groups making up the new local administrative leaders—the old hands, who had known a context largely devoid of such intra-administrative written schemes, procedures, and file-keeping; and the newcomers, most of whom were from state enterprises and were even less experienced in administrative matters than the old hands. Aside from being caught up in day-to-day business, the members of both groups probably tend to loathe such formalization of intra-administrative procedures, seeing it as a step towards a form of bureaucratization that they wish to avoid.

Activity at the senior administrative level indicates preoccupation with making decisions, even minor ones, at the expense of political, administrative, and organizational guidance. This inclination of administrative leaders to monopolize administrative decision-making instead of delegating seems to have two sources: (1) the apparent persistence of case-by-case improvised problem-solving that was ingrained in the administrative, economic, and everyday life in the former GDR, and (2) an underdeveloped ability to think and act in organizational and strategic contexts (Klinger 1994*b*). The potential to delegate remains undervalued and under-used in existing administrative structures because they lack formal instruments and experience to steer and manage the activities of the entire organization by administrative leadership and control of employees. This trend is sometimes reinforced by friction in the relations between the inexperienced new administrative leaders and the rank-and-file employees, most of whom are old hands.

The rank and file engage in two patterns of decision-making and activity that seem contradictory at first. Both are equally detrimental to the performance of the organization as a whole, but for different reasons. On the one hand, the attitude of the employees is to avoid taking decisions on their own where such responsibility has already been delegated. Probably still under the spell of the former GDR's administrative system, in which it was risky to stick one's neck out, many East German employees continue instead to prefer huddling with colleagues in order to share opinions and responsibility. The group protection that used to be afforded by the collective seems to surface in this practice. On the other hand, the rank-and-file employee may see reason to be an active decision-maker and problem-solver in individual cases. Conceiving of themselves as advocates of citizens and making common cause with them, public employees are apt to practise the improvisation-type of problem-solving that, in conjunction with previous beliefs and practice, might fall beyond and outside the existing legal framework in an attempt to beat the system.

POTENTIAL FOR ADMINISTRATIVE INNOVATION?

Do the socio-economic conditions and the socio-cultural givens of East German local authorities provide the experimental breeding-ground for administrative innovations that could transcend even the West German model?

Beyond Weber's Classical Model?

Counties and municipalities, particularly in West Germany, have recently been swept by debate about fundamental administrative reform that is bound to embrace formal organizations and capture the minds of the personnel (Reichard 1994 and references). Referred to as New Public Management (*Neue Steuerung*), this discussion is directed at

- ideologically and conceptually introducing economic thinking as a paradigm shift in the philosophy of public administration, which has hitherto been defined predominantly in legal terms;
- organizationally flattening the hierarchical pyramid by extensive delegation (decentralized resource management) to the bottom-line units;
- reducing public administration to its core function by having the greatest possible number of hitherto public responsibilities contracted out to private actors; and
- divesting the civil service of privileges by opening it to competition and introducing performance incentives.

Assuming that the formal organization and personnel of many existing administrative institutions are still conceived on Weber's model, one may call the reform scheme the post-Weber model. If existing bureaucracy is called the 'modern' type (again in Weber's sense), the next step could be seen as a step towards 'post-modern' administration.

East Germany as a Seed-bed for Post-Weber Public Administration?

The hypothesis that East Germany provides fertile ground for a post-Weber type of administration deserves consideration for a number of reasons. Take the socio-economic and institutional factors, for instance. First, current public administration has urgent problems. Drastic cut-backs are necessary in the number of personnel, which swelled, particularly in the social services, when local authorities were obliged to assume charge of institutions and staffs that had been the responsibility of other state and economic structures. Under pressure to become leaner, local authorities are compelled to adopt radical reform, including New Public Management. Second, the organizational and personnel structures of the local authorities have been in constant flux since 1990. Local and regional incumbents are still not as firmly entrenched in East Germany as their counterparts are in West Germany. The resistance of vested interests is less formidable.

Cognitive and socio-cultural factors also indicate East Germany's suitability as a laboratory for post-Weber public administration. Since 1990 local actors have gone through several waves of institutional change, including the paradigmatic transition from the model of the GDR to that of the FRG in 1990, the reform of county territorial boundaries and local-level organization in 1993 and 1994, the introduction of new municipal charters in the new *Länder* in 1994, and current functional and structural reform. Local actors have thus gained experience with institutional change. Consider, too, that the concepts of New Public Management are embedded in economic thinking. Hence, the administrative newcomers from state enterprises—the economists and civil engineers who account for more than half of the new senior administrators—might be regarded as an intriguing reservoir of administrative innovation that centres on economic thinking. Lack of professional administrative training or experience may enable them to shed outmoded administrative routines and mores and to embark on administrative innovation more easily than old hands can. If this premiss is correct, novices among local administrative leaders as a group might belie Max Weber's view of administrative 'dilettantes' as opposed to (and outdated with regard to) the administrative professionals (*Beamte*) in modern administration, who are essentially products of thorough training in a specialized field, special examinations, and expert qualification (*Fachschulung, Fachprüfungen, Fachqualifikation*) (Weber 1922/1978: 958–60; Wollmann and Jaedicke 1993: 107–13).

Moreover, the socio-psychological stage appears to be set for a rapid learning process. In addition to the previously cited psychological tests and surveys directly contradicting the cliché that the East German is slow to learn and move, mention must be made of research by Helmut Klages as reported by his collaborator, Thomas Gensicke (1994*a*,*b*), who constructed five types of people in their interpretation of representative surveys undertaken in 1990 and 1993. For the argument in this chapter it is suggestive that the surveys showed more than half (51 per cent) of the East German population to consist of the two types (the 'active realists' and the 'idealists') identified as being prone to active change, with 'despondents' accounting for one-third (Gensicke 1994*a*,*b*). Accordingly, East Germans are called 'psychologically robust, pragmatic, optimistic' (Gensicke 1994*a*: 46). Intriguingly, use of the Klages–Gensicke questionnaire and typology in my own project on local administrative leaders showed that as many as 58 per cent of senior local administrators are active realists and idealists, whereas the despondents account for as few as 7.3 per cent of that group (Berg, Nagelschmidt and Wollmann 1994: 107).

East Germany as Inhospitable Ground for Administrative Innovation?

The debate on New Public Management has recently been taken up by an increasing number of counties and municipalities in West Germany, but the number in East Germany has been insignificant so far (Reichard 1994: 79). Empirically, then, East Germany has shown itself to be rather barren soil for discussion of administrative innovation. A key reason for the hesitancy of East German counties and municipalities to jump on the New Public Management bandwagon may be that they simply have too many problems to cope with. Apart from unprecedented socio-economic challenges, they must struggle with the organizational repercussions and personnel-related impacts of other recent and ongoing administrative reforms. Local authorities in East Germany thus appear to have little political and intellectual attention and potential to spare for the type of administrative reforms envisioned by proponents of New Public Management.

Perhaps even more important is the question of whether efforts at post-Weber (i.e. post-modern) administrative reform can be meaningfully brought to bear *before* the structures of Weberian and modern public administration have become firmly rooted and before the related mind-sets and skills of the administrative actors have formed in the institutional, socio-cultural, and psychological contexts. Still tentative empirical evidence suggests that the delegation of expanded responsibilities (as 'decentralized resource management') can be successful only after the actors have learned and managed the traditional (Weberian) forms of organization that have been installed thus far (Berg, Nagelschmidt and Wollmann 1994; Lutz and Wegrich 1995). Similarly, making use of informal flexibility presupposes thorough knowledge and mastery of the formal rules. Skipping Weber's formal, or modern, stage of the institutionalization process would also leave out a related cognitive and socio-cultural learning process that helps structure the decision-making situation organizationally and cognitively. Without that phase, decision-making runs the risk of ending up in what could be called pre-modern chaos. In a way, one could speak of an internal logic to institutional modernization, a logic both parallel to and geared to the cognitive and socio-cultural learning process.

SUMMARY

With regard to institutional formation, which has been looked upon in this chapter as a dependent variable, it was shown that the corridor within which East German local authorities have been built up and reconstructed since the GDR's accession to the FRG have been largely defined by exogenous factors from West Germany. At the same time, the considerable variability of institutional formation in the many counties and municipalities of East Germany was shown to have been shaped by endogenous factors emanating from specific local political contexts, actors, and interests.

Using classical European bureaucracy and the advent of the rule of law as examples, I have asserted that new institutions and their related role prescriptions at the systems level are significantly mismatched with the cognitive and socio-cultural frames of reference operating at the actor level. The gulf between these two spheres still impairs the functioning of institutions.

It was concluded that East Germany does not offer organizationally or socio-culturally fertile ground for administrative innovation. Despite a number of favourable factors, the obstacles will probably prevail at least in the short run. The stage of modern (or 'formal') structures cannot be skipped in the transition to post-modern ('post-Weber' or 'informal') structures without risking pre-modern chaos in administrative and decision-making processes.

Against this background it does not seem justified to expect that the administrative dilettantism prevalent among local administrative leaders in East Germany will prove to hold cognitive and motivational potential to bypass (and belie) Weber's stage of bureaucracy and pave the way for its post-Weber form.

NOTES

This chapter draws partly on two empirical studies conducted under the author's guidance with support from the Research Commission on Social and Political Transformation in the East German *Länder* (KSPW). The KSPW was established in 1991 to prepare a comprehensive report on the transformation in East Germany since unification. It is funded by the Federal Ministry of Research and Technology and the Federal Ministry of Labour. The first project consisted of pilot studies that were carried out in a number of East German county and municipal authorities and were mainly based on questionnaires and semi-structured interviews conducted with fifty-seven 'administrative leaders' from June to Nov. 1992. For details, see Wollmann and Berg (1994). This first study is referred to in the following pages as the KSPW pilot project. The second project, referred to as the KSPW HUB project, is under way at Humboldt University. This research focuses on the institutional transformation of East German county and municipal authorities in what are now the *Länder* of Brandenburg and Saxony–Anhalt. Interviews based on a questionnaire very similar to the one used in the KSPW pilot project were conducted with about 100 political and administrative leaders from Oct. 1993 to early 1994. For details, see the project interim report (Berg and Nagelschmidt forthcoming).

1. This term was aptly introduced by Eisen (1996: 27) to denote the institutional concepts, transfer intentions, and administrative skills acquired and practised in the West German context, as opposed to the legacies that may persist in institutions and cognitive orientations carried over from the former German Democratic Republic (GDR).
2. A survey conducted by the Association of Local Authorities (Deutscher Städtetag) showed that at the end of 1991 all East German municipalities of more than 20,000 inhabitants, and 95 per cent of those between 10,000 and 20,000 inhabitants, had been 'twinned' with a respective municipality in West Germany. About half of these the partnerships involved material assistance and consultancy (see Scheytt 1993: 80–1).
3. Data from the KSPW pilot project show that about 7 per cent of the leading administrative personnel—division heads (*Dezernenten*) and section heads (*Amtsleiter*)—were West Germans. Data from the KSPW HUB project showed that the figures fluctuate from 8.8 per cent in the local authorities researched in Saxony–Anhalt to 21.4 per cent in Brandenburg.
4. According to data from the KSPW HUB project, more than 90 per cent of the newly elected officials came from state enterprises; 3 per cent, from institutions of higher education; and scarcely any from the Church. The data from the KSPW pilot project pointed in a similar direction (see Wollmann and Berg 1994: 248).
5. According to data from the KSPW pilot project, 36 per cent are old hands, 56 per cent are newcomers, and 7 per cent are West German (Wollmann and Berg 1994: 248). While the general tendency of these findings is confirmed by the KSPW HUB project, its data indicate considerable regional variation. Of the new incumbents of leading administrative positions, 25.8 per cent were old hands, 59.7 per cent newcomers, and 14.5 per cent West Germans (Berg and Nagelschmidt 1994:

Background	Brandenburg	Saxony–Anhalt
Old hands	32.1	20.6
Newcomers	46.5	70.5
West Germans	21.4	8.8

71). These percentages may vary considerably from one area to the next, as shown in the table (source: Berg, Nagelschmidt and Wollmann 1994).
6. Bärbel Boley, one of the most prominent dissidents and civic movement leaders in the GDR, coined the bitter and much-quoted phrase: 'We thought we were getting justice, but what we got was the West German rule of law.'

REFERENCES

BECKER, P. (1992), 'Ost- und Westdeutsche auf dem Prüfstand psychologischer Tests' (East and West Germans and Psychological Testing), *Aus Politik und Zeitgeschichte* (suppl. to *Das Parlament*), B-24 (5 June), 27–36.

BERG, F. (1994), 'Transformation der kommunalen Verwaltungsinstitutionen in Stadt und Kreis Strausberg' (Transformation of the Local Administrative Institutions in the City and District of Strausberg), in H. Nassmacher, O. Niedermyer, and H. Wollmann (eds.), *Politische Strukturen im Umbruch* (Berlin: Akademie Verlag), 239–71.

——NAGELSCHMIDT, M. and WOLLMANN, H. (forthcoming), *Kommunaler Institutionenwandel* (Opladen: Leske and Budrich).

BOHNE, E. (1981), *Der informale Rechtsstaat* (The Informal State Based on Due Process) (Berlin: Duncker & Humblot).

BUNDESVEREINIGUNG DER KOMMUNALEN SPITZENVERBÄNDE (1994), *Hilfe zum Aufbau der kommunalen Selbstverwaltung in den neuen Bundesländern* (Aid in Setting up Local Self-Administration in the New German *Länder*) (Munich: Rehm).

DERLIEN, H.-U. (1993*a*), 'Integration der Staatsfunktionäre der DDR im öffentlichen Dienst der neuen Bundesländer' (Integrating State Functionaries of the GDR into the Civil Service of the New German *Länder*), in W. Seibel, A. Benz, and H. Mäding (eds.), *Verwaltungsreform und Verwaltungspolitik im Prozeß der deutschen Vereinigung* (Baden-Baden: Nomos), 190–206.

——(1993*b*), 'German Unification and Bureaucratic Transformation', *International Political Science Review*, 14: 319–34.

EISEN, A. (1996), Institutionenbildung im Transformationsprozeß (Baden-Baden: Nomos).

GENSICKE, T. (1994*a*), 'Ostdeutsche: Psychisch robust, pragmatisch, optimistisch' (East Germans: Psychologically Robust, Pragmatic, Optimistic), *Psychologie heute* (Nov.), 46–50.

——(1994*b*), 'Pragmatisch und optimistisch. Über die Bewältigung des Umbruchs in den neuen Bundesländern' (Pragmatic and Optimistic: On Coping with the Upheaval in the New German *Länder*), in H. Bertram, S. Hradil, and G. Kleinhenz (eds.), *Sozialer und demographischer Wandel in den neuen Bundesländern* (Berlin: Akademie-Verlag), 120–42.

GÖHLER (1994), *Eigenart der Institutionen* (Particularity of Institutions) (Baden-Baden: Nomos).

GOETZ, K. H. (1993), 'Rebuilding Public Administration in the New German *Länder*: Transfer and Differentiation', *West European Politics*, 16: 447–69.

KLINGER, F. (1994*a*), 'Die unvollendete Integration—Grundprobleme institutioneller Erneuerung in Deutschland' (Incomplete Integration: Basic Problems of Institutional Renewal in Germany), *Wissenschaftliche Mitteilungen aus dem Berliner Institut für Sozialwissenschaftliche Studien (BISS-Public)*, 15: 67–103.

——(1994*b*), *Institutionen, Interessen und sektorale Variationen in der Transformationsdynamik der politischen Ökonomie Deutschlands* (Institutions, Interests, and Sectorial Variations in the Dynamics of Transformation in the Political Economy of Germany), MS, University of Constance.

KÖNIG, K. (1993), 'Transformation einer real-sozialisitschen Verwaltung in eine klassisch-europäische Verwaltung' (Transforming a Socialist Administration into a Classical European Administration), in W. Seibel, H. Mäding, and W. Benz (eds.), *Verwaltungsreform und Verwaltungspolitik im Prozeß der deutschen Einigung* (Baden-Baden: Nomos), 80–97.

LEMBRUCH, G. (1994), 'Institutionentransfer' (Institutional Transfer), in W. Seibel, A. Benz, and H. Mäding (eds.), *Verwaltungsreform und Verwaltungspolitik im Prozeß der deutschen Vereinigung* (Baden-Baden: Nomos), 41–65.

LUTZ, S., and WEGRICH, K. (1995), '(K)eine Reformkultur im Osten? Modernisierung der Kommunalverwaltung in Mecklenburg-Vorpommern' (Is there a Reformist Culture in the East? Modernization of Local Administration in Mecklenburg–West Pomerania), MS, Department of Political Science, Humboldt University.

MARZ, L. (1992), 'Dispositionskosten des Transformationsprozesses' (Costs of Coping with the Process of Transformation), *Aus Politik und Zeitgeschichte* (suppl. to *Das Parlament*), B-24 (5 June), 3–14.

MAYNTZ, R. (1994), 'Die deutsche Vereinigung als Prüfstein für die Leistungsfähigkeit der Sozialwissenschaften' (German Unification as the Acid Test of what the Social Sciences can Do), *Wissenschaftliche Mitteilungen aus dem Berliner Institut für Sozialwissenschaftliche Studien (BISS-Public)*, 13: 25–31.

RAPSCH, E., and SIMANSKI, C. (1991), 'Beratung in Kommunen der ehemaligen DDR' (Consultancy in Local Communities of the Former GDR), *Landes- und Kommunalverwaltung*, 6: 196–7.

REICHARD, C. (1994), *Umdenken im Rathaus. Neue Steuerungsmodelle in der deutschen Kommunalverwaltung* (Change of Thought in City Hall: New Models of Control in German Local Government Administration) (Berlin: edition sigma).

——and RÖBER, M. (1993), 'Was kommt nach der Einheit? Die öffentliche Verwaltung in der ehemaligen DDR zwischen Blaupause und Reform' (After Unification, what Next? Public Administration in the Former GDR between Blueprint and Reform), in G.-J. Glaessner (ed.), *Der lange Weg zur Einheit* (Bonn: Dietz), 215–30.

ROSE, R., ZAPF, W., SEIFERT, W., and PAGE, E. (1933), *Germans in Comparative Perspective*, Public Policy no. 218 (Glasgow: University of Strathclyde).

SCHEYTT, O. (1992), 'Städte, Kreise und Gemeinden im Umbruch. Der Aufbau der Kommunalverwaltung in den neuen Bundesländern' (Cities, Districts, and Local Communities in Upheaval: The Formation of Local Administration in the New German *Länder*), *Deutschland-Archiv*, 1: 12–20.

——(1993), 'Rechts- und Verwaltungshilfe in den neuen Bundesländern am

Beispiel der Kommunalverwaltung' (Legal and Administrative Aid in the New German *Länder* as Exemplified by Local Government Administration), in R. Pitschas (ed.), *Verwaltungsintegration in den neuen Bundesländern* (Berlin: Duncker & Humblot), 70–88.

SCHUBEL, C., and SCHWANENGEL, W. (1991), 'Funktionelle Probleme beim Aufbau von Landkreisverwaltungen in Thüringen' (Functional Problems in Setting up County Administrations in Thuringia), *Landes- und Kommunalverwaltung*, 8: 249–55.

STRATEMANN, I. (1992), 'Psychologische Bedingungen des wirtschaftlichen Aufschwungs in den neuen Bundesländern' (Psychological Conditions of the Economic Recovery in the New German *Länder*), *Aus Politik und Zeitgeschichte* (suppl. to *Das Parlament*), B-24 (5 June), 15–26.

WEBER, M. (1922/1978), *Economy and Society: An Outline of Interpretive Sociology*, 2 vols. ed. G. Roth and C. Wittich, trans. E. Fischoff *et al.* (Berkeley: University of California Press).

WEGENER, A., JAEDICKE, W., and WOLLMANN, H. (forthcoming), *Kommunale Arbeitsmarktpolitik* (Local Labour Market Policy) (Basel: Birkhäuser).

WILL, R. (1990), 'Stellungnahme' (Comment), *Staat und Recht*, 38: 30–5.

WOLLMANN, H. (1991), 'Kommunalpolitik und -verwaltung in Ostdeutschland. Institutionen und Handlungsmuster im "paradigmatischen" Umbruch' (Local Government Policy and Administration in Eastern Germany: Institutions and Patterns of Action in "Paradigmatic" Upheaval), in B. Blank (ed.), *Staat und Stadt* (special issue), *Politische Vierteljahresschrift*, 221: 237–58.

——(1994), 'The Implementation of the Unification of the Two Germanies: The Transformation of the former GDR between external determinants and endogenous factors, IPSA World Congress', to be published in F.A. Lazin (ed.), *Policy Implementation* (JAI-Press).

——(1995), 'Regelung kommunaler Institutionen in Ostdeutschland zwischen "exogener" Pfadabhängigkeit und endogenen Entscheidungsfaktoren', in: *Berliner Journal für Soziologie*, no. 4, pp. 497–514.

——(1996), 'Institutionenbildung in Ostdeutschland. Neubau, Umbau und "shöpferische" Zerstörung (Institution – building in East Germany. Construction, Reconstruction and "Creative Destruction"), in Kaase, M. *et al*, *Politisches System im Umbruch*, Opladen: Leske & Budrich (forthcoming).

——(forthcoming), 'The Transformation of Local Government in East Germany: Between Imposed and Innovative Institution Building', in K. Goetz and A. Benz (eds.), *A New German Public Sector?* (Aldershot: Dartmouth).

——and BERG, F. (1994), 'Die ostdeutschen Kommunen: Organisation, Personal, Orientierungs- und Einstellungsmuster im Wandel' (East German Local Authorities: Organization, Personnel, and Patterns of Orientation and Attitude in Flux), in H. Nassmacher, O. Niedermayer, and H. Wollmann (eds.), *Politische Strukturen im Umbruch* (Berlin: Akademie Verlag), 240–73.

——and JAEDICKE, W. (1993), 'Neubau der Kommunalverwaltung in Ostdeutschland—zwischen Kontinuität und Umbruch' (Rebuilding Local Government Administration in Eastern Germany: Between Continuity and Upheaval), in W. Seibel, A. Benz, and H. Mäding (eds.), *Verwaltungsreform und Verwaltungspolitik im Prozeß der deutschen Einigung* (Baden-Baden: Nomos), 98–116.

INDEX